THE SOCIOLOGY OF TEACHING

THE SOCIOLOGY OF TEACHING

BY

WILLARD WALLER, PH.D.

SCIENCE EDITIONS®

John Wiley & Sons, Inc., New York

Publication as a Science Edition paperback
authorized by Russell & Russell, Inc.

First Science Editions printing, 1965
Science Editions Trade Mark Registered U.S. Patent Office

Printed in the U. S. A.

INTRODUCTION

ONE of the qualities of a classic book is that it continues to do for the latest reader what it apparently did for the first. What Willard Waller's *Sociology of Teaching* continues to do is to give insight. In his preface to the first edition Waller stated his purpose this way: "To give insight into concrete situations typical of the typical school." This his work continues to do in generous measure. And more. For as an early bench mark study in the social life of the school the book now gives perspective. What Waller chose to talk must be talked about wherever and whenever the school as a social institution is examined. The topics found here continue to enliven the discourse of scholars and the folk talk of teachers. They constitute the on going agenda for the study of the schools.

But the *Sociology of Teaching* does more than *possess* the qualities of insight and perspective: it *teaches* them to the reader, or, more accurately, it teaches the reader to teach them to himself. Reading the book is a moving experience, even after repeated readings. Fresh insights and perspectives constantly appear, and the reader does precisely what Waller wanted him to do, be his own teacher. Almost unawares, one finds himself carrying on a dialogue with the book.

In a sense Waller makes every teacher an educational sociologist. He takes the common place events in the human life of the school and its surroundings, things many teachers might tend to overlook, and holds them up for examination like a good teacher does. He turns them around and inside out, he describes and relates them to people like teachers, students and parents, he places them in the larger context of many schools, many teachers, students, and parents, and suddenly the routine life of the school takes on excitement and magic, the gifts of insight and perspective.

Perhaps Waller's signal contribution is that he teaches us how to look at the school as a social institution. With him we begin to see that what happens among the human beings who constitute the school, or who are touched by it, is the single most important thing that goes on in the school. As he points out, these human beings are not "disembodied intelligences," "instructing machines," or "learning machines" but whole human beings interlocked in a network of human relationships. It is this network, and the individual relations and roles of the people within it, that really determines the outcomes of education.

This reminder could not be issued at a better time. It is an appropriate educational message for the sixties and seventies. These two decades will likely be characterized educationally by developments which tend further to impersonalize teaching and learning. In America the age of popular education is behind us, but the age of mass education has just begun. The legitimate demands put upon us to develop mass educational techniques will surely further depersonalize the education process. The danger is that we will come to regard the new developments as educational goals in themselves, rather than simply means for achieving a better human environment for learning. In a sense the real test of modern educational technology, curriculum change, and administrative reorganization is what they do to readjust the human equation in order to make for more effective learning. As Waller warns: "Let no one be deceived, the important things that happen in the schools result from the interaction of personalities." Today's educators, whether they be students in education, first year or veteran teachers, college or university scholars, will find here fresh perspective on the human and individual dimensions of mass education. Thus the *Sociology of Teaching* is more than a bench work, as was mentioned earlier; it is an educational beacon helping one to keep his eye trained on what is important and distinguishing it from the means to achieve the important.

One need not possess special powers to predict that this new edition will be reread in a way that one returns to an old friend and that it will attract a host of new readers among those who had not made its acquaintance before. And as in the past, new dialogues between reader and book will spring up, giving new insight and perspective, just as Waller thought proper.

Cole S. Brembeck
Michigan State University

PREFACE

WHAT this book tells is what every teacher knows, that the world of school is a social world. Those human beings who live together in the school, though deeply severed in one sense, nevertheless spin a tangled web of interrelationships; that web and the people in it make up the social world of school. It is not a wide world, but, for those who know it, it is a world compact with meaning. It is a unique world. It is the purpose of this book to explore it.

I believe that all teachers, great and small, have need of insight into the social realities of school life, that they perish, as teachers, for lack of it. Young teachers fail because they do not know how to keep order. Brilliant specialists do their jobs poorly because they do not understand the human nature of the classroom. Teacher training has done much to improve the general run of instruction, but it can do vastly more if it equips beginning teachers with social insight. For it needs insight to put advanced educational theories into practice when schools and communities are attached to the old and antagonistic to the new. Insight will help teachers to keep a good school and it will help them to hold their jobs.

If I am to help others to gain any usable insight, I must show them the school as it really is. I must not attack the school, nor talk overmuch about what ought to be, but only about what is. There are many things in the present-day school which ought to be bettered, many evil things which should be remedied, but my concern with them is expository rather than reformative. Nor do I intend to gloss over weak spots or to apologize for existing things. This presentation, if it is to be effective, must be unbiased.

But if one is to show the school as it really is, it is not enough to be unprejudiced. It is necessary to achieve some sort of literary realism. I think of this work, therefore, as an adventure in realism. To be realistic, I believe, is simply to be concrete. To be concrete is to present materials in such a way that characters do not lose the qualities of persons, nor situations their intrinsic human reality. Realistic sociology must be concrete. In my own case, this preference for concreteness has led to a relative distrust of statistical method, which has seemed, for my purposes, of little utility. Possibly the understanding of human life will be as much advanced by the direct study of social phenomena as by the study of numerical symbols abstracted from those phenomena.

This work is a study of the life of human beings in the school. The point of view of the analysis is primarily sociological. The work is, in one sense, a systematic application of the concepts of sociology and social psychology to the social phenomena of school life. The chief utility of the book, probably, will be as a textbook in Educational Sociology, but I hope that it may have some general interest as well. I have tried, indeed, to write such a book as would appeal to every teacher everywhere. The method that has been employed in gathering and interpreting material is empirical and observational. The style is as non-technical as it was possible to make it without the loss of essential meanings.

The purpose of the book, however it is used, is to give insight into concrete situations typical of the typical school. I have hewed to this line, and to no other. Whatever seemed likely to give insight has been included, and all else, however worth while in other respects, has been excluded. A certain amount of fictional material has been included. This must be judged as fiction; it is good fiction, and it is relevant to our point, if it is based upon good insight. A number of atypical cases have been included because of the illustrative value of such material.

This combination of an attempt to give insight and to call attention to its applicability to the every-day realities of school seems strongly to suggest the project method of teaching. I have therefore included projects covering most of the main points of the text material. In accordance with this theory of instruction, it is the function of the text and the teacher to furnish the student with preliminary insight which the student then checks, supplements, reorganizes, and assimilates by applying it to the data. Ultimately each student will work out his own evaluation of the point of view of the text, changing the analysis as he sees fit, and retaining in his mind only that which proves useful to him; this is exactly what I should wish him to do if I were teaching him directly. Each teacher, too, will probably want to furnish many of his own projects, and the projects given in the text should be regarded merely as suggestions. A further suggestion coming out of my own experience in teaching this material and using these projects in Educational Sociology is that it will be desirable to have students write out or otherwise very carefully prepare such projects as are presented to the class. I hope that the project-method feature of the text will take on, for I feel that effective teaching of sociology depends upon finding some way to make the student a collaborator of the text-writer and the teacher. This text, however, is not indissolubly wedded to the project method, for the field is broad, and will allow plenty of room for both teacher activity and student activity, no matter how it is taught. I am convinced that Educational Sociology is a fruitful and challenging idea, and I have tried to put the evidence for this belief into my book.

Many teachers, of many ranks and stations, have knowingly contributed their insight and their experience to this book; some others have contributed unwittingly. To all those who have contributed I am very grateful, but it seems best to leave them nameless. My debts in the general field of sociology are many, and their nature will doubtless be clear to the initiated reader. In the specialized field of Educational Sociology, I am particularly indebted to Clow, Smith, Snedden, and Peters for their books, and, in the case of Peters, for valuable suggestions given in conversation. Harold Alderfer, James W. Woodard, Clifford Kirkpatrick, Duncan Strong, Albert G. Dodd, Kenneth McGill, Henry Pratt Fairchild, and others have read all or part of the manuscript and have aided with constructive suggestions.

State College, Pennsylvania, 1932.

CONTENTS

PART ONE. INTRODUCTORY

PART TWO. THE SCHOOL AND THE COMMUNITY

PART THREE

SOME INTERPRETATIONS OF LIFE IN THE SCHOOL

PART FOUR. THE TEACHER-PUPIL RELATIONSHIP

Part One—Introductory

Chapter I

INTRODUCTION

Since the day of *The Hoosier Schoolmaster*, of "lickin' and larnin'" and "the three R's," American education has travelled far. Nor can there be any longer a doubt that the spread of teacher training and the improvement in its quality have had much to do with the improvement of the American school.

It is not to disparage teacher training that we remark upon the fact that teachers still learn to teach by teaching. The teacher gets something from experience which is not included in his "professional" courses, an elusive something which it is difficult to put between the covers of a book or to work up into a lecture. That elusive something is social insight. What the teacher gets from experience is an understanding of the social situation of the classroom, and an adaptation of his personality to the needs of that milieu. That is why experienced teachers are wiser than novices. That is what we must try to include in the regimen of those who aspire to be teachers.

The teacher acquires in experience a rough, empirical insight into the processes of personal interaction in the schools. For let no one be deceived, the important things that happen in the schools result from the interaction of personalities. Children and teachers are not disembodied intelligences, not instructing machines and learning machines, but whole human beings tied together in a complex maze of social interconnections. The school is a social world because human beings live in it.

That is the starting point of this book.

The insight that common-sense men and practical teachers get is fragmentary, needing to be fitted into a larger picture and to be pieced out with completer knowledge. And this insight is often crude, requiring to be sifted and sorted and refined. Perhaps the best procedure will be to attempt to draw a comprehensive picture of social interaction in the school, to analyze this as best we can, and to fit the empirical insight of teachers into the picture. We shall set ourselves, then, the following tasks:

(1) To describe with all possible care and completeness the social life of human beings in and about the school.

(2) To analyze these descriptive materials (particularly from the standpoints of sociology and social psychology).

(3) To attempt to isolate causal mechanisms involved in those interactions of human beings having their locus in the institution of the school. Many of our best clues to these causal mechanisms will be furnished by those bits of empirical insight which teachers have obtained in the course of their experience. We shall make much of this material, and we shall not hesitate to present it in the idiom with which it naturally consorts in the folk talk of teachers.

In attempting to work out a description of the social life of the school, we shall borrow every technique which promises to be of value. In some instances we shall apply ourselves to the description of social behavior in the manner of the cultural anthropologist, attempting to equal him in detachment and devotion to detail. In others, where fidelity to the inwardness of social behavior is desired, we shall not hesitate to borrow the technique or the materials of the realistic novelist. Otherwise we shall rely upon such descriptions and analyses of the group life of the schools as we may be able to work out for ourselves or to find in the literature, and for our understanding of this group life in its individual aspects we shall have recourse to life histories, case records, diaries, letters, and other personal documents. In our analysis of this material we shall be guided by such scientific concepts from the various fields of psychology, psychiatry, and sociology as seem to be clearly relevant, neither dragging any interpretation in by the heels nor failing to cross academic boundary lines in search of usable interpretations.

This book has been written from the point of view of the teacher. As a book primarily intended for teachers and prospective teachers, it has been directed at two somewhat different problems: first, the problem of understanding the school scientifically; and second, the problem of teacher control. It is hoped that no confusion will arise from this dual objective. Such advice as is offered relevant to the second problem is mainly incidental to exposition of a more strictly scientific character. The writer has tried to keep separate two phases of the practical problem, the question, "How should the teacher direct the life of the school for the best interests of all concerned?" and that more pressing, less ethical, question, "How can the teacher control school life at all?"

It is hoped that this book will be received as a frankly empirical first treatment of an important and neglected field of education. A first treatment of this sort must necessarily be rough and inconclusive. But this sort of empirical research must be done before more refined investigations can proceed; qualitative research must always go before quantitative research. We make here, then, no great claims either to accuracy or completeness. The book is a result of systematic wondering rather than of highly objective research. And it represents only what a reasonably acute observer cannot help seeing when he looks at the schools from this point of view.

If there is any merit in this book, it is the merit of the commonplace. A sociological writer cannot, in the present state of our science, hope to get very far ahead of common sense, and he is usually fortunate if he does not fall behind it. What we shall present here, then, is a sociology of common sense applied to an every-day theme. We shall say, as it happens, some things that have not often been said before, either because men did not think them worth saying, as, indeed, they may not be, or because people did not see them because they were so obvious.

And yet our undertaking is an ambitious one. It covers a broad scope and a complex phase of social life. If we are successful in this undertaking to make a first-hand study of the social life of the schools, this work will be useful. It is hoped that it may have two uses in particular: (1) to enable prospective teachers and school administrators to find their way more readily and accurately in the intricate maze of social life in school, and (2) to give an orientation for suggestions and experiments aiming at the reconstruction of the schools.

The materials of this study are mainly descriptions of life in the upper grades and the high school, but we have drawn occasional illustrations from college life. We have also confined our discussion very largely to the orthodox school, because it is our fundamental thesis that any far-reaching change in school methods must be based not only upon curriculum reforms and improved teaching techniques, though we do not belittle either of those, but also upon such an understanding of the social interaction of the classroom as will enable teachers to make intelligent modifications of that process. The case materials upon which the discussion of the relation of the school and the community is based are principally rural and small-town materials. This could be defended on the ground that the urban school is merely a transplanted country school, but our reason for choosing such materials was the quite other reason that they display attitudes of persons and mechanisms of social interaction more clearly than those from urban communities. Our generalizations concerning the school and the community contain a core of truth for the metropolitan situation, but would have to be modified considerably before being transferred. The place of the school in metropolitan life is a subject which awaits the scrutiny of sociologists. We have also used a number of private-school examples, and the reason for this is that certain mechanisms, though common in other schools, appear most clearly in the private schools.

This is an undertaking that is essentially constructive in its nature, an attempt to found a new understanding of the schools, and to find such remedies for existing ills as that new understanding dictates. It is not constructive if one means by construction an undiscriminating defence of the established order, for we shall have cruel things to say of that order. But it is based upon a fundamental philosophy of meliorism, and upon the belief that whatever contributes to the understanding of human life must one day contribute to its reconstruction. The duty of the social researcher is something akin to that of the physician; it is his to diagnose shrewdly and to tell the truth. If he does these things, no physician and no social researcher need be accused of pessimism because he sometimes returns a gloomy diagnosis.

PROJECTS

1. Describe the behavior of a young teacher confronting his first class. Could his students tell that he was inexperienced? How? Contrast this with the behavior of an experienced teacher.

2. Take notes on the behavior of a group of high-school students in a class. How much of their behavior seems to be concerned with subject matter? How much with social interchange with other pupils and the teacher?

SUGGESTED READINGS

(1) Betts, G. H., *Social Principles of Education.*

(2) Chapman, J. C., and Counts, G. S., *Principles of Education.*

(3) Finney, Ross L., *A Sociological Philosophy of Education.*

(4) Hart, J. K., *A Social Interpretation of Education.*

(5) Zeleny, Florence, "An Attempt to Relate Sociology to Teachers' Activities," *Journal of Educational Sociology*, Vol. V., No. 7, March, 1932, pp. 430-437.

Chapter II

THE SCHOOL AS A SOCIAL ORGANISM

The school is a unity of interacting personalities. The personalities of all who meet in the school are bound together in an organic relation. The life of the whole is in all its parts, yet the whole could not exist without any of its parts. The school is a social organism;[1] it is this first and most general aspect of the social life of the schools which we propose to deal with in this chapter. As a social organism the school shows an organismic interdependence of its parts; it is not possible to affect a part of it without affecting the whole. As a social organism the school displays a differentiation of parts and a specialization of function. The organism as an entirety is nourished by the community.

Changing the figure slightly, the school is a closed system of social interaction. Without pedantry, we may point out that this fact is of importance, for if we are to study the school as a social entity, we must be able to distinguish clearly between school and not-school. The school is in fact clearly differentiated from its social milieu. The existence of a school is established by the emergence of a characteristic mode of social interaction. A school exists wherever and whenever teachers and students meet for the purpose of giving and receiving instruction. The instruction which is given is usually formal classroom instruction, but this need not be true. The giving and receiving of instruction constitutes the nucleus of the school as we now think of it. About this nucleus are clustered a great many less relevant activities.

When we analyze existing schools, we find that they have the following characteristics which enable us to set them apart and study them as social unities:

(1) They have a definite population.
(2) They have a clearly defined political structure, arising from the mode of social interaction characteristic of the school, and influenced by numerous minor processes of interaction.

[1] We do not, of course, subscribe to the organismic fallacy, which Ward and others have so ably refuted. We have adopted the analogy here simply as a device of exposition. The school is like an organism; it is not a true organism.

(3) They represent the nexus of a compact network of social relationships.
(4) They are pervaded by a we-feeling.
(5) They have a culture that is definitely their own.

Schools differ widely in the degree to which they show these traits and in the manner in which they are combined. Private boarding schools exemplify them all in the highest degree. They have a stable and homogeneous population; the original homogeneity, produced by economic and social selection, has been enhanced by intimate association and common experiences. They have a clear and explicit political organization, sometimes expressed in a book of rules and a long line of precedents. The persons of the school live very close to each other, and are bound each to each by an intricate maze of crisscrossing social relationships. Intimacy of association, stability of the group, the setting apart of the group by a distinctive dress and its isolation from other cultural influences, combine to make possible a strong feeling of unity in such a school; it has often been remarked that a private school has something of the solidarity of the family. The isolation of the school from the remainder of the community, and the richness of the life which its members lead in their close-packed association, make the culture developed in such a school pronounced and distinctive.

The private day school sometimes represents such a closed corporation, and shows up very clearly as a social unit. It may not, for the day school is sometimes nothing more than a painless substitute for public school for the children of wealthy parents. But in the ideal case the private day school may be a functioning unity much more clearly marked off from the rest of the world than is the public school.

The various kinds and conditions of public schools differ in the degree to which they are recognizable and delimitable social units. The one-room country school is obviously such a unit. So likewise is the great suburban high school, and the high school of the small city described in *Middletown*. Sometimes, however, the public school is so split into divergent social groups that the underlying unity is somewhat obscured. This is possible where the school population is drawn from several sources and where there is no school program capable of welding these groups together.

The school has, as we have said, a definite population, composed of those who are engaged in the giving or receiving of instruction, who "teach" or "are in school." It is a relatively stable population and one whose depletion and replacement occur slowly. Population movements go according to plan and can be predicted and charted in advance. A bimodal age distribution marks off teachers from students. This is the most significant cleavage in the school.

The young in the school population are likely to have been subjected to some sifting and sorting according to the economic status and social classification of their parents. The private schools select out a certain group, and there are specializations within the private schools, some being in fact reformatories for the children of the well-to-do, and some being very exacting as to the character and scholastic qualifications of their students. The public schools of the exclusive residence district are usually peopled by students of a limited range of social types. Slum schools are for slum children. Country schools serve the children of farmers. In undifferentiated residence districts and in small towns which have but one school the student population is least homogeneous and most representative of the entire community.

The teaching population is probably less differentiated. In part, this is because the variation from the teacher type must be limited if one is to teach successfully. There is nevertheless considerable variation in the training and ability of teachers from one school to another and one part of the country to another. Teachers the country over and in all schools tend to be predominantly selected from the rural districts and from the sons and daughters of the lower middle classes. The teaching population is in some schools more permanent than the student population. There is nevertheless a large turnover among the teachers.

The characteristic mode of social interaction of the school, an interaction centered about the giving and receiving of instruction, determines the political order of the school. The instruction which is given consists largely of facts and skills, and of other matter for which the spontaneous interests of students do not usually furnish a sufficient motivation. Yet teachers wish students to attain a certain mastery of these subjects, a much higher degree of mastery than they would attain, it is thought, if they were quite free in their choices. And teachers are responsible to the community for the mastery of these subjects by their students. The political organization of the school, therefore, is one which makes the teacher dominant, and it is the business of the teacher to use his dominance to further the process of teaching and learning which is central in the social interaction of the school.

Typically the school is organized on some variant of the autocratic principle. Details of organization show the greatest diversity. Intra-faculty relations greatly affect the relations between teachers and students. Where there is a favorable rapport between the teachers and the administrative authorities, this autocracy becomes an oligarchy with the teacher group as a solid and well-organized ruling class. It appears that the best practice extends the membership in this oligarchy as much as possible without making it unwieldy or losing control of it. In the most happily conducted institutions all the teachers and some of the leading students feel that they have a very real voice in the conduct of school affairs.

Where there is not a cordial rapport between school executives and teachers, control becomes more autocratic. A despotic system apparently becomes necessary when the teaching staff has increased in size beyond a certain limit. Weakness of the school executive may lead him to become arbitrary, or it may in the extreme case lead some other person to assume his authority. The relationship between students and teachers is in part determined by intra-faculty relationships; the social necessity of subordination as a condition of student achievement, and the general tradition governing the attitudes of students and teachers toward each other, set the limits of variation. But this variation is never sufficient to destroy the fact that the schools are organized on the authority principle, with power theoretically vested in the school superintendent and radiating from him down to the lowest substitute teacher in the system. This authority which pervades the school furnishes the best practical means of distinguishing school from not-school. Where the authority of the faculty and school board extends is the school. If it covers children on the way to and from school, at school parties, and on trips, then those children are in school at such times.

The generalization that the schools have a despotic political structure seems to hold true for nearly all types of schools, and for all about equally, without very much difference in fact to correspond to radical differences in theory. Self-government is rarely real. Usually it is but a mask for the rule of the teacher oligarchy, in its most liberal form the rule of a student oligarchy carefully selected and supervised by the faculty. The experimental school which wishes to do away with authority continually finds that in order to maintain requisite standards of achievement in imparting certain basic skills it has to introduce some variant of the authority principle, or it finds that it must select and employ teachers who can be in fact despotic without seeming to be so. Experimental schools, too, have great difficulty in finding teachers who are quite free from the authoritarian bias of other schools and able to treat children as independent human beings. Military schools, standing apparently at the most rigid pole of authority, may learn to conceal their despotism, or, discipline established, may furnish moments of relaxation and intimate association between faculty and students, and they may delegate much power and responsibility to student officers; thus they may be not very much more arbitrary than schools quite differently organized, and sometimes they are very much less arbitrary than schools with a less rigid formal structure. The manifestations of the authority principle vary somewhat. The one-room country school must have a different social structure from the city high school with five thousand students, but the basic fact of authority, of dominance and subordination, remains a fact in both.

It is not enough to point out that the school is a despotism. It is a despotism in a state of perilous equilibrium. It is a despotism threatened from within and exposed to regulation and interference from without. It is a despotism capable of being overturned in a moment, exposed to the instant loss of its stability and its prestige. It is a despotism demanded by the community of parents, but specially limited by them as to the techniques which it may use for the maintenance of a stable social order. It is a despotism resting upon children, at once the most tractable and the most unstable members of the community.

There may be some who, seeing the solid brick of school buildings, the rows of nicely regimented children sitting stiff and well-behaved in the classroom or marching briskly through the halls, will doubt that the school is in a state of unstable equilibrium. A school may in fact maintain a high morale through a period of years, so that its record in the eyes of the community is marred by no untoward incident. But how many schools are there with a teaching body of more than—let us say—ten teachers, in which there is not one teacher who is in imminent danger of losing his position because of poor discipline? How many such schools in which no teacher's discipline has broken down within the last three years? How many school executives would dare to plan a great mass meeting of students at which no teachers would be present or easily available in case of disorder?

To understand the political structure of the school we must know that the school is organized on the authority principle and that that authority is constantly threatened. The authority of the school executives and the teachers is in unremitting danger from: (1) The students. (2) Parents. (3) The school board. (4) Each other. (5) Hangers-on and marginal members of the group. (6) Alumni. The members of these groups, since they threaten his authority, are to some extent the natural enemies of the person who represents and lives by authority. The difficulties of the teacher or school executive in maintaining authority are greatly increased by the low social standing of the teaching profession and its general disrepute in the community at large. There is a constant interaction between the elements of the authoritative system; the school is continually threatened because it is autocratic, and it has to be autocratic because it is threatened. The antagonistic forces are balanced in that ever-fickle equilibrium which is discipline.

Within the larger political order of the school are many subsidiary institutions designed to supplement, correct, or support the parent institution, drawing their life from it and contributing in turn to its continued existence. These institutions are less definitely a part of the political structure, and they mitigate somewhat the rigidity of that structure by furnishing to students an opportunity for a freer sort of social expression. These ancillary institutions are organizations of extra-curricular activities, and comprise such groups as debating societies, glee clubs, choral societies, literary societies, theatrical groups, athletic teams, the staff of a school paper, social clubs, honorary societies, fraternities, etc. They are never entirely spontaneous social groupings but have rather the character of planned organizations for which the major impetus comes from the faculty, generally from some one member of the faculty delegated to act as "faculty adviser." These "activities" are part of that culture which springs up in the school from the life of students or is created by teachers for the edification of students. Such groups are often hardly less pervaded by faculty control than classroom activities, and there seems a tendency for the work of such institutions to be taken over by the larger social structure, made into courses and incorporated into the curriculum. Perhaps the worst that can happen to such organizations, if they are viewed as opportunities for the spontaneous self-expression of students, is that they shall be made over into classes. But the school administrator often thinks differently; from his point of view, the worst that can happen to such groups is that they shall become live and spontaneous groups, for such groups have a way of declaring their independence, much to the detriment of school discipline.

The political order of the school is characterized by control on three levels. Roughly, these are:

(1) Theoretical. The control of the school by the school board, board of trustees, etc.
(2) Actual. The control of school affairs by school executives as exerted through the teaching force or directly.
(3) Ultimate. The control of school affairs by students, government resting upon the consent, mostly silent, of the governed.

The school is the meeting-point of a large number of intertangled social relationships. These social relationships are the paths pursued by social interaction, the channels in which social influences run. The crisscrossing and interaction of these groups make the school what it is. The social relationships centering in the school may be analyzed in terms of the interacting groups in the school. The two most important groups are the teacher-group and the pupil-group, each of which has its own moral and ethical code and its customary attitudes toward members of the other groups. There is a marked tendency for these groups to turn into conflict groups. Within the teacher group are divisions according to rank and position, schismatic and conspirital groups, congenial groups, and cliques centering around different personalities. Within the student groups are various divisions representing groups in the larger community, unplanned primary groups stair-stepped according to age, cliques, political organizations, and specialized groups such as teams and gangs. The social influence of the school is a result of the action of such groups upon the individual and of the organization of individual lives out of the materials furnished by such groups.

A rough idea of some of the more important social relationships arising in the school may be derived from the following schema:

I. Community-School relationships.
   1. Relation of community to school in general. (Mediated through tradition and the political order of the community.)
   2. Relation of community to students individually and in groups. The parental relation and the general relation of the elders of the community to the young.
   3. Relation of community to teachers.
   4. Relation of special groups in the community to the school. (The school board, parent-teacher clubs, alumni, self-constituted advisory groups, etc.)
   5. Relation of special individuals to the school. (Patrons, ex-teachers, patriarchs, hangers-on, etc.)

II. Pupil to pupil relationships as not affected by the presence of teachers.
   1. Pupil to pupil relationships.
   2. Pupil to pupil-group relationships.
   3. Pupil-group to pupil-group relationships.

III. Teacher-pupil relationships. (Including also pupil to pupil relationships as affected by the presence of teachers.)
   1. Teacher to pupil-group relationship. (The customary classroom situation.)
   2. Teacher to pupil relationship.
   3. Pupil to pupil relationship as affected by the presence of the teacher.

IV. Teacher to teacher relationships.
   1. Relation of teacher to teacher.
      a. Teacher to teacher relationship as not affected by the presence of students.
      b. Teacher to teacher relationship as affected by the presence of students.
   2. Relation of teacher to teacher groups.
   3. Relation of teacher groups to teacher groups.
   4. Relation of teaching force to administrative officers.

NOTE: All these relationships are reciprocal.

The school is further marked off from the world that surrounds it by the spirit which pervades it. Feeling makes the school a social unity. The *we*-feeling of the school is in part a spontaneous creation in the minds of those who identify themselves with the school and in part a carefully nurtured and sensitive growth. In this latter aspect it is regarded as more or less the property of the department of athletics. Certainly the spirit of the group reaches its highest point in those ecstatic ceremonials which attend athletic spectacles. The group spirit extends itself also to parents and alumni.

A separate culture, we have indicated, grows up within the school. This is a culture which is in part the creation of children of different age levels, arising from the breakdown of adult culture into simpler configurations or from the survival of an older culture in the play group of children, and in part devised by teachers in order to canalize the activities of children passing through certain ages. The whole complex set of ceremonies centering around the school may be considered a part of the culture indigenous to the school. "Activities," which many youngsters consider by far the most important part of school life, are culture patterns. The specialized culture of the young is very real and satisfying for those who live within it. And this specialized culture is perhaps the agency most effective in binding personalities together to form a school.

PROJECTS

1. Study the shifting population of one school for a year. Does student or teacher turnover affect the quality of instruction? How does this turnover vary from one school or one community to another? What problems does a high student turnover present to the school administrator?

2. Make a diagram of the political organization of a particular school. Write a constitution which would adequately describe the working principles behind that structure. Write the by-laws for that school.

3. Narrate some incident from your own community which helped to define the boundaries of the school or to show how far the authority of the school actually extends.

4. Fill in (orally) the schema of social relationship for a particular school, mentioning persons who stood in certain relations to other persons, incidents showing nature of relations, etc.

5. Show how school songs, yells, traditions, etc., express the *we*-feeling of your own school.

6. Make a study of a school situation in which the actual head is other than the theoretical head.

7. What happens to the teacher's relations with students when his relation to his superior is not cordial? Describe several cases.

8. Describe the actual working of a self-governed school. Contrast it with the usual type of school. Can a teacher dispense with the ability to discipline in such a school?

9. Make a chart of all the subsidiary organizations and institutions centered about a particular school. Which are teacher-controlled and which spontaneous? What is supposed to be the function of each of these? Does it perform that function?

10. Follow through a crucial decision on school policy. What persons had to be brought into line before it became a part of the working tradition of the school? How were they brought into line? What ones have stood out against the policy and what has been their position in the school since that time?

SUGGESTED READINGS

(1) Cooley, C. H., *Social Process,* pp. 4-28.
(2) Dawson, C. A., and Gettys, W. E., *An Introduction to Sociology,* Chapters XIV, II, and III.
(3) Dewey, John, *Democracy and Education,* pp. 22-26.
(4) Park, R. E., and Burgess, E. W., *An Introduction to the Science of Sociology,* Chapters VI and III.
(5) Peters, C. C., *Foundations of Educational Sociology,* Chapter II.

Part Two

THE SCHOOL AND THE COMMUNITY

Chapter III

THE SCHOOL IN THE SOCIAL PROCESS; VERTICAL MOBILITY

Causal relationships reaching from the man who first chipped flint to us who ride in self-propelled vehicles bind us and him together. We live on the heaped-up bones of uncounted generations of ancestors, and it is only by virtue of those ancestors and their achievements that we are what we are. Nothing is lost in the economy of nature; little in the economy of society. The evil that men do lives after them, but so, for the most part, does the good; in time, the good may become evil and the evil good. A beautiful phrase lives forever, and beautiful pictures and beautiful music and a beautiful character. Transportation franchises hold over from stage-coach days; good things become evil. Man and his heirs hold their common property in perpetuum. That is what we mean by the social process.

Upon analysis, the all-inclusive social process breaks up into a number of minor processes. We may note some of the more important sub-processes in their relation to the school. Our treatment of this aspect of the subject will necessarily be quite brief.

Park and Burgess lay particular stress upon the distinction between the political and the cultural processes. Conflict is the basis of the political process, and its end result is an accommodation, a living arrangement. The cultural process is one of interpenetration of persons and groups, and its end result is the sharing of experience and history.

Accommodation has been described as a process of adjustment, that is, an organization of social relations and attitudes to prevent or to reduce conflict, to control competition, and to maintain a basis of security in the social order for persons and groups of divergent interests and types to carry on together their varied life-activities. Accommodation in the sense of the composition of conflict is invariably the goal of the political process.

> Assimilation is a process of interpenetration and fusion in which persons and groups acquire the memories, sentiments, and attitudes of other persons or groups, and, by sharing their experience, and history, are incorporated with them in a common cultural life. In so far as assimilation denotes this sharing of tradition, this intimate participation in common experiences, assimilation is central in the historical and cultural processes.[1]

It will help us to grasp the meaning of the school as a social institution if we try to place it with regard to these processes. To be strictly accurate, we must think of these processes as going on within the school as well as without it, of the school as a microcosm that mirrors the macrocosm. We are here concerned with the macrocosm, and with the position of the school in the macrocosm.

When the political process is still in the stage of overt conflict, various conflict groups attempt to use the schools for passing on their truth to the unbiased younger generation. Sectarian schools are for the most part established for this purpose, but it is perhaps only of the worst of these that Ross's aphorism that they are means of conducting children into society through a tunnel holds true. Economic groups are able to influence profoundly the policies of established schools, and on occasion to establish chairs and schools for the promulgation of their doctrines. In a leading eastern college is a chair that was endowed for teaching the fallacies of socialism. One of the greatest of the business schools was established at least in part as a means of crushing out various heresies concerning the protective tariff.

Conflict groups likewise reach out their hands toward the public schools. The list of those who have sought to use the tax-supported schools as channels for their doctrines is almost as long as the list of those who have axes to grind. Prohibitionists, professional reformers, political parties, public utilities, sectarians, moralists, advocates of the open shop, labor unions, socialists, anti-vivisectionists, jingoes, chauvinists, and patrioteers—all have sought to control the curriculum, the composition of the teaching staff, and the method of instruction. In widely differing degrees all these groups have succeeded. The situation varies in a perplexing and contradictory fashion with differing local conditions, but the schools are always at the focal point of community conflict. To a degree, the explanation of the contradictions of the school is to be found in the conflicts that rage about it.

[1] Park, R. E., and Burgess, E. W., *Introduction to the Science of Sociology*, pp. 735-736 (1924). (Reprinted by permission of The University of Chicago Press.)

Opposing groups work out various compromises by virtue of which the schools can be made acceptable to all parties. Thus the school is shot through with accommodations, some of which have grown so old that their original purpose has been forgotten. When community-wide accommodations are worked out by the conflicting parties, thus bringing the political process to a temporary resting place, these accommodations are immediately transferred to the schools. When such accommodations as the Constitution of the country are incorporated into the curriculum and transmitted by the schools, that is already the cultural process.

In that assimilation of group to group which Park and Burgess think of as characterizing the cultural process, the schools play a most important part. That is particularly true of the schools of a nation which, like ours, is seeking to amalgamate into one whole the representatives of many diverse cultures. The main burden of Americanization falls upon the public schools, and there is every likelihood that it will continue to do so. The schools Americanize by immersing the young in the culture and tradition of the country, by inducing them to participate as much as possible in the activities of the American arena. The things that the children of the foreign born learn at school, and on the streets before and after school, are often in conflict with the tradition which their parents are trying to transmit to them. Children usually learn to speak English better than their parents, and they more rapidly acquire a superficial familiarity with American life, so that frequently they feel superior to their parents, and are most unwilling to take advice from them. Since the home plays a large part in the formation of law-abiding attitudes, and since the view of American life which these children get is at best incomplete and distorted, Americanization through the schools usually entails a certain amount of disorganization for the second generation of immigrants. Adult education of immigrants has also been organized on a wide scale. Though less immediately effective, it is yet a very powerful means of leading the immigrant to that participation in American culture from which Americanization results. It seems possible, too, that the concurrent education and Americanization of parent and child may furnish a partial remedy for the demoralization of the second generation which sociologists and social workers have so often deplored. It would be interesting to know whether the crime rate among sons of immigrant fathers who go to night school is as high as the general rate for the entire group.

The common experiences of a group of people living together under any circumstances which give a semblance of unity operate to give the group that sense of a common past which is the mark of assimilation. Time is of the essence of the cultural process. There is, however, in the cultural process a many-sided interchange of attitudes and definitions of situations, of techniques and knowledge concerning the elements of culture. It is this process of transmission and interchange which we shall have particularly in mind when we speak of the cultural process from this point on. The school serves as a medium in which this interchange takes place.

We may think of this process of transmitting mental and material objects of culture as occurring, principally, on two planes: (1) There is the distribution of cultural goods over society at large, a transfer of objects and attitudes from group to group, from region to region, from person to person. Cultural anthropologists have sought to describe the production and distribution of cultural goods in terms of the processes of invention and diffusion. Invention is the manner in which new culture traits arise; diffusion is the process by which they spread throughout society.

The ordinary school does not serve as a center of inventions, although there are many institutions of higher learning which, through the support of experimentation and research, are taking over this function. The ordinary school does not share in this, but serves rather as a very important sub-center in the process of cultural diffusion. It is partly the task of the local schools to keep the community *au courant*, or as nearly so as possible, in the greater society, to exemplify and to furnish information about the newer things. Teachers play an important part in the process of cultural diffusion.

Particularly on the mental side of culture is it the task of the schools to mediate new things to the local community. Commercial organizations take care of the purveying of newer material objects, and they do it most effectively. Sociologists have found that many of the unadjustments in modern society are traceable to what is known as cultural lag, to the fact that non-material, or adaptive culture, does not change so rapidly as material culture. Thus our systems of law, religion, and morals are authentic antiques, but our automobiles and radios and talking pictures are modern. Much of the maladjustment of society is due to this failure of the machinery of social control to change with a rapidity equalling that of mechanical culture.

Now the existence of cultural lag is ascribable to a number of factors. There is a low rate of invention in non-material culture. And it is also true that new ideas spread slowly and meet with much opposition because many of them are against the mores. The schools could do much to accelerate the diffusion of non-material culture, but they have not usually cared to assume this function.

(2) We come now to the second phase of the cultural process, which consists of the transmission of attitudes, techniques, and knowledge to the younger persons of the community. This process is incidental to the succession of generations and is necessitated by the fact that all men are born equally ignorant. Much of the work of forming the young is done by other institutions, and certainly the family is more significant in child life than the school, but the importance of the school in the cultural process seems to be increasing; its formal position has always been central in the process, and there are indications that the actual significance of the school in child life is not destined to diminish.

A different aspect of the social process is that of social mobility; we shall here discuss, more specifically, vertical mobility. There is in our society a rapid movement of individuals from class to class. Persons born to a low station in life move to a higher; others more fortunate in their birth are less fortunate in their affairs and consequently are degraded by several classes. These vertical movements of individuals in a stratified society we may think of as convection currents in society. This concept of vertical mobility is one of the most illuminating insights of sociology, and for its fullest and most authoritative exposition we are indebted to Professor Pitirim Sorokin. It seems worth while to analyze the rôle of the school in fostering and impeding the vertical movement of individuals. In the main, we shall follow the pattern laid down by Sorokin.

There are great variations in the amount of schooling which children get. Dr. Ayres has computed the elimination in the school system. For every 1,000 children in the first grade, there are

723 in the second grade.
692 in the third grade.
640 in the fourth grade.
552 in the fifth grade.
462 in the sixth grade.
368 in the seventh grade.
263 in the eighth grade.

189 in the first grade of high school.
123 in the second grade of high school.
81 in the third grade of high school.
56 in the fourth grade of high school.[1]

Death and the increase of the population would account for a ratio of 1000 in the first grade to 871 in the eighth, but we have in fact 263; the remaining 608 have been left behind.[2]

The amount of schooling which children undergo foreshadows, and some would say determines, their future earning capacity and the level of society on which they will find their life. A crude selection, then, goes on in the schools, a social selection of those destined to fulfill certain predetermined social functions.

Partly it is the schools themselves which select. The native intelligence of children sets certain absolute limits to their achievements. No amount of schooling can make the moron perform satisfactorily above his fated level. The schools, by their curriculum which must be mastered before the student can pass on, sift and resift their human materials, selecting on the basis of intelligence chiefly, but allowing considerable weight to other qualities such as a pleasing manner, emotional stability, and diligence.

The schools must sort all the human material that comes to them, but they do not subject all children to the same kind of sorting process. Other things being equal, the schools tend to bring children at least up to an intellectual level which will enable them to function in the same economic and social stratum as their parents. The children of the rich are carried by express elevators of prep schools which do not stop below the college level. The most stupid, indeed, sometimes fall off the elevator, but even these may ultimately ascend to the higher floors by dint of much tutoring and the offices of friends. But the children of the poor tend to drop out early, and very frequently for reasons quite other than incapacity to learn; they drop out because their labor is needed at home, because they are ashamed to attend school in shabby clothes, because there is no tradition in their group of going beyond the literacy stage in education. Equally important with economic factors are the social assets of a family, its standing in the community, its level of cultural participation, its traditions and ambitions—these factors likewise limit social mobility.

[1] Ayres, Leonard P., *Laggards in Our Schools*, p. 13, New York Survey Association, 1913.
[2] Cf. Sorokin, Pitirim, *Social Mobility*, p. 190.

It is clear enough that the native qualities and abilities of students are not the only factors determining their progress in school. Yet the showing that a child makes on the school yardstick, however that showing may itself be determined, usually proves roughly accurate as a measure of further achievement. In casting up our reckoning it is necessary to allow for a number of factors, for the large number of self-educated, for great and not measurable differences in the assimilation of the same subject matter, for the outside factors which affect the operation of the school as a sorting machine; but when we have made all these qualifications it still seems to hold true that the sorting process of the schools produces results which roughly conform to the (cultural or inherent) qualities of the individuals sorted, and it also seems that there is a high degree of correspondence between the point to which one progresses in school and the level on which he functions in society. One of the functions of the school is, then, to sort out individuals with reference to their fitness for certain occupations and social positions. Sorokin goes so far as to say that this distributive function is the essential social function of the school.[1] Hornell Hart demonstrates that we have recently made progress in our utilization of the abilities of individuals.

The functions of the school as an agency of the cultural process and as a channel of vertical mobility are sometimes blended; indeed, these two functions in their individual reference are often indistinguishable. Education brings one into touch with the main stream of culture. The aspiring student embraces this wider cultural participation in the hope that it will make of him something somehow different.[2] Yet this being different is indissolubly connected with having a different place in society. A university confronts a gifted freshman as a vast array of cultural riches; he may appropriate these and realize himself in learning to use them. The cultural process,

[1] Sorokin, Pitirim, *Social Mobility*, p. 188: "In other words, the essential social function of the school is not only to find out whether a pupil has learned a definite part of a text book or not; but through all its examinations and moral supervision to discover, in the first place, which of the pupils are talented and which are not; what ability every pupil has and in what degree; and which of them are socially and morally fit; in the second place, to eliminate those who do not have desirable mental and moral qualities; in the third place, through an elimination of the failures to close the doors for their social promotion, at least, within certain definite social fields, and to promote those who happen to be the bright students in the direction of those social positions which correspond to their general and specific abilities. Whether successful or not, these purposes are some of the most important functions of the school. From this standpoint the school is primarily a testing, selecting and distributing agency." (Reprinted by permission of Harper & Brothers.)

[2] See Martin, Everett Dean, *The Meaning of a Liberal Education.*

which must start anew with every generation, automatically assigns men to their proper posts. The manner and extent to which they assimilate the cultural heritage determine the niche they will fit into in the social structure.

One of the important things that the school does is to separate individuals into classes corresponding roughly to certain occupational and social strata. When the matter is pragmatically considered, that conclusion seems inescapable. One is tempted to inquire whether this view of education corresponds with that social philosophy which is known as democratic theory and which is regarded as the fundamental orientation point for discussions of social policy in our society.

If the democratic theory is an egalitarian theory, then this doctrine that the sorting of individuals for given social duties is a necessary function of the schools is most incongruous with it. But egalitarianism is not essential for democracy. Perhaps the better view of the democratic ideal is essentially Platonic, that it is a social arrangement that attempts to use each person in the social function for which his ability best fits him. Competition is the soul of democracy, competition which brings out all the differences of men. But it must be a fair competition, and not a competition of which the result is biased by the hereditary rank or the economic resources of the family. And the competition must be relevant to function, if it is to produce good effects. A democracy is not a society without classes, but a society of open classes. There must be the possibility that the person born in the humblest position may rise to the highest. Each generation must be resifted on its own merits. Theoretically, vertical mobility would be very high in a democracy.

No society has attained to this ideal form of social organization. It is always a matter for long debate as to whether one society or one period in a society is more or less democratic than another. The actual differences of social structure between nations theoretically quite differently organized may in fact be slight. Extreme ability enables an individual to rise in an aristocracy and extreme inability enables him to sink. Family background and tradition, and the opportunities for cultural assimilation that wealth can buy count heavily in a democracy. There is much inequality and injustice in capitalistic society, and altogether too much power over the destinies of others is placed in the hands of irresponsible persons. There is much arbitrary power in socialistic society, and it seems that it may be fully as difficult for ability to get itself recognized there as elsewhere. The only fair conclusion is that no modern society is completely democratic.

The best evidence that classes are really more or less open in the United States is the abundance of opportunities for education. The social ladder of the schools is open to all and it is relatively inexpensive to climb; there are many who do not want to use it or who cannot pay the fee, so that all do not have an equal chance at education, but the educational ladder is there, and its existence is something. Education, or what passes for education, is free and even compulsory in its lower reaches. The education that is offered is not ideally adapted to discovering and developing ability, but it is the same for all. On the higher levels, there are the state universities which grant admission readily and charge low fees. In some of the cities are universities which offer a high grade of instruction and charge no fee. Evening schools, extension schools, and correspondence courses extend the low cost service of these universities yet further. Opportunities for self-help are numerous, and the surveys consistently show a very large percentage of men students in colleges and universities paying all or part of their school expenses by their own efforts; a student does not necessarily lose caste by working his way, and the public is frequently very helpful. In every institution there are numerous student aids in the form of scholarships, fellowships, and loan funds. Now it may well be true that the education which we manufacture on so large a scale and distribute so widely is a cheap product. But it is much the same for all, and it destroys or it develops the children of all classes impartially.

If we follow out the line of interpretation laid down by Professor Sorokin, the importance of the schools as selective agencies is increased by the very fact of their accessibility. For if education were very expensive, then not the schools but the fees would select out the few chosen from the many desirous. Or if education were the privilege of a hereditary caste, then hereditary status rather than learning would determine one's place in the social organization. In our society, the importance of academic selectivity is enhanced by the lack of other selective agencies.

The kind of selection which goes on in the schools has a great deal of effect upon the tone of social classes and upon the way in which they perform their various functions. It behooves us, then, to consider what sort of selection takes place in the schools.

The social selection of the schools takes place largely upon the basis of intelligence. Although pleasing qualities of person and such incidental traits as stability, purposefulness, diligence, and ability to control attention, most of which accrue from the mode of personal organization, are always of the first importance, it is nevertheless true that the selective pattern of the schools is one which somewhat overemphasizes intelligence. Again, it seems very likely that the intelligence which the schools reward most highly is not of the highest type, that it is a matter of incomplete but docile assimilation and glib repetition rather than of fertile and rebellious creation. How many star students are grade-hunters and parrots rather than thinkers! For it is not only in the grades that teachers give good marks to good boys; the conformed intelligence sells everywhere for a higher price than the unconformed. The intelligence most useful in the schools is that which enables the student to recite well and to pass tests.

It can easily be established that the overemphasis of intelligence in the schools has serious effects upon some personalities. Stupid students, or even students who are merely slow, are made to suffer needlessly, and the effects are lasting. Clever persons of no great worth, or promising but entirely unproved persons, may acquire in college a conception of their rôle which will make it impossible for them to sustain the task of slow ascent in the world of toil; such persons, too, are frequently embittered by the discovery that the world is owned and operated by and for persons of lesser mentality. It may be, too, that the unrest of the mass of these able persons in minor positions constitutes a threat upon the established order.

The overemphasis of intelligence is lessened in American schools by the importance attached to activities; the able student never attains the recognition that is accorded a football captain or the editor of a student paper. And even on the academic side, the selectivity of the schools is not entirely a matter of intelligence, for a certain amount of doggedness and ability to stick to unpleasant tasks is always a requisite of academic success. This necessary amount of pertinacity is nicely graded for the various levels of academic achievement, for the higher one goes the more tedious, in spots, is the going. There is a cynical professor who insists that the most important thing a college degree proves is that the person who has it could stand the grind for four years. Since a feature of creative intelligence is perhaps a predisposition to ennui and a low tolerance for the tedious, a scholastic regimen that forces the dull and the clever to go at the same pace and imposes upon the capable a load of routine work intended only for the mediocre eliminates many brilliant persons by its very boredom.

The selectivity of the school is considerably affected by fellowships, scholarships, and other student aids. Nearly every scholarship is governed by a strict set of rules, and can be given to only a certain type of student. These conditions governing scholarships are very important from the point of view of vertical mobility. There are political scholarships, athletic scholarships, disguised athletic scholarships, unauthorized athletic scholarships, scholarships for the academically able, scholarships for the courageous, scholarships for those showing particular ability in some one direction, scholarships for the diligent, and scholarships for those entering some particular profession. Scholarships are excellent things, but when we consider them from Sorokin's point of view we are led to wonder whether moderation is not desirable. Some writers argue, for example, that the caliber of ministerial students has fallen off as the number of aids for prospective ministers has increased.

It is difficult to reconcile the selective function of the school with its other social functions. The selective aspect of the educational machine is one which theorists frequently overlook. Yet it cries out to be included in any real reckoning up of the social meaning of the school. Those who devise curricula will do well to consider the existence of this sifting and sorting process which is inevitably associated with school life, and they need to consider its relation to social welfare. Those who are interested in the debate concerning college entrance requirements in high school may unearth new material by studying the subject from this point of view.

There are some indications that the rôle of the school as a selective agency is more important in present-day western civilization than it has ever been before. In the first place, the democratic dogma requires equality of opportunity for education, requires, theoretically, that education shall be given to each man according to his ability. The schools must therefore play a part in deciding what education the ability of a particular individual warrants. In the second place, the lowering of the school age and compulsory school attendance have greatly reduced the importance of the family as an agency determining the amount and kind of education to be given to the child. They have reduced the influence of the family but have by no means destroyed it, for family tradition and background must always count for much. Nor have facilities by which parents can slip mediocre sons into the most desirable occupational niches decreased; it is still, unfortunately, the recognized function of many private schools to put boys into college whose ability does not warrant their going to college.

Since the school performs this selective function for society, it is obvious that the rigidity or laxity of the testing mechanisms which the school employs is a matter of great social importance. Sorokin is convinced that the testing process in vogue in America is entirely too lax.

> To summarize; by increasing the rapidity of production of university graduates; by making graduation comparatively easy; by singing hymns to the great significance of university graduation; by paying little attention to moral education; and by failure to place graduates in proper positions; our universities are preparing dissatisfied elements out of these graduates (the people cursing the existing régime, directly and indirectly helping its undermining), under emergency conditions capable of supplying leaders for any radical and revolutionary movement. Even now, the proportion of sympathizers in a radical "reconstruction" of a "reactionary and plutocratic United States" in this group seems to be much higher than in any other group. "The saloon-socialists" and "pink" and "radical" elements are recruited principally from this and similar groups. To check this result of a relative "overproduction" of élite or the pseudo élite, it is necessary either to find for them a corresponding place or to increase the severity of the demands necessary for passing through college or any other social "sieve." Contrariwise, instead of a social benefit, a further increase of graduates, B.A.'s, masters, Ph.D.'s, and so on, may lead to social harm. This may sound like a paradox, to a great many thinkers, and yet, it seems to be true.[1]

Sorokin's facts are unquestionable. His conclusions from the facts are very cogent, but perhaps not inescapable. His discussion presupposes that the stability of existing society is one of the ends of education; there are very many who would question this presupposition. All who have been affected by the doctrines of John Dewey will question it. We are not concerned with that argument, but merely with pointing out that from another point of view it is desirable that education should be widely diffused, and that there may be means by which its evil effects can be avoided. But Sorokin's indictment of our present procedure indicates plainly that great and challenging tasks face the schools. There is the task of placement and specialized education, of discovering and developing abilities, and of learning how best to utilize them for the benefit of society. And not less clearly indicated is the task of moral education, such moral education as will make each individual as satisfied as it is possible for him to be with his station in life.

We cannot take leave of this topic without noting what effect this selective function has upon the internal structure of the school. Some

[1] Sorokin, Pitirim, *Social Mobility*, p. 201. (Reprinted by permission of Harper & Brothers.)

schools, notably the state universities, feel such a pressure of students upon facilities that they must yearly eliminate a large percentage of their freshmen. Other schools eliminate in order to keep scholastic standards high; they eliminate automatically and according to schedule, for a large proportion of students dropped for poor scholarship is supposed to assure high intelligence in those who remain and to cause the indolent to bestir themselves. The teacher caught in such a system is supposed to have a certain number of failures at the end of the semester, and this leads him to set up objective, but often highly artificial, standards; he is crucified between the necessity of having a "scatter" and that of being able to justify his standards by some reasonable criterion. It may be doubted whether the selectivity of a school under pressure to eliminate is wholesome. It is certain that such benefits as it confers are obtained at an immense sacrifice of human values. It is certain, too, that pressure to eliminate makes teaching dry and factual, overorganized, and full of artificial barriers. All this is dead; real learning is alive.

The horizontal mobility of the teaching profession, as the statistics show, is enormous. We do not know how far this represents advancement, for statistical data are lacking, but we do know that the schools serve as a channel of vertical mobility for teachers as well as for students. Teachers rise in the schools, and the paths they tread are well worn by the many generations that have gone before them. Well known, indeed, are the testing mechanisms which determine who shall enter teaching, along what roads they shall advance, and how fast they shall go. Taking a cue from Sorokin, we may think of these testing devices as of three kinds:

(1) Such as determine fitness or unfitness for the work of teaching.
(2) Such as determine fitness or unfitness for the social position of the teacher.
(3) Such as determine the channel and rate of advancement.[1]

(1) The principal testing mechanisms by which fitness for a teaching position is established are academic training, professional courses, teachers' examinations, requirements for certification, recommendations, and the scrutiny of prospective employers. A good many are eliminated by these hurdles, those without sufficient academic or professional training, those unable to carry college courses, those able to carry courses but not to get recommendations, those unable to secure positions, those unable to pass teachers' examinations, etc. It

[1] Cf. Sorokin, *op. cit.*, p. 182.

will be noted that the hurdles are chiefly intellectual in nature. Gifted students get the best grades and the best recommendations; these enable them to secure the best positions available, and make it possible for them to find their way into the aristocracy of teaching.

A certain number of obvious misfits and persons with pronounced defects of personality are eliminated by the scrutiny of prospective employers. But most of the testing of the social fitness of the teacher for the teaching job is done by the job itself. Until some way is found to test social fitness, there must always be a high percentage of failures among beginning teachers. The study of teaching failures in relation to the personalities of teachers would seem to be a most promising line of investigation. In this connection it should be noted that many educators believe that there should be some way of weeding out timeservers and persons not in earnest about the teacher's mission. Smith goes so far as to suggest that teaching salaries be rearranged, making the starting salary lower and the salaries of experienced teachers slightly higher. This, he says, would interpose a "starving period" between the prospective teacher and the real rewards of teaching.

(2) Teaching is not only an occupation, for it is a status as well. It is in the truest sense a "position," for the fact of being a teacher places one neatly in the world. The position of teacher carries with it certain social privileges, and duties, and some well-known disabilities. Many teachers who are perfectly competent in their work fail because they do not measure up to the social requirements for a teacher's position. Negroes cannot hope to hold positions except in the negro schools, and not always there. The doors are only less tightly closed against Jews and recent immigrants. Radicals cannot usually hold teaching positions, and even moderately sophisticated views greatly limit the range of a teacher's choice of jobs.

School administrators desirous of securing individuals who conform to particular types have been most ingenious in devising testing mechanisms. It is necessary in some institutions to secure conformity in religion and in one's views upon such social problems as the family or the negro question. One sectarian university asks the prospective candidate to sign a statement to the effect that no good evidence has ever been brought forward in favor of the theory of evolution. Where beliefs are more free, social acceptability of a different sort may be even more fundamental. Some private school and college presidents never employ a teacher until they have eaten dinner with him. Others have devised techniques of showing a candidate about the school, introducing him to the faculty, or sending the individual to interview faculty members. If the individual passes these tests, the verdict is that he will be a useful addition to the faculty. If he does not pass, the verdict reads, "I'm afraid that he's just not our kind of fellow." If such tests were more searching, and if they were universally applied, they might lead to much wiser choices of faculty members.

The scrutiny to which the members of the school board subject the candidate constitutes exactly this kind of test. Every prejudice is likely to be given a hearing. "City slickers" find the going difficult. "You know," remarked an estimable lady of rural antecedents, "Why you know very well that a fellow with a funny little mustache like that couldn't get a country school." The cut of the hair, the handshake, the voice, dress, manners, manner, and mannerisms—all these are noted and evaluated.

Rarely is it perfectly clear whether a teacher has succeeded or failed in his work. More often it is a debatable question. The opinion of fellow teachers weighs heavily in the final judgment. Perhaps it is best that it should weigh heavily. The public has no very accurate way of rating the teacher; nor is the public likely, because of certain fundamental antagonisms, which will be discussed later, to rate him fairly. Therefore it is necessary for the teacher to be rated by his fellow teachers, but this, too, presents difficulties because teachers rate teachers largely from the institutional point of view. They judge him by the way in which his work conforms to institutional standards. And very rarely indeed are they able to separate the question of his social acceptability in the teaching group from the more objective question of the success of his teaching methods. The teacher's acceptability to other teachers depends upon his adherence to the teacher code, upon his keeping students at a distance and observing the proper ritual of aggression and recession in contacts with other teachers.

(3) The rate of the teacher's advancement is also important, and it may likewise be shown to depend in great part upon personal and social factors which for the most part are not of a strictly academic nature. The teacher's efficiency in his work does indeed have some effect upon the length of the intervals between increases in his salary. It is clear, however, that this efficiency is defined according to the institutional situation. A teacher who keeps order in his classroom is usually regarded as efficient, even if his instruction fails of any considerable effect upon the student mind. But a teacher who often troubles his superiors with disciplinary cases will rightly be con-

sidered inefficient. The ability to discipline is the usual test. The faculty of "fitting in," and a degree of dexterity in manipulating the social environment, of which the most significant part is the group of teachers, are traits which are known to help a teacher to get ahead in his profession. Ultimately, the teacher's advancement depends upon his ability to grow with his position, but that growth must be fully as much in social grace as in professional skill.

Personal qualities, of which the more important are intellectual and executive ability, rightly determine the channel of the teacher's advancement. It may also depend upon the traditions and connections of the teacher's family, and upon chance associations formed after entering the profession.

It is interesting to record the belief of rural school administrators that a teacher advances in her profession as she changes from the lower to the upper grades. Sometimes teachers are thus "promoted" against their will. Roughly, of course, advancement from one level of teaching to another, as from the grades to high school, does represent promotion.

The vertical mobility of teachers affects the social atmosphere of the school in a number of ways. Where there are careers there are careerists, and there are careers in teaching. The careerist, the individual who is overmuch preoccupied with his own advancement, may have a high degree of institutional efficiency, but he may be expected to handle human materials recklessly, with some resultant breakage. Again, a school which contains a number of teachers who have, as they think, been cheated of their advancement, has not the same moral tone as a school in which advancement is regular and satisfactory. Intrigue, rivalry, political maneuvering, and conspiracy also derive their chief meaning from their relation to the vertical mobility of teachers. Indeed, it seems a safe conclusion that, when the social history of the present-day school is written, the careers of teachers will make up a long and interesting chapter.

PROJECTS

1. Study some community conflict which has resulted in a change of school policy.

2. Make a list of the suggestions publicly offered for the improvement of the schools during a given period. How far do these represent the activities of conflict groups?

3. Study the groupings of children within a school. How far do these represent the carry-over of adult groups, and how far do they cut across adult groups?

4. Write a case history showing the influence of the American school upon the child of an immigrant family.

5. Inquire into the motives for college attendance of twenty-five students. How many are in college for purely economic reasons? How many for "cultural" purposes? Are there cases which cannot be so classified?

6. Make a table showing the family background of twenty college students. List such traits as occupation of father, yearly income, years in school of each parent, etc. Contrast with occupational aim of student, probable income, etc. Interpret.

7. Make a similar table for a group of established teachers. Interpret.

8. Construct a chart showing the relation between yearly income and number of years in school for a group of adult wage-earners. (Have each member of class contribute ten cases and then put all the data on a single chart.) Interpret.

9. Make a table for same group showing the relation between occupation and number of years of schooling. Interpret.

10. Tabulate all student aids, fellowships, scholarships, loan funds, etc., in your school. What kind of social selection do they favor?

11. Organize all the arguments for and against more rigid selection in the schools. (Refer to Sorokin, Pitirim, *Social Mobility* for further suggestions.)

12. Compare the I. Q.'s of a group of boys who came into college from prep schools with the I. Q.'s of an unselected group. Compare also for social background, as above. Interpret.

13. Make a study of a group of candidates for teaching positions, comparing them on the basis of traits listed in the text. Show the relative standings of those who did and those who did not get positions.

14. Make a chart showing the advancement of teachers in their profession. Correlate advancement with measurable traits of personality.

15. Make a case study of a teacher who is a "careerist."

16. From the census reports, ascertain the national origins of teachers, the proportion of foreign-born whites, native whites of foreign parentage, and native whites of native parentage. Prepare a chart showing nationality of foreign-born parents. Explain the distribution in terms of the sociological concept of assimilation. What does the distribution show concerning the place of the teacher in the cultural process? Would it be possible on the basis of these figures to reach any conclusions concerning the rate of Americanization in different nationality groups?

SUGGESTED READINGS

(1) Cooley, C. H., *Personal Competition,* American Economic Association, Economic Studies, Vol. IV, No. 2. Reprinted in Cooley, C. H., *Sociological Theory and Social Research.*

(2) Cubberley, E. P., *Public Education in the United States,* Chapter VI.

(3) Dawson, C. A., and Gettys, W. E., *An Introduction to Sociology,* Chapters VIII to XIII.

(4) LEWIS, E. E., *Personnel Problems of the Teaching Staff,* Chapters XIII to XVII.

(5) LINDEMAN, E. C., *Community Conflict.*

(6) MARTIN, E. D., *The Meaning of a Liberal Education.*

(7) OGBURN, W. F., *Social Change.*

(8) PARK, R. E., and BURGESS, E. W., *An Introduction to the Science of Sociology,* Chapters IX, X, and XI.

(9) SOROKIN, PITIRIM, *Social Mobility.*

Chapter IV

THE SCHOOL AND THE COMMUNITY: GENERAL

One who thinks about the relation of the school to the community which supports it will soon come upon questions of public policy which it would take an Einsteinian grasp of the calculus of felicity to answer. Difficulty arises because the aims of the school and the community are often divergent. It is very well to say that the school should serve the community, but it is difficult to decide what opinion should govern when school and community differ. The lights of the school authorities are often better than those of the community in general. School men have given some study to their own problems, and could reasonably be expected to know more about them than outsiders do. Yet the community is often wiser than the school, because the community is whole and the school is fragmentary. The school, as a fragment of the common life, is a prey to institutionalism. Institutionalism causes the school to forget its purpose; it makes the school give education for education and teaching for teaching, perhaps for teachers; in short, it makes an end of what is logically only a means to an end. This vice the community escapes because the community is whole, because it is not simply a place where teachers teach and children learn. The community is whole because whole men live in it. And the community is sometimes wise with a knowledge of the complete life that surpasses the knowledge of the schools. It becomes, then, one of the important questions of public policy as to how far the community should determine the policy of the school and how far the school should be self-determining. We have not yet the formula.

A complication of a different order arises from the fact that communities in general, perhaps especially American communities, have chosen to use the schools as repositories for certain ideals. The ideals which are supposed to have their stronghold in the schools are of several different sorts. The belief is abroad that young people ought to be trained to think the world a little more beautiful and much more just than it is, as they ought to think men more honest and women more virtuous than they are. A high-school student must learn that honesty is always the best policy; perhaps his father secretly believes that he knows better; perhaps the boy himself may be learning something quite different in the world of business, but it does the boy no harm to start with that assumption. We can teach him enough honesty to keep him out of jail all his life; later he can make such amendments to our principles as seem necessary to him. All must learn that the United States is the greatest and best of all the nations of history, unequalled in wealth or virtue since time began. Perhaps it does no harm for students to think that the world is getting better and better, though this is a very dangerous doctrine if one thinks about it very long.

Among these ideals are those moral principles which the majority of adults more or less frankly disavow for themselves but want others to practice; they are ideals for the helpless, ideals for children and for teachers. There are other ideals which are nearly out of print, because people do not believe in them any more. Though most adults have left such ideals behind, they are not willing to discard them finally. The school must keep them alive. The school must serve as a museum of virtue.

We have in our culture a highly developed system of idealism for the young. The young have not yet come into contact with a world that might soil them, and we do what we can to keep the young unsullied. There are certain things that are not for the years of the young. There are certain facts about human nature that they must not learn. There are certain bits of reality that they must not touch. There are certain facts of history that we think it best not to teach them. There is an idealized world view that it is thought best to pass on to adolescents. The notion that it is not proper to tell the whole truth is often carried over into college teaching, and it affects materially the point of view of many university professors. There is just enough apparent wisdom in the policy of hiding difficult facts from the young to justify it in the popular mind as a general policy. For it is often argued that character training must begin by the inculcation of an impossible virtue, in order that the individual may have a surplus of virtue to trade upon. The world, of course, is thoroughly committed to the policy of not telling the whole truth to youngsters, to the policy of telling them falsehoods which will make the world more attractive or themselves more tractable and virtuous.

The conventional belief, as we have noted, is that the young must be shielded from contact with the unpleasant and amoral aspects of the universe and that they must be kept in an ultra-conservative environment. These ideals may be justified by the fact that they prevent the demoralization of the young; as to that we have preferred to keep an open mind. But it is certain that the necessity of serving as the repository for these ideals limits the larger utility of the school. For if it is the purpose of education to prepare for life in the world, then the school must give its students that world in order that they may get themselves ready for living in it. Actually it cannot give students the world, but only an imitation or a representation of the world; in any case, it should be an accurate imitation or a faithful representation if the training which the student receives in school is to have any validity. The less the discontinuity between the life of the school and the life of the world outside, the better will be the training for life which the school gives to its students. Any ideal which cuts down the ability of the school to reproduce reality interferes with its real function of preparing students for life. The utility of such ideals may even be disputed from the moral point of view; the argument against them is the good one that the individual upon whom we have foisted off a too idealistic world view will be more readily disorganized by contact with a far from perfect world than will an individual who has already had some experience of the world; it is the old principle of inoculation. In almost any case, if a school man believes in the policy of training young persons to be virtuous by not telling them the truth, he sets very definite limits to his own continuing influence upon those who come in contact with him. There is reason for the bitter jest that a school teacher is a man hired to tell lies to little boys.

Our analysis of the relation between the school and the community has so far been very general. The possibilities of such analysis are limited. We may hope to achieve an analysis which will have greater concreteness by basing it upon the connections which are made between the school and the community by the lives of individuals. If we wish an analysis that will bite into reality we must study the roots which persons involved in school life have in the community at large and attempt to discover the interconnection of their lives within and without the school. Each individual represents a reciprocal channel of influence, an influence of the community upon the school and an influence of the school upon the community. Therefore we must study the relation of the school and the community by studying persons and attempting to learn what burdens they carry as they go back and forth between the community and the school. We turn now to an analysis of this sort.

The place of students as the young of a community we have already noted. Toward young persons the community in general has the conventional attitude of the elders, an attitude of protection mingled with regulation. Children live in glass houses. There is the desire to shield the young from all contaminating contact with the world, and this is one reason for the multitudinous restrictions upon the teacher in the community. Every older person tends to take a paternal interest in the young of the community, whether he has progeny or not. The students in a public school thus have a very definite place in the community, and the community conception of this place materially affects the kind of school which the community maintains.

But it is not enough, and it is not nearly enough, to say that the young occupy a peculiar position in the community. Each child has a position that is his and only his, and views life with unique perspective. A group of children leave the school house in late afternoon. A few ride off on bicycles toward the big houses on the hill; the rest walk toward the poorer section down by the railroad track. Social and economic differences separate the two groups. Some of the children make their way toward the mean houses and narrow streets where black people live; the white man's attitude toward them cuts them and him apart. One child turns to the left toward the Polish settlement while another turns right for "Little Italy." Ultimately each child finds his own street and his own family. His roots are in his family, and he lives always against the background of that "unity of interacting personalities."[1] Even within the family, each child has his own particular place, for no two children can ever occupy the same space. Diverse, indeed, are the environments of school children, and their personalities are diverse; but teachers are supposed to treat them all alike.

Differences of position in the community determine important differences in the school. The child's status as the son of a particular person affects his status in the school and his attitude toward school. The daughter of an influential man in the community does not expect to be treated in the same way as an ordinary child, and yet it is dangerous for a teacher to make exceptions. Thus arise many problems to perplex the teacher. Typical of these was the following:

The three-hundred-pound daughter of a member of the school board was also in that class—a daughter of the member in fact who allied himself with

[1] The student should understand the influence of the family upon personality. Excellent treatments of the subject are to be found in:

(1) Mowrer, Ernest R., *The Family.*
(2) Reuter and Runner, *The Family.*
(3) Goodsell, Willystine, *Problems of the Family.*

the man who hated me so. She had an inferiority complex of some sort, probably due to her size, and it was coupled with an insufferable conceit. She was a good student but you had to learn how to handle her. It was a nuisance too. She made trouble of some sort nearly all the time. The only thing to do, as I saw it, was to let her alone till she got over it.

For one project I had the class make pajamas. The heavy-set daughter of the school-board member got mad immediately. She refused, I insisted, she told her mamma and mamma said she didn't have to, that she wouldn't allow her to wear them, wouldn't have them around, etc., for six volumes. Above all things, I tried to cooperate with the parents, and especially in that class, for the townspeople were poor. I told her she had to make two nightgowns instead of pajamas. Her work was always in late. I was at my wit's end to know what to do with her. She had the idea, somehow, that the school was run for her convenience. She was a Junior until midyear. After Christmas, as Senior sponsor, I had her on my hands, and a sore problem it was when we came to give the Senior party.

To return to the sewing class. We finished in fine style, having a beautiful exhibit of all the work, with the room decorated very attractively. I had to threaten flunking to get my heavy-set pupil to bring in all her work. She would stand and argue and argue. I'd turn her off kindly but it did no good. I was rude to her more than once, trying to make her quit. She would get mad and go off and talk about me. Then she would try to bring me around by cutting me. If she knew how we laughed at her. She was so very adolescent and she thought she was so very mature. (Autobiographical document, *My First Year of Teaching,* furnished by a woman teacher.)

It is not unknown that such a tieup between the child's parents and the teacher should win for the child differential treatment that he does not desire. The daughter of the most prominent banker in a small town relates with some disgust the story of the favoritism shown her by different teachers; in her case it would seem that a teacher lost her respect and good will more thoroughly through favoritism than she could ever have lost it through impartiality.

The attitudes of students make very clear the cruel distinction between rich and poor. Many children attain an easy and unhealthy leadership through the use of the economic resources of their parents or merely through their parents' reputations. It is upon the basis of such distinctions that many of the cliques and social clubs of high-school children are formed; the competition is not a healthy one because it is not based upon the merits of the persons competing. Many parents who have the misfortune to be well-to-do or famous have longed to remove their children from this atmosphere. The private school presents a way out of the situation. In Washington it is no distinction to be a Congressman; in a private school it is not usually a distinction to have wealthy parents; competition must therefore ascend to a different plane.

The children of poor and humble parents experience the situation with the opposite emphasis. They are those whom the teachers do not favor; they are the ones excluded from things exclusive. These poorer children frequently drop out of high school because of their inability to sustain themselves in social competition with the children of wealthier parents.[1] Clothes make the student. Teachers sometimes take unusual pains with children who have few cultural advantages and little economic backing at home, and these efforts occasionally have remarkable and heartening results.

Students may likewise stand out as individuals. The high-school athletic hero achieves much distinction in the school, and his prowess is usually bruited about the community as well. Brilliant students may likewise achieve desirable status in the school, with some carry-over into the community at large. The girl who becomes implicated in any scandal is singled out for special attention both in the school and the community. Frequently the attention is an attempt to injure her, and it usually succeeds.

Such is the influence of the community upon the school, as mediated through the personalities of students. The opposite process is fully as significant. The school, through its influence upon individuals, exerts a tremendous influence upon the community. This is a process which has often been dwelt upon in the literature, and we need give it here but passing notice. The long-term influence of the school may be very great. Perhaps the school can have but little effect upon the inner make-up of the children who pass through it, but it can have a great effect upon certain specific beliefs. Thus the advocates of temperance strove wisely to get their doctrines incorporated into the curriculum of the schools. Perhaps it seemed futile at the time to show little children pictures of ulcerated stomachs and badly deteriorated livers, but when those children grew old enough to vote, they put prohibition into the Constitution. Likewise the representatives of the public utilities have chosen to make much of their propaganda easily available for teachers in the form of lessons ready planned; some have gone to the extreme of offering to grade the teacher's papers for him. The process of cultural diffusion has sometimes been hastened through the lessons of the schools; a particularly good example of

[1] Cf. The Lynds, *Middletown*, p. 185, Harcourt Brace and Co., New York, 1929.

this has been furnished by the rapid spread of the toothbrush in America in the last quarter of a century.

But the school does not always have to wait until a new generation comes into power before it can make its influence felt. Sometimes children seize upon particular doctrines and spread them with a missionary zeal which proves embarrassing to their teachers. The tendency of children to set their parents right on certain matters by reference to what the teacher says is well known. Some of the most effective work of the schools has resulted from enthusiastic teaching of such simple but important matters as personal cleanliness and methods of hygienic living, with a subsequent rapid spread of those doctrines from the just converted students as radiant centers. Occasionally sharp conflicts arise between parents and children on the basis of what the children have learned in school. Sometimes these conflicts destroy the effectiveness of the home as an agency of control. Particularly unfortunate is the immigrant home. The children have the advantage of schooling, and they rapidly become better adapted to the superficial aspects of American culture than their parents. They consider themselves, therefore, wiser than their parents in all respects, and a divisive conflict results which destroys the value of the home as an agency for the imposition of moral and ethical standards. This break in the process of social control may come about without any direct conflict between the school and the parents on moral matters; the school trains the children in a universe of values with which the parents are unfamiliar, and the children then emancipate themselves from their parents. Children are more rapidly drawn into the main current of American life than are their parents, and the children therefore leave most of their ethical and religious codes behind; unadjustment is produced by a differential rate of diffusion to successive generations.

On occasion, the doctrines of the school and the community come sharply into conflict. The result is that some members of the community attempt to discipline erring members of the faculty. Instances like the following could be multiplied without end.

In studying Caedmon, I asked them to read the Biblical version of the creation story and compare it with his. I especially reminded them that I wanted it read as literature and compared on that basis. I called for the papers the next day. Only three were available. I nonchalantly gave them the same assignment and an additional one. No papers came in. I reminded them of their neglect. Finally, after another day or two, I began to get papers of a distinctly sectarian version of the story. It was not what I wanted and I told them so. It could not be used to the same purpose.

One night after school a rap came at the Assembly room door. There stood three very indignant ladies, one of whom I recognized as the mother of one of my girls. She asked me icily if "The Professor" (everyone called him that) was in. Innocence itself, I took them to his office in my most gracious manner. Miss V and I laughed about how someone surely was going to get their everlasting, for those ladies were mad. Little did I dream! I was thoroughly surprised when, the next day, the superintendent told me what a terrible time he had convincing them that I was not trying to corrupt their daughters' morals. (Autobiographical document, *My First Year of Teaching,* from a twenty-five-year-old woman teacher.)

This incident leads naturally to a consideration of community school relations centering in the personalities of teachers. We may state our two most important generalizations concerning the relation of teachers to the community in this form: That the teacher has a special position as a paid agent of cultural diffusion, and that the teacher's position in the community is much affected by the fact that he is supposed to represent those ideals for which the schools serve as repositories.

Teachers are paid agents of cultural diffusion. They are hired to carry light into dark places. To make sure that teachers have some light, standard qualifications for teachers have been evolved. Not only must the teacher know enough to teach the youngsters in the schools competently according to the standards of the community, but he must, usually, be a little beyond his community. From this it follows that the teacher must always be a little discontented with the community he lives in. The teacher is a martyr to cultural diffusion.

It does not matter where a teacher starts, he must always take just enough training to make him a little dissatisfied with any community he is qualified to serve. And it does not matter much how far he goes, for there is, for most of us, no attainable end. A farmer's daughter decides to teach. It seems to her that a rural school would be just right; she is used to country life and it pleases her well. But she must be a high-school graduate before she is qualified to teach in a rural school. When she has finished her training in the nearby village she is no longer enthusiastic about teaching in a rural school. She goes to a normal school, and learns to live in a cultural center of that level. Then she can teach in the high school of a small town. She goes to a state university, which is a first-rate center of learning. What she learns there makes high-school teaching a little dull and life in the smaller community difficult. University teachers and public-school teachers in the large cities are partial exceptions, but for the rest there is rarely an end to the process. The teacher must always know enough to make his subject matter seem commonplace to him, or he does not know enough to teach it. He must always have received teaching a grade higher than he can give. He must always have adjusted his possibilities to a center of learning one size larger than the one he serves. The teacher must take what consolation he can from the fact, made much of by inspirational writers, that he is a carrier of the cultural values.

This nearly universal maladjustment is not without its effect upon the standards of success in the profession. The successful teacher makes progress; that is, he moves occasionally, and always to a larger community. That is one reason why teachers stubbornly go to school. They hope some time to make tastes and opportunities coincide. But the fact that they rarely succeed accounts in part for the fact that teachers rarely take root in a community. They hold themselves forever ready to obey that law of gravitation which pulls them toward an educational center equivalent to the highest center they have had experience of. That is partly why teachers are maladjusted transients rather than citizens. Although the stair steps of primary groups of children no doubt have more to do with it than the attitudes of teachers, this unadjustment of teachers may help to account for the fact that schools of each level ape the schools of the next higher grade, the grade schools imitating the high school, the high schools pretending to be colleges, and colleges trying to become graduate schools.

One may disagree as to the interpretation of the prevalent dissatisfaction of school teachers with the community in which they live, but the fact itself seems indubitable. Over and over again, teachers, asked to tell the story of their experiences in certain communities, relate the same story. Especially keen is the disappointment of the teacher in his first school. The young teacher comes fresh from the training school to his first position. He has accumulated a great fund of idealism during his training; he is enthusiastic over his work and the self-fulfillment it will represent. He is usually elated over the prospect of at last receiving a salary for his services. When he arrives at the scene of his labors, which he has pictured with a certain glitter, as having upon it some of the tinsel of Utopia, he sees that which gives him pause; the community seems barren, sordid, uninspiring; the school itself is uninviting. "The school building displayed that peculiarly drab and unpicturesque deterioration which comes from a generation or so of school children, as if the building, too, were sullen and unhappy because of the unwilling children who entered it. It made me think of a tattered, old-young woman, frowsled and down-at-the-heels, worried from the care of so many children.'' But the teacher struggles to keep up his courage; he is determined to be pleased. This is a typical situation. A woman teacher phrased it briefly thus: ''The two weeks before school opened were not quite so appealing to me as I had hoped. Had I been disillusioned after my visit to the town? I tried to keep up my courage, and say, 'It'll be better than you think.' '' But there is no mistaking the fact that disillusionment has already set in. It needs now but a row with the school board, a set-to with a parent, and a wrangle with a colleague, plus, perhaps, a few weeks of following the course of study, and the discovery that the community does not approve of his progressive methods of education, to make a discontented professional of the erstwhile enthusiastic amateur.

This is the theme of many of the novels that deal with life in the school. The teacher goes out with a vigorous idealism, determined to pass his values on to others, eager to find his own place in the give and take of the universe. But he finds the world without comprehension of his values, unready to receive them, interested in coarser things managed by duller, harder men. He tries to begin at the beginning and explain his values to those about him. He finds this very difficult. He struggles in vain against disillusion, finally yields to it. The Messianic spirit dies, his own grasp upon his ideals is enfeebled, and he sinks into a stubborn and unreasoning discontent. Sometimes the hero of these novels is so weak and so self-pitying that one finds it difficult to sympathize. *Chimes* is a study of such a feeble personality very sure that he has received the light—at Harvard—and wanly desirous of the society of others who have received the same light. He is swamped in the upsurge of new things at the midwestern university, presumably the University of Chicago. He is bleakly unhappy, and more than a little rebellious, but never does anything about it. He is forever misunderstood, forever lost, forever bitter, and profoundly unhappy because others are not as he.

A truer pathos appears in the struggles of teachers to ''keep up.'' Young teachers fan the little spark burning feebly in their bosoms to keep it alive. Realizing their isolation from the main stream of cultural development, they fall into a sort of intellectual valetudinarianism where reading a good book or a serious magazine acquires a religious significance. The tragedy of those who strain to keep up is that they were never ''up.'' One has more difficulty in sympathizing with those specialists who demand not merely that they shall pass their days in the society of cultured men, but that these men shall have exactly the same kind of learning that they themselves have. Not that the specialist is particularly happy in his relations with those in his own field, for rivalries sever him from them. The college professor criticizes one half of his colleagues, as a witty friend suggests, because they have written books, and the other half because they have written none. The cultural isolation of the new teacher is further complicated by the breaking of personal ties in transplantation, by a conflict of urban and rural behavior norms, and by the teacher's status as a newcomer.

Our second major generalization is that the teacher is supposed to represent certain ideals in the community. These ideals differ somewhat from one community to another, but there is an underlying similarity. The entire set of ideals in their most inclusive form is clearly stated in the contract which teachers in the public schools of a certain southern community are asked to sign. The contract follows:

> I promise to take a vital interest in all phases of Sunday-school work, donating of my time, service, and money without stint for the uplift and benefit of the community.
>
> I promise to abstain from all dancing, immodest dressing, and any other conduct unbecoming a teacher and a lady.
>
> I promise not to go out with any young men except in so far as it may be necessary to stimulate Sunday-school work.
>
> I promise not to fall in love, to become engaged or secretly married.
>
> I promise not to encourage or tolerate the least familiarity on the part of any of my boy pupils.
>
> I promise to sleep at least eight hours a night, to eat carefully, and to take every precaution to keep in the best of health and spirits, in order that I may be better able to render efficient service to my pupils.
>
> I promise to remember that I owe a duty to the townspeople who are paying me my wages, that I owe respect to the school board and the superintendent that hired me, and that I shall consider myself at all times the willing servant of the school board and the townspeople.[1]

The contract quoted above is so extreme that it will seem incredible to persons who are not familiar with the moral qualifications which teachers in general are supposed to fulfill. Those a little closer to the facts will be willing to credit its literal truth. In any case, the contract itself is so explicit that comment upon it is unnecessary.

The demands made by the smaller community upon the time and

[1] Quoted by T. Minehan, "The Teacher Goes Job-Hunting," *The Nation*, 1927, Vol. 124, p. 606. (Reprinted by permission of *The Nation*.)

money of the teacher are unremitting. The teacher must be available for church functions, lodge functions, public occasions, lecture courses, and edifying spectacles of all sorts. Not infrequently he is expected to identify himself closely with some particular religious group and to become active in "church work." School executives occupy an even more exposed position than do underlings. Yet some unbelieving superintendents in very small communities have been able to work out compromises that satisfied the community and yet involved no sacrifice of their own convictions. One tactful agnostic declined to attend any church services at any time, but made it a point to be present at all church suppers, "sociables," and other non-religious ceremonies. Such a policy would need to be coupled with a great deal of skill in evasion and putting off if it were to work successfully; the teacher must not only avoid the issue and wear out those who urge church attendance upon him, but he must do it without giving offence or getting himself classed as an adherent of the devil. The teacher is also under considerable pressure to contribute to good causes. The difficulty is that he is not always permitted to judge of the goodness or badness of a cause. Quite aside from any such factor of judgment, the very multiplicity of the good causes to which the teacher is expected to contribute may make them a heavy drain upon his resources.

These demands are often resented, and with reason. But an interesting dilemma presents itself in this connection. A part of the solution of the problems of the teaching profession depends upon the assimilation of teachers to the community. Is not this conscription of teachers for edifying occasions a step in that direction? Where the participation of the teacher is quite unforced, as it sometimes is, it would seem that such demands work out favorably. Yet such participation will never really assimilate the teacher to the community, because it is not the right kind of participation. The teacher participates as a teacher, always formally and *ex officio*, too often unwillingly and by force. What is needed is participation by the teacher as an individual in community groups in which he is interested. If the teacher is ever really to belong, he must join in local groups as John Jones and not as the superintendent of schools.

The moral requirements that go with school teaching are extremely important. A colleague sometimes says, half in jest, that the schools of America are primarily agencies for moral and religious instruction. If anyone accepts the challenge laid down by that proposition, he points out the fact that the most complete ineffectiveness as a teacher does not always constitute a valid ground for dismissing a teacher from his position, whereas detection in any moral dereliction causes a teacher's contract to be broken at once. Undoubtedly the fact that teachers must be models of whatever sort of morality is accepted as orthodox in the community imposes upon the teacher many disqualifications. With regard to sex, the community is often very brutal indeed. It is part of the American credo that school teachers reproduce by budding. In no other walk of life is it regarded as even faintly reprehensible that a young bachelor should look about for a wife, but there are indications that courtship is not exactly good form in the male teacher. The community prefers its male teachers married, but if they are unmarried, it forbids them to go about marrying. With regard to the conduct of women teachers, some communities are unbelievably strict. Youth and beauty are disadvantages. Husband-hunting is the unpardonable sin. The absurdity of this customary attitude, as well as its complete social unsoundness, should be apparent from its mere statement; it becomes all the more significant that, in presenting the subject of sex prejudice against school teachers, one must usually go on to point out that this is a situation almost without parallel in modern life. Women teachers are our Vestal Virgins.

Conduct which would pass unnoticed in a young business woman becomes a matter of moment when the young woman is a teacher. Rarely does an entire community pause to inquire into the affairs of a nineteen-year-old stenographer, but it can, as the following incident shows, become tremendously excited about the affairs of a nineteen-year-old school teacher.

During the summer when Mr. Blank, our superintendent, was on vacation, Miss Jones came to apply for a position. Miss Jones was a very good looking young lady, nineteen years of age, and just graduated from a small sectarian university. She, herself, belonged to the sect. The school board had one fellow sectarian, and, as the principal remarked, two others who were susceptible to good-looking young women. Miss Jones was hired. Mr. Blank had intended to fill her place with a young man.

Miss Jones, being the only member of the high-school faculty belonging to this sect, chose to room alone. From the first it was noticeable that the young men frequented Miss Jones's room in the mornings and noons before school had taken up and after school evenings. That started talk. The story was passed around that Mr. Blank hadn't wanted her in the first place and that she had better be careful. Some of the teachers passing through the hall or otherwise near her classroom reported that she had noisy classes.

Several of the teachers talked to her in order to get her to confide in them. Then the rest of the teachers were informed of what had occurred. She remarked that there wasn't a single man in town that she hadn't dated. Several times she had accepted rides with high-school boys. If she walked up the street with one of the boys at noon this was further cause for gossip. One teacher was reported to have said that she had better leave her gentleman friend alone or she would scratch her eyes out.

One of the mathematics teachers was on hall duty right outside Miss Jones's door and each day she had something to report about Miss Jones.

The first six-weeks examination time came. The examinations were sent to the office to be mimeographed. Miss Jones's questions were considerably revised. Naturally she became bitter. She remarked that she knew that the superintendent and principal were out to oust her. Her conduct was reported as worse and worse. The teacher on hall duty reported that she had heard the principal chase a number of boys out of her room. It was decidedly noticeable that the principal and superintendent were in the hallways a great deal of the time.

Every move she made was watched and catalogued. A teacher told the others that at one of the class parties some boys had come up to her and politely inquired as to how she had enjoyed the party, then turned to Miss Jones and asked her to go riding with a group of them after the party.

Toward the end of the year she started keeping company with a young man reported to be of questionable character. It appears that a member of the school board remonstrated with her, telling her she shouldn't be seen with him. As Miss Jones stated in her own words, she "gave him to understand where he should head in."

By established custom, public dancing was not allowed among the teachers. Miss Jones was seen numerous times at public dances.

Once she told a group of teachers that she was not cut out for a teacher and that she was not coming back.

The school teachers, principal, and superintendent were all brought forcefully to the attention of the public through this unfortunate affair. The town took sides on the question, which disturbed the entire school and the entire community. (Document submitted by a school teacher.)

Miss Jones, perhaps, merits scant concern. But hers is a story that repeats itself every year or every few years in almost every city and village of the nation. In other instances some particular points would stand out more clearly. Cases could easily be found in which much greater injustice was worked upon the individual teacher and a much less charitable attitude taken by the community at large. This community had some cause to be concerned. There were numerous complicating factors, including the young woman's religion, her isolation from the other teachers, and the bad blood between her and them. But this case will serve to show how a storm may descend upon the head of an adolescent girl who is a teacher and who nevertheless behaves as another adolescent girl might behave.

This story calls to mind many others of a similar nature. There is, for example, the not uncommon case of the teacher who is quite efficient in her work and quite discreet in her relations with students, but inclined to lead a somewhat emancipated life outside the school room and the circle of school contacts. The efficient teacher who somehow gets the reputation of being "fast" often becomes a storm center too. Sometimes this reputation is founded upon nothing more tangible than the fact that this teacher prefers to live in a hotel than in a private home, that she does not go to church, that she plays cards, or that she occasionally takes weekend trips. The list of taboos is endless; the president of a certain teacher's college in the south is reputed to look with the utmost disfavor upon any association outside of school between his male and female teachers, though he does not disapprove, apparently, of other arrangements they make in their love life. This seems a fine distinction. Smoking is an issue of importance. It is sometimes disapproved even in men, and the conservative members of some communities still think with horror of "the teacher who doesn't think anything of walking down the street with a big cigar in his mouth." The preference of such communities is very definitely for men who do not smoke, but their sense of moral outrage is not so keenly aroused by smoking in men as by a similar indulgence in women. A not unprogressive eastern community was recently thrown into a war of words by the moral issue of women teachers who smoked. The president of a teacher's college in Michigan not long ago announced his intention to refuse to recommend any girl who smoked. This would probably prevent such a girl from ever obtaining a teaching position. A ludicrous example has been reported from a state university of the middle west. A number of faculty wives smoked at a meeting of the faculty dancing club. A faculty busybody reported the incident to the president, and furnished a list of names.

PROJECTS

1. Recount a dispute between school authorities and community leaders over some question of school policy. Analyze the implications of the dispute.
2. Tell the complete story of the campaign made by a school executive to introduce a needed school reform in a particular community. Interpret.
3. State the code of morals to which the children of a given community are expected to adhere. Be explicit. Compare with the working moral code of the adult community.

4. Secure statements from a group of teachers on the question, "When is it necessary or desirable to lie to children?"

5. Make a case study of a young man who has absorbed the cynicism of an older man. Interpret your material.

6. Determine by observation of cases what happens to the idealist when he meets disillusion. What principles of school policy do your conclusions establish?

7. Describe and compare the home environments of ten unselected school children.

8. Analyze the membership of a high-school social club. How much bearing has the economic status of parents upon admission to membership?

9. Make a list of the recent changes in our customs in which you believe school instruction played a part.

10. Do you know of high schools with "varsity" teams? What does this show?

11. Make observations to check upon the generalization that the discontent of school teachers is partly produced by the teacher's peculiar position in the process of cultural diffusion.

12. Tell the story of a teacher who lost his position because of "unprofessional" conduct. Interpret.

13. Keep a record for one month of the demands made by the community upon the time (outside of school hours) and the money of a small-town superintendent.

14. Is it politic for a teacher to engage in church work? Support your contention with concrete evidence.

15. Analyze the personality of a teacher who is reputed to be "too fast." How did he get this reputation? Interpret.

16. Find out the attitudes of twenty unselected adults toward smoking by men and women teachers. Interpret your results.

17. "Describe some community you have known where teachers are recognized as the *élite*." "Describe some community where teachers are regarded as an inferior class." (Quoted from Clow.)

SUGGESTED READINGS

(1) Hart, J. K., *A Social Interpretation of Education,* Chapters VII to XI.
(2) Herrick, Robert, *Chimes.*
(3) Lynd, R. S. and H. M., *Middletown.*
(4) Park, R. E., and Miller, H. A., *Old World Traits Transplanted.*
(5) Steiner, J. F., *The American Community in Action.*
(6) Steiner, J. F., *Community Organization.*
(7) Wissler, Clark, *Man and Culture.*
(8) Young, Kimball, *Social Psychology,* pp. 347-52.

Chapter V

TEACHERS IN THE COMMUNITY

Enough has been said to mark out the general position of the teacher in the community. It will be readily understandable that the teacher is usually more or less isolated in the community in which he lives. He is isolated because he is often an outsider hired to mediate certain skills and certain specialized lores to the young of the community. He is mentally isolated from the rest of the community by his own set of attitudes. But, most important of all, he is isolated because the community isolates him. This the community does by making him the carrier of certain super-mundane values, and by imposing upon him certain humbling restrictions. The community can never know the teacher because it insists upon regarding him as something more than a god and something less than a man. In short, the teacher is psychologically isolated from the community because he must live within the teacher stereotype.

The teacher stereotype is a thin but impenetrable veil that comes between the teacher and all other human beings. The teacher can never know what others are really like because they are not like that when the teacher is watching them. The community can never know what the teacher is really like because the community does not offer the teacher opportunities for normal social intercourse. The cessation of spontaneous social life at the entry of the teacher, and the substitution for it of highly artificial and elegant conversation, is very evident in the following record:

I was listening to a group telling jokes customarily heard in a barber shop, when a man approached the door. At once the barber stopped working and said, "Sh! Sh! Boys, the principal of the high school is coming in." All was quiet. The principal entered and sat down. The barber broke the spell by saying, "Well, I suppose, professor, you are glad school will soon be out?"

"Yes," he replied.

The barber remarked, "If you are as anxious as that boy of mine is for it to let out, why it can't be too soon." The principal had come to pay a bill. He started out. The barber said, "Professor, you need not hurry off. There is just one ahead of you and then you're next. Won't be over twenty minutes."

"Oh, I'll be back later," the principal remarked.

"All right, come in about twelve-fifteen. Business is lax at that time and I can fix you out right away."

After the principal had left the barber turned to the group and said "Boys, I enjoy a good story myself but this is a public place and we've got to treat such men as the one that left with respect. *Besides that I have many women customers.* It is embarrassing to them and, too, it throws the responsibility upon me. You understand what I mean. All right, now go on with your jokes and stories!" The barber laughed. (Unpublished manuscript by Charles Zaar, *The Social Psychology of the Barber Shop*, stenographic report of conversation.)

The constant use of the title "Professor," the obviously artificial conversation, the lack of interest of the teacher in those banal remarks that he had heard so many times before, the assimilation of the teacher to the female character ideal, the suppression of normal activity when the teacher entered the room—all these things make the above stand out as an interesting and significant incident. It has been said that no woman and no negro is ever fully admitted to the white man's world. Possibly we should add men teachers to the list of the excluded.

But it is not only in his public appearances that the teacher feels the gulf between himself and other men. When the teacher must live in a private home, the teacher stereotype still isolates him from the people with whom he lives. A woman teacher narrates the following incident:

Soon supper time came and the family and I were seated at the table. There was a small boy of three in the family and much conversation was directed to him in which the mother and the father remarked that he must behave because the teacher was watching him. The fact that I was the teacher seemed to be foremost in the minds of these people. That barrier between the teacher and the rest of society was much in evidence. I was the teacher. Towards me there was a somewhat strained attitude. I didn't see much of the family, for as soon as they were through eating they had chores to do and when the chores were finished they all went to bed. (Student paper, *My First Year of Teaching.*)

The objective side of the isolation of teachers in the community has nowhere received a better statement than that of the Lynds in *Middletown*:

Indeed, few things about education in Middletown today are more noteworthy than the fact that the entire community treats its teachers casually. These more than 250 persons to whom this weighty responsibility of training he young is entrusted are not the wise, skilled, revered elders of the group. n terms of the concerns and activities that preoccupy the keenest interests f the city's leaders, they are for the most part non-entities; rarely does one un across a teacher at the weekly luncheons of the city's business men ssembled in their civic clubs; nor are many of them likely to be present at he social functions over which the wives of these influential men preside. Iiddletown pays these people to whom it entrusts its children about what it ays a retail clerk, turns the whole business of running the schools over to School Board of three business men appointed by the political machine, nd rarely stumbles upon the individual teacher thereafter save when a paricularly interested mother pays a visit to the school "to find out how Ted s getting along." The often bitter comments of the teachers themselves pon their lack of status and recognition in the ordinary give and take of ocal life are not needed to make an observer realize that in this commercial ulture the "teacher" and "professor" do not occupy the position they did ven a generation ago.[1]

In smaller communities the teacher's difficulty in finding a place n the community is objectified in his difficulty in finding a room in which to live. Much hinges upon the choice of a rooming place, and nuch upon the choice of a boarding house, for the teacher, although e has no value as a person in the community, may acquire a symolic value on the chessboard of community factions and antagonisms. A story with some unusual features and many common ones is the ollowing:

About this time my rooming problem had to be settled. I couldn't stay here I was. The house was too small, having only one bedroom and a bed n the dining-room. After a time I grew used to coming to breakfast and ating in the same room where the over-grown, twelve-year-old daughter of he house lay sprawled across the bed in regal slumber. There was a time, ater in the year, when the man of the house (a perfect giant of a fellow who worked on a railroad gang) was ill, and then we ate all three meals or days on end with his huge form draped on the bed. No, I couldn't stay here. That girl got on my nerves, and everyone's else. When I was in my oom she kept up a continual going in and out. She did it merely out of uriosity. I could not stop her, for that was the only bedroom and all of their hings were in there.

The superintendent tried his best to get me to stay with some member of he numerous X—— family, if they would condescend to keep me. I found ut he didn't stand well with that faction and wanted to use me as a "club." refused, and yet there seemed to be no place to go. Finally, Mrs. C., the irst- and second-grade teacher, asked me to room there. I was delighted.

[1] The Lynds, Middletown, p. 209. (Reprinted by permission of Harcourt, Brace Company.)

She and her husband appealed to me as very fine young people and of a high type unusual in that town.

The room was large and full of sunshine. They had a lovely home with a grand piano that appealed to me. I found it to be sadly out of tune, like the rest of the place, underneath, but it was far better than nothing. I had a stove in my room. At first an oil heater that nearly asphyxiated me one Sunday afternoon when I took a nap. Another day it smoked and blackened up the new wall paper upstairs and all my clothes. It nearly set the house afire. The bathroom wasn't heated. One week end I returned from a visit home to find the lavatory had been blown clear across the bathroom. It was a long time before we had water after that. We had to get it from a well. I kept two stew kettles full in my room. They put up a trash burner for winter. It burned cobs and the cobs brought mice galore. I couldn't sleep for the noise they made. Until January, when he left, Mr. C. came up and made my fires in the morning. It bothered me at first, but I got over that along with a lot of other things.

When I first went to live with the C.'s I saw that a separation was inevitable, but I didn't think it would come for a year or so at least. She made no home for him. The house wasn't even clean most of the time. It had a stale and musty odor. I kept my room well-aired and cleaned to counteract it. There was no need for her to teach. She herself was wealthy. She put away every cent she made, making her husband furnish everything for the house, even postage stamps. She kept the roomer's rent till the year I came and then he decided he was going to keep it.

She talked incessantly. How it got on my nerves! Always telling of her "sacrifices" for Mr. C. Time and time I heard such remarks as, "I always take the milk that's a wee bit sour, Peg, and give him the sweet. True love is like that, Peg." I got so I stopped up my ears and let my sixth sense nod my head at the proper intervals.

Then her father was eternally coming in. He came in before breakfast, again after breakfast, as soon as it was time for school to be out, before supper, and a couple of times after supper. If she wasn't home after school when he thought she ought to be he gave me no peace till she arrived, coming in and out or calling up (after Mr. C. insisted on having a phone put in so he wouldn't have to go over to the old man's every time he wanted to phone). There was a terrific battle over it, and Mrs. C. alternately pouted and snapped for days over it.

I had to be decent to the old gentleman because he was on the school board. He used to quote scripture to me by the yard, and especially after the trouble began to break out. I used to think I was religious, but he cured me. Every time he came over he would shout upstairs at me. He talked incessantly. I soon learned to make excuses to get up to my room when he arrived. He didn't like it, but I smoothed it over by saying I didn't want to intrude.

From the first there was a constant bickering at the house. There were trained silences, slammed doors and all the rest that goes with it. I ignored it s best I could, keeping to my room. Mr. C. began staying out later each ight and then failed to come home at all one night. And what an uproar hat caused!

Mrs. C. was always complaining of her heart. I heard heart symptoms ntil I didn't see how anyone dared even to walk fast. They still bother me hen I suddenly discover that I have run up a flight of stairs. Of course, had to be very sympathetic. After nine months of it, day in and day out, got so I didn't care if her father was on the school board.

If it had been just heart symptoms I shouldn't have complained. As she egan to realize he was definitely slipping away she tried other bits of trategy. One was falling downstairs in a sort of stupor. She begged me ever to tell a soul about it. What brought this symptom on, she said, was he finding of a note which he had written to the fifth and sixth grade eacher, a Mrs. B. She regularly went through his pockets, saying, "That's he only way I have of keeping track of him, Peg."

More trouble developed when he refused to speak to her. He talked to me nd so did she; also she talked to him. She tried to get me to talk to him nd find out what the difficulty was—as if any woman with a grain of sense ouldn't see it! I refused to be drawn into it. Then her father begged me o talk to him. Night after night I came in from supper to witness terrible cenes by Mrs. C. and hear her beg me to talk to Mr. C. and find out what he trouble was. Over and over they told me their side of it and asked me f they'd done right. I dreaded coming home.

I had troubles of my own. I began actually to fear that big old bridge cross the angry river down the road. I was going to resign. The superinendent told me he couldn't recommend me if I did. He tried to force me o move, for by now gossip was getting around the town. I couldn't find ny place to go. No one had a room or wanted a roomer. Also, I feared to eave because of what Mrs. C. might then say. If I left she'd say she had o ask me to move because she had begun to be suspicious of me. Although refused to take sides in the case, that very fact made her suspect me, think. He left in January, telling her that he was getting a divorce. I can ear that scene yet. One other night when he was there (he came back to eep up the fires) she asked me to go in and talk to him. I refused. She gave ne a push that sent me flying into the room.

She began to talk, and how she did talk! The whole town was abuzz before knew it. I would come home from a long hard day at school to spend the ime until late at night hearing her rant and tear and moan and groan. I vent to sleep to the noise of that every night. It did no good to try to talk o her.

She spied on the bank to see if "the other woman" was there. I recall one ight she got me to walk up and down the one main street of the town with er for that purpose. I soon learned better. He and she played in the town and. She insisted that I go to practice with her so that she would not have to go alone. Dreading to stay all alone in that big house, I went. She got s she stayed over at her folks' home evenings and I was glad to get out eve on such an excuse.

The superintendent told me to quit going to band practice with her. H said that people were talking horribly about her and that they "looked side wise" at me for going out with her. I protested that it got mighty lonely nigh after night in that big house. It made no difference, so I stayed at home. I made Mrs. C. angry and more suspicious than ever, for again she though her husband had come to see me. He did not; but she had the lady next doo watch every move I made while she was away. I saw her in the yard one nigh looking at my windows. Heaven knows I didn't want that man.

I went home nearly every week end. Mrs. C. always slept in my bed whe I left, even asking company to sleep with her. When she was gone Mr. C slept in my bed, I discovered. This was after he quit staying at the house One Monday morning the superintendent came in and said, "I hear you ha company over the week end at home." I looked aghast and denied it. Mrs. C had gone up to the city with me on the same train to visit a friend. She ha told several, and the news had travelled that I had asked her to visit my home He said everyone was talking and that he couldn't understand why I ha done such a thing. I was mad as blazes.

The same morning he said someone started the tale that I was going to marry "Tabby," her brother. Their folks were redecorating their house and the townsfolk had it that I was going to marry him. I didn't even go with him. The superintendent's wife told me late in the spring that if I'd ever gone with him alone once, I'd have had to leave town.

All the time the talk and sentiment grew steadily worse. I went on my way as serenely as I could. I refused to talk with anyone about it in spite of pumping. I knew more of the straight facts than anyone in town. The rest got only what Mrs. C. wanted to tell to help her case along. I was afraid to speak to folk on the street for I didn't know which side of the story they believed. No one ever snubbed me, however. Not even the bully on the school board.

Mrs. C. thought she found more and more convincing proof of Mr. C.'s and Mrs. B.'s affair. She told me all the dirty details over and over till I could say it all backward. I tried not to take sides. She thought I did underneath, and behind her back, and treated me accordingly. However, to my face she couldn't be sugary enough. She started weird tales. She talked terribly of Mrs. B. Finally that madame, after many trials, got Mrs. C. cornered one night after school and told her what was what and threatened a law suit. That squelched the open work of Mrs. C. for fear of court. It didn't stop the underground work, however.

It was painful at school. Mrs. B. paid no attention to Mrs. C., but Mrs. C. went miles out of her way to avoid Mrs. B. Mrs. C. pestered the third and fourth grade teacher nearly to death, telling her all about it, over and over. I had a school orchestra. Mrs. B. and Mrs. C. were in it. Each was bound the other was not going to run her out of it. It made the atmosphere very strained. Finally, Mrs. C. pled "much work" and stopped. Then Mrs. B. was ill and dropped out. Mrs. C., after much questioning me, returned. She always insisted upon sitting in the front row, and, as she played the saxophone, it was awkward. Their changing about was hard on the orchestra, for it was small enough at best.

By this time all the students knew of the turmoil and watched it with interest. In spite of everything, bits of gossip would stray out in my sewing class. The girls used it as a clearing house for town gossip. I tried at first to stop it. Then I decided that it was hard enough to hold their interest in school, so as long as they talked quietly and worked I let them alone. I think very much more is accomplished in a class like that if easy, friendly relations are established. . . .

The preacher was a nice little old fellow, but his wife did more harm than his preaching could ever rectify. She and Mrs. C. got together and between them told such tales on me as are impossible to print. I didn't know about it until a day or so before I left, in fact, I heard of it in the midst of the rush and worry of the last day of Senior play practice. I thought I couldn't find strength to go on. Just before I heard of it the preacher's wife asked me to come over to dinner. I had no boarding place then, as the lady with whom I boarded had had to go out of town for the week. I accepted and was sorely condemned for it. Another evening I was passing, and she asked me to come in and sit down a minute. No one called on them and she was very lonely. I knew she was trying to pump me every time she saw me for inside news of the C. trouble, but I was lonesome so I decided to ignore all reference to the C.'s and stop for a while. No word was mentioned of them. The next morning the superintendent's wife stopped me en route to school and told me the preacher's wife had gone up to her house after I left, to a committee meeting. She let it be understood that I came for counsel, and talked things over with her. The superintendent's wife wanted an explanation, and she said that that woman was not my friend. I denied that one word had been mentioned of the C. affair. It got so the superintendent's wife stopped me every morning with some new development, some new rumor in connection with the C. trouble. It made a fine starter for the day. It remained for me to get myself in hand, for the day, during the time which it took to eat breakfast, what little I could eat after that, and walk the block to school. (Autobiographical document, *My First Year of Teaching,* furnished by a twenty-five-year-old woman teacher.)

This story has some unusual features, but it also serves to illustrate some common mechanisms. A further sidelight on this case is that the school board had been divided as to the advisability of hiring a music teacher, and that bitter dissension had arisen. This young woman had become a bone of contention in the community before she was asked to sign a contract; she had already acquired an unusual value in terms of a community conflict. The attempt of the superintendent to use her as a stopgap in his own political fences by inducing her to room with a member of the X—— family, if it were possible, is typical of a certain level of political machination. In the family with which she finally decided to room, she stepped again into a conflict situation. Accordingly her symbolic importance as the focal point of one community conflict became reenforced by a like concentration of attention upon her through her connection with the C's. Were it not for her exposed position at the crossing of all these lanes of machine-gun fire, her sudden prominence in the community would seem fantastic. It is noteworthy that her attempt to be neutral alienated the members of both factions from her, and made them all the more willing to listen to gossip about her. Typical, too, were those who attempted to extract information from her and, failing in that, invented a story according to their own ideas. Perhaps the most trying of all, for the person living through such a crisis, are those self-appointed mentors, those warners and talebearers of the community who come to one with reports of gossip, thereby increasing the sense of their own importance at the cost of the unhappy individual who is the subject of the tales they carry. Interesting, too, are the revelations made by some of the words and phrases which recur in this young teacher's story. It was "the preacher's wife," "the superintendent's wife," etc., throughout the story. One judges that the union of the woman and her husband's official position is not, in these isolated, small communities, a mere formal connection, but an intermingling of parts resembling, almost, a chemical combination.

In view of the reluctance of communities to receive teachers into fellowship with them as human beings, the tendency of teachers to form cliques is not surprising. In the society of other teachers, at least, the teacher can be spontaneous and relatively unreserved (supposing these other teachers to be intimate friends and equals). There are limits to the freedom one may have in the society of teachers, but that society usually offers the teacher his best opportunity to be accepted as a person. Therefore the teacher group comes to constitute a close-knit in-group, a fellowship. (This tendency is increased by the fact that all the teachers in a system are engaged in a common struggle against those enemies of the social order, the students.) This group stands out very clearly against the background of the community in general; its members are young, well-educated, mostly unmarried, transient, and discontented. They are strangers.

The teacherage, a community-owned home for unmarried teachers, serves a useful purpose in supplying to these unattached members of the community reasonably good quarters and relatively pleasant surroundings at a minimum price. It is interesting that in many communities something more or less akin to the teacherage springs up spontaneously. Some home is thrown open to one or two teachers, who report favorably upon it, and soon all the teachers are rooming and boarding at the same place. This arrangement has its uses, but it strengthens the tendency of teachers to form themselves into a clique. Where one or more of these unplanned teacherages spring up, they often become the headquarters of hostile factions on the faculty. A relatively harmless example of this was the following:

When I arrived in the town where I taught, I secured a room at the house where three other high-school teachers roomed. The rest of the lady high-school teachers, who did not have their homes in the town, roomed at the place where nearly all the high-school teachers took their meals. My intentions were to be friendly with all the teachers, as I had been given this advice. I came in contact with the teachers rooming at the boarding house more than with those who took only their evening meal there. I noticed almost immediately that the teachers where I roomed began to crab the teachers at the boarding house. Miss F. was so dumb. Really she was repulsive to them because of her lack of intelligence. They gave Miss F. some pretty nasty snubs. "Poor thing," they said, "she was the kind who went to church, merely because she didn't know any better." Miss F. and Miss J. had been in college together, and Miss F. hadn't been able to make a sorority because she was so dumb. Then Miss S. was pretty, but she was also dumb. Some better than Miss F., but not much. They couldn't bear Miss M. because she was so homely. Finally, they told me if I wanted to run with the other group to go ahead, but I couldn't be one of their members if I did. Then our landlady decided to give us breakfast there and I became more intimately associated with the rooming-house group, and so without any intention on my part I was considered of that group and not of the boarding-house group. (Life history document furnished by a teacher.)

The tendency of teachers to associate with teachers has its advantages. Unquestionably these associations help to make life bearable for the teachers in the less hospitable communities. And in the company of teachers, the teacher feels less any stigma that attaches to his calling in the popular mind. Bagley even champions these associations on the ground that they foster the craft spirit. The primary group of teachers gives a sub-group sanction to the attitudes of the teacher toward students and community; they support him in his struggle for mastery, comfort him in defeat, and advise him as to ways and means of further struggle. But from this very fact arises the danger of these groups to education as service to the community; where the ties between those belonging to the personnel of an institution become more important than the relation of those persons to the community the institution serves, institutionalization rapidly ensues. The teacher teaches for teachers and thinks that school is for the school men. But as a court poet once implied, the palate may be better served if one does not dress his meat for cooks.

Concerning the low social standing of teachers much has been written. The teacher in our culture has always been among the persons of little importance, and his place has not changed for the better in the last few decades. Fifty years or more ago it used to be argued that teachers had no standing in the community because they whipped little children, and this was undoubtedly an argument that contained some elements of truth. But flogging, and all the grosser forms of corporal punishment, have largely disappeared from the modern school, and as yet there is little indication that the social standing of the profession has been elevated. It has also been argued that the social standing of any profession is a pretty accurate mirror of its economic standing, and that therefore the low financial rewards of teaching are a sufficient cause of its being considered one of the less honorable pursuits. This, however, is an explanation that may not be pushed very far; it holds some truth, but there are other facts that limit it. In the smaller communities, the superintendent of schools often occupies a financial position far superior to that of most of the villagers, and yet the villagers both pity him and condescend to him (the while, perhaps, they envy him his easy means of livelihood). And it happens that the group among the teachers who are most respected in the world at large, the college and university professors, are but little better-to-do in most cases, and in some cases are much poorer, than secondary school executives, who nevertheless, except in the larger cities, have less social standing. The Lynds have a simpler sort of economic explanation, which is that there is simply no place in this commercial culture for the teacher and the professor.

In analyzing the opinion people have of teachers, it is necessary to reckon with the teacher stereotype which partly reflects and partly determines that opinion. This stereotype apparently represents a caricature of the methods used by the teacher to maintain control over children, and of the personality worked out by the teacher as a solution for the problem of control. This problem of control arises, of course, out of the supposed necessity of conducting schools along the lines of teacher domination and pupil subordination. From the means which the teacher has to use to obtain control and to keep it arises a generalized conception of the school teacher which perdures in the minds of all the graduates of the school. This is an idealized and not a factual portrait, because the memory will not hold all the flesh and blood of human beings for so long a time; the general impression remains, but details fade. The idealized conception tends to become a caricature, and an unpleasant and belittling caricature, because a real enmity exists between teacher and taught, and this enmity transmutes the work of memory into irony. In accordance with this theory, each generation of teachers pays in its turn for the sins of the generation that has gone before; it would require some decades of sensible and friendly teaching to remove the stigma from the occupation. There are some indications that this process has already begun, but antagonism toward teachers is still widespread. It is a hostility not unmixed with a certain respect, but it is a real hostility, and apparently it is as universal as is the school itself. A passage in *The Road Back*,[1] in which the mayor and some other villagers endeavor to make the new teachers drunk, might well have been, with certain changes, a passage in *The Hoosier Schoolmaster*.

Teachers lack respect in the community because of the teacher stereotype which comes between them and other persons. The stereotype is something of a caricature, and its distinguishing features arise from the fact that the teacher must be a despot ruling over the petty concerns of children. Where the relation between the teacher and the taught is unfriendly, the caricature may be sharp, and this is one basis for the argument that popular opinion of teachers will rise as the schools come to use less arbitrary and cruel means of enforcing discipline. However sound this reasoning may be, this principle has only a limited applicability, for there is another cause, and a deeper one, that operates to cut the teacher off from commerce with his fellow men. And the more successful the teacher is, the more he is cut off. The teacher must live in a universe of adolescent attitudes and values. He can teach, it is true, and remain essentially adult, but to do that he must interpose between himself and his students an immense distance, and then the teacher-pupil relationship becomes one of dominance and subordination in its strictest form. If the teacher is to control understandingly it must be by the sacrifice of some of his own adulthood. This is not to say that an individual with sufficient insight might not be able to have his cake and eat it too, in this

[1] Remarque, Erich Maria, *The Road Back* (translation), pp. 227 ff., Little, Brown, & Co., Boston, 1931.

case, to make adjustments to boys on a boyish level, and to adults on a slightly different level; but this is insight which is rare, and it could lead to the complete isolation, in feeling, of the individual from society.

The teacher must talk to boys of the things in which boys are interested. He must understand adolescent rôles, and live vividly rôles of his own not wholly incompatible with the rôles of adolescence. The persons who are happiest in these rôles, and perhaps most successful in playing them, are individuals who have never wholly made the transition from their own adolescence, the college heroes, the football players, the track stars, and the debaters who have never quite forgotten their undergraduate conception of themselves. These persons are able to live adolescent rôles vividly because there is no discontinuity in those rôles in their own lives. More introspective teachers may resent the parts they have to play. But the teacher must always take very seriously the social system designed for the edification and control of children. He must speak seriously and even prayerfully of examinations, grades, credits, promotions, demerits, scoldings, school rituals, making good, etc. And it is difficult for the teacher to take such things seriously and yet keep them from entering his soul. In the main, the better a teacher he becomes, the further they will enter.

It is not only that the teacher must have social traits which enable him to enter a little way into the society of boys, but that these same traits exclude him from the society of men. A banker and a lawyer may converse together with interest and profit, because they live in the same universe of values, but any contact between either of these and the professional teacher must be more difficult. Of what is the teacher to talk? When teachers meet they talk shop, but that is excluded when the teacher and the banker meet. After the introductory commonplaces, the conversation may go on to platitude, possibly to politics; very likely it languishes. Individual teachers learn to transcend these boundaries, but for teachers as a class they continue to exist.

The situation is made somewhat worse by the fact that much of the communion of men in general is on the level of certain vices, or certain sporting interests which are more or less taboo for the teacher. One who does not smoke, drink, swear, or tell risqué stories is excluded from the confraternity of men in general, from all barber shop, pool room, and men's club fellowship. Now the mere possession of vices may seem a poor recommendation for any person as a human being, but the fact remains that these vices are very important in determining the friendly opinion of other persons; they are important because they open the portals of personal contact. Some teachers realize that these vices are important, and have set themselves to cultivate an indulgence or so. They are not nicotine addicts, as they explain it, but they relish a good cigar once in a while. It is heart-rending to watch them relishing a good cigar.

A further element in the popular prejudice against teachers, for the disrespect in which the profession is held amounts to that, is that teaching is quite generally regarded as a failure belt. There is some justice in this belief. A popular epigram of a few years ago had it that teaching was the refuge of unsaleable men and unmarriageable women. The epigram is unjust to many individuals, as any generalization so sweeping, but it mirrors accurately a general belief. Unjust or no, the low social standing of teachers, and the belief that teaching is a failure belt among the occupations, which is a part of that low standing, contribute much to make the personnel of the profession represent a lower gradus of the general population than would otherwise be the case. These social handicaps of teaching eliminate some undesirable teachers, but it could hardly be gainsaid that they also shut out many individuals of pronounced character who would be very useful in the schools if they could be induced to take up or to continue teaching. As to the truth or untruth of the statement that teaching is a failure belt, that is a question which we must leave unanswered. Certainly for many teachers it is a failure belt, for they think of teaching as an unpleasant or boring occupation from which they are unable to extricate themselves. For them, it is the occupation of second choosers.

It remains to note one other factor of great importance in determining the low standing of the teacher in most communities. Teachers have usually a very insecure tenure in their positions. It is not only that this insecurity causes them to be more subservient and less self-assertive in their relations with influential persons, and not only that it forces them to kowtow to business men and others who are permanently established in the community. Important as is this necessity for toadying to keep one's position in destroying the teacher's self-respect, and consequently the respect of others for him, there is another aspect of the teacher's feeble hold upon his position which is even more significant. That is that the teacher is often unable to remain long enough in the community to make the transition from categorical to personal (otherwise called sympathetic) contacts. There is, as we have said, a teacher stereotype, and in the absence of actual personal knowledge of a particular teacher, the opinions of the community regarding him tend to be determined almost wholly by the prevalent stereotype. If a teacher remains long in one group, he gradually builds up about him a set of personal impressions, and, though the teacher stereotype influences these impressions, there is a tendency for the human and personal element in those impressions to increase in value while the stereotyped element decreases. When John Jones enters a community as a teacher, his fellow townsmen tend to see him at first almost altogether as a teacher. But as he grows acquainted with his neighbors, they tend to see him more and more as a person; when they have come to think of him as John Jones who happens to be the superintendent of schools, and not as the superintendent of schools who happens to be called John Jones, the transition is complete. But if John Jones remains in the community only a year or two, his acquaintance will be limited largely by his official capacity, and his fellow townsmen will never have an opportunity to arrive at a just estimate of his qualities as a person. The transition from categoric to personal contacts will never be made. The low social standing of teachers, then, is partly conditioned by the fact that they never put their roots down in particular communities, and those communities therefore never learn their worth as persons. A partial solution of the problem presented by the lack of social standing of teaching may be obtained by adding together the two facts that the school teacher stereotype is peculiarly unfavorable, and that the teacher rarely remains long enough in the group to substitute personal for stereotyped contacts.

Every teacher, indeed, will find study of the rôle of the stranger rewarding, and it will have special significance for the teacher who is going to a small town. The stranger may have great importance in the community, but it is not a personal importance. The stranger's importance often derives from the fact that he is not a person; that is why confidences come easily to the stranger. "The newcomer" is a special variety of stranger. Blumenthal has discussed the apparent contradiction between attentions paid the newcomer and his actual personal unimportance. When the newcomer is a teacher, the attention paid him is explicable as respect for his position compounded with curiosity as to his cultural attainments and the intimate peculiarities of his character. During the first few days that the teacher spends in his new community, the members of the community watch him furtively and attempt to assay him. Many questions are in their minds as they spy upon him from curtained windows and quiz the children for news of his doings. What new cultural goods are offered this year? Will the new teacher stir up unpleasantness and become a center of community strife? Or will he be that long-awaited paragon who shall satisfy all the demands of the community, cultured, but not too cultured, edifying in tone, but along the established channels, pleasant but not too pleasant, enthusiastic over his mission, but not inclined to create a disturbance about it; will he, crushing out altogether any impulses of his own, live the life the community has laid out for him? It follows that the status of the teacher as a stranger and a newcomer is not inconsistent with low standing as a person.[1]

The distribution of teaching positions conditions the insecurity of tenure of the teacher. School boards and individuals may deal harshly with the teacher, for they know that he will then have to remove himself from the community. A merchant must be a little careful how he dismisses clerks, for the unjustly used employees will remain in the community and as long as they remain they will continue to be his enemies and they will continue to raise other enemies up against him. But the same merchant as a member of the school board can treat other employees of a much higher grade with much less consideration, for he knows that though there may be some hard feeling at the time, it will subside when the teacher leaves town. And the teacher must usually leave town, or quit teaching, for no other teaching positions are available in that community. If teachers were accustomed to remain in the communities where they lost their positions, school boards would be much more reluctant to dismiss them. (This conclusion is substantiated by the fact that home-town teachers usually have a better hold upon their positions than imported ones.) Many other elements enter, of course, into the explanation of the insecurity of the teacher's tenure of office. There is the fact of tradition, for it is traditional in some communities to change teachers frequently, at least in the responsible positions. There is the unadjustment of the teachers themselves, which makes it difficult for them to put their roots down in a particular place. There is the faulty human engineering of the schools, as a result of which the school executive is put in a position to make many enemies and few friends. There is the fact of frequent dissensions among the faculty themselves. There is always the influence of teachers who are using teaching as a temporary occupation, for they hold their positions lightly, and correspondingly decrease the hold which other teachers have upon their positions. There are

[1] Suggested readings on this topic: Park and Burgess, *Introduction to the Science of Sociology*, pp. 294-298, 322-327. Blumenthal, Albert, *Small Town Stuff*, pp. 121 ff.

the very difficult moral and social qualifications of the teacher; in some communities they are so very strict that it seems that the most docile and conformed of all the saints could not have fulfilled them.

It is sometimes proposed to remedy the low social standing of the teaching profession by making teaching a real profession. Let it be known that teaching is a difficult art, and one that requires years of expensive training, say those who argue for this remedy, and the people will esteem their teachers accordingly. As a part of this program, it is usually proposed to increase the amount of teacher training necessary for obtaining a teaching position. This savors a little of the curative principle of "the hair of the dog that bit me." For it is partly the failure of teachers to register as human beings which accounts for the low opinion which their contemporaries have of them, and this failure to make an impression as human beings is partly due to the fact that the narrow social and intellectual training of teachers has destroyed some of their essential qualities of human beings. Perhaps the solution is to be found in the very opposite procedure; perhaps what will do the teacher most good will be for him to have an opportunity to take leave of his profession, both during his training and after he has begun to practice his trade, and to mingle with his fellow men as an equal.

Special members of the teaching staff have a special relation to the community. The responsible heads of the school system stand often fairly close to the community, always on the negative side and sometimes on the positive side as well. The chief school executive must work with the school board, who are the representatives of the community, and so must often those minor executives who stand at the head of parts of the local school system. The superintendent of schools, and the principals of the various schools, have frequent contacts with parents of students and so-called "patrons" of the schools. In the list of those members of the faculty who stand in a special relation to the community we must by all means include the coach, who is, to the sporting element in the community, the most important individual in the school, and usually, to the alumni, the hero of all the pool rooms when he has a winning team, and hard put to it to defend himself against the wolves of the barber shop when his team loses.

The crisscrossing pattern of social relationships between community and school becomes even more complicated when teachers are involved who are teaching in their home community. Such teachers usually occupy a very solid position by reason of long acquaintance in the community, by reason of friendships there, and family alliances, and the influence of kinsmen; perhaps greatest of all the advantages which the home-town teacher enjoys is simply his membership in the community as an in-group and in particular small groups of the community. These advantages are partially balanced by the fact that such a teacher is also subject to rivalries and family feuds which are older and stronger than he. A further disadvantage of note is the unwillingness of those who have known a person as a boy ever to realize that he is now become a man. And though the small-town community includes all who live in it, barring none because he is a fool, it is reluctant to honor any very much above the others, so that the home-talent teacher usually lacks the prestige that would be his if he were an outlander. But on the whole, the home-town teacher enjoys a favorable position. For the foreign-born superintendent, these native teachers are often a thorn in the flesh. In the first place, superintendents are often handicapped, or they often feel that they are, in their efforts to develop a really efficient school system because of the fact that school boards override their recommendations and employ or retain "home-talent" teachers of very limited qualifications. Home-talent teachers, also, are very frequently involved in political intrigues affecting the position of the superintendent. Their acquaintance in the community makes intrigue easy for them, and their possession of a place in the community not dependent upon the superintendent's good will makes them less loyal to the superintendent than transplanted teachers. They frequently are stronger in the community than those who rank above them in the school system, simply because they are more permanent. On the basis of their superior political influence, they often demand favors which the school executive finds it difficult, in fairness to other teachers, to grant. The position of the teacher who is the superintendent of schools in his home community is also one of special interest. He has at his command a greater personal following in the community than the alien executive, but he has also a greater assortment of rivals and enemies. Furthermore, his position is somewhat more likely to be owing to the political influence of personal connections, so that he does not have quite so free a hand in determining school policies or administering details as a determined man who stood under no such obligations might have. On the whole, when one considers the fact that a person does not secure adult status in his home community until he is quite old, and that the native superintendent of schools is somewhat more under fire than an outsider by reason of the jealousies and personal spites that follow him into office, one must conclude that the situation of such a person is not enviable.

There are certain devices by which those individuals who occupy positions worthy of some wire-pulling usually endeavor to maintain their hold upon the community. One of the greatest of these is church work, and unquestionably activity of this nature immeasurably increases the teacher's prominence as a person and enlarges the following that he is able to gain in a community. Where the churches are the rallying point of local factions, however, as is so often the case, a teacher may lose as much as he gains by identifying himself closely with such a group. Particularly is this true if the right people belong to one church and the wrong ones to another; the teacher must then belong with the right people or he must not belong at all. Other men use lodge connections as an outlet, and lodge work has the twin advantages of giving the teacher an opportunity to mix with his fellows on a common human basis and of giving him a highly organized group of backers in the community. On a smaller scale, teachers may attempt to ingratiate themselves by judicious "entertainment," and by such social activities as are open to them in the community. The personal techniques of flattery and deference are devices which some teachers are able to use with convincing effect upon influential individuals.

PROJECTS

1. Begin a street-corner conversation with a stranger. Lead him to express himself as freely as possible. Midway of the conversation, remark that you are a school teacher. Record results. Repeat the observation. Interpret.

2. Record the comments made by members of a community about teachers. Interpret.

3. Give examples of "made" talk between tradesmen and teachers. Contrast with freer conversation of same persons. Interpret.

4. Tell the story of a school-teacher's clique. Analyze.

5. Tell the story of your relations with some family in which you boarded while you were teaching. Analyze.

6. Describe some community conflict centering around a particular teacher. Interpret.

7. Have a group of teachers living in a small community make lists of their closest friends, noting occupations. Do the same for a larger community. What conclusions do you draw?

8. Analyze the social contacts of a teacher. Is the teacher a "stranger"?

9. List the occupations of the members of the leading men's clubs of a small city. How many are teachers? Interpret.

10. Gather statistics on dismissals of teachers in a particular school system over a period of years. Interpret.

11. Take notes on the shop talk of teachers. How much of it concerns the "universe of adolescent attitudes and values"?

12. Analyze the personality of an athletic coach. Upon what things, judging from his conversation, does he chiefly pride himself? Keep a record of community comments upon him. Analyze and interpret.

13. Analyze the hold upon the community of some prominent teacher who is secure in his position.

14. Write a case history of a teacher illustrating the transition from categorical to sympathetic contacts.

15. Write the history of a campaign for a new school building.

16. Tell in detail why some school superintendent lost his position.

17. Analyze the situation of a "home-talent" teacher.

18. Analyze the relation of a particular school superintendent to the members of the school board.

19. Analyze the teacher's position as a "newcomer" in the community. Read Blumenthal, Albert, *Small Town Stuff*, pp. 122 ff.

20. How many incompetent teachers can you name who continue to hold their jobs although their inefficiency is known and conceded? By what techniques do they hold their jobs?

SUGGESTED READINGS

(1) Blumenthal, Albert, *Small Town Stuff*.

(2) Park, R. E., and Burgess, E. W., *An Introduction to the Science of Sociology*, Chapter V, particularly pp. 294-298 and 322-327.

(3) Sumner, W. G., *Folkways*.

(4) Young, Kimball, *Social Psychology*, Chapters XVII, XVIII, and XIX.

(5) Young, Kimball, *A Source Book for Social Psychology*, Chapter XVI.

CHAPTER VI

PARENTS AND TEACHERS

A MARKED lack of clear thought and plain speaking exists in the literature touching the relation of parents and teachers. From the ideal point of view, parents and teachers have much in common, in that both, supposedly, wish things to occur for the best interests of the child; but, in fact, parents and teachers usually live in a condition of mutual distrust and enmity. Both wish the child well, but it is such a different kind of well that conflict must inevitably arise over it. The fact seems to be that parents and teachers are natural enemies, predestined each for the discomfiture of the other. The chasm is frequently covered over, for neither parents nor teachers wish to admit to themselves the uncomfortable implications of their animosity, but on occasion it can make itself clear enough.

The reasons for this rarely admitted enmity are not hard to find. There is the fact already mentioned, that parents and teachers wish the child to prosper in different ways, that they wish him well according to different standards of well-being. Parents and teachers want to do different things with the child. The teacher, perhaps, wishes to further the intellectual development of the child by vigorous or unpleasant measures; this the parent resists because he has before his eyes the whole child, and sees that the child is made unhappy by the sacrifice of one phase of his development to another. But parents are supposed to support the school, and conscientious parents must often have some difficulty in arriving at a rational attitude toward the program of the schools. In a sense, this is the individual side of the old conflict between the institution and the community. The teacher, as a member of the institutional faculty, desires the scholastic welfare of children even at the expense of other aspects of their development; parents usually take their stand for a more harmonious development. (This is not to say that there are not cases enough where the opposite situation presents itself. Parents are particularly unreasonable where their own ego feelings, or their own projected ambitions, have become involved in the scholastic standing of a particular child.)

This fundamental conflict between the school and the parent is accentuated by the fact that parents and teachers are involved in different alignments of group life affecting the child. For the parent, the child is a fellow member of the closest of all the primary groups, and a warmly personal attitude toward him is the result. But the teacher, however much he may strive to do his duty by the child, still sees him mainly as a member of a secondary group over which the teacher must exert control by the mechanisms of secondary group life. The parent, further, is buttressed in his personal attitude toward the child by his involvement in various social groups in which that is the customary attitude to take toward children. The teacher is involved in the group of teachers, and the indicated attitude in those groups is impersonal. From this arises the essential futility of parent-teacher work as it is usually carried on. Parent-teacher work has usually been directed at securing for the school the support of parents, that is, at getting parents to see children more or less as teachers see them. But it would be a sad day for childhood if parent-teacher work ever really succeeded in its object. The conflict between parents and teacher is natural and inevitable, and it may be more or less useful. It may be that the child develops better if he is treated impersonally in the schools, provided the parents are there to supply the needed personal attitudes; that is at least the theory upon which the school practice of our time has been based. But it would assuredly be unfortunate if teachers ever succeeded in bringing parents over completely to their point of view, that is, in obtaining for the schools the complete and undivided support of every parent of every child. This is not to say that parent-teacher work of a certain kind might not be very helpful. If parents and teachers could meet often enough and intimately enough to develop primary group attitudes toward each other, and if both parents and teachers might have their say unreservedly, such modifications of school practice and parental upbringing might take place as would revolutionize the life of children everywhere.

The antagonism between parents and teachers is sometimes overt, and in such cases it presents some delicate problems. With parents of some education the antagonism toward teachers still exists, but it appears in disguised form. Some very interesting crystallizations and oppositions of attitude appear at times. Typical are those described in the following narrative:

One of the most troublesome phases of my private-school life concerned tutoring. . . . What I always objected to was the fact that if I tutored a boy his parents, and he, would expect that he would then pass the course, even if thereafter he neglected to do his work. I felt also that tutoring was slightly degrading, and that the boy I was tutoring felt that he had the upper hand of me by being able to hire me to do the unpleasant job. And I felt quite sure that the parents, who had contributed a few extra dollars, felt that they had a claim upon me for all time to come. I therefore developed a technique for keeping tutoring at a minimum. It was not to my taste. It was dull enough teaching classes, but it was ten times worse to spend hours on some of the more stupid students, repeating again and again the simplest explanations and things that a brighter boy could have learned from a text.

In the typical case, things would happen about like this. A dull, but perhaps not altogether hopeless boy would neglect his Latin for a few days. I would "get after him" at once, but not always with a good effect. Perhaps he picked up for a day or so, but he would fall behind again more rapidly than before. Perhaps he was ill for a few days and could not attend class; that gave him a double task. I would see the boy's faculty adviser, and he would exhort the boy to do his back work in Latin. Things would go on that way for a month or two, and by that time the boy would be hopelessly behind the class. I would be ready to have him drop out, because I realized that just a few weeks in a rapidly moving language class is a hopeless handicap.

A little more time would drag by, and then the routine reports would go to the boy's parents. His parents would come out to have a talk with me about the boy's failure in Latin. They promised to "put pressure on the boy" to make him bring up his Latin. By this time I would begin to be wearied of the whole affair, and eager to have done with it, but I dared not say so. I would promise to give the boy every chance, which I must say that I always did. The next couple of days the boy would prepare his lesson diligently, but without the least understanding of what it was about. At the end of the month he would fail more miserably than before. I then gave him up as hopeless, quite. Too soon, perhaps, but after all there were others to worry about.

When the second failing report went home, the boy's father would write back and ask if there could not be some special arrangement for Tommy to do special work in Latin in order to overhaul the rest of the class. Tommy's adviser would then call me in and ask if I would care to do the tutoring. I was hardly in a position to refuse point-blank. I would have the adviser write a letter to the boy's father, explaining my position with regard to tutoring. It became somewhat formalized. I stated first that I was willing to do the tutoring if the boy's father wished it done, but that I felt that in general such tutoring was inadvisable. In the first place, tutoring was a crutch which a boy ought not to come to depend upon; it would injure his morale in most cases. In the second place, tutoring was expensive, and one could not by any means be sure that it would produce the desired effect. I could go over the work of the course with the boy, but unless he found some extra time for studying, and worked diligently on his own account, no particular improvement would be forthcoming. One could buy a suit of clothes if he had the money to pay for it, but one had to pay for academic advancement in another coin. I would want all this explained to the boy beforehand if I were to tutor him. If he could be made to see that tutoring represented merely an additional opportunity to bring up his work, and not a means of having me make his credit for him, I would undertake to go over the work of the course with him.

If these formalities were complied with I would do the tutoring. Usually I would have two or three boys at the same time who would be asking me to tutor them in beginning Latin. I would get them together and bring them over the material they had missed in as short a time as possible, but usually that would be long enough to run up a good-sized tutoring bill at best. I would write a letter to each parent, informing him that the tutoring had begun and would continue until the boy had brought up his back work in Latin, or until the attempt proved hopeless.

When we had finished, I failed to send in a bill for my services. Sometimes payment was offered (not often), but I finally came to refuse payment in nearly all cases. I found that those accounts were always difficult to collect, because the parents really felt that such special tutoring should have been included in their tuition fee, which was fair enough except for the fact that ours was not a tutoring school, and did not pretend to be one. So I did not really sacrifice much money by refusing payment for tutoring, and I gained a great advantage over those parents in my dealings with them. They, at least, could never again ask that I tutor their youngster, and they could not again ask any sort of special dispensation for him. Since the number of parents who insisted upon tutoring was small in any case, this seemed to be the best way out. It did not take a great deal of time. I had to tutor perhaps one group of boys every semester, and I felt that the expenditure of time was more than justified by the results.

In general, I adopted toward the parents a somewhat reserved and cold attitude. I felt that if they cultivated me they did it with the intention of getting favors for their children, and I resented that. I therefore adopted a pose toward them that was at once respectful and aloof.

The victory was not always with me. Some parents, in fact all who made a determined attempt, were able to break through my shell. I must admit that whenever they did I always adopted a more human attitude toward the child; in those cases I always assumed with the boy the rôle of the friend of his father. I did not win always on the tutoring, not even there, where I had worked out my defences so elaborately. The fact was that I was contending with parents who were accustomed to getting their way in business and politics, and an insignificant teacher was hard put to it to preserve his integrity against such assaults as they could make upon it. The direct assault, by telling me what was what, what I should do about a particular boy, how I should run my classes, etc., always failed, because I was then able to fight the battle on my own ground. But an indirect assault might win. For instance, some parents got around my refusing payment for tutoring, perhaps correctly evaluating my attitude for what it was, a defence against patronage in personal relations and against any further demands on their part. Understanding this, they sometimes tried to wipe out the obligation by making payment in the form of presents, invitations, etc., making it difficult for me to refuse.

Some of the parents were able to manage me in spite of my attempts to retain control by remaining aloof. I might know very well what they were doing, and yet be unable to keep them from having a considerable influence upon my attitude toward their child. I might explain that I always felt that I should resist such influences because I needed to be impersonal with students in order to maintain discipline, and because I always desired to be fair with all students, something which I knew I could not do if I established intimate relations with some of them. I feel now that I was mistaken in both these attitudes, but I was very young and very teacherish at that time.

The most crushing and the most pleasant defeat that my policy of isolation suffered was administered by a famous physicist who was the guardian of a boy who entered our school as a Senior. The boy's name was Reiman, and he and I came to be at sword's points the first week of school, and continued in that state for some time. He insisted upon enrolling in my third-year Latin, and although he had the necessary credits, I knew that he was not really prepared to carry the work of the class. I advised him to drop out, but he elected to continue and take his chance. I decided to show him how little he actually knew, and began to ride him unmercifully. Since it was a very small class, he had no chance to slip by. I corrected his every error, and they were very numerous. I assigned make-up work to him, and demanded that he complete it in jig time. He had a very thick shell, and that very shell exasperated me, and urged me to make even more determined assaults upon it. I wanted to make him admit that he was not prepared to carry third-year Latin. I could have flunked him, of course, but he managed to do work that was on the margin and I did not wish to be unjust.

The upshot of it all was that I drove the youngster so hard that I began to grow a little ashamed of myself, but he still maintained his defiant attitude and left me no choice but to continue in the same course. But just the same I felt rather badly about the boy; I knew I must be making him somewhat unhappy and my conscience hurt me over it. Just before Christmas, his guardian, happening to be in the city, came out to the school to visit us and the boy. I heard that he was on the campus, and made myself hard to find; I did not relish the possibility of being called to account for my treatment of Reiman. I should have had a defence, of course, that I was trying to make him work, but I should not have believed that defence myself, and could hardly expect anyone else to believe it.

But they caught me. Just after dinner the superintendent came over and told me that Reiman's guardian was here and was inquiring especially for me. With fear only partly concealed beneath the aloof manner, I went over to meet him. There was no smile on my face. I expected to hear a vigorous complaint. We were introduced. The guardian was a fine, jovial gentleman, and he seemed genuinely glad to see me. He said,

"So you're Reiman's Latin teacher?" I braced myself for a scolding. He continued, "Well, I've been wanting to meet you ever since Reiman began writing home about you. You've done more with that boy than any teacher he ever had. I believe you are the first person who has ever scared him enough to make him work since he has been going to school. I congratulate you. Keep it up and you will be doing a service to all of us."

That was all, but it was enough. I expanded under the influence of that man. It changed things for Reiman, too. It gave me an excuse for making a slight break in my policy with him. I still made him work, but it was a friendly driving now. I do not ascribe all the change to the intervention of the guardian, for I was, as I said, already looking for some way of ameliorating my discipline with regard to that particular boy, but that intervention marked a turning point. I made a mental note as to how I should handle the teachers if I ever had a boy who went away to a private school. Other parents used a similar technique, and it was never wholly without effect. But so far as I know, no parent ever made me change my policy by making a direct issue of it with me.

There was an army officer in the school who was particularly fine at handling parents. One day he gave me one of the best demonstrations of practical psychology that I have ever seen. One of the boys in the school had a somewhat irascible mother, and on occasion she told off the teachers or administrative officers to the queen's taste. My friend had disciplined her son quite severely a day or so before, and apparently he was expecting her to call him to account. He and I were sitting in his quarters one afternoon listening to the radio. Suddenly he jumped up, pulled on his coat, and started looking for his overcoat. I asked him why he was in such a rush. He said, "There comes Mrs. H." I sympathized. I thought he was going to make a run for it; I think that is what I should have done. Imagine my surprise, then, to see him walk right out of the house and go toward Mrs. H.! They talked for a moment or two, and then he tipped his hat and walked on. Later I asked him for an explanation of his conduct. He said, "I wanted to catch her before she got set. If she just happened to run onto me on the campus, we could talk about her boy's problems just in passing. But if I let her come in here and walk up to my door, she would have to get set for a quarrel with me. She's coming over to lodge a formal complaint. She has to get ready for a fight. And I have to defend myself accordingly. But I caught her before she got set, and we had no quarrel, but a little friendly chat. I was in a hurry because every step that she took toward my quarters made her get a little angrier." (Life history document.)

The above document seems to contain some fragments oı a sound and realistic empirical psychology. Its meaning for our immediate purposes is quite clear.

A good technique for handling irate parents is an essential for success in any responsible post in the school system. The irate parents is not a mere creature of literature; he is one of the facts of the social life in which teachers are involved. The many jokes about the conflict between parents and teachers should be taken as showing the reality of the conflict situation. Such conflicts occasionally arise concerning the subject matter and the point of view of the school curriculum, and we have already alluded to such an instance. But by far the most fruitful source of disagreements between parents and teachers is the matter of school discipline (in which are included academic requirements, which are dealt with in more or less the same manner as disciplinary problems). Here the attitudes of parent and teacher come into their most irreconcilable opposition. The teacher must see the child as a part of the school group, and must treat him as one of many involved in the school situation; he must treat the child more or less impersonally, and must perhaps inflict some hardship upon him for the sake of maintaining a consistent stand with reference to other students. The parent stands out for the immediate welfare of the particular child as the parent sees it. To some extent it is the old conflict between the whole community and the school as an institution; the teacher sees that fragment of the child which is involved in the school situation, and must judge him from that point of view, whereas the parent is trying to see the whole child of which the school personality is a part; the teacher represents the school and the parent represents the community. A long-term process of adjustment between school and community takes place, and the conflict of parents and teachers is part of the long-term process.

It is not enough to develop a philosophy of conflict; we must attend to the details of this personal interaction and of the technique by which it can be controlled if we are to offer anything of value to those who wish to understand the school. The school executive must learn, in the first place, to meet disgruntled patrons with a poised and friendly air that effectively discourages their definition of the situation as a personal quarrel. There are many disarming devices which may be adopted for the purpose; the chief of these is a willingness to grant the other person's point and an attempt to draw him into a cooperative attempt to work out a solution for a situation. Sometimes a fine line must be drawn; it is certainly desirable that a complainant should be received in a friendly manner and that he must be assured of a fair hearing from the outset, but it is fatal for the teacher if he shows any sign of fear or any tendency to fawn upon an influential but disgruntled parent. (Good executives need stable vasomotor systems.) This can perhaps be summed up by saying that the person who must hear complaints must learn to receive them with the utmost poise and balance; he must seem glad to listen, but there must be no indication that he is surrendering his own point of view. The cause should certainly be heard, and it should be heard in detail. Many executives have had good success in handling angry parents by the simple technique of allowing them to sit down and pour forth their whole story; when the story was told, the parents had experienced a catharsis and their attitudes toward the school were changed for the better; in some cases, something approaching the analytic phenomenon of transference took place. There is always a danger, of course, that a person in such a case will be carried on by the uprush of emotion and will say many things that he would not say in his calmer moments, and then, having committed himself, be more antagonistic than ever before. As a corrective against this, it is desirable that a friendly rapport be established if possible before the interview. This may sometimes be done by the manner of receiving the complainant, or by small talk before the interview reaches its point.

There will be numerous cases, however, in which any attempt to get the angry parent to assume a rational and cooperative attitude will be fruitless. It is, after all, a severe emotional upset that brings a parent away from his daily pursuits to remonstrate with a teacher or a school executive. The teacher should above all avoid allowing his own emotions to become aroused in the process. If the teacher's own emotions are involved, the procedure will degenerate into a personal quarrel, and possibilities for a constructive attitude on either side will be immeasurably decreased. While the angry parent states his grievance, the teacher should remain silent, respectful, sympathetic enough to allow the cathartic procedure its full emotional value for the other person, but aloof enough to prevent becoming personally involved in the situation. An interviewer should in every case avoid joining issue on particular points; no matter how absurd the charges that are made, they should not be controverted at this time. He should bear in mind that he is trying to win his point through a psychological technique and not through argument, and should refrain from even the most tempting opportunities to take up the thread of the argument. Ready confuters do not make good "peace-talkers."

When the complaining parent has at length stated his grievance fully, the interviewer should attempt to bring the discussion around to the question of what is to be done. (He thus substitutes a from-this-point-on orientation for the praise and blame orientation which prompted the complaint.) This may involve disregarding what has gone before, though this should not be obvious to the other person. The interview can then be changed into a calm discussion of future policies instead of a heated debate concerning what is irremediably past; it can gradually acquire the tone of a cooperative attempt to arrive at a policy for the future. Such a discussion will give the teacher an opportunity to introduce indirectly an explanation of his position before the public, and a statement of the aims of the school as he sees them, together with some information concerning the problems of the teacher, the school problems of a particular child, or other material calculated to win over or to impress the parent. After a discussion of this sort, when parent and teacher have arrived at some agreement concerning general matters, or at least some mutual understanding concerning what each thinks to be involved in them, the interview may again be directed at the personal issue, which may very likely be resolved easily.

The mistakes which teachers usually make in such situations are in the line of allowing themselves to become personally involved in the situation. They feel that an attack has been made upon them and that they must meet the attack at once. They feel that unjust and preposterous charges have been brought against them or their school, and that the only possible answer is a direct refutation of those charges. They see force arrayed against them, and feel that they cannot with due regard to their own dignity meet that force with anything but force. Above all, they are afraid that by allowing the other person to speak in anger without themselves speaking in the same vein they will lose control of the situation. They are quite wrong, of course. The individual who controls such a situation is the individual who retains his poise. Stability, and a friendly but judicial attitude, are greater advantages in such a situation than all the anger in the world. It is really odd that the policy of arguing disgruntled customers into being satisfied customers has prevailed so much more widely in teaching than in any other mode of life. Business long ago realized the value of the initial assumption that "the customer is always right," and of a technique that was directed first at finding out the customer's grievance and then at trying to work out a satisfactory compromise. A number of factors have operated, of course, to make teachers, and the school executives who meet the public for them, unreasonable. There is the fact that the school is an artificial social system maintained by the force of a few personalities, therefore an arbitrary system to be defended by arbitrary tactics. There is the fact that teachers develop a technique of carrying their points by arbitrary means in their dealings with students; leaving aside the question whether those methods are desirable in any case, they certainly are not to be recommended for dealing with those who are adult and equal. There is, further, the fact that the teacher has such a limited status in the community that any attack upon him makes him rally to a desperate defence. He has not confidence enough in the essential security of his position to allow attacks to be made upon it without at once sending out a punitive expedition. Then there is the fact that many of those to whom the delicate problem of handling public relations is entrusted are themselves problem cases, and bristle with indignation at the slightest suggestion of a personal affront.

It remains to note some special cases, and some qualifications and corollaries of our general principles. A special case is that of the school executive hearing a complaint about the conduct of one of the teachers working under him. This case presents some problems. The tradition of the school requires that the superior defend the subordinate. The unwritten law of teachers is that "the superintendent must back his teachers up." The faculty of a school must present a unified front to the public. On the whole it is a good rule, for without such backing the teacher is hopelessly lost. Many exceptions are made. The school executive may openly repudiate the action of the teacher, frankly saving his own standing at the cost of that of the subordinate. Or he may, and this is far more common, lead the person complaining about the action of the teacher to understand that he does not himself endorse that action but that he may have to seem to support the teacher. Thus he saves his own face by undercutting the under teacher, a procedure very common among those executives who strive to please everybody. A device from which executives derive both ego gratification and popularity is that of multiplying rules, sternly forbidding subordinates to make exceptions, and then making exceptions. The executive gets the thrill of magnanimity. The recipient of the favor goes away feeling that underlings are always unreasonable while higher-ups are human, and this again is just what the executive wants.

The executive must be ready to hear complaints, and he must hear them respectfully. He must go as far as he can toward satisfying them. But he must also, if he is to retain the loyalty of his teaching force, defend his teachers before the community. He must follow a subtle policy, but he must not arouse the antagonism of either of the conflicting parties or let either of them suspect that he is following a subtle policy. Sometimes, by all reasonable standards, the teacher is badly in the wrong. Here is a case for the utmost in diplomacy. The best solution seems to be a conference in which the executive boldly takes hold of the situation and directs it into what seem to him the proper channels.

There need be nothing unmanly in a receptive attitude toward complaints. A willingness to hear the other person's point of view, and an unwillingness to quarrel until one knows what he is quarrelling about, and is reasonably sure that the other person knows also—these qualities do not denote an absence of moral fiber. One does not compromise his own position by allowing another person to state his; usually a position seems stronger if it can be maintained by conceding much to the person attacking it. Nor should either a teacher or a school executive feel that he convicts himself of cowardice by being slow to take personal offence. He will do well, then, to overlook personal affronts in order to perform his official functions properly.

There are cases in which, in spite of the most friendly and reasonable attitude on the part of the teacher, the parent persists in quarrelling, cases enough, in most communities, to give the most heroic a chance to demonstrate the stiffness of their spines. When he meets such individuals, the teacher must as far as possible avoid participating in a vulgar quarrel, but he must also stand his ground. Such teacher-baiters are well known in the moderate-sized communities and are usually unpopular. More than one young teacher has found that he has quite suddenly and unexpectedly gained standing in the community by successfully resisting the town bully.

PROJECTS

1. Analyze the demands made by parent and teachers upon you as a student. In what way are these demands alike and in what are they inconsistent?

2. Assemble the comments of a group of parents about teachers, and the comments of teachers about these same parents.

3. Tell the full story of a quarrel or dispute between a parent and a teacher. Analyze and interpret.

4. Induce a group of teachers to talk about calls that irate parents have paid them. Record and analyze their techniques and results.

5. Outline a program of parent-teacher work.

6. Discover by observation of cases whether teachers' attitudes toward children are modified by acquaintance between parent and teacher.

7. Analyze the devices which teachers work out for defending themselves from parents.

8. Make observations upon the manner in which complaints are handled by department stores, telephone companies, power companies, etc. How can you apply this technique in teaching?

9. What verbal formulae have successful school executives evolved for meeting complaints? Analyze these formulae.

10. Certain people are said to be "disarming." Observe them closely and analyze their disarming qualities. Contrast with people who are not disarming.

11. Describe the social situation which resulted in some community when a superintendent failed to support his teachers.

12. What is poise? Determine by observing and analyzing persons considered to have poise. What is its value in a disagreement?

SUGGESTED READINGS

(1) BINGHAM, W. V. D., and MOORE, B. V., *How to Interview,* Chapters VII to IX.

(2) BUTTERWORTH, J. E., *The Parent Teacher Association and Its Work.*

(3) CHAPMAN, J. C., and COUNTS, G. S., *Principles of Education,* Chapter XIII.

(4) HART, HORNELL, *The Science of Social Relations,* Chapter XVIII.

(5) OPPENHEIMER, J. J., *The Visiting Teacher Movement.*

(6) PETERS, C. C., *Foundations of Educational Sociology,* pp. 290-293.

(7) SCOTT, ELEANOR, *War Among Ladies.*

(8) SHERMAN, RITA, *A Mother's Letters to a Schoolmaster.*

(9) YOUNG, KIMBALL, *Source Book for Social Psychology,* pp. 374-379.

Chapter VII

THE FRINGES OF THE SCHOOL

We have elsewhere noted that the school community contains some hangers-on, some marginal members who from one point of view are members of the school as a social body and from another are complete outsiders, some persons without any fixed legal status in the group but often with a good deal of influence. These marginal members of the school community are of particular importance in determining the relation of the school to the community.

The janitor is a person of no little importance in any school system, and in smaller communities he may be a power. The janitor has, it is true, a very limited theoretical status, but his actual influence is often out of proportion to this theoretical place in the school system. Largely this disproportionate importance of the janitor is derived from the fact that the janitor is always a member of the local community, whereas teachers belong rather to the outside world. The primary groups and compact social units of the community stand behind the janitor; although these groups are not always powerful, they are sometimes more than any the teacher can mobilize in his own interest. The janitor is important, too, as a talebearer. Often he regards himself as an official lookout for the community; it is his to see what he can and to report what he observes to his friends and connections by way of gossip. In large school systems, janitors have been known to serve as stool-pigeons for principals and superintendents. Instances of spying by janitors can be multiplied without end.

That the janitor sometimes exerts a veto power upon school policy is shown by the following story:

Another New England school center was nearly wrecked in the launching by an old janitor with a large local following who worked openly to discredit everything it did. He stood in the hallways and insulted the patrons; he locked school rooms and refused to open them even when ordered to do so by authority; and on the occasion of the first big neighborhood gathering, he locked up the stereopticon and hid the cables, nearly breaking up the meeting. He boasted that the school authorities would not dare to discipline him because he had too many friends in the neighborhood, and he was right. When the authorities threatened to try him under civil service rules, several prominent neighborhood leaders made a counter-threat to boycott the center. Personal loyalty was stronger than public spirit.

The difficulty was solved for a time by the appointment, as supervisor, of a woman who had even a stronger neighborhood hold than the janitor. She knew her people and bided her time. One day when she had the trouble maker conspicuously at a disadvantage, she suddenly turned on him with a tongue-lashing that held him wild-eyed and speechless; when he turned to the neighborhood for sympathy, he found most of the sympathy already aligned on the other side. But a year later the supervisor married. Her successor knew nothing of the neighborhood line-up; the janitor easily worsted him and disrupted the center again. (From Barrows, E. M., "Backyard Battlefields," *The Survey*, Vol. 51, Oct. 15, 1923.) (By permission of The Survey Associates, Incorporated.)

The keepers of school stores and those customary "hang-outs" frequented by grade and high-school students figure often and prominently in the life histories of students. These individuals are rarely of a high social type, and their influence upon students is frequently a factor in cases of juvenile delinquency. Sometimes they take an active part in corrupting the young, obtaining income and personal satisfaction by purveying to youngsters contraband articles; sometimes they are relatively innocent and merely allow their premises to be used by groups of students who get into mischief quite on their own initiative. The influence of these marginal persons upon students is sometimes great, far surpassing the influence of teachers and occasionally outweighing the influence of parents. An explanation of this power is not easy to find, for it may rest upon subtle and contradictory factors. The hard-boiled restaurant keeper of the university community, a figure present around nearly every university, is often a more important person than the president of the college. In one such case it was possible to make detailed observations of his technique in dealing with boys and to arrive at some tentative conclusions concerning the nature of the influence which he exerted over them.

Phil B.'s restaurant was one of the famous spots in the recent history of Blank University. It was just a little hole in the basement of one of the business buildings near the university, but it was a hole which many visited and all remembered. "Phil's" was so tiny that it could seat only twelve persons at one time, but its habitués preferred standing in line there to immediate service in one of the larger eating houses located round about the university. Phil's was always steamy, it was usually dirty, the floor was filthy and the dishes were not so clean as they might have been. Customers elbowed each other at the counters and got spots on their clothes when they sat down in the chairs. But the steady customers always came back. It was amazing.

One of the great drawing cards was the fact that Phil served a good, plain, nourishing meal at a low price. It helped also that tipping was not encouraged. But the chief attraction was Phil. Phil had been a bartender in the old days, and he had that combination of rough and ready camaraderie, robustious lewdness, sympathy, pugnacity, and quarrelsome joviality that used to make some bartenders known the world over as "characters." He still had the paunch, and he still wore an apron rather than a white coat. He was equally ready to tell a vulgar story, to make a wager, to give an insult, or to lend his money to a person who happened to be in trouble. Small wonder that boys who had found no other warm and human place about the university campus swarmed about Phil for such companionship as was to be had from him and in his place.

Phil's manner of giving service to his patrons was unique. When a customer entered, Phil would ask him gruffly, "Well, what's yours?" No smile was on his fat, round face.

If there was any delay in giving the order, Phil would walk over to the customer, stand over him pugnaciously and inquire, "Well, well, make up your mind. Make up your mind. What the —— do you think this is, a clothing store?"

One had to be wise to the ways of "Phil's" or he would call down a storm on his head, and this was equally true whether it was a member of the faculty or the greenest freshman who made the break. So innocent a question as, "How's your soup today, Phil?" would throw Phil into a pretty good imitation of a rage. He would answer, "Well, how the —— —— —— do you suppose it is? Do you think I'd be serving it if it was poison? Several guys has had some already today and I ain't seen none of 'em dying from it."

But Phil was as ready to take as to give abuse, and he received a great deal of it from students who thought themselves sharp tongued. He heard the same stories over year after year, and as politely as he heard any stories at all. He was a great sportsman, and not only made many bets of his own, but acted as intermediary and stake-holder in many others.

Many students borrowed money from Phil, or used the credit which he freely extended as a means of tiding themselves over for a few weeks or even months. Nearly everyone used Phil as a bank, and he cashed hundreds of dollars worth of checks for every dollar's worth of food that he sold. This was a real service, for students often have difficulty in cashing checks. Phil always cashed them without question. Several times a year he would get a bad check. He never prosecuted, and he never complained to the university authorities. "Why should I complain to those guys?" he would say. "That would just get the boy in trouble and wouldn't get me my money. I'll get the money if I have to break the —— —— ——'s neck." Though there was no memory in the community of his ever having resorted to such violent means of collection, he usually got his money.

Phil's was the place where many of the students really lived. It was the place of all places about the campus where they relaxed and entered completely into the situation. The boys took a great delight in "kidding Phil," and revelled in the torrent of obscene abuse that a direct hit would set off. It was plain also that many of the students made of Phil a father substitute. But it was no ordinary father substitute; it was rather a father substitute with whom one could be perfectly familiar, a father substitute that could be cursed out roundly, deceived, imposed upon, and belittled with perfect impunity. It seemed Phil's function to fill this place in their lives, to enable them to have their father near, but at the same time to be free of all the repressive aspects of his personality, perhaps to even up old scores. Phil's personality was also very interesting to the boys because of the fact that he represented an offshoot of the sporting world, a world with which their upbringing had kept them from being familiar, but about which they were very curious.

At Phil's the boys could be perfectly free; they were known there, and they were included. It was perhaps the most human place that any of these students had found on the campus. This is the greater part, apparently, of the explanation of Phil's influence over his customers. But as has been suggested, the man had also a certain influence because he represented a harmless and easily manipulable father substitute; he enabled youngsters to maintain an emotional rapport with the older generation and at the same time to even scores with it.[1]

There is a custom around universities and colleges of hiring an elderly woman to act as "house mother" or "matron" in all university dormitories. The almost openly avowed purpose of this woman is to serve as a mother substitute, something which her status as a high-grade servant and, usually, her lack of social background enable her to do with less than indifferent success.

The campus policeman is a personage of great meaning in student eyes. Students engage in friendly conflict with him, but know that they can count on his sympathy if they need it. Alumni of New York University, according to a recent article in the *New York Times*, always inquire for John the Cop when they return to the campus.

In all schools of high-school rank and over, the alumni exert a real, though problematic, influence. The interest of the alumni is usually in the athletic welfare of their alma mater, and the bulk of the benefactions, as well as of their attempts to dictate policy, relate to this more spectacular aspect of the life of the school. For universities and

[1] Pop Jenks, keeper of "The Sugar Bowl" in the comic strip, appears to occupy a similar position in the adolescent group centering around Harold Teen.

colleges, and for private preparatory schools, the alumni are very important in that they furnish both endowments and enrollments. Various attempts are therefore made to cultivate them, through such devices as alumni journals, alumni days, class reunions, anniversaries, etc. Public high schools may also attempt to cultivate their alumni, but they do not usually succeed in maintaining the interest of any but the most recent.

Indeed, there seems to be an inherent necessity that the better sort of alumni, the more intelligent and the more successful, should always elude the tentacles of the alumni secretary. There are exceptions, of course, but the rule seems to hold. When a man goes back to his alma mater for a reunion, whether that alma mater be a prep school or one of the most advanced professional schools, he does it for a taste of the joys that were his when he was a youngster in school. But if he has attained a satisfactory adjustment of his life on the adult level he will not be likely to hanker for a revival of adolescent associations. Thus it is the unadjusted and the failures in life who are in general most enthusiastic about keeping up their school connections; if they have adjusted themselves to adult life their interests and desires will have moved on irrevocably from their school-day memories. Indeed, it may be argued that a man who after five years still persists in telling stories of his college achievements has failed in life. He may not have failed to secure position, or professional advancement, or wealth, but if his emotions and his intellect have not become involved in situations of life far more interesting than those old situations of school, he has failed in life. If nothing else keeps them away, the mere press of engagements in a full and interesting life suffices to prevent those alumni whom one would like to see from gathering with the others around the banquet board at the reunion. So it comes about that those who plan and engineer reunions and gatherings of the clan are disappointed not only in those who stay away but in those who come. But a whole art, and a difficult one, concerns the use of alumni connections. Individuals use such devices for political and business advancement, and schools use them for getting students and money.

There is some difference between the active and interested alumni of a college and those of the high school or preparatory school. Those who remain interested in the adolescent athletic and social activities of the prep-school level are almost sure to be of a lower grade than those who are interested in carrying on the athletics of a college. For one thing, the higher-grade alumni of the high school go on to college, and become thereby alumni of a college; it is only natural that in later years they should prefer to identify themselves with the more distinguished institution. It is those who remain quite adolescent who care most for the recognition and applause they can get from being one of the active alumni of the preparatory school. In the alumni of the prep school, as contrasted with the alumni of the college, this status motivation is clearer and less mixed with other motives, and as the life of the school in which they wish to shine is more juvenile, their activities verge more definitely upon the feeble-minded. A college, too, is a bigger thing to be interested in, and college life is after all the life of young adults, sometimes young adults at the most liberated and creative period of their lives; no stigma should attach to the blameless attempt to hold fast to the values of undergraduate days—some should perhaps attach to the failure to form other attachments. While we are attempting to generalize about alumni, we should state that there seems to be a considerable difference between those alumni who merely hold to the values of school life because that was the most interesting time of their lives, and those alumni who break away, are inducted into a rapidly expanding world of adult interests, and afterwards encounter their alma mater in their expanding social world. From this latter group are gathered those excellent individuals who, though weighed down by a thousand and one other interests, persist in serving their alma mater as a means to a wider social service. From this latter class are recruited those lay advisers and administrators without whom it would be very difficult to conduct the work of any school.

In every community are certain individuals who take it upon themselves to stand sponsor for the school and the teachers. Partly this is a pose which identifies them with the so-called finer things of life, with the cultural values which the school is supposed to carry. Partly this attitude reflects a real interest in the school and in the work which it is doing in the community. Sometimes the desire to sponsor the schools assumes the form of a paternal or protective interest in the teachers or in a particular teacher, which may be due to a real affection or to a desire to bask in his reflected glory. It is not uncommon that these individuals, while protecting the teacher from any onslaughts made upon him by others, should privately try to dominate him. Often enough this sponsor is a member of the school board, but he does not always have an official connection with the schools. The following narrative furnished by a teacher who has had extensive experience in rural communities brings out some aspects of this situation very clearly.

One situation which existed throughout Williams's teaching career both gratified and embarrassed him. This was the circumstance where an individual of the district adopted a paternal attitude toward Williams as the teacher. This person, the "teacher's pappa" as Williams jokingly called him, took it upon himself to look after Williams much as a father, mother, or fond relative might. Williams was never completely decided whether to be joyful or chagrined over the relationship thus set up between teacher and patron. He wondered if other teachers were fathered in a similar fashion. It was flattering enough to obtain so much attention from a middle-aged or influential adult of the district, and it was often very helpful to be told the attitudes of the community, but at times this fatherliness was like a bridle to a young colt.

Walt Maxson, of the Mart School District, was the first to take up the paternal rôle toward Emmet Williams as a teacher. Williams was teaching his first school then, and it was some time before the full portent and potency of this relationship became clear to him. Walt was fifty years of age, a small man, a moron, and the father of seven children, four of whom were in school. Walt had not been successful as an independent farmer and was reduced to the level of working for the other men of the community. He was a great conversationalist, but since he, incapable of having many valuable thoughts and opinions of his own, had become an artist at putting together the talk he heard from others to make up his own wise-sounding speeches, none of his neighbors accredited any importance to what he said.

Walt had never fathered a teacher before, though he had often tried. The new teacher, however, inexperienced in the ways of the school teacher's world, readily accepted Walt's definition of the situation. This was Walt's chance. What prestige, what status it gave him, this close contact with the teacher, this privilege of talking intimately and confidentially to the teacher whenever he saw him, this business of helping the teacher along and looking after him!

Williams knew the four older Maxson children before he became the Mart School teacher, but he had never met Walt. The first indication Williams had of the attitude Walt was going to take was the Saturday before school, when Walt scraped an acquaintance with him in a nearby town.

"Say, you're Emmet Williams, ain't you? Well, my name is Walt Maxson. You know my boys, and I know your dad. We live out in the Mart School District. My kids'll go to school to you, you know. Boy, that's a hard school! They're tough down there. Why, them kids had a fight with jackknives last spring. . . . But, oh! They ain't bad kids; the teacher didn't keep 'em busy. That's the big trouble. Then there are two bunches of kids. The Marts and the Sistons, all related to each other, ganged up against the other kids. If you can handle the ringleaders, you'll be all right. Anyway, we all expect you to get along fine."

Williams had heard rumors before, but here it was first hand. He carried Walt's words to school with him the next Monday morning and all through the year. As a result, he vigorously attacked the problems that arose, kept order in the school, and won a reputation as a disciplinarian. Walt was an excellent mouthpiece for the community. Every time he saw the teacher, he would stop and talk. From his talk Williams gleaned the neighborhood attitudes toward the school, and he got also both sympathy and encouragement. When Williams learned of Walt's standing in the community and Walt had told Williams's own father in a proud way how he was trying to help the teacher, Williams began to resent Walt's attitude. Then, too, when the community gathered at the school house or when the teacher was in town, it was more or less of a nuisance to be subjected to an attempt at conversational monopoly on the part of Walt Maxson. But a teacher cannot be rude toward his patrons—especially before his reputation has been established, and when the patrons are as good hearted and helpful as Walt Maxson was. When Williams needed furniture from a home to use at school, Walt furnished it. When Honidays were going to take their children out of school because the teacher didn't keep them from playing with those dirty Farney children, Walt passed the low-down on the situation to the teacher. When Williams was looking for a boarding and rooming place with a family that was neutral, as far as the two school cliques were concerned, Walt mentioned Kraders. In several other instances Walt functioned in a helpful manner and gradually established himself through this fatherly rôle as a hanger-on of the school.

The next experience of Williams as a teacher was in the Arizona School, four miles from the Mart School. The Arizona neighborhood was strongly organized about its school. Williams had now spent a year at a university and was the upper teacher in the two-teacher grade school of this well-organized village community. His year's experience in teaching, his relationship with Walt Maxson, his college training, and his position as upper teacher, all combined to make him less susceptible to the fatherly overtures of a patron of the school. Nevertheless he was fathered. John Speck, a congenial old fellow, usually looked after the Arizona teachers because his home was the customary boarding and rooming place for the teachers of the village. Williams and his younger sister, who was the lower teacher, drove an automobile each day from their home six miles away, and this left John Speck out of it. The "school teacher's pappa" this year must necessarily be someone else. Strangely enough it turned out to be a woman, a Mrs. Ed. Wixer, a lady of no small physique and personality. Mrs. Wixer mothered the lower teacher more than she did Williams, but he came in for his share of her maternal attention on occasion.

Before her marriage Mrs. Wixer had been head nurse in a hospital. Now her duties as a farmer's wife, though he was the outstanding man of the community, did not sufficiently take care of her executive drive. She, therefore, transferred her interests to her daughter Betty, who attended the Arizona school, to the teachers of the school, to the school itself, and to the neighborhood in general. She mothered everything and everyone in the village. Well, she had been taken away from what had been her life, and introduced to a life which was unsufficient and had to be supplemented by some sort of paternalistic, philanthropic, pseudo-social welfare work. Mr. Wixer was a school-board member, and through him Mrs. Wixer, having heard of Williams's reputation as a handler of unruly children, and his sister's reputation as a teacher of little folks, almost forced the community to hire the two Williams teachers. Then she had to justify her choice. She visited the school frequently and told the community of its good work. Thus while the Williamses were in the school her transferred interests centered around them. She was a go-between she acquainted herself with the work of the school and sold the school and the teachers to the neighborhood. She did not convey the true attitudes of the patrons of the school to the teachers; she brought them only words of praise. What she heard averse to the school she discounted. Her school was perfect.

Praise was Mrs. Wixer's technique. "Oh, you two children," she would say, "what a wonderful school you do have. Why, I never saw anything like it. When I was a child, we never did all these things. It just rests me to sit and watch Miss Williams teach. She does it so easily. And Mr. Williams goes about it so systematically. Now you two must come down to supper next week. Mr. and Mrs. McGinty will be there."

She didn't suggest, as did Walt Maxson (who had moved into the Arizona district, and would have suggested again if the energetic Mrs. Wixer had not eclipsed him as the "teacher's pappa"), but she praised, and she inspired by presenting the teacher to himself as an ideal. A teacher cannot disappoint that kind of feeling.

Mrs. Wixer wished the teachers to live with her during the cold months, but fate had given her too small a house for that. She did the next best thing. She invited the Williamses to her home for dinner every two weeks. At the same time she would entertain an influential patror and his family. The village was amused at Mrs. Wixer, but was kept in actual touch with its teachers, and consequently gave them good support. When at the end of the year the Williamses declined to sign a contract because no increases in salary were forthcoming, Mrs. Wixer forced the resignation of the two members of the board who were responsible for the no-raise policy.

Neither before the Williamses came to Arizona, nor after they left, did Mrs. Wixer so vigorously mother the village teachers. It should be added that neither of the Williamses knew Mrs. Wixer before they entered the community as teachers.

Williams became more accustomed to the school-teaching rôle. He became less influenced by its attendant paternal rôle, but the paternal rôle continued to exist nevertheless. Williams's third year of teaching was spent as the lower teacher in the two-teacher Blackstone Rural High School. The community about this school was very disorganized because of its unyielding provincialism and its sharp and gossiping tongue. In this community two tall, raw-boned, middle-aged men took Williams under their wings, and Williams took it upon himself to be paternal toward the upper teacher.

Carl Willy and Bill Lemon assumed the paternal rôle toward Williams. Carl Willy was a traditional "teacher's pappa," a busybody, and a gossip. He wanted someone to whom he could tell the scandal of the neighborhood. At first he surpassed his rival, Bill Lemon, in looking after the teacher, because the teacher roomed and boarded with the Willys. Williams had not known Carl Willy before he came to Blackstone, but Carl was an old friend of his parents. At night after supper as the Willy family and Williams sat around the living room, Carl would light his pipe, call up a twinkle in his eye, and tell that he had heard that Clarence Hanson had quit school because he just couldn't get along with Miss Neerey; she was too strict and unreasonable. Now in reality Williams was the stricter of the two. Carl's procedure was just an easy way of letting Williams know the anti-school and anti-teacher feeling at Blackstone. He never related a pro-school sentiment. "It wasn't any fun to tell nice things to folks, because such things never bothered them any." Carl took a mild delight in seeing people squirm. The Blackstone High School had been conducted much on the everyone-do-as-you-please plan in the past. When Williams and Miss Neerey attempted to make a well-disciplined and business-like school of it, the pupils and their parents protested vigorously. It was these protests which Carl Willy passed along to Williams. The younger man was usually annoyed by such gossip. He would go to school, however, and try to bring it into accord with the public opinion of its patrons as much as he could and still keep it a school. Thus he popularized the school and himself. At the end of the year he was asked back, but Miss Neerey was not. Carl's son, Ronald, went to high school, and he would tell Carl of the corrections made in the policy of the teachers. Of course, Carl was pleased. He got much more pleasure, however, from relating hearsay than from the fact that what he told had caused Williams to make a bid for community support for the school.

Cold weather forced Williams to move closer to the school building. He began to live with Bill Lemon's married daughter. Bill had had two daughters of his own who taught school. That made him more a listener than a talker. Bill had early in the year taken a liking to Williams, whom he spoke of as a "good kid." The young school master, usually reticent about talking of school troubles, soon found himself speaking freely to sympathetic Bill Lemon. When Williams expressed uncertainty concerning the wisdom of some action taken by the teachers, Lemon would philosophize as follows:

"Aw, don't pay any attention to the —— fools in this neighborhood. I know them all from A to Z. None of them got any kick coming, and half of them don't know what it's all about anyway. Shucks! You folks have had a good school. Alice [his daughter in high school] is getting along fine and so's everybody else's kids. Go ahead and do as you please, and tell them all to go to —— if they don't like it."

This was all there was to Bill Lemon's fathering. It was sufficient, however; and to this day Emmet Williams thinks more of Bill Lemon than of any of the others who assumed the paternal attitude toward him.

Miss Neerey, the principal of the Blackstone High School, was inexperienced in school administration. She soon began to bring every problem to Williams. Williams could have taken the principal's place and worked out an actual solution for these problems. For some reason he avoided this. He only suggested ways of solving problems, and the principal worked out her own solutions and retained her place as the nominal head of the system. Miss Neerey was so shut-in that no one in the community was moved to take a parental attitude toward her. The man to whom she was engaged was attending a university in a distant city. This caused her to be extremely moody at times, and for this the only cure was to talk to some one concerning this young man. All these things contributed to make Williams assume a brotherly, if not a fatherly, rôle toward the principal. Thus he became addicted to a practice which he had many times lauded and as many times condemned.

Williams next taught two years in the Riverview High School. The first year, when he was just an instructor, he was looked after by the "big boy" of the school. Wilbur Carrol, the boy, was a senior in high school and was eight years Williams's junior. Williams had known Wilbur for several years. As a result of this relationship, Wilbur thought at first that the presence of his friend in the school constituted an opportunity for levity. Williams turned on him savagely, and the unexpectedness of the action, together with the biting tongue of the teacher, reduced Wilbur to tears before the whole class on the very first day of school. This was a lesson in discipline to the school as well as to Wilbur Carrol. Wilbur set about hating Williams as hard as he could, but he had to tolerate him. Eventually the "fieriness of this little school-dad Williams" stirred up a real affection. Wilbur was always fathering someone or something anyway, so it was quite natural for him to look after the teacher.

His chief care was toward the physical well-being of Williams. At a public gathering at the school it was, "Say, Williams, don't you want to comb your hair before you go on the stage? It's all mussed up. You've been fussing with those curtains again and that's those blamed juniors' job. Seems like they don't attend to their business at all." On clean-up day, he'd bellow, "Hey, you guys, get hold of this piano. Ain't Williams done enough without having to help lift this too?" At a picnic, he attacked a group of little boys thus, "Now listen, you kids, don't be so rough. It's all right to throw dirt on us high-school boys, but that fellow over there is our teacher. If you hit him we'll clean up on you." Whether Williams was there or not,

Wilbur was the same. One time before Williams had arrived at a class party, he said, "You guys cut that out or you'll break something, and Williams will get the blame."

The second year at Riverview Williams was the principal of the high school and had a score of pappas. A group of young men with children, who would one day be in high school, took upon themselves the paternity of the principal. At a public meeting Williams said something about electric lights in the school building to take the place of the antiquated gas system. The school improvement bug there and then bit these young men hard. They persuaded the young principal to push their program for a modernizing of the school plant. He agreed. The elderly men and the church people of the town—this community was organized more or less about its wealthy old men and its church—met the issue with bitter opposition. Williams and the young men supported each other well. They finally reached a state of mind where they were willing to fight for each other. Or rather the men had backed Williams until they would have perished rather than see him fail. He, in turn, was very grateful for their support. The elderly and church elements had the advantage of numbers, solidarity, and vested interests, and they discouraged Williams from returning to Riverview for a third term. His "pappas" resented what they called his "being made the goat." Eventually they gained control of the school board. Riverview now has a modern school plant. The letters of recommendation that Williams secures from the Riverview board are little short of eulogy. Each year the Riverview board offers the superintendency of the Riverview Public Schools to Williams.

It may be safely said that every community has an individual, or individuals, or a group of individuals, who are concerned with fathering, mothering, or brothering—looking after and helping out—the teacher or teachers of the community. These school teacher's pappas may be only on the fringe of the school population, but they are very real persons and have a significant relationship to the teacher, the school, and the community. Sometimes their influence is good, and sometimes bad. They may be relatives or friends of the teacher, or they may never have known him before his advent into the community as a teacher. They may act in a customary capacity, or they may do the job for a single term. They may have some official connection with the school or they may have none. Often they are the persons with whom the circumstances of the teacher's life in the community have happened to bring him into close contact. Their techniques vary greatly, according to their object in taking up the job of sponsoring. They may suggest, they may praise, they may gossip, relay gossip, coax, support, tease, threaten, or do any one of a hundred other things as they father the teacher. But however that may be, the school teacher's pappa must be considered a part of the social system of the school. (Graduate student, *The School Teacher's Pappa,* unpublished manuscript.)

PROJECTS

1. Make a case study of a janitor, indicating clearly his relation to teachers, executives, students, and community.

2. Make an extended study of the social atmosphere of a "hangout" popular among school boys.

3. Study the personality of a campus policeman. What is his meaning in the school?

4. Describe the channels by which alumni exert influence upon your own school.

5. Relate the problem of the overemphasis of football to the attitudes of alumni.

6. Study several issues of an alumni quarterly or other alumni journal. What mechanisms are employed to keep the alumni in line?

7. Observe closely the behavior of a high-school principal on alumni day. Analyze and interpret.

8. Make a case study of some individual who stands sponsor for a particular teacher before the local community.

9. What campus character do alumni of your school inquire about when they return for a visit? Make a study of his relations to students.

NOTE: The influence of marginal persons and groups upon school life seems to have received no serious and extended treatment. References are therefore omitted.

CHAPTER VIII

OTHER ASPECTS OF THE RELATION OF THE SCHOOL AND THE COMMUNITY

IN THEORY, the ultimate authority of the school system is vested in the school board, a group of local citizens elected by the community to oversee the schools. In fact, the most important function of the school board is usually to see to the hiring of a superintendent. Once the superintendent, a specially trained teacher vested with authority over other teachers and titular headship of the schools, has been employed, a sharp struggle usually ensues between him and the outstanding members of the school board over the right actually to determine the policies of the school. The advantage is with the superintendent so far as this issue is concerned, for he is a specialist, and can claim the specialist's right to carry his point over those who have not had equal or equivalent training; he is in fact the titular head of the schools, and bears the responsibility before the community if anything goes wrong; he is on the scene constantly, and must deal with many minor matters without consulting the board except, perhaps, for routine ratification afterwards, and he usually carries on dealings with teachers and students single-handed, from which he acquires a considerable amount of prestige with both bodies.

By mediating to the school executive the sense of the community concerning the administration of the school, the school board may perform a legitimate function and one that in no way interferes with the initiative or the efficiency of the school administrator in his specialized field. It is part of the superintendent's technique so to define the situation as regards himself and the school board as to make an extended and bitter struggle over the control of the school system seem unnecessary and fruitless; he should accept the principle that he should have sufficient authority to deal adequately with all school situations and that he should not be interfered with in the legitimate performance of these functions, and he should take his authority so much for granted that others will be disposed to grant it as legitimate and in the scheme of things. The technique of avoiding major conflicts with a school board is apparently similar to the technique which the teacher uses in avoiding such trials of strength with his students;

it consists in settling minor details so swiftly and with such assurance that no question ever arises as to one's competency or right to deal with the greater. This is the question of dominance and subordination, and it is settled in most cases, or it may be settled, without an actual trial of strength by the assurance and completeness of detail in the alternative plans of action presented by the persons involved in the situation. In this matter, as in many others, there appears to be a great difference in personalities. Some superintendents have their way with their school boards over many years, and no one arises to contest their claims; in fact, authority is genially taken and genially granted. Other superintendents are always in difficulty with the board, and we must conclude that it is a difference in their personal techniques which accounts for this difference of results; this is what we are attempting to analyze. (It may be suggested, too, that the ability to dominate a school board pleasantly is a greater factor in determining personal advancement in this walk of life than the ability to administer a school system of students and teachers.) A judicious superintendent will be able, by devices subtle and hard to recognize, to avoid any conflict over policy, taking that matter and others very largely into his own hands. He will then be able to make his board see that running a school is a cooperative enterprise, and to direct them into various lines of cooperative endeavor with him, thereby not only avoiding conflict, but actually making use of the collective intelligence and community connections of the board, and letting the members feel that they are being of use. But between this and a policy of asking advice which will lead to conflict, or permitting interference which in the end can only handicap the executive, is another line that is not easy to draw. The line is there, and many persons know how to draw it, but it will require acute powers of observation and much tact to draw it in the individual instance.

Some board members are captious, and some superintendents let relations with the board get out of hand; there is, besides, in many communities a tradition of interference which effectively precludes any school executive from ever obtaining a quite free hand. Superintendents caught in such situations have evolved many interesting devices whereby they get their own way and yet preserve their position with the board relatively undamaged. In discussing some mistake which he was alleged to have made, one young and inexperienced "principal" remarked to his school board, "Why, I thought that would be all right, so I went ahead and did it." A member of the board, anxious to preserve the right of the board to dictate all policies, came out upon him roundly, "We didn't hire you to think. We hired you to be the principal of this school. Hereafter you leave the thinking to us. We'll do all the thinking for you." Thereafter he adopted a policy of making a great show of consulting his board members on all minor matters, and of pushing essential matters so far before consulting the board that only one decision was possible. His position was then something like that of the president, who can involve the country in war, but cannot declare war.

Another policy which has many converts is that of pitting one faction of the board against another. It frequently happens that bitter personal enemies and business rivals are asked to serve together on the school board; it is then possible for an adroit manager to play many tunes upon these personal oppositions and antagonisms. Often enough it is one man who controls the board; the superintendent's problem is then to maintain some sort of hold upon this one man. For this, many hundreds of devices have been evolved by harassed superintendents. These devices cover almost the whole gamut of human possibilities, ranging from identifying one's self with the leading member's church to buying supplies from his store or failing to pay a note. One small-town superintendent invariably selected a leading grocer from among the members of the school board, and patronized him with the intention of maintaining a hold upon him; it was a device which did not, because of the personality of the superintendent, have by any means unfailing success; this man might have done better, it would seem, to have kept the upper hand of this grocer, as of any other, by the threat of removing patronage, or at least to have kept the grocer from coming to believe that he was cleverer than the superintendent. A less obvious policy was that of a small-town superintendent who kept a hold upon the president of the board, a banker, by refusing to pay a note at the bank. Though the banker hated this teacher, as he had almost from the first, he wanted to keep him in the community, until he had paid his note; since this man was the most influential member of the board, the superintendent retained his position as long as the note was unpaid. A more general sort of policy is that adopted by many executives of showing a great deal of interest in the scholastic and personal welfare of the children of influential members of the community.

It is a difficult thing to succeed a man who has been popular in the community, and this is a fact which often affects the fortunes of individuals who fill prominent positions in the schools, such as the position of superintendent, high-school principal, coach, etc. One's friends do not at once forget him, and often they think to benefit him by making things hard for his successor. A lax superintendent is a hard man to follow, for he has allowed the school machine to disintegrate. He has allowed authority to escape from his hands, and his successor will always have a difficult time in restoring the school system both internally and externally. Added to this is the fact that such lax superintendents have usually made a number of friends in the community who, though perhaps not numerous or powerful or devoted enough to prevent his dismissal, are still ready and able to raise the cry that he has been dismissed unfairly and to work a reprisal for the injustice upon the man employed to take his place. Since this new man comes from the outside, he is usually, of all the persons involved in the situation, the most innocent of wrong. This mechanism is most noticeable within the faculty, and the carryover of old loyalties is one of the most difficult things which the new executive has to face. Sometimes the teachers who still preserve the memory of the former superintendent band themselves together in order to handicap the new executive; such fights are usually carried over into the community at large, and they often become very bitter. Such a case is that described in slightly fictionized form below.

During most of the year it was noticeable that the "old timers" were particularly clannish. Mr. Woof and family were self-sufficient. Miss Please and Mr. Out were excluded from the rest of the group because of their support of the administration. Their attitude might be stated in this way: They did not entirely approve of Mr. Adams, the then superintendent, but he was their superior and the head of the school system. As such he deserved their cooperation whenever possible. There was at least no necessity for open opposition.

The situation stood so when spring-time came, with its annual puzzle concerning the reelection of teachers. After some quibbling the board elected Mr. Adams for another year. At their request he then presented each teacher with a slip requesting the following information:

"Are you a candidate for reelection?"
"If so, at what salary?"
"If reelected at that salary will you immediately sign your contract?"
"Remarks."

One might have thought that a bomb had been set off. Such frothing at the mouth could hardly be imagined over such a trivial matter. To several of the teachers it was not entirely unexpected. Mr. Saith admitted that the board had wanted Mr. Laxman (the previous superintendent) to do the same thing the year before, and added that he had refused.

"Well, what do you think of such a questionnaire?"

"Well, I'll tell them one thing and that is that I won't bow down and ask them to reelect me. If my being in the system four years isn't recommendation enough, I'll go somewhere else. If they want me to leave why don't they say so?"

After each teacher had finally filled out his slip and returned it to Mr. Adams, the board dilly-dallied along before determining the reelections. After considerable delay contracts were handed out to Miss Blough, Miss Please, and Mr. Out, as well as all the grade teachers except two.

Then feeling did mount. Each faculty member rejected sought, from the members of the board, to know why. They also had troubles to unburden to the members of the board concerning ill treatment at the hands of the superintendent.

The special board-faculty meeting was the result of all this. Through all the events of the year the board had shown itself rather weak. Each member seemed to fear speaking his mind, perhaps for reasons connected with his business. After each of the "outlandish" things Mr. Adams did, some of the group of teachers would carry the information to the president of the board. They also carried to him a number of remarks that Mr. Adams was supposed to have made about members of the board, teachers, and others. As some of the reported comments charged the president of the board with drinking, he finally took action. He called a special meeting of the board and faculty for the purpose of ironing out the difficulties between them.

The offended teachers nursed their grievances until the appointed time. Some of those reelected had received increases in salary; others had not. Miss Please had received an increase of fifty dollars; Mr. Out, of a hundred dollars. Miss Blough had been reelected at no increase. All this added fuel to the fire.

In the meantime rumor was rife among both faculty and students. A fantastic tale went the rounds to the effect that Mr. Out, the debating coach, was to have charge of football the next year. Several students asked him about this possibility, but he had heard nothing of it.

On the evening set for the show-down, the joint meeting of faculty and board was called to order by the president of the board. He stated in a hang-dog manner that there appeared to be some dissatisfaction and that this was an opportunity for all to have their say.

It began slowly, but soon the fireworks were sparking. The trend of the meeting seemed along very childish lines. "I understand that So-and-So said such and such about me—I want to know if that is true." And then So-and-So would arise and gravely deny the charge.

One of the grade teachers was moved to defend her reputation. "I want to know if Mr. Adams said that I have been keeping company with the high-school boys? I want to say that I have not. Yes, I'll admit I go to dances, but I don't see that that is any worse than playing cards or playing pool." This last was aimed at Mr. Out, who had occasionally played rotation pool with the boys.

Some remarks which had been made in confidence to members of the faculty concerning the inebriety of the president of the board were brought up and similarly dismissed.

A choice incident of the proceedings occurred when Miss Blough arose to her feet, eyes flashing.

"I have only one question which I wish the board to answer." (Her manner made it clear that she expected a negative answer.) "Did Mr. Adams recommend me for reelection?"

The president: "He did."

This reply completely befuddled Miss Blough for the moment, but then she took up the task of determining why she had not been given an increase. She asked some questions which she evidently considered very pointed, whether or not there was a salary schedule or a scheme of promotions, etc.

All the teachers in the group of "grievers" wanted to know what the vote had been on their applications. In every case the count had stood at four to two.

Unable to tolerate this child's play any longer, Mr. Out arose and said, "As this is a meeting for the purpose of having everyone express his or her opinion, I should like to make a few remarks, although I realize that I am not fully acquainted with all the conditions.

"First, I think this meeting is mere child's play. What good can come from each one demanding to know whether a certain remark was made about him, when the accused immediately denies. We might pursue such a course indefinitely without arriving anywhere.

"I propose to cut through to underlying motives and to present an analysis of the present situation in the school as I have studied it. To begin with, we have on the faculty several members who served under Mr. Laxman, who evidently was very satisfactory, to the faculty, at least, for four years. They came to hold him in high esteem. Some of them, I am sure, feel that he received a 'raw deal' in not being reelected last year. That is as it may be, and I know nothing whatever about it. But from the comments of these teachers and from chance conversations with several students and members of this community, I have gathered that these persons have developed a high loyalty to Mr. Laxman. So great, in fact, that they expected the new superintendent to do everything exactly as his predecessor did. And when he didn't, these persons proposed to raise trouble for him. Possibly they were determined to make it tough for the new man anyway. At least that is what they have done. They have done all that they could to antagonize Mr. Adams. They have been quite open in their disapproval of his ideas and methods and they have refused to cooperate as they should have done." . . .

Mr. Out entered the school café a few days after the above meeting to find some other teachers already seated there. He wanted to show them that it was possible to speak one's mind and still be sociable, so he chose to sit at the table with North, Blough, and Saith.

"Hello, everybody," said Mr. Out, seating himself.

Silence.

The preceding evening an all-school party had been held, which had been taken charge of by Mr. Out because of the fact that none of the other members of the faculty had put in an appearance before the evening was well on. A conversation was begun:

Saith: "How was the party last evening?"

Blough: "Dumber than usual."

Saith: "I had a headache and didn't feel like going out."

Blough: "I don't know whether to sign my contract or not. What I would like to do would be to come back and raise all the disturbance possible."

Saith: "Yeah, won't Laxman get a kick out of things as they are?" (Fictionized student paper.)

The opposite situation to the above is that of the person succeeding a man who has left many enemies in the community. The enemies of the former superintendent, especially if they are members of the board or otherwise prominent in the community, attach themselves at once to the new superintendent, as if determined to prove that they are not trouble-makers, that it is possible for this new man to get along with them, and that it therefore should have been possible for his predecessor to do so. This type of situation is often found when an executive of some vigor and aggressiveness has just been at the head of the schools. Such a man pushes the program of the school energetically, he fights for needed supplies, equipment, and salaries, and he insists upon centralization of authority in his own hands. He integrates the school machine at the expense of the independence of some of its parts. But such an energetic man makes enemies. Sooner or later his enemies oust him. His successor finds a well-organized and smoothly functioning school system, and a community ready to receive him cordially. This mechanism comes out particularly in smaller communities where there has been a fight for a new school building. The superintendent, let us say, becomes convinced that there is need of a new building, or for extensive improvements upon the old one. He argues the case strongly. He enters into the fight for the new building. He wins, but in the process he makes many enemies. These enemies oust him from the school system. Then he goes to a new community and repeats the process. It is significant that in teaching and in the ministry certain individuals early acquire a reputation as "builders."

It is a fact that has sometimes been remarked upon that certain communities change the chief executive of their school system very frequently, perhaps every two or three years. (Sometimes other members of the faculty are involved in these changes, and leave for the same reasons, though this is not necessarily true.) This tendency of the community to oust a man when he is just beginning to know his way around in the community has often been inveighed against, but its reasons and its causes have not been analyzed. It seems worth while to point out that this insecurity of the school executive inheres in the nature of his relationship to the community. The relation of the superintendent to the community which he serves is one in which alienation is always implicit, and the alienation begins to work at once when he appears in the community, but it reaches its culminating point two or three years later.

We may say that the superintendent has a typical life history in the community. This typical life history repeats itself again and again in the life of one executive, and in the community with different executives. The life history seems to be about as follows: When the new executive takes charge of the school system, he has the support of nearly the entire community (except in such a situation as the one described above, where the outgoing executive has left behind him a considerable and well-organized opposition to the new one). The board is usually with him to a man. This undivided support is his until some incident occurs which brings him into conflict with an individual or an organized group in the community. It is not long before such an incident occurs; the executive metes out some disciplinary measure with which individual parents disagree, or supports a teacher who becomes similarly embroiled (or refuses to support her), or he refuses to cooperate with some group in the community in the program they are promoting, or he launches some school policy which proves to be unpopular with students or teachers. The essential weakness of his position is that it gives him an opportunity to make many more enemies than friends. Opportunities for becoming unpopular, to the point, almost, of infamy, are numerous, but opportunities for gaining friends are few.

The life of a superintendent is from spring to spring. At the end of his first year the superintendent has made some enemies, but the majority of the community, let us say, is still satisfied with the manner in which he is conducting the school. He has made some bitter enemies, as, apparently, he unavoidably must. Those enemies are criticizing him severely. But as yet they are not powerful enough to dislodge him from his position. During the second year of his incumbency, the superintendent continues to be harassed by these same enemies, who become increasingly bitter. Perhaps he becomes embroiled in something of a feud with them; in any case the opposition group becomes increasingly compact and well organized. The superintendent has by now acquired certain enemies on the school board and they serve in the community as further radiant points of antagonism toward him. But the important fact, and the inexorable tragedy of the superintendent's life is that in the second year he usually makes a few more enemies, but he rarely has an opportunity to restore the balance by making friends of those who have previously been inimical to him. At the end of the second year, the opposition is sufficiently powerful to "make a fight on the superintendent." Making a fight on the superintendent usually implies an open attempt to elect persons to the school board who will vote against his reelection; it implies a great deal of gossip and poisonous whispering, and, usually, conspiracies to discredit him in the eyes of the community. Not infrequently teachers become involved in these conspiracies. Let us say that the superintendent has given the community a satisfactory school and that he is able at the end of the second year to win the fight. Sometimes he is not, and the process, for him and the community, can begin again. But if he does win at the end of the second year, he stands a greater chance of losing at the end of the third, for his position is continuously weakened. He makes more enemies than friends. And he makes decided enemies, if not bitter enemies, and only lukewarm friends.

In the larger communities, the mass of the community is large enough to absorb without damage those individuals who have come into conflict with the superintendent over personal matters incidental to school administration or concerns of general school policy, so that his enemies will have less hope of removing him, and therefore less motivation to organize an opposition to him. (His enemies are likely also to be scattered and without acquaintance with each other, which would make organization difficult.) Greater security of tenure is also assured in the larger communities by the very unwieldiness of the political machinery, which is so cumbrous that it is rarely set in motion for trivial reasons. Further, if the school executive manages to remain in a smaller community for as long as, let us say, five years, he becomes pretty stable in his position, for he is then accepted as a member of the community and there is as little thought of discharging him because of disagreements concerning school policies as there is of running a farmer off his land because of his politics; he is a member of the local in-group, and he is something of a fixture; he has had time to develop firm and enthusiastic friends, and is not easily to be removed. We may, however, allow for all these exceptions without destroying the truth of our generalization, that the relationship of the school executive to the community has within it the elements of its own destruction. And as long as the traditional conception of the school, and the conception of school administration which goes with it, persists, and as long as the school continues to be controlled by the local community, the school systems of the smaller communities are doomed to frequent changes of head.

PROJECTS

1. Analyze the techniques worked out by successful superintendents for handling school boards.

2. Observe carefully the behavior of some person who gets his own way without antagonizing others. Analyze and interpret.

3. Describe a heated campaign in a school-board election. What hinged upon it?

4. Tell the story of a teacher who had to succeed a popular man. An unpopular man.

5. Outline a program by which a school executive may hold his position in a community which has a tradition of changing school executives frequently.

6. Write the history of a school system, in terms of aggressive and lax executives, for a number of years.

7. Write the life history of a school superintendent who is known as "a builder."

8. Show how the visiting teacher may help to explain the school to the community.

SUGGESTED READINGS

(1) LINDEMAN, E. C., *Community Conflict.*

(2) LINDEMAN, E. C., *The Community.*

(3) PATRI, ANGELO, *A Schoolmaster of the Great City.*

(4) PERRY, A. C., *The Status of the Teacher.*

(5) WHITNEY, LAMSON, *The Growth of Teachers in Service,* Chapters VI and VIII.

PART THREE

SOME INTERPRETATIONS OF LIFE IN THE SCHOOL

CHAPTER IX

THE SEPARATE CULTURE OF THE SCHOOL

TEACHERS have always known that it was not necessary for the students of strange customs to cross the seas to find material. Folklore and myth, tradition, taboo, magic rites, ceremonials of all sorts, collective representations, *participation mystique*, all abound in the front yard of every school, and occasionally they creep upstairs and are incorporated into the more formal portions of school life.

There are, in the school, complex rituals of personal relationships, a set of folkways, mores, and irrational sanctions, a moral code based upon them. There are games, which are sublimated wars, teams, and an elaborate set of ceremonies concerning them. There are traditions, and traditionalists waging their world-old battle against innovators. There are laws, and there is the problem of enforcing them. There is *Sittlichkeit*. There are specialized societies with a rigid structure and a limited membership. There are no reproductive groups, but there are customs regulating the relations of the sexes. All these things make up a world that is different from the world of adults. It is this separate culture of the young, having its locus in the school, which we propose to study. To work out all the details of this culture would be a task long and difficult, and, for our purpose, not altogether necessary. We shall be content to mark out the main lines of the cultural background of school life.

In part the discussion of the school in cultural terms has been anticipated in a preceding section. We have advanced the notion that the school is a center of cultural diffusion; we have shown that the school serves as a point from which the cultural standards of the larger group are mediated to the local community. The organization of higher and lower schools for the purpose of cultural diffusion may be thought of as analogous to the organization of wholesale and retail merchandising for the distribution of material goods. The goods, here certain cultural traits, are sent out from centers in job lots, to be distributed by retailers by their own methods at their own price. There is a certain amount of central control of education, as there is central control of the merchandising of certain material objects. We have noted also that the school is engaged in the transmission of a vast body of culture which is passed on from the old to the young. The school must pass on skills and it must implant attitudes; most of these are not new in the community. At any time and in any community the major portion of the work of the school is that of imposing these preexistent community standards upon children.

Certain cultural conflicts are at the center of the life of the school. These conflicts are of two sorts. The first and most obvious is that which arises from the peculiar function of the school in the process of cultural diffusion. A conflict arises between teachers and students because teachers represent the culture of the wider group and students are impregnated with the culture of the local community. Where the differences concern matters of religion or of fundamental morality, the struggle which then ensues may become quite sharp and may seriously affect the relation of the school to the community. A second and more universal conflict between students and teachers arises from the fact that teachers are adult and students are not, so that teachers are the bearers of the culture of the society of adults, and try to impose that culture upon students, whereas students represent the indigenous culture of the group of children.

The special culture of the young grows up in the play world of childhood. It is worth while to note that it arises in the interstices of the adult social world. Thrasher's *The Gang* is a study of the conflict between the established social order and the interstitial group which has sprung up and grown strong in the sections of society where the adult order does not hold. But this is by no means a complete explanation of the behavior norms of childhood groups. Another fact of importance is that the child does not experience the world in the same manner as does the adult. The child perceives the world differently from the adult in part because he sees it in smaller and simpler configurations. The adult sees social situations as falling into certain highly complex configurations; the child, with a simpler mental organization, does not see these, but breaks up his sensory data into different wholes. The sensory patterns of childhood, then, arise in part from imperfectly experienced adult situations. What the child appropriates from the cultural patterns around him must always be something which it is within his power to comprehend. This is usually one of the simpler and more elementary forms of adult behavior, as the criminal behavior followed out by the gang, or it is a split-off part of a more complex whole common in the culture of adults.

The culture pattern followed out by children may be a survival, for when culture changes it often happens that what was formerly a serious activity for adults is continued in the play of children. Indian fighting, sword play, Hallowe'en festivities, fairy tales, and the use of the bow and arrow have lost their worth in the adult world, but they have retained a certain value in the mental world of childhood. Sometimes economic activities survive and are continued in play because they have great intrinsic interest and have disappeared from the adult world only because they were unable to hold their own in competition with more efficient and prosaic means of getting a living. This has been true of hunting and fishing. There is in the developmental process a gradual evolution in the complexity of social situations and of the adjustment which the person makes to them; the fact that these social situations sometimes reproduce the actual situations of an earlier state of society has led some common-sense observers to believe in the theory of recapitulation.

Between mental processes and the cultural milieu in which they take place there is at all times a nice adjustment. As one's mind approaches the adult form of organization, he is increasingly assimilated to the culture of adults. Koffka, in *The Growth of the Mind*, has ably described the intellectual processes by which the child approaches mental maturity. The very young child sees the red ball against the indifferent background; it sees its mother's face and hears her voice. It is conscious of only the most elementary discomforts. As the child grows older, it acquires more objects in its world, and those objects are more complicated; interrelations appear between those objects in the form of new configurations. Mental life develops by a series of "Aha moments." As a result of these moments of insight, material objects may pass through a long series of metamorphoses. The little round glass backed with mercury is for the very young child something to pound with; a little later it is a mystery, and later yet a thing with which to play a prank upon the teacher; at one time it is a thing that it is slightly disgraceful to be caught looking into; for the adult it is just a pocket mirror. It is this difference in mentality which determines the different uses of cultural products among groups of different age levels.

Age is not the only factor that separates people who nominally drink of the same cultural stream from actual community of culture. Mental ability, education, subtle differences of interests and of personality may likewise sort people into cultural pigeonholes. So completely is the individual immersed in the culture of his own age and social level that he often has difficulty in realizing that any other kind of culture exists. He is separated by invisible walls from those about him who follow different gods. Persons living in different segments of our culture, as determined by age and life situation, may find difficulty in communicating with each other or in understanding each other at all. The old cannot understand the young, the prudent cannot understand the heedless, the married can have little sympathy for the unmarried, parents can never commune with non-parents; each person in the world is surrounded by many with whom he must communicate by smoke signals and by only a few with whom he can converse. But the greatest chasm is that which separates young persons and old.[1]

The journey from the world of the boy to the world of the man

[1] The fact that the world of the child is organized into configurations of a different kind from the configurations composing the base of the adult's universe seems to constitute, by the way, the best justification we have for lying to children. The greatest argument for the teaching of falsehood seems to be that different orders of truth exist for different mental levels. Children should therefore be taught the kind of truth they are able to understand. There is truth in this argument in that children are likely to break up into simpler configurations the complicated configuration which results for the adult mind in the weighing of virtue against vice, and they are likely to get a final result which is, for the adult, distorted and beside the point. No one who has seen the demoralization produced in some not overly intelligent youths by contact with cynical but well-balanced and earnest adults can fail to see that there is some argument for the simple virtues, even if they are based upon falsehoods. But one wonders whether demoralization is not even more likely to result from building up in the child's mind a structure of beliefs which he is likely to take sometime for complete lies because they are partly false. That such demoralization often occurs will be apparent to all who have ever been in a position to witness the changes wrought in the moral fiber of students when they enter the greater world or make the transition from secondary schools to universities. Nor should we fail to remark in this connection that the policy of lying to children presupposes that one should be intelligent enough and dexterous enough to deceive them completely. This is often not the case at all, for shrewd children, judging their elders by their behavior rather than by their words, are frequently able to cut through the adults' rationalizations to the amoral core of their behavior. Since children, even the shrewdest of them, do not make allowance for rationalizations as rationalizations, as phenomena beyond the conscious control of the individual, they judge their elders more harshly, sometimes, than they deserve. They think their elders both knaves and fools when those elders are in fact too high-minded to admit their selfishness to themselves. Perhaps, when all the alternatives are considered, we shall do better to stick to the simple virtues ourselves, and to speak truth, while taking such precautions as we may against unwarranted generalizations from facts which run contrary to the accepted views of ethics. The virtue that we shall so engender will be a tough-minded virtue. It may be less comprehensive than some would desire, but it will not be brittle.

is rarely smooth and continuous. But it has fewer sharp corners to turn if the members of the adult world are able to project themselves back into the psychic world of childhood. The adult who can live in the childish world with sufficient intensity to understand children from within can help them intelligently to develop those complex and unstable syntheses upon which the adult adjustment depends. Teachers have tried to make the transition easier by presenting to children a finely graded and continuously evolving culture, organized into ever more complex configurations. (They have succeeded very well in grading and sorting academic subject matter.) So have arisen those teacher-initiated and teacher-managed "activities," ceremonials, traditions, etc. So were produced, in fact, most of the things which we shall treat in discussing the culture of the school. The purpose of all these things is to soften the conflict of cultures between old and young.

Though an enlightened pedagogy may ameliorate the conflict of adults and children, it can never remove it altogether. In the most humane school some tension appears between teacher and students, resulting, apparently, from the rôle which the situation imposes upon the teacher in relation to his students. There are two items of the teacher's duty which make it especially likely that he will have to bring some pressure to bear upon students: he must see to it that there is no retrogression from the complexity of the social world worked out for students of a certain age level,[1] and he must strive gradually to increase that complexity as the child grows in age and approximates adult understanding and experience. Activities may reduce conflict, but not destroy it.

Children have something which can be regarded as a culture of their own. Its most important loci are the unsupervised play group and the school. The unsupervised group presents this culture in a much purer form than does the school, for the childish culture of the school is partly produced by adults, is sifted and selected by adults, and is always subject to a certain amount of control by teachers. The culture of the school is a curious mélange of the work of young artisans making culture for themselves and old artisans making culture for the young; it is also mingled with such bits of the greater culture as children have been able to appropriate. In turning to more concrete materials, we may note certain aspects of

[1] A strong tendency toward such retrogression in the direction of simpler and easier structures seems to exist, especially in the intermediate stages. This retrogression appears as "silliness." Much conflict between teachers and students arises from the desire of the teacher to eliminate "silliness."

tradition in the school. It will illustrate well this mingling of cultures if we divide the tradition which clusters about the school into three classes: tradition which comes entirely, or almost entirely, from the outside; tradition which is in part from outside the school and in part indigenous; and tradition which is almost entirely indigenous. It is roughly true that tradition of the first class exists in the community at large, that of the second class among teachers, and that of the third class among students.

Tradition of the first class, that which for the particular school comes altogether from the outside, is a manifestation of a culture complex diffused throughout the whole of West European culture. The historic school has of course had a part in the formation of this complex, but any particular school is largely the creation of it. Tradition of this sort governs the very existence of schools, for, without such a culture complex, schools would not exist at all. This traditional culture complex governs also the general nature of the life in the schools. It determines that the old shall teach the young, and not that the young shall ever teach the old, which would be at least equally justifiable in a world that changes so rapidly that an education twenty years old is out of date. Tradition governs what is taught and it holds a firm control upon the manner in which it is taught. Tradition determines who shall teach; we have already discussed some of the traditional requirements for teaching. It is this same sort of tradition also which largely determines how students and teachers shall think of each other.

The best example of a mingled tradition in part absorbed from the general culture of the group and in part produced in the particular institution is the tradition of teachers. In so far as this tradition of teachers is derived from outside a particular school, it is drawn by teachers from the general culture, and from association with members of the teaching profession everywhere. In so far as it is a purely local product, it is produced by the teachers in the institution and is passed on from one teacher to another. We may mention some cardinal points of the teacher tradition as it is usually encountered, making due allowance for local variations. There is a teacher morality, and this morality regulates minutely the teacher's relations with his students and with other teachers; it affects his relations with other teachers especially where the standing of those teachers with students might be affected. There is a character ideal of the teacher; nearly every group which lives long in one stereotyped relation with other groups produces its character ideal, and this ideal for teachers is clearly observable. When teachers say of a colleague, "He's a school teacher," they mean that he conforms to this local character ideal. (It usually implies that the individual puts academic above other considerations, is conscientious in his duties, and exacting in the demands he makes upon himself and others.) There is a taboo on seeking popularity among students, and this taboo operates with dreadful force if it is thought that popularity seeking is complicated by disloyalty to the teacher group. There is a traditional attitude toward students; this attitude requires that a certain distance be kept between teachers and students. The desire to be fair is very likely not the strongest motive that teachers have for keeping students at a distance, but it is certainly one of the consequences of the policy, and it has in its own right the compelling value of an article of faith. None may violate the code of equality with impunity. Teachers have likewise a certain traditional attitude toward each other. The most obvious manifestation of this traditional attitude is the ceremoniousness of teachers toward each other and toward the administration of the school. It seems clear that this is the ceremoniousness of a fighting group which does not care to endanger its prestige with underlings by allowing any informality to arise within itself. Another interesting observation that has often been made about particular groups of teachers is that they discriminate markedly between veterans and new men. This distinction is in the folkways. Occasionally there is a more or less definite ceremony of initiation, more rarely, actual hazing.

The indigenous tradition of the school is found in its purest form among students. This tradition, when it has been originated on the spot, is passed on, largely by word of mouth, from one student to another. Some of the indigenous tradition has been originated by the faculty, and then imposed upon the students; once it has been accepted by students, however, it may be passed on by student groups. Some of the traditional observances which students follow are not home-grown; there is a great literature of school life, and students occasionally appear who are obviously playing the parts of story-book heroes. Besides, there exists in the culture of any community a set of traditional attitudes toward school and school life, varying from one social class to another, and from family to family; these attitudes influence profoundly the attitudes which students have toward school life. Nevertheless the tradition of students is very largely indigenous within the particular school. Although this sort of tradition varies much in detail from one school to another, we may mention certain characteristics of the fundamental patterns.

Like teacher morality, student morality is the morality of a fighting group, but differences appear in that the student group is subordinate, and its morality is relevant to that situation. Social distance between student and teacher seems as definitely a part of the student code as of the teacher code. The student must not like the teacher too much, for that is naïveté. There is the well-known school-boy code, the rule that students must never give information to teachers which may lead to the punishment of another student. Certain folkways grow up in every group of school children, as the folkway of riding to grade school on a bicycle or of not riding to high school on a bicycle, and these folkways have a great influence over the behavior of all members of the group. These groups of children are arranged in stair-steps. Membership in the older group implies repudiation of the folkways of the younger group. No one more foolish than the high-school boy on a bicycle, or the college boy wearing a high-school letter! Interlocking groups look forward only, each group aping its elders and despising its juniors. In modern schools, there is a whole complex of traditions pertaining to activities; it seems that all activities are meritorious, that they are in some way connected with the dignity and honor of the school, that some activities are more meritorious than others.

Sometimes a whole social system is carried in the tradition of students, and such social systems are very resistant to change. The fagging system, or a system of any sort of hazing, may persist for decades against the best efforts of highly efficient teachers and administrators to change them. A collegiate institution comes to mind which has conducted such a struggle for upwards of a hundred years. We are led to believe that hazing, at least, having its roots in the desire of those already in the group to dominate new members (and having its parallel on the faculty), would be destined to have some place in the culture which the young work out for themselves even if it had no sanction in tradition. In other words, the manner in which the young experience the universe recreates a hazing problem in every generation of students.

An interesting sidelight upon the importance of tradition is afforded by the fact that certain universities have recently become aware of the beauty of old tradition and have tried to establish traditions overnight. Thus the student daily of one of the great western universities recently announced that it had become a tradition in that university for cowbells to be rung by loyal students in the stands when a touchdown was made by the home team; this tradition, one gathered, had been established on the preceding Saturday. Regulations concerning the wearing of caps by freshmen, likewise, become traditions as soon as the regulations are promulgated. Tradition from time immemorial, that is from time beyond the memory of a particular generation of students, determines the relations of classes, sets the day for the class fight of the freshmen and sophomores, and reserves for seniors the right to sit upon a certain bench or to walk with their sweethearts along a particular path across the campus. In American universities, which have mostly not had a long history, such traditions are rarely aged in the wood.

Less dignified than tradition, and less old, but of a fascinating diversity, are those bits of folklore which circulate among students. A few years ago there walked upon this very spot a marvellous being, a student who defied the school authorities, laughed when the principal flogged him, finally ran away from home and has never been seen again. There was formerly a teacher in this school who was so near-sighted that the boys played leap-frog in the rear of the classroom. Such and such a teacher has a glass eye. The principal has an artificial foot. A certain male teacher once killed a man in a boxing bout. Much of this folklore centers about teachers. By its spread to adults, which occurs only occasionally, it gives rise to some of the fantastic gossip concerning teachers which circulates in the small town.

The cultural anthropologists have taught us to analyze the actions of human beings living in a certain culture into culture patterns. Those partially formalized structures of behavior known as "activities" will serve as excellent examples of culture patterns existing in the school. Among the "activities" to be found in most public schools may be mentioned athletics, work on the school paper, oratory and debating, glee club work, Hi-Y work, dramatics, participation in social clubs, departmental clubs, literary societies, fraternities, etc. Each of these activities may be thought of as representing a more or less ritualized form of behavior carried out by the individual as a member of a group and, often, a representative of the larger group. There is a set form for these activities. There is merit in these activities, and that merit seems to rest ultimately upon the notion that group welfare and group prestige are involved in them; the honor of the high school is damaged if the team loses. ("Our team is our fame-protector, On boys, for we expect a touchdown from you—"

is unpoetic, but explicit on this point.) But there is intrinsic, irrational merit in them, too, as in the trading of the Trobiand Islanders. There is distinction in these activities for individuals. That distinction rests in part upon the prominence which participation in them gives the individual in the eyes of the school at large, and in part upon the recognition which the adult group accords them. The variety of activities is almost endless, for each of the activities mentioned above has many subdivisions; these subdivisions are sometimes arranged in something of a hierarchy as in athletics, where the greatest distinction attaches to football, a little less to basketball, less yet to baseball and track. These activities are commonly justified on the grounds that they actually prepare for life, since they present actual life situations; their justification for the faculty is in their value as a means of control over restless students. It is noteworthy that a competitive spirit prevails in nearly all activities. Not all activities are really competitive, but the struggle for places may make them so, and the desirability of having some place in some school activity makes the competition for places keen. One "makes" the school orchestra or glee club quite as truly as one makes the football team.

These culture patterns of activities are partly artificial and faculty-determined, and partly spontaneous. In so far as they have been evolved by the faculty, they have been intended as means of control, as outlets for adolescent energies or substitutes for tabooed activities. They represent also the faculty's attempt to make school life interesting and to extend the influence of the school. Any activity, however, which is to affect the life of students at all deeply, any activity, then, which aspires to a greater influence than is exerted by the Latin Club or the Cercle Français, must have a spontaneous basis, and must appeal to students by presenting to them behavior patterns of considerable intrinsic interest. Each activity usually has some sort of faculty connection, and the status of the faculty adviser is thought to rise or fall with the prosperity or unprosperity of the activity which he promotes. Activities, then, increase in importance and gain recognition from the faculty through the efforts of interested faculty members, as well as through their own intrinsic appeal to students. (A change is taking place in our teacher idiom. The young teacher now refers to himself not as the teacher of a certain subject, but as the coach of a certain activity.)

Of all activities athletics is the chief and the most satisfactory. It is the most flourishing and the most revered culture pattern. It has been elaborated in more detail than any other culture pattern. Competitive athletics has many forms. At the head of the list stands football, still regarded as the most diagnostic test of the athletic prowess of any school. Then come basketball, baseball, track, lightweight football, lightweight basketball, girls' basketball, girls' track, etc. Each of these activities has importance because the particular school and its rivals are immersed in a culture stream of which competitive athletics is an important part. Each school has its traditional rivals, and a greater psychic weighting is attached to the games with traditional rivals than to those with other schools. Schools are arranged in a hierarchy, and may therefore win moral victories while actually suffering defeats. Pennsylvania wins, but Swarthmore triumphs.

Games, the most interesting phase of competitive athletics, are complex and elaborate cultural patterns. Other culture patterns reside in them. Some form of game is to be found in most cultures. The history of games is one of the most fascinating chapters of anthropology of the historical sort. Enthusiasts of the modern games played with balls claim for them a most ancient origin. (Basketball is an exception.) The game acquires a clearly defined pattern, and this is passed on with little variation. (Even minor changes in the rules usually meet with determined opposition.) Skill is relevant to the culture pattern of the game; if the form of the game is changed, skill vanishes. It is interesting, too, that a "form" which is partly cultural comes to reside in every feature of competitive athletics. The most flexible and skillful performance, with irrelevant motions most completely eliminated, represents "form" in a particular performance. Lack of form usually limits the perfectability of a performance sufficiently to keep the athlete out of competition. Thus there is "form" for batting a baseball, for a drop-kick, for putting the shot. It is possible that an athlete, by long practice, might develop this form through trial and error and the gradual removal of imperfections in his performance. But it is more likely that the athlete gets this form through cultural diffusion. Form itself may represent the accumulated improvements in technique of many generations of athletes. Form, produced by the internal mechanisms making for the perfection of responses, has thus a cultural character as well.

Competition between schools in athletics comes to a focus in games. The game is in fact disguised war. There is a continual tendency for the game to revert to actual war. "Now go out and fight," says the coach. "Fight," says the school orator. "Fight," scream the spectators. Everyone treats the game as a fight and thinks of it as a fight except perhaps the referee. It is small wonder that the political order worked out for this conflict situation, the political order consisting of the rules and the referee to back them, is maintained with such difficulty and only by penalties which impose the direst disabilities upon the offenders. There is, it is true, a whole code of sportsmanship which arises from this conflict situation, a code which internalizes the rules and makes for the principle of fair play. This code of sportsmanship is a central part of the athletic tradition, and as such an important aspect of the cultural life of the school.

The code of sportsmanship becomes a very important ethical principle, one almost says the very source and spring of all ethics, for youngsters and for those adults who hold to the conflict theory of human life. There are men who insist that they learned the most important lessons of life upon the football field. They learned to struggle there and to hold on, and they learned to respect the rights of others and to play according to the rules. It may be surmised that men who have such a conception of life do not live in a very complex world. It is difficult to generalize about the effect of athletics upon the personalities of those participating. One might guess that it is in general favorable, and that its favorable effects are in the line of a growing into such rôles as those mentioned above. Part of the technique, indeed, of schools and teachers who handle difficult cases consists in getting those persons interested in some form of athletics. This constitutes a wholesome interest, opens the way to a normal growth of personality, and inhibits abnormal interests and undesirable channels of growth.

There arise some problems of the relations of professionals and amateurs in school athletics, and these have their effect upon the culture patterns of the game and sportsmanship. All coaches are professionals, and live by the prowess of their teams. All players are forced to be amateurs. It often happens that the preachments concerning the sporting code which drop so frequently from the lips of the coaches are more than neutralized in practice by the pressure which these men put upon their players to win games. A more serious indictment of a social system which allows the livelihood of a man and his family to depend upon the athletic achievements of boys is that the coach is so pressed that he uses his human material recklessly. He trains his "men" (aged sixteen) a bit too hard, or he uses his star athletes in too many events, or he schedules too many hard games; all this he does from a blameless desire to gain a better position or a rise in salary for himself, but he often fails to consider the possible effects upon the physical well-being of the rising generation.

The various forms of athletics have been established as a means of control in American schools on the pragmatic principle. The system of control through athletics works. The extension of activities, of which the most important are the athletic activities, has helped to make the schools pleasant places in which young people may pass their time. But this extension has not been attended by the development of a wholly satisfactory theory of the use of athletics for school control. The theory which is perhaps most in vogue with the school men is that athletic activity makes students more tractable because it drains off their surplus energies and leaves them less inclined to get into mischief. This we may call the physical-drain justification of athletics. It founders upon the fact that in most schools the participation of most students is vicarious, almost entirely vicarious for girls, largely so for boys. It is difficult to see how athletics can constitute a pronounced physical drain upon those who do not play. A slightly more sophisticated theory is that athletics furnishes a diversion of attention from undesirable to desirable channels, that it gives students something to think about and something to do with their time. Spectators, according to this account of the process, attend the games and get from them a catharsis; their souls are purged. This theory has value and must be incorporated into any final reckoning up of the influence of athletics upon school life.

The author would be inclined to account for the favorable influence of athletics upon school life in terms of changes effected in group alignments and the individual attitudes that go with them. It is perhaps as a means of unifying the entire school group that athletics seems most useful from the sociological point of view. There is a tendency for the school population to split up into its hostile segments of teachers and students and to be fragmented by cliques among both groups. The division of students into groups prevents a collective morale from arising and thereby complicates administration; the split between students and teachers is even more serious, for these two groups tend to become definite conflict groups, and conflict group tensions are the very antithesis of discipline. This condition athletics alleviates. Athletic games furnish a dramatic spectacle of the struggle of picked men against the common enemy, and this is a powerful factor in building up a group spirit which includes students of all kinds and degrees and unifies the teachers and the taught. In adult life we find the analogue of athletics in war; patriotism runs high when the country is attacked. Likewise we find the most certain value of punishment to be the unification of the group which punishes.[1] Athletic sports use exactly the same mechanism in a controlled way for the attainment of a more limited end.

By furnishing all the members of the school population with an enemy outside the group, and by giving them an opportunity to observe and participate in the struggle against that enemy, athletics may prevent a conflict group tension from arising between students and teachers. The organization of the student body for the support of athletics, though it is certainly not without its ultimate disadvantages, may bring with it certain benefits for those who are interested in the immediate problems of administration. It is a powerful machine which is organized to whip all students into line for the support of athletic teams, and adroit school administrators learn to use it for the dissemination of other attitudes favorable to the faculty and the faculty policy.

In yet another way an enlightened use of athletics may simplify the problem of police work in the school. The group of athletes may be made to furnish a very useful extension of the faculty-controlled social order. Athletes have obtained favorable status by following out one faculty-determined culture pattern; they may be induced to adopt for themselves and to popularize other patterns of a similar nature. Athletes, too, in nearly any group of youngsters, are the natural leaders, and they are leaders who can be controlled and manipulated through the medium of athletics. Those who are fortunate enough to be on the squad of a major sport occupy a favored social position; they are at or near the center of their little universe; they belong to the small but important group of men who are doing things. They have much to lose by misconduct, and it is usually not difficult to make them see it. They have, too, by virtue of their favored position, the inevitable conservatism of the privileged classes, and they can be brought to take a stand for the established order. In addition, the athletes stand in a very close and personal relationship to at least one faculty member, the coach, who has, if he is an intelligent man or a disciplinarian, an opportunity to exert a great influence upon the members of the team. The coach has prestige, he has favors to give, and he is in intimate rapport with his players. Ordinarily he uses his opportunities well. As the system usually works

[1] Mead, G. H., "The Psychology of Punitive Justice," *American Journal of Sociology*, Vol. 23, pp. 577-602, March, 1918.

out, the members of the major teams form a nucleus of natural leaders among the student body, and their influence is more or less conservative and more or less on the side of what the faculty would call decent school citizenship. The necessarily close correspondence between athletic prowess and so-called clean living is another factor which affects the influence of athletes upon non-athletes. We have here stated a theory of the ideal use of athletics in school control, but it is the part of common sense to concede at once that it does not always work out so. An anti-social coach, or a coach who allows his players to believe themselves to be indispensable, so that they wrest control of athletics from his hands, can vitiate the whole system. When the system does go wrong, athletes and athletics become an insufferable nuisance to teachers. A teacher who had had numerous unpleasant experiences with athletes summed up the situation in her school by saying, "I learned that whenever I ran into some particularly difficult problem of discipline I could look for a boy wearing the school letter."

There are other activities. Their effects upon the school group, and upon the personalities of the individuals who participate in them, differ widely. There is the school paper, which, for all its repetitiousness and banality, its absurd aggrandizement of the heroes of the hour, its use of clichés and sloppy reporting, serves a useful purpose in maintaining group morale and training its reporters to observe and to use language in an effective if not an elegant manner. There is debating, and debating needs careful management if it is to be useful at all. A choice must be made between the shallow and superficial smartness of the clever high-school boy and a serious intellectualism forced to bloom too soon, a choice which avoids both of these extremes if possible. And it takes great discrimination to keep debating separate from mere contentiousness. There is also a danger that high-school debating will give its participants final opinions upon subjects about which they are not yet qualified to pass judgment.

There are the various social clubs, apparently the early form of the sifting and sorting agencies of adult society. They give a great deal of ego gratification to those fortunate enough to be elected to them, probably detract from the efficiency of the school as an agency for the passing on of learning, and give those excluded from them an excellent basis for an inferiority complex. The least important of the social clubs, as the Lynds have remarked, are those fostered by particular departments. There are the various musical activities, the school orchestra, the glee club, the band, and possibly the minstrel show. Many of these furnish an excellent opportunity for the expression of the bursting heart of adolescence; the difficulty from the point of view of school administration is to find a person able to promote such activities who is also able to preserve the respect of students and to carry his teaching load successfully. There are dramatic societies; these have some value, and could have a great deal more if the technique for their promotion were better developed and contention concerning the desirable rôles did not so often arise. There is that old-time favorite among activities, half dramatic, half musical, the minstrel show, to which many administrators still pin their faith. The minstrel show gives a very great deal of ego gratification to participants, probably much more than conventional drama, and this makes those participating a bit easier to live with while the production is in progress. It gives no great amount of musical training. Conservative teachers are probably justified in their negative reaction to minstrel shows in that they bring to the fore a relatively undesirable personality type and one that cannot stand popularity. It needs to be pointed out in passing, though with all the emphasis possible, that minstrel shows or other dramatic productions in which boys play the rôles of girls or girls take the part of men are very undesirable in high schools and grades because of their possible influence in fostering homosexual attitudes.

The most important consideration affecting our judgment of any particular activity is its effect upon the personality of the participant, and this effect is usually beneficial in proportion as the activity gives to the individual opportunities for wholesome self-expression and growth through interested self-activity. A further value of activities is that they may often give a sense of solidarity to a wide group, which is an essential part of the training of the young; it is a part which is doubtless overdone at present, but it would be very regrettable if it were to be omitted altogether. From the faculty point of view, activities have a very great value in facilitating faculty control of school life. The growth of school activities in recent years, and not the development of new theories of education, would seem to have been chiefly instrumental in making school interesting for the student, and undoubtedly helps to account for the recent success of the public schools in holding their students through the years of high school. There is added the fact that most of the activities carried on in the schools would probably exist in one form or another whether the faculty fostered them or not. If the faculty is able to foster and control them, there is at least a greater likelihood that they will subserve ends acceptable to the faculty than there would be if activities were quite spontaneous. Activities are indeed so thoroughly a part of the school system at the present time that school administrators have grown superstitious about them. They have learned to expect trouble when there is a lag in the activities. In the private boarding schools, a relative lull in activities occurs somewhere in midwinter, usually just after the onset of wintry weather has put a stop to widespread participation in athletics. The experience of these schools seems to show that serious cases of discipline and general discontent with school life are more likely to be encountered in this period than in any other.

Unquestionably, activities contribute much to make the schools livable and are more effective than any other feature of the school in the molding of personality. But we should not allow these facts to blind us to the truth that they often tend to interfere with other important features of school life. Every activity has its faculty sponsor, who in addition to his teaching is charged with the promotion of that particular activity. His prestige among the faculty and students, and often his salary as well, are largely determined by the success of that activity; it is no wonder, then, that activities accumulate and make increasing demands upon the school time and the attention of students. It would, of course, be perfectly possible to educate through activities alone, and the present writer would be the last to argue against such a system if one could be devised, but we must not forget that education through activities as at present organized is at best scattering and sporadic, and needs systematic supplementation through the basic training in facts and skills which it is the formal purpose of the schools to give. And it would not be possible to take even so tolerant an attitude toward activities whose chief motivation is a business one, as seems to be the case with college football.

Projects and references will be at the end of the following chapter.

Chapter X

THE CULTURE OF THE SCHOOL: CEREMONIES

In the culture complexes which make up the separate culture of the schools, ceremonies and activities are usually associated. School ceremonies are now largely subsidiary to activities, but this was not always so, for ceremonies have apparently a longer history. Ceremonies accumulate rapidly in the school, being easily devised and readily absorbed into the main current of tradition. Ceremonies may relate to any phase of the school life, traditional or otherwise, but the most colorful and significant ceremonies in the school of today are those ceremonies associated with activities; the commonest and most interesting of these are associated with athletic activities. It should be remarked that school ceremonies mostly have value, or are thought to have value, in the mobilization of individual attitudes with reference to group objectives.

Analysis of these ceremonies reveals some of the psychological mechanisms upon which they depend for their effectiveness. There are, first, numerous identification mechanisms which act upon the individual by casting him in a particular rôle for which he receives group approval or by causing the individual to wish to play such a rôle because of the public praise supposed to be connected with it. Closely allied to these, and in many cases indistinguishable from them, are certain formal expressions of attitudes in which all are required to participate; the underlying philosophy of such ceremonies is apparently that there is a tendency for such attitudes to be carried over and made permanent.

In all school ceremonies appear numerous collective representations, insistently repeated and brought to the attention of the individual in many different guises. According to Park and Burgess, "Collective representations are the concepts which embody the objectives of group activity. The totem of primitive man, the flag of a nation, a religious creed, the number system, and Darwin's theory of the descent of man—all these are collective representations. Every society and every social group has, or tends to have, its own symbols and its own language. The language and other symbolic devices by which a society carries on its collective existence are collective representations. Animals do not possess them."[1] Collective representations which appear in school ceremonies are: "the honor of the school," "our place on the honor roll," "the Central High School Spirit," "the Bearcat spirit," "the school that builds personality," "what I owe to Central High School," "our fighting team," "Fighting Illini," "ready to fight, bleed and die for dear old Siwash," "the fair name of our university," "our untarnished escutcheon," etc. Most of these phrases will not stand analysis, for they have in fact no meaning at all beyond their ability to command emotions; it is perhaps more correct to say that they have an emotional meaning but no intellectual content. Some of these phrases are objectified in symbols such as school colors, banners, trophies, etc. Victory in certain competitions often has an objective symbol such as the famous little brown jug that changes hands with football superiority. Much is likewise made of mascots, who lend a picturesque character to ceremonies, and help to batter down the walls about the emotions of the spectators. Many of these collective representations, accepted and tinged with a high emotional coloration during the years of youth, are carried over into after years; indeed the suspicion is not wholly absent that some schools cultivate them with an eye toward future endowments.

Underlying the logic of collective representations is the unquestioned belief that there is merit in activities, a notion which it would be very difficult to justify on rational grounds. There is added the belief that those who enter the competition for places on the team do so for motives altogether altruistic, and at an immense (but always unnamed) personal sacrifice. Usually, too, it comes out that the coach of a certain activity "has given freely of his time and energy," and that without thought of material reward. Such is the logic of emotions which makes the wheels of activities turn around.

Let no one smile at these adolescent phenomena. This is a real world, and there is in these ceremonies and activities a serious meaning that fades out with routine description and analysis; the emotion that clusters here is strong enough to stand attack from without and hardy enough to weather ridicule; what it cannot stand is objectivity. There is herein contained a hint that the proper conductance of such proceedings as those we are here concerned with implies that all must be taken very seriously indeed. The adults involved must really participate; if the adults who are charged with the duty of engineering

[1] Park, R. E., and Burgess, E. W., *Introduction to the Science of Sociology*, pp. 167-168. (By permission of The University of Chicago Press.)

such performances cannot participate because of the constant interference of their critical intelligence, then the work is better done by adults who have less intelligence or are able to keep such intelligence as they have under better control.

We turn now to a description and analysis of certain typical ceremonies. A short account of the ceremony with which the school day was invariably begun a few years ago, the so-called ''opening exercises,'' now old-fashioned and but little used, follows below:

When I was in C—— High School, we always began the day with "opening exercises." This was then the invariable custom, and the daily grind began in every school room with a few minutes, from a quarter to a half hour, devoted to singing and pleasant speech-making.

Directly the last bell had sounded, the principal called us to order by clapping his hands together. There was a last minute scurrying to seats, a hasty completion of whispered conversations. The principal stood on the platform in the front of the room and watched us. His assistant, Miss W., whom we all knew to be the kindliest of souls, but whom we nevertheless feared as if she were the devil himself, stood up behind her desk and regarded us coldly.

When the room was quiet, the principal turned to the music teacher, Miss M., and said, "All right. Go ahead, Miss M."

Miss M. advanced enthusiastically and announced, "We will begin with Number 36 in the paper books. That's an old favorite. Now, please, let's all sing."

The accompanist began to drum out the tune, none too expertly, to be sure. Miss M. began to sing. A few joined her. Then a few more. When we came to the chorus, Miss M. said, "Now everybody join in the chorus!" We did. We sang two or three songs. Miss M. usually started with things we all knew and tried to work up to more difficult selections. We did not like that; we thought it much more fun to sing the simple songs which were already our favorites. As we sang, the principal and one or two of the other teachers joined in timidly, always along toward the middle of the song after the volume of sound had risen to a point that made it certain their errors would be inaudible. Miss W. made no pretence of singing, but merely allowed herself to assume a more benevolent look.

After the singing, the principal or one of the other teachers would make a few remarks supposed to be inspirational in nature. Perhaps he read a passage from Elbert Hubbard or Henry van Dyke. (Bible reading was forbidden by law in that state; otherwise, as he made it perfectly clear, he would have read from the Bible at least occasionally.) Perhaps he would make a little speech about the team or some other school activity. Perhaps he exhorted us about some matter of school discipline, beginning his speech, "Now there's one little matter I'd like to speak to you about." Along toward the end of the year, when our interest in school began to sag, he would urge us to keep up our morale, saying, "It's a poor race horse that can't hold out till the end." Perhaps he asked the coach or one of the members of the team to make a little speech. Then he said, "Miss W., are there any announcements?" in a tone that gave us to understand that if there were any announcements they would be very important announcements indeed.

There usually were announcements. The sewing class should bring materials with them to class. The glee club would meet that afternoon at four. Tryouts for debating would take place next week.

Sometimes we ended by singing the school song. Sometimes it was merely, "That concludes the opening exercises for today. At the sound of the bell you will pass to your first period classes." (Life history document.)

It would be a pity that the old-fashioned "opening exercises" have so nearly passed away if their place had not been taken by other and better-adapted ceremonies. Formal as opening exercises were, with their Bible-reading and their speech-making, they may have served a purpose in focussing the attention of the group upon school matters before the even more artificial procedure of classwork was begun. Beyond that, barring a possible favorable effect in occasional cases of the sermonizing that accompanied them, opening exercises served little purpose. The same may be said of chapel exercises. Their place has been taken in the modern high school by "assemblies" called for a particular purpose; the better organization of "assemblies," and their more clearly stated objectives, enable them to attain a degree of meaning and efficiency unattainable in the more formal and more generalized opening exercises. The specialization is tending to be carried even further, particular weeks being set apart for a series of assemblies devoted to particular objects.

An interesting ceremony that has long been in use in a certain private school has as its purpose to make the boys acquainted with each other and at the same time to get them committed in the eyes of others to certain activities. The ceremony is briefly described below:

On the first night of school all the boys assemble in the chapel for New Students' Night. They are all very tired, as they have spent the day in registering for their courses, getting straightened up in their rooms, and in general getting set for a year of living. But they are all interested, for the beginning of a new school year is always a momentous occasion, and doubly so for those who are for the first time in a boarding school.

The proceedings are initiated by the superintendent or the commandant or some older member of the faculty. The appointed person makes a little speech welcoming the newcomers, and wishing them well. He then explains that in accordance with an old custom he will now ask every boy to rise in his turn and to give his name, tell where he comes from, and state what school activities he intends to go out for this year. And each boy in his turn rises and says, "My name is Tom Brown and my home is in Marsden and this year I intend to go out for heavyweight football and basketball and track and be a reporter for the school paper."

The statement of intentions is usually a bit more comprehensive than the boy's ability or energy would justify, but it is nearly always respectfully received by both students and teachers. As the scheme works out in practice, it is an excellent device for obtaining a high degree of participation in activities at the very start of the school year.

The ordinary pep meeting, probably the commonest of all ceremonies in high schools, is also one of the best adapted to its ends. A crisis situation looms; the group must be organized for that crisis. The team is to act as the defender of the group in the coming crisis. It is necessary that they be sure that the school is with them to a man, or the members of the team will not be able to put forth their best efforts. The technique of conducting pep meetings is pretty well standardized, though subject to some variation. It is necessary that the team be present; if possible that they should sit together on the stage or in some other prominent position. It is part of the pep meeting to give the members of the team boundless ego-gratification, which may, following out a mechanism previously described, make them good citizens. Playing up the members of the team as the set of heroes standing between the school and disgrace also stimulates interest in athletics by making every other boy who is present wish that he were in the place of some member of the team. There is a speech by the coach or a member of the faculty interested in athletics; it may be a red-blooded, fighting, he-man sort of speech, or it may be the sort of speech that recites the cold facts for the consideration of the group. The facts are just about the same in either case. It is made clear that the team approaches a severe trial, perhaps a desperate trial, a situation that calls for reckless deeds of derring-do. But fighting spirit and team play, the willingness to sacrifice individual glory for the benefit of the team, will win. And the team is ready to fight and not a man on it is a grand-stander. The team is ready. Smith, there, will fight like a lion. The great-hearted Jones will give his last drop of blood. He mentions others. To a man they will die in their tracks rather than surrender; they will fight to the last tooth. . . . All the collective representations come in. But the team must have support. Success in athletics depends upon student support. The speech ends. There are cheers, the school yell, a yell for the team, a locomotive, a cheer for the speaker, a cheer to keep in practice. The cheer leader urges the students to make more noise; he points out the increased effect of synchronized cheering. The master of ceremonies calls upon the captain of the team for a speech. He states that the team is going to do its best, that he hopes that it will win, that the team badly needs the support of the student body. The other members of the team make briefer speeches or perhaps merely rise in their places. Perhaps there are more speeches. Certainly there are more yells. Very likely the school song is sung. The meeting ends with everybody's emotions aroused, and all the students live in a state of collective insanity until after the big game and are very easy to manage and very inattentive. Students enjoy the pep meeting. What permanent effect it has upon the valor of men and virtue of women we can only guess. But it gives the student body an enemy to hate that is not on the faculty.

Organized cheering is a minor culture complex subsidiary to the ceremonies connected with athletic sports. In the days when war was personal or group combat and not an industry, the battle cry was very important in maintaining the morale of the group and in terrifying the opposition. The ancient battle cry was commonly a collective representation, a brief statement of a slogan or perhaps merely the name of the person the combatants were fighting for or that of the deity whose aid they invoked. Organized cheering in the schools is formed on the analogy to the ancient battle cry and carries out further the analogy between the game and war. But the object of the cheer as a statement of a collective representation has more or less faded out, since it is rarely clear what the contestants really are fighting for. And since the players usually profess to be entirely unconscious of the cheering, it may perhaps be concluded that the main effect of organized cheering is the effect produced upon the spectators. Instances are on record where a contagious group enthusiasm seems to have affected the result of a game, but it may well be doubted whether such enthusiasm usually works the miracles which are credited to it. Cheering, then, is for the spectators; it is a part of the gigantic mobilization of will, and a feature of the large-scale expression of emotion which the game furnishes. The crowd at an athletic spectacle excites itself to a frenzy over the incidents of the game; the occasion is a thrilling one because it furnishes a holiday for all the inhibitions. The ego is expanded a thousand times. Hidden wishes are expressed. The process is facilitated by the mechanism of organized cheering. The intellectual content of the cheers which make people so wildly enthusiastic is very thin indeed. Beyond the mere statement of the name of the school or of the names of members of the team, beyond this and an occasional repetitious slogan such as "We want a touchdown! We want a touchdown!" or "Fight! Fight! Fight!" or "Hold that line!" there is nothing in the cheer which suggests the faintest residuum of rationality. The tendency, indeed, is for the cheer to go over into the ludicrous, to take refuge in nonsense syllables and patent absurdities, and it must be that the element of the utterly mad in these cheers which are repeated by the multitude has something to do with the psychic thrill which they make it possible for the spectators to experience in the game.

But let us abandon evaluation and the wonderment that goes with it and return to simple description. A great amount of time is spent in the preparation of college and high-school yells; the aim is always to have something which will produce an effect on the crowd, a euphonious or cacophonous array of syllables having a certain rhythm lending itself easily to group expression. Most favored, perhaps, are plays upon and recombinations of the school name. There are often yell-writing competitions to supply new yells when those in vogue are adjudged to have become trite and ineffective. The yells are then carefully selected and tried out on the group. Those which take on are officially adopted. In most schools the position of cheer leader is a coveted one, and is obtained only after considerable effort and some wire-pulling. The cheer leader is often carefully trained in the antics which he is supposed to perform in order to wring a greater volume of noise from the crowd; these antics have been selected out through the group experience as means of loosening the inhibitions of the crowd. Associated with organized cheering in recent years has been a great deal of pageantry and the display of gorgeous colors; all this has its meaning in terms of the logic of the emotions.

Oddly enough, people build up an affection for the cheers of their school. Usually it is only one or two of the favorites that are remembered, but it seems a little strange that even so much of crowd emotion could be carried over. In no case, however, does a cheer retain its hold upon the emotions of the alumni as does the school song. The school song usually extols the virtues of the school, states what a wonderful time those singing it have had there, expresses a feeling of gratitude for benefits conferred, and ends on a note of loyalty. The melody must be a simple one, and must be adapted to singing by large or small numbers of persons. In addition to the orthodox school song, there are usually a number of unauthorized versions. Some of these uncanonized songs are wanderers, being found, with alterations to fit the local situation similar to those made in certain jokes, from coast to coast and from grade school to college. Occasionally a fever of parodying popular or standard songs will arise in a high school, and the school will be blessed with a large number of school songs capable of being sung to ragtime. This parodying is occasionally cultivated as a means of inducing participation in school life by certain persons who could not otherwise take part in activities. The life of these parodies, however, is usually short.

The ceremonies connected with the athletic life of the school are very numerous, and it is not possible to analyze all of them here. In the smaller schools, much is made of the presentation of emblems. There is a post-mortem on the season, usually favorable, a recollection of dramatic incidents in crucial games, and a statement of prospects for next year. Then each player is called to the front, congratulated, perhaps made the subject of a short eulogy, and given his emblem. Such public praise of the successful helps to sustain interest in athletics; what it does to the unsuccessful we cannot say. Frequently, too, there are banquets and other special affairs at which the members of various teams are entertained. Much ceremony accumulates around these in some schools.

The problem of getting recruits for the team is central in the management of athletic affairs. The most successful devices apparently depend for their effectiveness upon getting the individual to commit himself publicly to a statement of his intentions. We have already mentioned one such ceremony used in a private school with the avowed purpose of getting every student to participate in some activity. In larger schools the problem is different, and a different kind of social pressure is used to get a large number of candidates for the football squad. Usually an appeal is made for strong, determined men to volunteer for football; they are to signify their willingness to serve by coming and standing upon the platform. The speaker congratulates those who come forward, and shames the able-bodied who do not. By implication, or directly, those who refuse to play football are called yellow. All the arts of the evangelist urging converts to hit the sawdust trail are employed, with the difference that here persons are solicited to come forward for the sake of the school rather than the salvation of their souls. Sometimes the social pressure of the girls is discreetly used; in no case is it absent in a mixed assembly. The effectiveness of devices of this kind is almost entirely dependent upon the ability of the orator to command the crowd. In any case, it must be followed up by personal pressure tactfully brought to bear upon those who have once gained public praise by promising to participate in athletics.

Some ceremonies of a different nature remain to be described. Wherever a number of persons must be organized for collective movement or collective action, a number of more or less military ceremonies naturally arise. Some of these concern the movement of peoples' bodies. These are such ceremonies as fire drills, filing out of the room, passing to classes, etc. Bagley has pointed out that the efficient management of the school demands that these be as thoroughly routinized as possible. Military or quasi-military ceremonies whose function is the regulation of social relationships are also found in the school. These are developed through the formalization of routine contacts and are basic in the school where much is made of dominance and subordination. Of these ceremonies we may distinguish two types: the one, that in which the ceremony is the relationship; the second, that in which the ceremony is designed to be an externalization of a desirable internal state and to produce an effect upon that internal state. Where contacts between persons are quite limited, as between students and some administrative officers, it is often possible to formalize them completely; each person goes through a certain social ritual upon the occasion of every encounter with the other; in that case it is possible to say that the ceremony is the relationship. In the second case, never entirely separable from the first, the relationship is not so completely routinized, but certain aspects of it are committed to an iron-bound and invariable ceremony. The purpose of this ceremony is to insure a due amount of respect on the part of the subordinate for his superior; the thought behind it apparently is that the show of respect will make the respect.

A number of ceremonies are found whose purpose is simply the maintenance of the general morale, a rather ill-defined purpose although the ceremonies themselves seem beneficial enough. Among these we may mention the reading of letters, martyrdom ceremonies, grade and distinction ceremonies, ceremonies leading up to particular events, and school spirit ceremonies. High-school principals and the superintendents of prep schools generally make much of the reading of letters from the alumni, especially recent alumni. In these letters there is generally some reference to the benefits derived from the school and some wholesome advice to the boys still in school. There is often a space in the school paper or in the school bulletins for printing such letters in order to give them wider publicity.

These letters are buttressed by frequent reference to the achievements of these alumni, and the inference is usually clear that the school takes a large part of the credit for the success of the alumni.

When a school athlete has been severely injured in a game, the incident can be a serious liability to athletics in the school, but it may, through the use of proper martyrdom ceremonies, be made a very important focal point for the school morale. Thus one high-school principal, when a prominent athlete familiarly known as "Nigger Jones" had been in the hospital for several months with a football injury, made on the average about one speech a week concerning him. He told of the boy's courage under difficulties, of his desire to return to Central High School, of his fine spirit, his great athletic ability, his desire to be able to play football again next year, etc. The effect of such speeches upon school morale was very noticeable. The school had a martyr.

Special ceremonies have likewise been worked out to give public recognition to those who have distinguished themselves scholastically, the criterion of scholastic distinction, unfortunately, being nearly always the average grade. Such ceremonies are usually localized on commencement day, but they are sometimes carried throughout the year as well. One private school makes a practice of reading weekly the list of boys making the ten highest grades for the week previous, and competition for a place on "The Upper Ten" is sometimes keen. Unfortunately, such a list is likely to contain the names of the seven boys who have chosen the easiest courses, but the system does set up a competition for high grades. Specialized ceremonies have likewise been developed for honoring those who have distinguished themselves in other ways, as by debating, serving on the school paper, making an unusual conduct record, showing exceptional courtesy, etc. None of these ceremonies have the intrinsic appeal or the effectiveness of ceremonies centering around athletics, because none of these activities has an interest comparable to the interest in athletics.

When some special school event is planned, there may arise a number of ceremonial observances whose function is to whip the group into line for it. These follow the plan of the preexisting culture pattern for ceremonies. Thus, when it had been determined that a certain school should follow the team on one of its trips away from home, there ensued a rapid growth of ceremonies of preparation. These ceremonies were at first directed at working up enthusiasm about the trip. Then the emphasis was changed, and the school administrators tried to work up an equal enthusiasm among the students over the idea of earning the privilege of attending the game through good conduct. Then there were unanimity ceremonies; the administrators wanted to make it one hundred per cent; everybody had to want to go; everybody had to earn the privilege of going by good conduct for the two weeks previous to the game. At the last moment, there was a purification ceremony as a result of which those who had amassed demerits which would otherwise have prevented them from attending the game were interviewed, and the extent of their delinquency was assessed, after which those who had been able to give no good excuse for their derelictions were given a somewhat foreshortened punishment which made it possible for them to attend the game. This last ceremony was apparently necessary if a perfect attendance at the game was to be obtained without insulting the gods of discipline.

School spirit ceremonies are numerous, and are among the most picturesque and affecting of all the ceremonies centering around the school. Many of these recur according to the calendar rather than the occasion. In one college for young women a great deal is made of a doll ceremony. A doll represents the L—— spirit. The sophomores hide the doll. Until the freshmen find it, they have not the L—— spirit. Great interest attends the game, and apparently it is not without its permanent effect. More dignity is attached to those ceremonies in which, after certain preliminary rites, a torch is passed from the hands of the outgoing senior class to the new senior class; this ceremony is very affecting to the participants and spectators alike. Variants of these ceremonies are numerous. A special set of ceremonies, supposed likewise to be related to the induction of new members into the spirit of the school, tends to grow up to symbolize the relation of classes to each other. Many of these ceremonies were introduced by school authorities as substitutes for hazing.

The commencement season is the focal point of many ceremonies. The traditional ceremonies pertaining to graduation, commencement exercises, class day, the baccalaureate sermon, are so well known, and their supposed function so well understood, as to require no additional comment here. These are among the oldest and best established of all the ceremonies to be found in the school; there is a tendency for such ceremonies to go over into formalism. One ceremony of graduation week preserves its power to control the emotions, and that is the ceremony in which the senior class takes leave of the school. Particularly affecting is the practice in a certain private school. Here all the seniors join hands around the flag pole and sing Auld Lang Syne. They pass round the circle shaking hands with all their friends. There are few who go away from the ceremony with dry eyes.

PROJECTS

1. Work out in detail culture conflicts which become classroom conflicts between student and teacher.

2. Describe culture conflicts which are the basis of conflicts between teachers and members of the community.

3. Make a list of the cultural survivals to be found in a group of children.

4. Write the folklore of a group of children.

5. Attempt to codify the so-called "traditions" of your own school. Determine by inquiry how long it takes for a "tradition" to become established.

6. Write the history of the culture complex of the school.

7. Account for the survival of the country school in an urban civilization in cultural terms.

8. Formulate the principal points in "the code of equality." What place does this code occupy in the culture of the school?

9. Review cases in which a student has adhered to "the school-boy code" to his own disadvantage. Cases where he has violated the code.

10. Determine by questioning and observation what "activities" mean to a college fraternity.

11. Write the history of hazing in one particular school. What are the social and psychological roots of hazing? What attitude should teachers take toward it?

12. Tell the story of a campaign waged by a faculty against some school tradition.

13. Study minutely the behavior of some "activity" group and interpret it in terms of its meaning for the participants and its relation to other occurrences in and about the school.

14. Determine by study of the behavior of the athletes in a particular institution whether athletics is a useful control mechanism in that school. How does it work?

15. Describe the process of competition for places in some school activity. Does that competition, in your opinion, have a healthy effect?

16. Record the public utterances of coach, team members, and "friends of the team" throughout an entire season. Interpret your results.

17. Study the public utterances of leading coaches concerning proposed changes in football rules. Interpret.

18. Make a study of "form" in track events. How does one acquire "form"? What is the history of "form"?

19. Narrate incidents in which a game has turned into a fight. Interpret.

20. Verbalize the code of sportsmanship. Narrate incidents illustrating it.

21. Make a case study of a boy whose personality was improved by participation in athletics.

22. Study the personality of an athletic coach in relation to the morale of a particular school.

23. Analyze several issues of a school paper. What social functions does the paper subserve?

24. Write the history of a school play, class play, or minstrel show. Analyze.

25. Make a chart showing the temporal incidence of cases of discipline during one year. How do you explain the variations?

26. Record and assemble all the collective representations which seem to have importance in your own school.

27. Make a catalogue of ceremonies for one year, indicating the place of each ceremony in the rhythm of the year.

28. Take careful notes on a pep meeting. Determine by observation and inquiry the meaning of this ceremony to spectators and participants.

29. Make a case study of a teacher who is particularly successful in conducting pep meetings. What marks him off from other teachers? Analyze his technique.

30. Discover the rationale of such a series of assemblies as go to make up "Better English Week," or "Four C's Week."

31. Assemble data to show whether or not success in athletics actually depends upon student support.

32. Describe the process by which cheering is organized in your own school.

33. Describe and analyze the behavior of a crowd at a football game. Explain.

34. Record the yells of your own school and analyze their effect.

35. Analyze your school song, or songs.

36. Has your school a mascot? Describe his position in the school community.

37. Assemble material for a comparison of the position of athletics in large and small high schools. In what size high school does the system of control by athletics work best?

38. Describe the ritual of ceremonies and phrases that has grown up about some school martyr.

39. What ceremonies surround the enforcement of discipline in your school?

40. Make a careful record of commencement week at your own school. Analyze the various ceremonies with regard to their real or intended social functions.

SUGGESTED READINGS

Anthropology

(1) KROEBER, A. L., *Anthropology.*
(2) KROEBER, A. L., and WATERMAN, T. T., *Source Book in Anthropology.*
(3) LEVY-BRUHL, LUCIEN, *Primitive Mentality.*
(4) LOWIE, R. H., *Primitive Society.*
(5) MEAD, MARGARET, *Coming of Age in Samoa.*
(6) MEAD, MARGARET, *Growing Up in New Guinea.*
(7) WISSLER, CLARK, *Man and Culture.*

Sociology, Psychology, and Education

(1) FERRIÈRE, ADOLPH, *The Activity School.*
(2) JORDAN, R. H., *Extra-Curricular Activities.*
(3) KOFFKA, KURT, *The Growth of the Mind.*
(4) KOHLER, WOLFGANG, *Gestalt Psychology.*
(5) LYND, R. S., and H. M., *Middletown,* Chapter XVI.
(6) MEAD, G. H., "The Psychology of Punitive Justice," *American Journal of Sociology,* Vol. XXIII, pp. 577-602, March, 1918.
(7) OGDEN, R. M., *Psychology and Education.*
(8) PETERS, C. C., *Foundations of Educational Sociology.*
(9) RAINWATER, C. E., *The Play Movement in the United States.*

CHAPTER XI

THE FOUR WISHES IN THE SCHOOL

IT IS a sociological truism that the social organization is an arrangement for the satisfaction of human wishes. The vitality of institutions, and the very life of the formal structure of society, depend upon the closeness of their connection with the needs of mankind. It is, then, very much in point, when we essay a description and evaluation of the social life clustering about a major institution, to study the involvement of impulse in that segment of society. According to the conception of social psychology nursed by one school of social interpretation, it is the major task of social psychology to trace the workings of original nature in society. Original nature for these thinkers means instinctive nature, but the task of following out original nature in society is no less important for those other social philosophers who are unable to believe that social interpretation is advanced by the positing of definite instincts in the hereditary constitution of mankind.

The most sceptical observer is able to see certain of the facts of human life in the school as reflexive or instinctive behavior in the strictest sense of the term. Children and teachers cough and sneeze, their mouths water, their eyes accommodate to the variations of light; the youngest children rub their eyes when they are sleepy and on occasion close them as perfectly as do the oldest. Rainy days make restless school rooms, and perhaps this restlessness has a reflex basis. The sex interplay of children and their elders in the classroom has no doubt a complex instinctive basis, but if it is traceable to an instinct (or instincts) it is to an instinct whose pattern cannot be so easily described as can the instinctive patterns of the mason bee. It is possible that much of the social interchange of human beings in the school has its basis in reflex or instinct; we should not at once exclude from consideration the notion that there may be innate patterns in social interaction, that our awareness of the mental states of another, and our penetration into his inner life through sympathy and insight, may have a foundation in inherited mechanism.

It is well established, however, that we are not at the present time able to identify any specific instincts with certainty, or to make sure that any given acts are expressions of particular instinctive patterns. This is not to say that we shall never find complex, patterned activities corresponding to instincts in the original nature of man. At the present time we have not found them, for not even the instinct psychologists can agree as to what instincts are or how many of them there are. Scientific precision will be better served, therefore, if we adopt a concept of a different order as the basis of our analysis. Such a concept was furnished by Thomas in his doctrine of the four wishes.[1] Thomas once proposed that there are four wishes which represent the totality of human conation. These wishes are: the wish for response, the wish for recognition, the wish for new experience, and the wish for security. All human activity may be thought of as coming within the bounds of these categories. The wishes are all found in every human being, and some arrangement for the satisfaction of each one is necessary for normal living. The extent to which a satisfaction relevant to one wish can be substituted for a satisfaction relevant to another is limited. The wishes are not substitutes for the instincts, although they are used in that way by many writers; they are frankly environmental categories relating to the things men want. Unlike the instincts, the wishes are not intended to have finalistic value in social interpretation. We cannot explain acts by tracing them to a particular wish. Evidence that the wishes are in original nature in specific form is wanting. The point of the doctrine of the wishes is that the normal human being develops these wishes in social interaction very early in life.

The wish for response, according to Thomas, is "the most social of all the wishes." It is "primarily related to love." It "shows itself in the tendency to seek and to give signs of appreciation in connection with other individuals." The wish for response includes most of the impulses which the Freudians classify as sexual, but, like the Freudian notion to which it roughly corresponds, it includes many phenomena for which there seems no organic sex basis. The wish for response is the desire to be close to others; it is a craving for intimacy, a hunger for acceptance. It includes all behavior that has as its aim the rapprochement of personalities, and responsive behavior ranges from the most grossly sexual to the most highly refined and subtilized

[1] This notion has received little attention in his recent work. The point of view which the present writer has consistently maintained is that the wishes are in fact classifications of attitudes. The four wishes, however, present a very convenient schema, and it seems best to orient our discussion from that point of view.

forms of personal interplay. The wish for response is most clearly expressed in the relationship of parent to child, in courtship, mating, and marriage, and in small in-groups of a congenial nature.

The desire for recognition is more definitely egoistic in nature, but it is social in that it can be satisfied only in society. It ranks with the wish for response as one of the most important handles by which the group takes hold of the individual. The wish for recognition is the wish to stand high in the group; its movement is vertical whereas the movement of response is horizontal. It is "expressed in the general struggle of men for position in their social group, in devices for securing a recognized, enviable, and advantageous social status." The wish for recognition is the prideful motive; as such it is almost equivalent to the status drive which Adler makes the basis of his system of social explanation.

Nearly all thinkers are willing to admit the existence of the motives of recognition and response, or of some other motives corresponding closely to them. These are tangible motivations, and they seem to be universal. Everyone has some pride, and he arranges his life to protect and enhance it; everyone has likewise some need of close personal attachments. It may well be questioned whether the motives of security and new experience are of the same nature. Faris has pointed out that the wishes for security and new experience are in fact derived wishes of a different order from the pervasive and fundamental wishes for response and recognition. The wish for security is a mechanism that is called into play wherever a fear appears. The desire for new experience is a mechanism of a kindred nature that is called out by fatigue resulting from monotony or routine. It is closely associated with ennui. But these are not primary wishes; they are mechanisms for protecting or altering the life structures which we work out for the satisfaction of other wishes.

Faris has called attention to another wish of a social nature, which is the so-called desire for participation. It appears as the yearning to be attached to some super-personal entity, a group, a cause, a movement, something larger than one's self. It is an intangible motive, and one that has therefore been long overlooked, but it corresponds to real things in human nature. Faris has also pointed out that Thomas's classification is incomplete in that it does not allow for the wishes arising from and perhaps localized in definite parts of the organism, the segmental wishes consequent upon hunger, the physiological tensions of sex, excretory tensions, fatigue, thirst, etc.

These modifications furnished by Faris seem important contributions to the theory of the wishes.

We include Krueger and Reckless's paraphrase of Faris's schema of the wishes:

(Faris) found that we may recognize (1) the segmental wishes, such as appetites and craving (i.e., hunger and thirst); (2) the social wishes which include (*a*) the desire for response, (*b*) the desire for recognition, (*c*) the desire for participation (i.e., the wish to be attached to or identified with a cause, a movement, something larger than oneself); (3) the derived wishes for new experience (developing from the effects of monotony and routine) and for security (arising from the undermining effects of crises).[1]

It is our present task to trace out the processes of wish satisfaction in the schools. We shall survey the social life of the schools in the attempt to discover what opportunities it offers for the satisfaction of the various sorts of human wishes, and we shall see how personalities fare when they become involved in the institution. This is no mere academic inquiry that we are undertaking, for we should be able to get from it some light, at least, upon two very important problems:

(1) We should be able to come to some conclusions concerning the success or failure of the school as a social organization to provide adequately for the needs of human nature. From this point of view, the success of the school may be measured by the contributions it makes to the growth of personality through the satisfaction of wishes.

(2) We should be able to discover how well the formal social order of the school stands up under the impact of undisciplined impulse welling up from original nature. How far does the established order of the school stand in need of supplementation by spontaneous arrangements for wish satisfaction? What conflict is there between the established channels of wish satisfaction (the social order) and spontaneous social organization? What are the processes of breakdown and rebuilding in the formal order of the school? In short, how does the school survive the attack of "the wild raiders, Beauty and Passion"?

Nearly all the intimate and informal attitudes that spring up in the school could be classified as manifestations of the wish for response. Thus there grow up friendly and affectionate attitudes between teachers and students and between students and other students, but the fact that such friendly attitudes arise should be taken only as an indication that the affectional dispositions of human beings

[1] Krueger, E. T., and Reckless, Walter C., *Social Psychology*, p. 175. (By permission of Longmans, Green, and Company.)

are strong and will assert themselves in any accustomed milieu. Certainly the school is not a favorable environment for the flowering of those personal rapprochements expressed by the easy give and take of response. In proportion to the importance of the wish for response in human life, response arrangements are scanty in the schools; such arrangements as there are are not ordinarily in the formal order of the school, but spring up unplanted in the interstices of the great system, and thrive as they may upon whatever nourishment their situation affords.

There is a general thwarting of the wish for response in the schools, and this involves not only sex, perhaps not sex so much as the less ponderable and more fragile phases of response, but all channels of personal interchange as well. The social distance between teacher and student hinders interaction of a spontaneous and human sort, and leaves both parties disappointed and a little bitter. The presence of the teacher, to whom subordination is owing, and from whom secrets must be kept, operates to cut down personal interchange between students. Such interchange takes place, but it is furtive and limited. It is perhaps this lack of human responsiveness which accounts for the feeling many new teachers have that they have come to live in a desolate and barren world. We may pause to remark that the welfare of students is no better served than that of teachers, for most possibilities of personal growth through participation in group life are lost in such a school; character training, in the rigid school, is either accidental or it is a myth. Response is thwarted, but it is not wholly blocked. Some friendliness, some camaraderie, some pleasant and unsought rapport, some selflessness, some interest of persons in each other there is within the walls of every classroom, because such things are everywhere. And sex, which refuses to be cheated, is there.

The sex wishes, although they undergo considerable distortion, suffer less from the restriction of the school than other segments of response. Nearly all sexual activity in the schools is of the unsanctioned sort, and much of it is directly in conflict with the formal order of the school. That which is sanctioned is rather suffered than encouraged. That which is in conflict with the established order is usually regarded as a serious menace to the school as a social institution.

In spite of the illuminating discoveries of the psychoanalysts and other researchers, our knowledge of the sexual life of children remains meager. The analysts have thought to distinguish several different stages in the sexual development of the young. There is first the diffuse sexuality of infants, which persists through the first five, six, or seven years of life. The sexuality of this period has been called "polymorphous perverse," which means merely that it has not been canalized as have the sexual activities of the normal adult. Theorists of the psychoanalytic school have shown that the erogenous zones, or pleasure zones, are widely distributed over the body during this early period, and, identifying pleasure and sex, they have regarded these pleasure zones as sexual in nature. But since adult canalizations have not been established at this time, the question whether any of the pleasure sources of the infant can be called sexual in the adult sense remains debatable. It is possible that the original of all pleasure is sex, but it is also possible that sex pleasure is a differentiation of generic pleasure of a different sort.

The few years of life from infancy until the approach of puberty are known as the latency period. There appears to be at this time a marked falling off of sexual activity as contrasted with the previous period. The energy, interest, and activity of the personality seem to flow, for a time, into other channels, and sexuality lies below the surface. Opinions differ as to the depth and duration of the latency period. Some say that sexual activity disappears from the personality almost entirely during the latency period. Congruous with this notion is the belief that the latency period may be quite prolonged, if the familial and cultural life in which the child is immersed favor such prolongation; there are persons of much insight and experience who believe that it is possible to rear a child to maturity without once exciting sex curiosity (and this without inducing such splitting of personality as would be brought about by repression). Whether this should be done or no, supposing it to be possible, is a question that our generation must take time to answer. Obviously there are marked differences in the latency period of children in different social groups and different cultures. And there are individual differences within the same culture and the same social group. For some individuals there is apparently no latency period at all, but a continuous development from the diffuse sexuality of infancy to the highly structured behavior of maturity.

A complex series of changes is ushered in by the coming of adolescence. On the physiological side, the coming of adolescence is marked by the tonicity of those internal organizations from which sex tensions arise. Most of the partial wishes which go to make up the sex urge of the adult are awakened at adolescence; numerous problems of control and of the reorganization of personality and the scheme of life are precipitated by this change in the system of working attitudes. There ensues a considerable period in which attention is directed toward the redefinition of sex attitudes and the finding of proper objects for them. At the very onset of adolescence the personality is subjected to considerable strain by the urgency of the unaccustomed tensions of sex. Renewed interest is shown in infantile sex outlets; there is a regression toward the polymorphous perverse channels of earlier days. Often there is masturbation, and mental conflicts arise which seriously rend the personality. Sometimes a homosexual adjustment is made during this period, especially if there is a severe inhibition of the normal flow of affection or a failure of the heterosexual outgo to find an object. The homosexual adjustment is much more evident among girls than among boys; it probably appears in a larger number of cases and its character is less masked. Some writers maintain that all girls pass through such a period. The reasons for the greater prevalence of this phenomenon among girls are probably: that the earlier onset of puberty in girls gives them a longer period between the time when sex tensions arise and the time when courtship, with which is involved some sort of heterosexual outlet, is permitted by our customs, that our folkways permit a much greater affectional interchange between women than between men, and sometimes enforce it, that the primacy of the genital zones is less completely established in the girl, so that her sexual aim is less specific than that of the boy.

The observation that adolescence brings with it severe problems of personal adjustment has now passed into platitude. The theory has been that the sudden awakening of sex at adolescence necessarily entailed personal disorganization. Such an explanation overlooks the fact that two factors are really involved: the inner needs of the individual and the frames of behavior which society presents to him. In a society which imposes less rigid controls upon the sexual behavior of adolescents, adolescence is apparently not a serious personal crisis.[1] Without going to extremes, it seems that we might provide many more acceptable outlets for the sexual interests of adolescents. If we wish to divert these interests into other channels, and to postpone the upheaval of personality by sex behavior, it will be necessary to present adolescents and sub-adolescents with much better conceived and much more consistently worked out schemes

[1] See Mead, Margaret, *Coming of Age in Samoa*, and *Growing Up in New Guinea*.

of life than the resources of our society at present afford. This is one of the issues upon which the local community must decide, and the social structure of the school must be planned in accordance with the policy of the community.

The account which we have given of the sexual life of the young has thus far been in terms of the interaction of internal motivation and the social patterns which are presented to it. A different view of our problem results if we study the sexual life of the child more subjectively, and attempt to find out how sexual phenomena present themselves to the consciousness of the child at different age levels, for the man-woman relationship appears in different guises and changes its form throughout life. To understand the sexual life of the school child, we must know in what configurations his conception of sexuality is organized, we must know what dilemmas it presents to him, and how he thinks of it.

In the earliest years of life, over a period corresponding approximately to that of infantile sexuality, there is an acceptance of the male-female relationship with complete naïveté. There is, however, almost no comprehension of sex functions, and no idea of the meaning of sex differences. This ignorance, however, by no means precludes the possibility of a very pleasant and meaningful cross-sex rapport.

During the latency period, there appears a surface antagonism between the sexes, but this antagonism usually covers both interest and diffidence. There is between the sexes at this time an immense social distance; the worlds of male and female are more completely separate and differentiated than they are at any other period of life. Among groups of boys, at least, there is an inexplicable taboo upon association with girls, accompanied by an attitude of depreciation of women and all their works; there is a time when a boy's most embarrassing moment is when he meets his mother on the street. However incomprehensible to the adult, this attitude remains one of the central facts of boy life. But along with this goes an inner idealization of the opposite sex which far surpasses adult idealization. There is a rich phantasy life, although these phantasies are very difficult for the adult investigator to tap. Ideas concerning sex functions are nearly always vague at the beginning of this period, and such knowledge as the child obtains concerning the physical side of sex is rarely complete or accurate. Some of the childish theories concerning sex processes have been found by the psychoanalysts to be of great importance in the further development of personality; of these the cloaca theory of birth and the castration complex are perhaps the most important. Certain devices commonly used for getting the attention of the opposite sex at this time are: showing off of physical prowess, persecution of the opposite sex, mock combat, loud talking, boasting, self-inflicted torture, etc.

Between the latency period and the stage of adolescence appears a transitional stage of sub-adolescent courtship. This is the stage of puppy-love, the silly stage and the gawky age. Some barriers have been broken down between the sexes; the veil of antagonism has begun to wear very thin. There is a very limited amount of social and physical contact, but such contact as there is is very meaningful and is often reworked into endless phantasy. There is a tendency to worship from afar.

In adolescent courtship there is much greater contact. Starting out with an even greater idealization than before, there is a tendency for adolescent love to run easily into cynicism, especially if there is great physical contact and that contact is taboo. There is a stage, nearly inevitable, in which the adolescent thinks of the association between male and a female as a game which that person loses who first allows himself to become emotionally involved. In this game, pretense is allowable, and it is long before a boy is as truthful with girls as he is with other boys. "Petting" is part of this game.[1] The adolescent courtship group has its own peculiar folkways and mores, which are rigidly enforced. A light affair passes through a crisis when one person begins to take it seriously; it enters a new stage when the other person becomes likewise involved; if he does not, it usually breaks off. A noteworthy fact concerning adolescent love is that it very readily submits to sublimation.

School life is immensely complicated by these intellectual transitions in accordance with which sex relations are conceived of in ever more complex and definite configurations. The problem of administration is rendered yet more difficult because children grouped together for instruction almost never represent the same level of sophistication; sophistication does not follow the mental age. In accordance with different levels of social development, there are rapid shiftings in the significant social groups of the child, and this introduces a further complicating factor in school life.

Since teachers are usually adult, or nearly so, they might be expected to have attained to a much more mature and normal attitude toward sex than even the most mature of their charges. It is true

[1] Cf. Blumenthal, Albert, *Small Town Stuff*, p. 246.

that a large proportion of teachers have become reasonably adult in respect to their sex life. It is only fair to include in this normal group of teachers as large a number as possible; let us suppose that it includes all married teachers and all who expect or hope to be able to fulfill their biological destiny in marriage. Let us add to the group those fortunate spinsters and bachelors who have been able to preserve a normal attitude toward sex. There remains a large and pitiful group of those whose sex life is thwarted or perverse. The members of this group, often consciously and usually with the best of intentions, carry sex problems into the schools, and transmit abnormal attitudes to their pupils because they have no other attitudes to transmit.

It is unnecessary to go into details concerning the sex life of teachers. There are many of them who are involved in normal love affairs with persons outside the schools; such affairs do not usually add to the value which the community puts upon their services and they do not increase their prestige among students. There is also a large group of teachers whose normal sex interests have led them into personal disasters of one sort or another. There are numerous teachers whose love life is definitely perverse. This perversity and the mental conflict arising from it must seriously affect the teacher's influence as a person.

Unmarried teachers, usually women, often fall in love with their principal, who is perhaps the only man of their acquaintance. Sometimes the principal is a married man. An interesting give-away resulting from such a situation is related in the following anecdote:

One afternoon we were sitting together in a room talking over some of the happenings of the day when the principal walked in, smiling as if to say, "Now I have a good joke on someone."

"Well," he said, "Miss Berger, I should like to know what relation you are to me, be it aunt, cousin, or what-not."

Miss Berger was about thirty-five years old and had been teaching for fifteen years, but still possessed a sense of humor.

"Now what kind of a joke are you trying to pull?" she asked laughingly.

"Joke?" he said. "This is no joke." And he read the following note that he held in his hand: "Mr. Wells, please send me two monthly report blanks. (signed) *Mrs. Althea Wells.*"

"You sent me this note, did you not, Miss Berger? It is your writing. Tell me, when did you change your name?"

Miss Berger was stunned. She finally said, "I wrote that note so hurriedly and had my mind on many other things at the same time."

The rest of us thought it was a very good joke, but we wondered if Miss

Berger might not be harboring a secret passion for Mr. Wells, who was already very much married.

A rapport based upon sex attraction frequently arises between teachers and students. Usually it is cross-sexual and entirely normal. It may be a strictly one-way rapport, as in the case of the high-school girl who falls in love with her handsome teacher, or in that of the elderly teacher who privately worships one of his young students. Because, as we elsewhere explained, a sex-based rapport between students and teachers is inconsistent with a continuance of teacher control, and because of the taboo upon affectional interchange between teachers and students, teachers usually attempt to suppress or to disguise such feelings as have too personal a reference. Over-compensations whose meaning is obvious enough to the analytical observer are thus produced. There is the common case of the spinster lady whose affections are attached to one of her larger boys, and who thereupon proceeds to use the machinery of discipline to impress her personality upon him. She reprimands him for the slightest offence, sends him to the principal, lays hands upon him, keeps him after school in order "to have a heart-to-heart talk with him and appeal to his better nature." Her interest in disciplining this one youngster amounts almost to an obsession, and the conflict which originated in her own mind has internal reverberations which keep her nervous system taut. She confides to a friend that she just can't stand that boy, the while she arranges her life and his so that they spend many hours together in an association that is at once hostile and very personal, and so that she has a great deal of him to stand.

A different kind of over-compensation is apparent in the following incident.

I was detailed to go to a Mr. Johnson's class to observe the teaching of Modern History to students of the Junior College. Mr. Johnson was a most unprepossessing fellow, very small and scraggly, and endowed with a huge, hoarse voice. He struck me as a bit crude, both in his manner and in his use of English, but he did everything he could to be pleasant to me. I sometimes wondered if he was afraid that I might carry back an unfavorable report of him and his teaching.

I soon began to suspect that Mr. Johnson was struggling against an attachment to Miss Deveau, who sat in the front row just to the left of the center. I was first led to suspect this because I noticed that his eyes rested upon Miss Deveau more often than upon any other person in the class. Miss Deveau was a 1922 flapper, if you remember the type. Thin and boyish, enameled face, and hard as nails. She kept combing and recombing her hair—the

Lorelei effect. She combed it on me once as we were coming up in the elevator together. Not a serious thought in her head, and very likely not many frivolous ones. Altogether an unsatisfactory resting place for the affections of a serious-minded gentleman like Mr. Johnson.

Directly I began to suspect this situation, I became more interested in Mr. Johnson's personal behavior than in his methods of teaching Modern History. At the end of the term I had made the following notations, among others, concerning this affair:

"Mr. Johnson let his eyes rest upon Miss Deveau rather too often today. At the end of the hour she went up to his desk to complete her conquest. She leaned over his desk gracefully, smiled and looked at him admiringly. Mr. Ross waited for her. I gathered from the expression on his face that he might know what was happening.

"Miss Deveau was late to class today. She and Mr. Ross entered together, somewhat breathlessly. Mr. Johnson refused to look at her once. He was very severe with Mr. Ross for the non-preparation of his lesson.

"Mr. Johnson digressed today and talked a long time about his wife and baby. He seemed a trifle over-emphatic. He gazed at Miss Deveau several times when he talked. (This happened more than once.)

"I have noticed that Miss Deveau's presence in the room hinders the free movement of Mr. Johnson's gaze over the classroom. He starts to look the class over from left to right, but he stops when he comes to her. With some effort, he tears his eyes away, but as likely as not he does not complete the movement, but begins another in the reverse direction, showing a very great distraction. This happened several times today, and he appeared a bit nervous.

"Mr. Johnson called upon Miss Deveau three times today. Her name seems to come very easily to his lips, and when he is at a loss for a person to whom to address a question, he puts it to her. Each time she was called on today she gave a rather absurd answer, but each time he twisted it around in such a way as to give her credit for much more background than she really has; this he did by supplementing, correcting details, taking sentences out of their setting, reorganizing, etc. He required of her, while he completed her recitation, only an occasional halting, 'Yes.' At the end of each recitation he commended her. Mr. Ross and Miss Deveau always enter and go out together, and always sit together in class.

"Miss Deveau and Mr. Ross talked audibly in class today. Mr. Johnson looked at them very sternly.

"Mr. Johnson is very friendly with Mr. Ross now. He calls upon him frequently for expressions of his opinion, and gives him every possible opportunity to make a showing in class. He always asks Mr. Ross and Miss Deveau the easy questions.

"Mr. Johnson was looking directly at Miss Smythe, the homely girl with spectacles, and absentmindedly called on Miss Deveau. Everybody was surprised and Mr. Johnson was flustered. I wonder if any of these people know what a Freudian error is?

"Miss Deveau was absent today, and Mr. Johnson kept looking at the vacant chair. He seemed to have an unusual interest in the door and watched it narrowly. Finally he gave up and settled down to the dull business of a class meeting without Miss Deveau.

"Mr. Johnson repeated his error of a few days ago, but with different individuals. He looked at Miss Perkins, and called on Miss Jones. I wonder if he did it to cover up?

"Today Mr. Johnson gave a short quiz at the beginning of the hour. While the students were writing he sat with his hand over his eyes. But his fingers were not quite together and it seemed to me that he was looking at Miss Deveau. At the end of the hour Miss Deveau and Mr. Ross went up to the desk and talked to Mr. Johnson. I followed them out of the room and heard her say, 'Well, I hope the old coot don't flunk me. I didn't know beans about that first question.' To which he replied, 'Same here. Funny old buzzard, ain't he?'

"Mr. Johnson's friendliness toward Mr. Ross continues. But it rather came out today. He called him Mr. Deveau!"

These were not all the notes I took, but they cover the incidents most in point. It seemed to me unmistakable that Mr. Johnson was in love with Miss Deveau and that he was fighting it down with all his power. I do not know, but it seemed that he was clearly conscious of the state of his affections. (Unpublished manuscript supplied by a graduate student.)

Discerning observers report that such affairs are very common. The present tradition permits coeds of high school and college age to use their feminine lure to get grades and harmless favors from their male teachers. Many teachers, aware of the attacks constantly made upon their standards, have erected strong defences, and meet all such advances with chilling distance. Often enough the technique of students who would be clever is so rudimentary that it would not deceive a tyro; students make it too obvious altogether that they are cultivating the teacher with friendly intent around the time of examinations or when final grades are about to be turned in. In the case detailed above, the whole affair was probably conscious, although it may have been, and on general grounds one is inclined to say it very likely was, of unconscious origin. Where unconscious factors are more definitely in play, some very peculiar and disquieting events take place. Highly conscientious teachers complain of definite compulsions with reference to students of the opposite sex. These unshakable prepossessions are often enough of a harmless nature in themselves, but the conflict engendered by them may endow them for a time with all the importance of inevitable disaster. These teachers find it impossible to take their eyes from the face of a fair student, or to preserve the academic standards where she is concerned, or to rid themselves, in their off hours, of the thought of her and the sound of her name and the vision of her face. Pinching impulses are not uncommon. Such mental phenomena are very likely pathological, and they certainly do much to destroy the efficiency of the teacher as a social personality, but they are common. There is no remedy except in some kind of psychiatric guidance and reeducation for teachers. The most wholesome teachers, however, find it difficult to avoid picking favorites on the basis of personal attractiveness. In every class certain faces stand out; a class itself appears as a constellation of a few outstanding faces against a background of mediocrity, and it is to be expected that this selection of faces which are high lights should be made in part on an esthetic basis. The selectivity, however, is not wholly in terms of abstract beauty, for it is also based upon intelligence and responsiveness, and it is possible for any alert and reasonably intelligent student to conduct himself with reference to the teacher in such a manner as to make his face one of the accustomed resting places for the teacher's gaze. The teacher looks at him rather than the others because he registers as a significant personality, which the others fail to do.

An account of the various kinds of sexually based rapport between teachers and students must include mention of the emotional involvements of the latent homosexual. The latent hemosexual is here taken to be an individual who has a large homosexual component in his make-up, so that he readily develops sexual attitudes toward members of his own sex, but who has not gone over into overt homosexual practices. Apologists for homosexuality have pointed out that this quality might have a use in the personality of the teacher, in so far as it prompts him to a greater solicitude over the welfare of his charges, and is diffused into a general sweetness and kindliness toward them. It apparently does not work out so in practice, for the homosexual teacher develops an indelicate soppiness in his relations with his favorites, and often displays not a little bitterness toward the others. He develops ridiculous crushes, and makes minor tragedies of little incidents when the recipient of his attentions shows himself indifferent. The favoritism which these crushes entail is of course fatal to school discipline. But that is by no means the worst danger that the homosexual teacher brings with him; the real risk is that he may, by presenting himself as a love object to certain members of his own sex at a time when their sex attitudes have not been deeply canalized develop in them attitudes similar to his own. For nothing seems more certain than that homosexuality is contagious. Some school administrators, committed to a policy of employing no individual with a marked homosexual component in his personality, have cast about for suitable means of making an accurate diagnosis on short acquaintance. Although this is a task which would not usually be difficult for a trained person, it presents some perplexities to the common-sense man. One man with an experimental turn of mind evolved what he thought to be a satisfactory formula for men teachers. "Do you like boys?" he would ask. Often the answer betrayed the applicant. An over-enthusiastic answer was taken as probably betraying a homosexual, latent or active, while an under-enthusiastic answer bespoke a turn of mind that could not bear association with children cheerfully. It is also possible for such a question, suddenly injected into the conversation, to precipitate a conflict, and to obtain a confused, emotional, delayed or unduly hurried answer that is very diagnostic. In using such a device, it is necessary to have in mind an answer that is neither too thick nor too thin and to have a sharp eye for all kinds of self-betrayal. A more sophisticated technique would probably depend somewhat more upon such personality traits as carriage, mannerisms, voice, speech, etc.

At yet another point the sex attitudes of the teacher affect the sex adjustment of his students. The attitude which the teacher takes toward the young student's first tentatives at an understanding with a member of the opposite sex may inhibit or delay the formation of a heterosexual adjustment or it may encourage and abet him in this crisis; in any case, the attitude of the teacher can profoundly affect his future happiness. The attitude which teachers take toward the harmless love affairs of young students is generally not an understanding one, and the best that the youngster can hope for is an amused tolerance. Teachers are frequently given to outspoken ridicule of "puppy-love" and of all persons suffering from it; they do not realize, perhaps, the cruel hurt they can give to sensitive youngsters. The intolerance of teachers may be ascribed to two sources: first, it is an unconscious product of the teacher's own love thwart; and, second, it is a part of the teacher's rational judgment that it is better for a young person who has intellectual work to do to postpone an awakening of the sex interest as long as possible. It hardly needs to be said that the teacher's intolerance toward the love affairs of his charges can have regrettable and perhaps lasting effects upon the attitude of the students toward him. Some teasing any lover enjoys, even the youngest, but it must be a very friendly teasing, for there is a line which none may cross with impunity; it is the reward of those who ridicule unfairly to be held in lasting detestation. The loss of rapport with the teacher, however, is a lesser consideration when compared with the possible permanent effects of an environment definitely unfriendly to a heterosexual adjustment. The transition from homosexual and autoerotic activities is not an easy one under the most favorable circumstances, and the school, if it cannot aid that transition, at least should put no obstacles in its way. And if the schools ever decide to take their task of character education seriously, they will need to set it up as one of their major objectives to produce individuals normally heterosexual.

We should not take leave of the topic of sex in the schools without mentioning certain considerations affecting those social affairs, dances, parties, ceremonious occasions, etc., commonly given in high schools with official sanction and supervision. Where these affairs are properly managed, they supply a satisfactory outlet for the sex tensions of youngsters, and prevent them from seeking other and less desirable outlets. But a number of difficulties arise. The spontaneous give and take of response will stand only so much supervision, and that supervision must always be both friendly and tactful. If school affairs are too well supervised or too rigidly conformed, the social life of youngsters betakes itself elsewhere, and their unauthorized affairs, wholly or in part removed from adult supervision, show some tendency to degenerate. Thus arise those "love cults" and other illicit arrangements which make such good copy for the tabloids. The teachers themselves present some problems, for not many teachers care to assume extensive social duties outside the school, and few of them can perform such duties gracefully. It is a difficult rôle, that of the chaperon, and it takes great social facility to carry it off. If, however, school affairs are loosely supervised or too frequent, there is certain to be criticism, and the school may possibly err by coaxing the sex interests of children to become too early or too thoroughly aroused; where this occurs, the school not only suffers some moral degradation in the eyes of the community, but it also performs haltingly and imperfectly its basic task of imparting facts and skills. It requires an ear close to the heart of the community and an eye finely adjusted to the behavior norms of children to decide what social affairs there shall be and what load of chaperonage they will bear. Even then no more than a day-to-day adjustment seems possible. Often a wavering course between the most conservative and the most radical elements of the community is the best that the most adroit politician can manage. How many parties there shall be, what activities shall be permitted at those parties, how they shall be supervised; when spontaneous social arrangements of children arise (as they will) what shall be done about it—these are perennial problems.

In closing our discussion of the sex life of persons in the school, we may say that there is an active personal interplay on a sex basis in the school. It is an interplay, however, which is often hidden and sometimes disguised. Some of the sex manifestations in the school are perverse; of these a certain number are necessary incidents in the process of growing up, and others are definitely pathological and would not be if the school presented the individuals involved with greater opportunities for response gratification or if the community did not interpose barriers between those individuals and the satisfaction of their wishes. The sexual interaction of the schools leaves out numerous persons, who in part compensate through phantasy, and in part remain unconscious of the sex-laden interaction going on about them. Those persons left out are often not interested, and this lack of interest corresponds to the diminution of sex motivation in the latency period. In every school group, there is a certain number who are actively interested in sex, and a certain number who definitely are not. It would seem that the size of these groups is susceptible to some control. The life of the community conditions the number in each of these groups; in the disorganized community there is a larger number of children actively interested in sex than in the community whose life is arranged in normal patterns. And the nature of the life which children and teachers lead together in the school greatly affects the number of children in each of these groups; some schools apparently confront their youngsters with such a full and interesting round of activities in which sex is not involved that the latency period is much prolonged. We should add also that a sane system of sex education would probably obviate much sex curiosity.

We shall now attempt to trace out some of the more important manifestations of the wish for recognition in the social life of the schools. The involvement of the recognition motive in the schools is even more manifold and devious than that of response, but the forms which it assumes, obvious though they are to the observer, are less tangible and less accessible than the forms of response, and therefore we must treat of recognition in more general terms. The schools depend much upon the wish for recognition; they depend upon it, in fact, for the motivation of the formal tasks of school and for that of most "activities." Recognition is the one string of the human instrument which it is permissible for the schools to play upon at will. The pitting of one individual against another in the schools, and the attempt to determine each one's standing exactly in the form of a percentage, the giving of prizes and of medals and of special privileges—all these have no other purpose than the stirring up of emulation. They are the means of involving the child's ego feelings in the achievements of the schools, of catching him up by his status feelings and making him do things he would not otherwise want to do. The wish for recognition is a strong enough motive and a dependable one, but it is difficult to control without access to all the child's social groups. This difficulty arises from the human tendency to grow away from relationships in which one does not obtain favorable recognition, and to make those relationships meaningful in which one does get recognition. The group in which one has satisfactory standing is a significant group, and standing in one group enables one to dispense with standing in others. It is also unfortunate for slow or stupid students, and for those whose ability does not show in the routine of school achievements, that students should be ranged in a rigid ranking system, for those students who are left at the bottom of the class develop inferiority feelings which affect their behavior unfavorably throughout life. Contrariwise, it is none too fortunate for those who rank toward the top to become accustomed to the easy conquests of the school, and many of these have a hard time later in finding themselves; that is, in most cases they have difficulty in reconciling their actual rôle in life with their conception of their rôle. There are some for whom the ranking system is definitely advantageous. Those who are thwarted elsewhere may compensate for their disabilities in other lines by marked success in formal subject matter, and their success will be measured and turned into an arithmetical grade. It is not always so, but it is true in many cases that children who like school do so because of its flattering implications for themselves. If they have an inferiority drive, they may like even the difficult and esoteric subjects, for these, more than others, give them an opportunity to demonstrate their superiority.

Some of the conflicts between teachers and students are directly traceable to their different aims in the mutual association. These arise because the teacher wants one thing and the student wants another. In all these conflicts the wish for recognition of the opposing parties sooner or later becomes involved, and there are other conflicts which apparently consist of nothing more than a struggle over status.[1] Given the hostile definition of the situation as between teachers and students, a student may rebel in order to win the plaudits of his fellows, and the teacher is equally motivated to crush out the last traces of rebellion in order to prove himself an efficient teacher and a powerful personality. Those long and pointless struggles over disorder in the classroom, in which many teachers spend their time and that of their students so wretchedly, have for the most part this explanation and no other. The teacher's use of epithets, threats, and rodomontade, varied by benignant poses, and the students' use of nicknames, mimicry, and take-off, are all part of a death struggle for the admiration of their little world. (Part of the struggle arises because the groups in which teachers and students want status are different groups, and have different standards.)

The involvement of the teacher's prideful feelings in his profession we discuss elsewhere, and we shall here only summarize a few of the more important features of that discussion. Teacher pride is very great, great enough to make the task of keeping the peace among a number of teachers a task for a very Solomon of an administrator. This pride of the teacher arises in part from the authoritative rôle that the teacher plays in his little group, in part from the superficial respect which the community pays to the teacher; in large part, perhaps, teacher pride is the obverse side of an inferiority feeling arising from the teacher's only partly conscious realization of his actual low standing in the community. Unable to secure greater things, the teacher makes the most of the little that is his by right—from this, teacher pride. The teacher is infallible. It is not permitted to talk back when the teacher has spoken. Teaching is the noblest of all the occupations. The ego feelings of the teacher soon come to be involved in the matter of his adherence to rigid academic standards; teachers are soon made to realize that their standing with other teachers depends somewhat upon the red ink they use. Something dries up in the teacher's heart when he realizes that students believe him to be easy; it needs only some definite incident added to this state of mind—as of

[1] "Teaching," wrote a woman teacher, "is a game that almost all of us wish to play again. We never know whether we are to win or lose, but we learn to watch every move with an eagle eye cast upon the opponent and play ourselves against his hand. It keeps us wondering what experience lies right ahead. It makes us alert. We have to be to stay in the game and be a real player. Who likes to play and not play well? The poor player soon has no opponents and is out of the game. . . . School teaching is a great game. I like it, and may I play the game well!"

a student begging a favor and then boasting of having gulled the teacher—to make the teacher feel with his fellows that low grades are a proof of his efficiency.

There are persons who are more concerned over status than others; these are sufferers from that state of mind known as the inferiority complex. It is characteristic of persons who have pronounced feelings of inferiority that they are very sensitive to real or imagined slights or affronts to their personal dignity and quick to scent out any implication derogatory to themselves. Such persons take offence easily and often. When a teacher is afflicted with an inferiority complex, as so many teachers are, he makes a deal of unnecessary trouble for himself in his classroom. There is no disciplinary officer of any experience who cannot tell endless stories of "oversensitive" teachers who kept themselves and their students in a continual stir over the most trivial matters. Short of a psychiatric overhauling which could give these individuals insight enough and control enough to enable them to conquer their difficulties, there is little that can be done in such cases. Sometimes a redirection of the compensatory drive welling up from the hidden feeling of inferiority can be effected by manipulation from without; the technique here is to give the individual constructive experiences in another line, thus diverting his compensatory energies from useless struggles.

A student with an inferiority complex is likely to be a behavior problem. There is here no place for an extended discussion of the rôle of the inferiority complex in the production of juvenile behavior problems, and, since this matter has been discussed very ably in the numerous books dealing with problem children, we may omit it here. We should merely mention that some of the most stubborn and pernicious behavior problems are traceable to feelings of inferiority and the compensatory urge built up as a negation to them; this inferiority drive has been found at the basis of such behavior as persistent lying, stealing, fighting, truancy, sexual delinquency in girls, etc. Students with inferiority feelings are often difficult, and the best-poised teacher in the world is sadly put to it at times to avoid friction. What happens when a child with exaggerated status feelings meets a teacher of the same constitution has been seen again and again, but if it had never been seen, it could not for a moment be doubtful.

In the less extreme cases the manifestations of the inferiority complex are still puzzling. A certain boy at the beginning of his senior year announced an intention to give up all athletics "in order to have more time for his studies." A shrewd teacher managed to cut through to the underlying motive: The boy had gained favorable recognition in lightweight football and basketball, but he had grown out of the lightweight class. He was unwilling to face the competition upon this next level of status. He admitted the truth of this diagnosis. Persons with overstrong status drives seem to create problems for teachers all along the way from the kindergarten to the graduate school. A very distressing situation arose in a graduate class in philosophy not long ago, which was entirely due to the peculiar personality of one individual. He kept fairly quiet when the regular teacher was present, but when a substitute, a younger man whom he had known before, took charge, he made himself a problem at once. He had taken up his position in the rearmost part of the class, separated by two rows of seats from all the others. Since the room was arranged in the form of an amphitheater, this gave him complete command of the situation. Taking advantage of his unusual position, he constituted himself an assistant teacher. When questions were addressed to the teacher, he would quickly repeat them, and relay them to him. When the teacher did not at once answer questions, he volunteered his answers. Frequently he took it upon himself to explain the teacher's answers to the class, thus presuming a greater familiarity with subject matter than other students had, and a greater verbal facility than the teacher. The teacher was frequently irritated but determined to be polite. On one occasion, as a fellow student put it, "he stood up and orated till the bell rang, and then he just kept on talking. All the students started to leave, but he just kept on talking." Talkative students and self-constituted teacher's helpers have, of course, a more ruinous effect upon classes conducted by the lecture method than upon classes where other teaching methods are employed.

Students who are not clever may, as we have intimated, escape from the pressure put upon them in the school by making some other relationship more significant than the school relationship, thus maintaining their mental equilibrium by a rearrangement of their social world. The school often attempts to follow up these persons, to "carry the fight to them," in teacher language. The pressure built up around the slow and unwilling student during school hours is often tremendous, and one wonders how such a one can find life bearable at all. Yet when one looks at him, one is convinced that he keeps his sufferings well hidden. When an opportunity is given to look within, one finds perhaps a little more concern than appears on the surface, but one finds also some well-worked-out defence reactions which function perfectly in keeping out the hurt. Some of the attitudes which come between such an individual and the teacher who is trying to put pressure upon him are the following: that it does not really matter because school is not like life and many successful business men never did well in school anyhow; that it is all really very funny; that one "could do as well as anyone else if he would work, only he won't work"; that teachers are nobodies and what they say doesn't matter anyhow; that the teacher is "cracked on scholarship"; that the teacher did well in school but never amounted to much; that it is an unfriendly world and that one is treated unfairly; that one can really get by just as well on his personality as on his brains, etc. There are many others, and although we must recognize their psychological character as defence reactions, we should do well to remember that even truth may be arrived at pathologically.

Faris has pointed out that the desire for security and the wish for new experience do not deserve to be ranked with the wish for response and the wish for recognition as basic categories of desire. They are simple mechanisms which are set off by the conditions of life. The wish for security is called into play wherever there is fear, and the points at which fear arises are determined almost wholly by the configurations affecting the life of the individual. The mechanism of fear is apparently inherent in the human organism, for it is the same kind of fear that one feels before the firing squad and in the presence of a declining market, but it is an emotion that one does very well without, and it builds up no cumulative tension in the absence of stimulus as do the wishes for response and recognition. Once started, fear persists in the organism, and cannot be dealt with by the simple refusal to recognize it. It is hard to eliminate fear, too, because it tends to equalize itself from one scheme of life to another, and to attach itself always to the shakiest point in the structure. However safe they may be in fact, those social buildings in which we pass our days are all condemned in our own minds. And it is worthy of remark that individuals who have grown accustomed to fear tend to reproduce their fears under any circumstances of life, however inappropriate. There are pathological fears, likewise, which are thought to be disguised affects or inverted wishes; although these fears are always experienced as arising from the environment, they are in fact of internal origin, and may for our purposes be considered as fears arising in one part of the self from a realization of the nature of certain split-off impulses.

Without entering upon that deeper question, "What makes men fear one thing rather than another?" we may briefly characterize some of the fears of teachers and students. This discussion, again, must be merely a summary included for the sake of completeness, for it has seemed best to give this topic more extended treatment elsewhere. Teachers fear two things above all others: the loss of control over their classes, and the loss of their jobs. Why either of these fears should become so important, we cannot pause to inquire now; our point is that each of these fears extends itself into other departments of life, and gives rise to security mechanisms which grow weightier with use and end by becoming central features of the personality. Students' fears are more scattering in nature; students fear punishment, the disapproval of the teacher and of their parents, they fear being shown up as stupid, and they fear examinations and failure and the disgrace of being left behind.

The manifestations of the so-called wish for new experience are likewise puzzling. Writers on educational subjects have frequently spoken as if there were an instinct of curiosity, a desire to master subject matter wholly divorced from social motivation, and unrelated to the beginnings of acts. (Thomas's use of this term is further complicated by his inclusion of the reaction to monotony, the mental state of ennui, which is best thought of as neural fatigue consequent upon protracted attention to a limited range of stimuli.) There is little evidence that there is in human beings anything corresponding to an instinct of curiosity. We shall hold here, with Faris, that curiosity is no more than the tendency to complete an act already in a sense begun. Mental life is organized into certain patterns, and these patterns tend to be complete; one aspect of the tendency to complete them is curiosity (as imagination and memory are other phases of the same tendency). This completing tendency differs for different patterns, and it matters greatly what portions of any pattern are presented; there might also be individual differences in the strength of the tendency to complete configurations, and in the ability to conjure them up from their rudiments. The connection which a suggested pattern has with the remainder of the personality is also an important determinant of the curiosity which it arouses; that learning comes easiest which is based upon our dominant complexes.

The attitude of the eagerly learning student is not all curiosity, and we should do well to recognize its composite character. The motivation is partly social; the child learns to please his teacher, and to excel his schoolmates. The desire to learn has thus a social basis. But curiosity mechanisms are set off in the learning process. Learning proceeds by wholes, and these wholes are units complete in themselves. When one perceives a part of such a whole a desire arises to perceive it more completely, to see its details, or to know its relation to other wholes; this desire is curiosity. The desire to understand is a desire to see things in a causal configuration.

The mode of presentation of subject matter affects the extent to which curiosity is aroused. An interesting presentation is one which from moment to moment gives suggestions of wider horizons and makes one think of problems yet unsolved. It is a method of incomplete wholes gradually completed. One must not present too little, for then the materials suggest no pattern, and, if there are many of them, they befuddle, nor must one present a satisfying completeness until the proper time has arrived. The peroration must always come at the end. The interest with which we read a book or listen to a speaker depends upon a rhythm of suggested and completed configurations which first excites and then allays our curiosity. Two contrasting techniques with which all are familiar are those of the newspaper writer and those of the novelist. The newspaper writer tells the story in the first sentence. He keeps our interest, in so far as he does keep it, by furnishing ever more minute details. He must be increasingly specific or he loses us. He presents us first with a structurally perfect whole, and then sketches in the details; the general pattern remains the same but the internal structure becomes more detailed. The novelist operates on the principle of suspense. He gives us incident after incident, each perfect in its detail, but underneath we have the sense of a greater configuration taking shape piece by piece as we travel through the pages. The more incidents he relates the greater the suspense and the more compelling the suspended configuration. Each of these techniques sustains interest and avoids ennui; ennui arises only when the mind is confronted with too many facts of the same order, or when it is compelled to attend too long to the same thing.

Each of these techniques may be of use to the teacher. Teachers will find some experimentation with incomplete configurations of value in their social relationships. They may stimulate interest in their classrooms, as Willa Cather does in her books, by never saying too much. Or they may use the suspended configuration to discipline and to make their students sit forward in their seats, as Clarence Darrow does when he mumbles his best epigrams. Teachers must remember, however, that more than merely intellectual processes are needed to secure sustained interest; if it were not so, there would be many more good teachers than there are. The real art of the teacher is to manipulate the social interaction of the classroom in such a way as to favor the expansion of the students' personalities along desired lines. To do this well requires some insight, and also a certain amount of self-discipline, for it may necessitate the sacrifice of the teacher's own immediate impulses in the situation. To discuss this subject fully would require more space than we can give, but we may summarize it by quoting some of the rules which a teacher who had had considerable success in this line had worked out for himself.

1. To be strict without being unpleasant.
2. To receive all student contributions respectfully and interestedly, and to magnify their importance.
3. To find something to praise in every performance, to condemn with caution.

The desire for group allegiance has been advanced by Faris as a third sort of desire capable of being classed with recognition and response. This is the wish to be loyal to some group or some cause, to be incorporated into, perhaps to lose one's identity in something greater than one's self. This is sometimes called the desire for group superiority. It finds expression in all the impassioned loyalties of school days and displays itself most strikingly in the ethnocentrism of the young. It helps, perhaps, to account for the popularity of competitive athletics. The loyalty of the school child reaches ecstatic fulfillment in those school ceremonies and moments of collective insanity when the entire group feels and acts as one. (For a full description of such occasions see Chapters IX, The Separate Culture of the School, and XII, Crowd and Mob Psychology in the School.)

PROJECTS

1. Observe a school room on a rainy day. Compare with the same school room on a day when the weather is fine.
2. Make a chart showing the daily incidence of disciplinary cases and compare with a chart showing various weather conditions.
3. List all reflex behavior in a classroom. What social meaning has it?
4. Take notes upon cross-sex attraction or antagonism between a teacher and a student.
5. Tell the story of some school scandal and analyze its effect upon school, students, and teachers.
6. Make observations upon "puppy-love." What should be the teacher's attitude toward these manifestations?
7. Take notes upon "crushes" which students have upon teachers. What is the indicated behavior of the teacher?
8. Describe the disciplinary troubles of a teacher with an inferiority complex.

9. Verbalize the folkways and mores of an adolescent courtship group.

10. What happens when a teacher with an inferiority complex meets a child with an inferiority complex? Describe minutely.

11. Determine by study of cases the actual motivation of children eager to learn.

SUGGESTED READINGS

(1) Adler, Alfred, *The Practice and Theory of Individual Psychology* (trans.).

(2) Freud, Sigmund, *A General Introduction to Psychoanalysis* (trans.).

(3) Krueger, E. T., and Reckless, W. C., *Social Psychology*, Chapter VII.

(4) Low, Barbara, *Psychoanalysis and Education.*

(5) Thomas, W. I., and Znaniecki, Florian, *The Polish Peasant in Europe and America*, Vol. I, pp. 72-74; Vol. III, pp. 33-35, 55-61.

(6) Thomas, W. I., *The Unadjusted Girl*, pp. 4-32.

Chapter XII

CROWD AND MOB PSYCHOLOGY IN THE SCHOOL

One of the most fascinating chapters of social psychology is that which deals with the mentality peculiar to the crowd and the mob, for the mind undergoes a strange metamorphosis under the impact of many other minds, and people do things when the mob has heated their passions white that would be impossible if they were sober. It may appear surprising that we should treat of the mob spirit in connection with the school, but experienced teachers will not be astonished. We shall find here no fiery crosses and no negroes hanged and burned, but things happen in the school which mark the crowd and the mob, and we shall speak of these.

The crowd is much more common than the mob. What makes a crowd, apparently, is the condition of attention to the same stimulus. There may be also like response to this like stimulus, and there is usually a process of interstimulation and response which heightens suggestibility and at once stimulates and narrows mental activity. Most classes are crowds at times, and nearly all lecture groups are crowds most of the time. The class is usually the kind of crowd known as an audience. Social interaction in the audience takes place, of course, in all directions at once from any individual, but the most significant interaction is always that between the individual in the crowd and the one person (or the small group of persons) at the focus of attention. The art of holding one's audience is that of keeping this relationship significant to the exclusion of others. He who would move an audience must do a little more; he must utilize the interstimulation and response of the crowd to reenforce his own appeal. The teacher is often at the focus of attention. Newcomers to the profession do not always know how to bear this Argus gaze, but learning to move gracefully in the limelight is part of learning to teach.

The condition of interstimulation and response in the audience heightens receptivity. Investigations show that the back fringe of the audience tends to be partially excluded from the interaction. There is good evidence that this is particularly true of the classroom audience, for the highest proportion of failures in lecture sections is found on the back row.[1] Where the group is engaged in some definite activity, as in doing tests or writing examinations, the advantage is probably with the individuals seated toward the center of the group, for they are completely surrounded by other persons doing the same thing, and favorable interstimulation and response are at their height. But where the group is merely listening (though there is no evidence for this generalization beyond the common-sense observations of teachers), the present writer would venture to assert that the advantage is with those persons who are physically closest to the teacher. They are involved in more intimate rapport with him, and are able to attend to him more closely because there are fewer competing objects in their field of attention. They have the further advantage of more complete communication based upon facts of gesture and posture too subtle to be observed from a distance. Griffith's results seemed to show that no such advantage existed, and he offered the explanation that a too close view of the lecturer might cause the attention to be directed at irrelevant details unnoticeable from a distance; it is possible that this attention to details irrelevant for purposes of academic instruction would facilitate personal interchange at the expense of subject matter. (The importance of gesture in the supplementation of the meaning of words and sentences is not generally realized. There are few of us who are not misunderstood over the telephone. There are few of us who can put our thoughts down on paper, for gesture is excluded from written expression; perhaps that is why writing makes an exact man.)

Human ecology is the study of the distribution of men and institutions in space and time as determined by the process of competition. There appears to be a characteristic ecology of the classroom. We should distinguish this from the position psychology described above, for it does not concern variations in the effect of classroom interaction with different position, but variations of position determined by different grades and types of personality. In large classes where students are left free to choose their own positions, the author has found a certain distribution to recur. In the front row is a plentiful sprinkling of overdependent types, mixed perhaps with a number of extremely zealous students. In the back row are persons in rebellion, commonly persons in rebellion against authority and ultimately against the father image; if not that, perhaps in rebellion at being

[1] Cf. Griffith, C. R., "A Comment on the Psychology of the Audience," *Psy. Mon.*, Vol. 30, 1921. Reprinted in Kimball Young, *Source Book for Social Psychology*, pp. 679-684.

assimilated to the class. Those who use the responsive technique for constellating the teacher's attention usually distribute themselves about midway of the class. A number of timid students have stated to the writer that they habitually sit next the wall. The effect of this distribution upon classroom interaction depends upon the instructor's rapport with his students and the manner in which he distributes his attentions over the group, but it is always a significant effect. Further study would doubtless reveal other patterns. Quantitative investigation of these phenomena would be long and difficult, but not impossible.

A class, as a crowd, develops a definite personality, and that personality can very easily be observed from where the teacher stands, for a class is never a sea of faces after the first day. It is a pattern, a structure of high lights and shadows, a configuration with shifting points of tension, a changing equilibrium of ease and unease, of beauty and loveliness. The maintenance of discipline depends upon the emergence in the teacher's mind of configurations enabling him to keep the whole class in view without sacrificing any of its parts. For the beginning teacher, the class is confusion and very likely a "big, booming, buzzing confusion." For the experienced teacher, it is an orderly, patterned whole. Within this configuration of the class as a whole are many minor centers of tension, and the whole field may come to be organized around any one of these. The teacher who has good command over his class preserves the balance by merely shifting the center of his attention to points of incipient confusion.

Very shortly, on the basis of the give and take carried on by the more aggressive members of the class and the teacher, the class develops a personality of its own. What personality a class shall have is partly determined by that chance and it is not all chance—which decides which students shall be in a particular class at a particular time of the day under a particular teacher. And a very important determinant of the personality of a class is in the teacher's mind, for different attitudinal sets are called forth in the teacher by classes which shape themselves in different configurations, and the teacher shows a different side of himself to different classes. The differences in the teacher's attitude are often so slight that they defy the keenest observer to isolate and describe them but the effects of these differences are neither slight nor difficult to observe.

Every teacher has observed that there are some classes that are easy to teach, and some others upon which his best efforts produce no effect. There are hostile and receptive classes; sometimes these are obviously produced by some small action of the teacher at the first meeting of the class which defines the situation in one way or another. There are live classes and dull, and this seems to be partly a matter of arithmetic, for five or six alert students make a class that moves, and a class with a smaller number of good minds is likely to be dull. There is a numerical point, too, beyond which the mere size of the group crushes out student participation; this is a statistical clue deserving of further investigation.[1] There are classes whose members are disposed to argue with each other, and in these it is never difficult to pass the class hour. The seating of the habitual disputants has a noticeable effect upon the character of the discussion. If the argumentative ones are seated on opposite sides of the room, there is some likelihood that the discussion will be carried on on a high level, and that other persons will enter into it, but if the persons who are usually focal points of discussion are seated together there is more likelihood that the discussion will degenerate into the ridiculous and the personal. There are classes that are eager to learn, and others whose nature it is to be dumb and driven; there is a superstition among college teachers that a class of the latter species is largely made up of so-called "activities men." The nature of the participation of the teacher and the student will differ according to the configuration to which the class conforms in the eyes of the teacher, and according to the side of himself which he correspondingly shows to the class.

Park has said that when a crowd acts it becomes a mob. The crowd observes and feels; the mob acts. There occurs in the mob a much higher degree of interstimulation and response than in the crowd, and there is consequently a much greater loosening of inhibitions. Attitudes and emotions that do not ordinarily come to consciousness are expressed when one is a member of a mob. From this expression of long-repressed impulses there arises an exaltation of feeling that is unusual and that leads easily to further excess. Kimball Young has remarked upon the expansion of the ego in the mob; this, too, is a significant part of the explanation of mob behavior. Where the group of school children entertains much latent hostility toward the teacher, where there is much antagonism between teachers and students but the students do not dare to let this antagonism come to expression as an ordinary thing, the problem of the teacher may be said to be that of keeping the group oriented as a crowd rather than as a mob. In such a combustible situation, the slightest misstep on the part of the teacher will be enough to turn the crowd which faces him into a mob.

[1] Cf. Peters, C. C., *Foundations of Educational Sociology*, pp. 264 ff.

In general, the chief danger is that of reacting emotionally to the group. What distinguishes the crowd and the mob is the more complete emotional participation of the individual in the mob; if the teacher reacts with those segments of himself which should not be in play, he will call out in others emotions that are similarly inapropos. It is these tabooed emotions which make the crowd into the mob. The teacher may change his school-room crowd into a mob by treating it as a mob. If, for instance, he shouts at a group, or makes an unsuccessful attempt to discipline a group, he becomes the leader of a mob, and organizes the mob in opposition to himself. A benefit of military or quasi-military organization is that it assembles and controls a crowd that can only with the greatest difficulty be turned into a mob.

The place in the school where a mob is most likely to arise is the study hall or assembly room. The technique of managing a difficult study hall involves, therefore, a careful schooling of one's habits of social expression in order that all that is not pertinent to the situation may be eliminated at will. The mask which the teacher wears in study hall is characterized by impassivity and imperturbability. This, then, is the reason for those peculiar set expressions which one observes on teachers' faces, for those expressions which enemies call wooden and friends call granite-like: these men are forced to pose much as symbols of authority, and they have chiselled their faces into the pattern of authority. Fear, after all, is a great teacher, and one learns under duress to obviate the possibility of the entry of anything personal when that might detract from one's validity as a symbol. The struggle to remain poised and impassive is a struggle to limit the social interaction of the study hall to the significant issues. It is to the interest of would-be disturbers of the peace to bring other matter into play if they can, but it is the business of the teacher and the policeman to go straight to the point.

For those who have not had experience of mobs in the school, some descriptions of such episodes will be in order; those who have seen and experienced them will have no need of these narratives, for those are things that teachers never forget.

A Disorderly Study Hall

I graduated from college at the Midyear's, very happy to have a contract to teach in Central High School at E——. Central High School, the principal wrote, was a very fine place to teach; there were about twelve hundred students, and sixty teachers, and the morale was excellent.

It was a fairly sophisticated high school in a city larger than any in which I had ever lived before. I was little prepared to cope with the problems that faced me, and presented myself at Central High School that February morning without the slightest suspicion of what was going to happen to me. I was very young, and the conformation of my face made me look even younger. I was taken for a student several times during the first day of school. I was extremely green, and showed it plainly. For this reason I have often wondered how so efficient and tactful a principal happened to assign me to the hardest study hall in the school.

I drew the study hall in 217, the third hour of the day. It was a boys' study hall, and it was supposed to be difficult, but I knew nothing of that. My instructions were about as follows: "Now, Mr. J., come down on them. It's easier to ease up later than to tighten up. Watch carefully for any disorder, and if there is any let me know. I think, perhaps, the best practice is to take a seat in the back of the room and go on with whatever work you have to do when things are quiet. We want a careful report of absence and tardiness. You turn those in on blanks that you can get in the outer office. Good-day, Mr. J."

Study hall 217, when I found it, seemed overlarge. The boys were apparently a bit slow about taking their seats and settling down. I had some difficulty in finding the teacher's desk, for it was not a desk, but only a table. I fumbled in the drawer till I found the roll. The boys gradually came to realize that I was the teacher, and straggled to their seats. They had, however, no intention of beginning work immediately. I was not concerned about that, because I was concentrating just then on taking the roll. I had decided to turn in all my reports so faithfully and accurately that the office would realize at once what manner of man they had to deal with.

I began the semester a week late, and the study hall had been in the hands of a substitute teacher during that week. Older teachers told me that my troubles really began that week, because the substitute teacher let the boys get a start. I have no complaint to make, however, for the substitute teacher probably did a much better job with 217 than I was able to do. That first hour there was a good bit of talking, and a little sporadic mischief here and there. Several students were frankly idling, and I tried to deal with them with stern looks. There was also a great deal of shuffling of feet, and one or two boys changed their seats without permission. Unfortunately, I was unable to deal with this situation, or even to notice carefully what was taking place, for I was taking the roll. The roll was very complicated, and it was not possible to see the entire room from the teacher's desk, so that I had my troubles. I spent nearly all the first hour in taking the roll and making out absence reports.

The second day I began to realize what was happening. The disorder started the next day about where it had left off the day before. I discovered that I could best keep the whole room in view by stationing myself over in the front corner, to the left of the room, but the trouble with that was that it left the other side too little supervised, and there were some troublesome boys over there. I allowed myself to be drawn from one side of the room to the other. When I was on one side of the room, things would quiet down there, and I would be much encouraged and would entertain the hope momentarily that I was getting the situation in hand. But then noise and disorder would arise on the other side of the room. I began to be desperate, for I could never catch anybody, and too many were involved for me to be able to punish them all, even if all were apprehended. From time to time I tried to deal with the situation masterfully, saying, "Now this has got to stop," "You fellows dig in and get to work," or, "Now I want to have it quiet in here." These masterful speeches, coupled with the fact that I was gradually increasing the tempo of my movements from one side of the hall to the other, must have been very ludicrous. It was not funny to me, however amusing it may have been to the boys; I was frantic.

The third day I had a cold and high fever, and these symptoms disabled me for several days, perhaps enough to dull my perception of the tragedy that was taking place with myself as the chief tragedian. That my emotions were swirling in my chest, and that I was none too anxious to take up the struggle again, must have been obvious to all my young charges as I entered 217 that third day. That day I definitely abandoned the attempt to take a roll; I had decided that I had better concentrate upon establishing order and let the attendance go for the time. I stood in front and tried to watch everything that went on. Following out the advice of an older friend, I tried to bluff the boys by looking at them and writing names on a slip of paper. For a while it looked as if the ruse might work. But the boys must have known that I did not know their names, and they were having too much fun to be easily dissuaded. I was beginning to be frightened, for I knew that my professional career was at stake. I looked about me for a friendly face, but all the faces seemed to have an evil look upon them, and every youngster there seemed determined to torment me if he could. Then the first inkwell fell. I went over to the place where it had fallen and investigated. I became very excited, and that fact must have been obvious to all about me. Shortly after that another inkwell fell, and I investigated. And then came another, and I decided not to investigate, but to stand in front and try to catch someone throwing one of them. But they were thrown somehow, and I could not see who did it. I made a plea for order. Those about me listened with some show of respect, but there were derisive hoots from anonymous sources in the back of the room. I coupled a threat against persons unknown to the pleas. Then trouble began. Evidently all doubt that I was fair game had been removed. There was disorder of every kind, talking, laughing, throwing paper wads, and moving about the room, but the most troublesome thing was that they kept throwing those inkwells around the room. I got hold of two or three boys who were unquestionably guilty of some minor offences and sent them to the office. My action was greeted by the Bronx cheer. I knew that I was getting my baptism of fire, and I wondered how long this situation could last.

My questions were answered the next day. I knew that it could not last long. Inkwells were thrown all through the hour. I was desperate. I threatened and cajoled. I resorted to every ruse that I could think of in the effort to catch someone red-handed. I failed. I got up in front and asked for their attention for just a moment. I made a memorable speech. I said that it wasn't fair for those fellows to attack me from behind, that if anyone had anything against me I would step outside and fight him at once. As for me, I had nothing against anybody, but I could whip any of the dirty skunks who were causing all this trouble. I was so angry that I nearly cried. The issue was in doubt, for a while. Evidently the boys considered my speech. But the inkwells kept falling, falling, falling, and I didn't know where one of them came from. When my head was turned in one direction, a number of inkwells would come from the other side; when I looked the other way, the fire would be returned. The boys thought that it was uproarious fun. Of course no one thought of studying. The room was as noisy as a basketball game that hour. It was beginning to be dangerous, too, for one or two of the boys were hit and hurt slightly.

The fifth and last day of my torture came. It was pandemonium that day from the first bell on. I was perfectly helpless, and saw nothing to do but stand up and take my punishment. The inkwells were flying faster than ever. I tried to make a plea, but it was unheard. I couldn't make my voice carry above the din. I smiled grimly and settled down to hold on for the forty-five minutes. There were signs that the more timid boys were genuinely concerned about the danger they ran. One boy was hit and had to go out of the room with a slight cut over his eye. An inkwell came very close to my head. Midway of the hour a boy got up, looked at me indignantly, and cried out, "I'm not going to stay in here any longer." Then he fled from the room. A dozen others rose and started to follow him. I stood in front of the door as if to bar their exit. Then the whole assembly room arose and rushed angrily out of the room, whooping and stamping their feet. I did not try to stop them. I was glad that it was over.

A School Strike

The events that I shall relate took place in a private school shortly after the war. Strikes were common among students in those days, for the unrest which affected the rest of the population had had its reverberations within the schools as well.

What grievances the boys had it would be hard to say. When put down on paper they do not appear to have been momentous. But there was much discontent among the boys, so much is sure. One would see sullen groups standing around in the dormitory and talking. There was a bitter note in the voices of the boys when they talked about the school. Offences of all sorts multiplied, and the number of boys forced to walk the bull-ring in order to rid themselves of demerits, or detained upon the campus for bad behavior, was large. The morale of the school was poor.

The commandant seemed to be the subject of special hatred. He was accused of playing favorites, which may or may not have been true. That he was weak and uneducated, and did not handle cases of discipline tactfully, was certain.

There was a succession of cooks at the school. Some of the cooks were not very expert. The quality of the food declined, and there were a few meals which were very thin indeed. This was made worse by poor table service, for there had been trouble with the student waiters.

In addition there were some very "bad actors" among the boys. They were unmanageable under any system and would have stirred up dissension within the pearly gates. They became embroiled with the commandant or with other members of the faculty. There were several serious cases of impudence. These same boys, not too secretly, circulated a number of alleged jokes in the nature of plays upon the commandant's name.

Then, for some unknown reason, all the cockroaches in the kitchen began to die at once. And to choose the most inconvenient places in which to die. They died in the food. Everybody began picking pieces of cockroach out of the soup. This lasted two or three days, and everybody was thoroughly exasperated. It was reported that one of the bolder boys took his bowl of soup to the man in charge of the commissary and showed him the cockroach that was in it.

The grumbles among the boys increased a hundred fold. It required no seer to perceive that trouble was brewing.

Wednesday came, and the boys' free time. The boys went away. Pretty soon they returned, a motley crew in a pseudo-military formation. They carried banners stating their grievances and mentioning the commandant by name. They gave vent to jeers and catcalls as they marched by the school. Faculty men noted down their names.

A strong executive took hold of the case. He put the striking students under arrest, depriving them of communication with each other. He handled each case separately, dealt with grievances, real or fancied, and meted out what seemed to be a just penalty in each case. The ringleaders he expelled summarily, as I remember, and other cases were handled on their merits.

After the mob had been broken up as a mob, an attempt was made to deal with the morale of the group.

Similar manifestations to these related above are those periodic outbreaks of college students which attract so much attention and occasionally have such serious results. It is interesting that the tradition of different schools calls for such outbursts on quite different occasions and that the activity associated with them has nearly always a traditional pattern. In one midwestern university such mob phenomena are known as "Rallies," and take place before important games. In another university, the name given is "Rowbottom," and a Rowbottom may take place at any time, but is most likely to occur on a Saturday night after a big game. The patterns of the activities are different, the Rally calling for the disturbance of school classes, and the Rowbottom for the destruction of furniture. In numerous universities certain activities are traditional after victory in important games, snake dances, raids upon movies, etc. These are activities for which there is a traditional pattern, but they are also phenomena of the mob, and are associated with many unplanned and uncontrolled expressions of buried wishes.

In the incidents which we have described at length, it is interesting to note certain features which social psychologists have found to be typical. In the first place, none of these phenomena was wholly spontaneous and without precedent; it might be doubted if such things could ever take place without the influence of a cultural pattern calling for or sanctioning such behavior. Secondly, we observe that these coming events cast their shadows before them; the definite outbreaks were preceded by a long series of occurrences preparatory to them. The milling process described by Park and Burgess[1] was obvious in both these stories. We may note that this preparatory process is a circular interaction resting upon dramatic incidents. It is a process of a summatory nature, so that each succeeding incident but reenforces those which have gone before. There come out of these stories some implications as to the technique of dealing with a mob. It is obvious that the members of the mob must be treated as individuals; this prevents them from feeling mob backing, or the unanimity of the group; it shuts them off from martyrdom, and it removes the sanction of the conflict group from their behavior. The mob, contrariwise, struggles as does any other group to prolong its life as long as possible and to keep its ranks unbroken.

C. C. Peters has given us an excellent discussion of the technique by which school mobs may best be handled. It follows:

> The teacher needs to utilize the laws of group psychology in controlling the potentially omnipresent crowd spirit, even turning it to good account. Many teachers do this intuitively, having picked up its technique unconsciously in the give-and-take of social experience.
>
> (1) The tactful teacher will avoid unnecessary conflicts with the group. The best disciplinarian gets on without any show of discipline. When crises arise, it is, of course, necessary that the teacher handle them with vigor and courage. Weakly to back down would mean irretrievable loss of prestige. But it is no credit to a teacher to be continually having crises to meet. While

[1] Park and Burgess, *Introduction to the Science of Sociology*, Chapter XIII.

the writer was principal of a high school he had a teacher who could not get on with one of the boys. She knew very well that he hated her. Nevertheless, when she wanted someone to do her the favor of carrying the phonograph downstairs, she asked this boy to do it. He refused; she then insisted that the principal ought to expel him. It is such unnecessary crises that it is the part of tact to avoid.

(2) The crowd can be handled better if dealt with good-humoredly than if defied. Aggressive opposition always intensifies the crowd spirit. Conceivably the teacher might break down a mob by the weight of his attack, but ordinarily he will have better success if he meets it good-humoredly. The writer knows a teacher who was once threatened with a hazing by his students. When they came around for the purpose he maintained his calm, laughed at them, and joked with them, and they changed their minds.

(3) The crowd should be broken up into individuals. Get the members apart and talk with them separately. Do not direct requests or disciplinary measures at the class as a whole, but isolate single persons and deal with them one at a time. Individuals will be reasonable, or at least tractable, when the crowd will not.

(4) In your class work do not give opportunity for the spirit of chaos to get started. See to it that things move on in routine fashion. It is when the teacher must hunt for laboratory equipment, or for a reference, while the class is idle, or when he has so poorly planned the lesson that it does not move on smoothly, or when in some other way there are hitches, that there is danger of spontaneous development of mob mischief. As long as the teacher keeps things in his own hands and keeps them moving, there is little danger.

(5) Maintain your own calm. Nothing else is so contagious in a crowd as the calmness of one or more persons, especially those with great prestige. The calmness of a commander in war, or of an individual person at a fire, can reduce to rationality the whole ebullient multitude.

(6) Seek to enlist the support of the natural leaders of the group. Not all persons of a crowd have equal influence. Its character is usually determined by a few members, and often by a single one. It will pay the teacher to discover who these are, have talks with them explaining his hopes and purposes, and particularly inviting their cooperation and support. If these bell sheep can be caught, the crowd will follow.[1]

That the individual derives psychological benefits from participation in the mob is undeniable. He expresses therein emotions that would otherwise remain repressed, and his mental health must attain at least a temporary betterment. Practically the same ends are obtained, and with much less danger to the social order, by those orgiastic ceremonies connected with athletic contests. A pep meeting

[1] Peters, C. C., *Foundations of Educational Sociology*, pp. 345-6. (Reprinted by permission of The Macmillan Company.)

is devised to arouse the crowd to frenzy; it is itself a controlled and ordered frenzy; the mob spirit displays itself at a game, and the occasion is often an orgy for the spectators. The great advantage of all this, for the school administrators, is that it is harmless, and that it may even have beneficial effects upon the discipline of the school at other times. But the furious passions of the mob need to be carefully bridled, or they become dangerous. Breaking loose, the least that they can do is to make it difficult to carry on school for a certain time. More serious excesses are not at all uncommon and include such things as fights, destruction of property, vandalism, and rowdyism of all kinds. It is not unknown that mob spirit originating in the school should spread throughout the community.

Minor manifestations of the crowd spirit in the schools are those psychic epidemics which sometimes sweep through a body of students. A few years ago a boy of low mentality coined a word and a gesture that were a significant part of the mental environment of a generation of students. He carefully prepared three paper wads, which he put on his desk. He then pushed them about with jerky movements of two extended fingers of his left hand. As he went through this mystic rite, he murmured to himself the word of words, "Toods." The teacher observed this strange behavior, and asked him what he was doing. He repeated the gesture, and said, "Toods." The word and the gesture took on. The motivation is obscure, to say the least, but there was a year in which any student in the school might at any time be expected to prepare three paper wads, and push them about with murmurs of "Toods." The gesture and the word were copied carefully at first, but later they were used separately and out of their setting. The gesture came to be used as one of those little devices for relieving the tension of a social situation that are so common in groups of the young. A young man talking to a young woman made this little gesture with the two fingers of his right hand when at a loss for anything else to do, and a young woman desirous of being considered jolly and sophisticated gestured in like manner. The word "Toods" came to be used as a word of some derision. (Sometimes it had a meaning that bordered dangerously upon the vulgar.) When a story was told that strained credulity, or a request was made that showed a lack of contact with the actual situation, the indicated answer was "Toods." A phrase of derogation or denial was, "Oh, Toods on that!" The pattern of behavior held its own for some years, and was taken up by many who were utterly unaware of its origin.

A similar nonsense word which became the vogue in a certain group of boys was "Purrp!" The sound was made in a high falsetto, with the lips nearly closed. So rendered, it had an explosive quality, and carried well. There was an element of humor in it, and it was accepted as a witticism, or at least as a stroke of humor, whenever it was given. "Purrp" apparently started in the study hall kept by a man whom the boys disliked and found a bit ridiculous. It was at first merely an occasional means of tormenting this gentleman during his study period. Its vogue increased during that hour, and there came to be a pandemonium of "Purrps" at the beginning and the end of the hour. Then all boys entering and leaving this man's classes did so to the accompaniment of this yell. It had a personal connection, and this man's life was made an agony by the "Purrps" of unseen origin which followed him everywhere he went. It then became epidemic, and was heard everywhere and on all occasions. Other teachers intervened, and the behavior was suppressed.

Where there is a little bad blood between teacher and students, take-offs of the teacher have especial point for students. The teacher's mode of shrugging his shoulders, his smile, or any other slight mannerism may be taken up and satirized; this is usually reduced to a conventional gesture, and whenever the gesture is made the members of the group laugh. It is agreed that it is a joke. (How much of our most sophisticated humor is founded upon consensus! Say "priest" in a certain tone of voice to a member of the Ku Klux Klan, say "Rotarian" to a sophisticate, say "social worker" to a certain kind of sociologist or "sociologist" to a certain kind of social worker, and the joke has already begun.) These conventional gestures then degenerate and pass away, although they may persist for some time after the individual against whom they were first directed has passed from the scene. An ill-considered speech, or one too often repeated, is likely to be subjected to the same treatment. A certain man had difficulty with his students which came near blows. Not wishing to resort to such brutality, he told the boys a story of a chap who had made him really lose his temper just the year before. In his recital occurred the statement, "He was a great massive fellow, with the most massive shoulders and arms!" This was repeated hundreds of times among the boys and it never failed to evoked laughter. A high-school principal talked too often of what would happen after the partition was erected in the high-school auditorium; that became a stock joke. The president of a small college discoursed so often and so long upon the subject of a Carnegie library which he hoped to secure for the institution that the very mention of a library came to arouse the risibilities of the students, and finally some of the more enterprising ones secured an alleged library building, and located it by night in a prominent place on the campus.

Disorder itself is epidemic in a school. Teachers know well that certain behavior, once started, tends to go through the entire school, passing from one room to another with little loss of time and none of intensity. (The time that such an epidemic lasts, and the seriousness which it assumes, vary greatly according to the effectiveness of the teacher.) Such behavior is that of pitching pennies, dropping shot on the floor, throwing stink bombs, etc. When the school is located in a ramshackle building, it is possible for students to shake it by small and almost undetectable movements if these movements are properly synchronized; when behavior of this sort is once started it is very difficult to stop. Various kinds of laughter, mostly artificial and with that raucous quality connoting bitterness or disrespect, may become epidemic.

Yet other fads and crazes may happen quite inexplicably to fasten themselves upon the school and to compel the consent of all its members. Thus fads arise which call for certain kinds of pencil boxes, or colored crayons, or bookstraps. Or fads arise that call for certain articles of wearing apparel, and the child unable to procure such clothes feels quite out of place in his little world. A few years ago it was toreador trousers, a variant of the bell-bottom trousers, that became the rage in some of the high schools. These fads of school children furnish much interesting material for the social psychologist, and they might, if they were studied properly, cast much light upon the fashions of adults. The spread of rumor in the school, whether in the form of stories circulated by grapevine, or of tall tales about teachers, may also prove of considerable interest to social psychologists. We regret that our space does not permit an extended treatment of rumor.

In closing, we may indicate briefly certain considerations concerning the implications of this topic for school and social policy. We have noted that, for purposes of control by the faculty, crowd mind is much superior to mob mind. We might add that we shall very likely not be able to reduce crowd-mindedness in the school below a certain minimum. But we shall do well to remember that crowd-mindedness is dangerous, and that such mechanisms of crowd psychology as we employ for the control of the young may be laden with the most dangerous consequences for the future. For the mind of the crowd is slavish, and as susceptible to anti-social propaganda as to any other sort. Ultimately, education must individualize. And in the ideal school every member of the educative group will participate as a complete person, and not as the part of a person that makes a part of a crowd.

PROJECTS

1. Chart the interpersonal relations of love, hatred, fear, confidence, mistrust, rebellion, etc., in one classroom.

2. Study the distribution of personality types in a lecture section of one hundred or more.

3. Analyze the "personality" of a class and relate incidents showing how it was established.

4. Relate an incident which changed the tone of a class.

5. Study the underlying selective processes which, in an elective system, attract students to the classes of particular teachers.

6. Determine by questioning teachers and by study of grades whether teachers more easily establish cordial relationships with morning or afternoon classes.

7. Analyze the reaction of different classes to slight mishaps, such as stumbling, etc., of the teacher. Show type reactions which go with different kinds of rapport between student and teacher. Devise informal tests for teachers upon this basis. How must the teacher pass off these mishaps?

8. Take notes on a supervised study group. How does this form of organization reduce the tendency to mob-mindedness?

9. Compare successful and unsuccessful teachers in study hall. Describe the technique of keeping a study hall.

10. Write the complete story of a study hall or class that got out of hand. Interpret.

11. Describe a "psychic epidemic" in a school.

12. Give instances of fashion in the school.

13. Record "take-offs" of teachers and analyze their meaning.

14. Give examples of remarks or gestures which come to symbolize humor in the school.

15. Determine by statistical investigation what size of class is most favorable to voluntary participation of students in class exercises.

16. Inquire of some twenty or twenty-five students where they habitually sit in classes where they are allowed to choose for themselves. Characterize their personalities. Formulate some generalizations concerning the ecology of the classroom.

SUGGESTED READINGS

(1) Dawson, C. A., and Gettys, W. E., *An Introduction to Sociology,* Chapter XVII.

(2) Le Bon, G., *The Crowd.*
(3) Park, R. E., and Burgess, E. W., *An Introduction to the Science of Sociology,* Chapter XIII. (See bibliography.)
(4) Young, Kimball, *Social Psychology,* Chapters XX, XXI, and XXII.
(5) Young, Kimball, *Source Book for Social Psychology,* Chapters XXII, XXIII, and XXIV.

CHAPTER XIII

PRIMARY GROUPS AMONG SCHOOL CHILDREN

THAT those persons are most meaningful who are closest to us is not a startling bit of wisdom, but the science of sociology was overlong in discovering it. There are some associations in which we participate fully and without reserve, and there are others to which we parcel out only a grudgingly delimited segment of ourselves. Complete participation makes what Cooley has called the primary group. Partial participation makes the secondary group.[1]

Primary groups are intimate and personal in that they demand of the person his whole allegiance and his unreserved participation. In them the individual attains his most complete fulfillment as a person; bathed in the warm, rich flow of response which permeates the group, he can be conscious of no lack which is not immediately supplied. Because of the close person-to-person rapport that exists in them, primary groups tend to unanimity. Primary groups are usually face-to-face, for some physical intimacy and the supplementation of verbal communication by gesture are apparently necessary for primary group rapport. Primary groups are informal, for the intervention of social frames and forms, if in the least obvious, interferes with the spontaneous give-and-take of persons which constitutes the primary group. Primary groups are usually permanent and are very resistant to all the forces of change.

It is the personal attitude, however, which makes the primary group, and not the mere conditions of association. As people feel the life of a group to be unplanned and spontaneous, unlimited and without reserve, the group tends to become primary. Conditions of physical association make primary group life possible, but they do not ensure it. Secondary group attitudes can enter into the most intimate association and make of it a secondary group; this is exactly what happens in the family when discipline and the upholding of secondary group norms is too much at issue.

The life of primary groups, as Cooley states, is ubiquitous. Every human being tends to be drawn into some primary group relations,

[1] Cooley does not use the term "secondary group."

and those tend to be the significant relations ordering his life. This ability of primary group norms to establish themselves under the most unfavorable conditions has caused the failure of many social schemes which had as their goal the inculcation of virtue by machinery, for the distances which social arrangements are able to set up between men are melted away before attitudes which arise from the internal necessities of the men themselves.

The child participates in the life of many groups on his way to maturity. From time to time he enters new groups and leaves old ones behind. His personality must adapt itself, often by radical changes, to the demands of the new group and the new rôles which he assumes in it. In the best-ordered life there is some discontinuity and some lost motion in the development of personality. Where the change which is forced upon the personality is far-reaching, a considerable distortion, if not a definite splitting, of personality ensues. The continuity of personality is assured by such factors as make possible the continuity of rôles from group to group, and by such influences as limit the completeness of change of group connections at one time. Physical and mental characteristics which do not change, and previous social experiences which have given the personality a definite stamp, are things which cause one to assume similar rôles in group after group and therefore limit the change of personality. The replacement of one set of group connections by another is rarely complete in the history of the normal child, so that abrupt change of his social adaptation is not the rule. He makes the transition from one group to another gradually, or the membership of the group itself changes slowly. Some groups, as the home, persist while all others change. Investigators have thought that they could distinguish certain typical rôles customarily played among groups of school children. Among these are the rôles of the leader, the clown, the goat, the bully, the man of property, the man about town, the athlete, and others. It is thought that investigation might reveal a considerable consistency in the rôles selected by particular individuals in different groups.

It seems possible to speak of a certain order of succession of social groups as typical. Each of these groups appears in the life of the developing child at a particular time; each has its own peculiar contribution to make to his social experience, and each in time loses its importance. Each should, relatively, decline in importance when other interests intervene, but there are many cases in which this does not occur, and the individual is arrested in one developmental stage.

The home is the starting point of all excursions. In the home, the child is at first almost entirely passive in his reception of the cultural patterns impinging upon him. He is at first little more than an extension of his mother's personality; at this time he is perhaps more completely included in the group life of the home than he ever is in any later group. In the home the child learns, usually, the technique of response fulfillment, the interplay of one person with another. In the home, likewise, are absorbed the basic cultural tools without which later participation would not be possible; language is the most important of these. The child forms in the home the basic pattern of his personality; Burgess has suggested that the differentia of personality patterns are the modes of satisfying wishes. It is also important to note that social techniques have their beginning in the home. The home is the most important of the social groups with which we shall deal, and primarily for two reasons, that it forms the child before other groups touch him, and that it persists while other groups fade out. The importance of the home is not based upon its overwhelming influence at every period of development, for there are periods when the child participates with much greater interest in the life of his own age-group outside the home.

The home is soon supplemented by the pre-school play group. Here the social training of the child is continued, but with this difference, that he is now definitely among equals and has to learn lessons of a different sort. He acquires at once a technique of self-assertion in an environment where his wishes are less important than they are in the home, and some elementary knowledge of the rights and duties of others. Some inhibitions the home has supplied, but if the home has failed, the play group attempts to socialize the individual by imposing restraints upon him. The extreme penalty of the pre-school play group is probably not blows but isolation, and the genesis of many shut-in personalities is often explicable on the basis of unadaptability in the pre-school play group.

When the child goes to school he is confronted with a relationship of child and adult that differs radically from that existing between the child and the parent. For a few years the teacher may constitute a satisfactory mother substitute, but this does not last beyond the first few grades. The teacher-pupil relation has in it a much greater element of impersonal domination, and as time goes on the relation between child and teacher is increasingly a secondary group relation governed by secondary group norms. Therefore the primary group attitudes of the school child attach themselves more and more completely to his contemporaries. The child lives most really in the play group composed of children of his own age, and he comes to shut adults from that world with an impenetrable wall.

Primary groups of children are stair-stepped as to age; the tendency is for children to consort only with children of about their own size and age.[1] Membership in the group is usually denied to the younger child, something which mothers, who try to make older brothers include younger brothers in their activities, can never understand. Sometimes an overlarge child or an exceptionally bright one is admitted to the fellowship of those slightly older than himself, but this is rare. The child precocious in school is usually found in association with children of his own age outside of school. The group is a little more open at the top, but older children do not usually care to belong to it. The play group at different ages has different norms, and achievements are graded to the age and physical development of the members of the group. Ethical and intellectual norms differ and develop. What is permissible among nine-year-olds is not permissible when one is twelve. What was an interesting game when one was twelve is absurd when one has entered his teens. Humor differs and develops; the humor of the eighth-grader fails to amuse the grown-up boy in high school. Status in the group is seriously undermined by any failure to measure up to the standards of the age group. (It is always a serious symptom when a child prefers to associate with children younger than himself.) Emulation looks invariably to the next higher age group. The great heroes are children a few years older. There is little carry-over of status from previous age groups; the high-school sweater is ridiculous in college. Laurels do not stay fresh in childhood. Within the age group, rivalry is very keen. Competition becomes particularly bitter, and may go over into conflict when it takes place under the eyes of those a few years older. The following incident is typical:

I recall one peculiar fight that I had at this time. Another boy and I were playing around a tree and a young man was watching us. I tried to be funny and made up some silly little rhyme about the other boy's name. He started denying it and I kept repeating the rhyme. Then we began to slap at each other's hands. Then the fists began to fly and words stopped. There were some mighty hard blows struck. I hit him hard in the eye and he hit me hard on the forehead. That was enough for me. I went home crying and the other boy soon followed. I never did see why he should be crying. The young

[1] Cf. Blumenthal, Albert, *Small Town Stuff*, p. 226.

man moved on his way laughing heartily. Not only did I cry because of the physical hurt but also because of the hurt to my pride coming from being humiliated with that young man as an audience. I still hate him in memory. (Autobiographical document furnished by college student.)

Various writers have treated the types of association that arise among students of grade and high school. Thrasher has studied the life of boys in the play group which has become a gang. A gang is a conflict group which has arisen in the interstices of the adult social order by reason of the conflict between the wishes of the youngsters and the law-enforcing agencies of the community. Given a play group with opportunities for certain forbidden activities and for few others, it tends to fall into these forbidden activities and therefore to run afoul of the law. In consequence, it becomes a gang. Where there are more opportunities for interesting activities, or where the social order does not press so heavily, as in rural districts, the group does not become a gang because it does not come into conflict with the law. The present writer feels that the gang makes an indispensable contribution to personality, and a contribution which adults sometimes overlook. One learns morality in the gang and one learns to take punishment. Even a vicious gang is better than no gang at all. There is a progression in the activities of the gang conforming to the age, social maturity, and criminal experience of the members. The gang usually disperses at adolescence, because sex interests intrude and predominate.

Kimball Young has noted the congenial group, bound together by similarity of tastes and interest. Congenial groups are common among girls, where they manifest themselves particularly in the form of cliques. These girlhood cliques, however innocuous their activities by comparison with those of a boys' gang, and however silly their behavior norms to the outsider, are very important both to those who belong and those who do not belong. The group relations of youngsters of both sexes often take the form of one-to-one relations. The chum is very meaningful, perhaps more so than a friend is afterwards. Sometimes this has a homosexual basis, but if this generalization is limited to those cases in which overt behavior of a homosexual nature takes place, it is necessary to conclude that the homosexual explanation of the one-to-one rapport falls down.

Excellent examples of the congenial group are found on the college level. A student informant has furnished an account of such a group:

My group—since I am not a fraternity member—includes my room-mate and four fellows who live in rooms near my own. We eat together, go to the movies together, discuss any and all events together, and know each other's intimate friends. It results from such close contact that we comprise a very highly associated and connected primary group.

Within this primary group are institutions. These permanent behavior patterns which hold us together are such as common interest and desirability demand. A knowledge of good modern literature to the extent of being able to converse intelligently upon same is essential. This includes titles by Tolstoy, Eugene O'Neill, Mayo de la Roche, Conrad, Anne Parrish, Morley, and possibly H. G. Wells. We *must* have read something by each. Also, we are required to eat particular foods in a particular manner. If we are not very hungry we drink a tomato juice cocktail, eat a toasted sandwich, and drink a cup of coffee, eating as a finishing touch either pie, cake, or a baked apple with cream. We pass everything—slide nothing, never tip the waitresses. As to conversation—never use gestures, never point, but at least one curse is imperative in every conversation. Among other things a lie is absolutely not allowed. We must have had some intimate association with women, but must not dissipate as far as "the limit." The drinking of intoxicants is permissible but requires an apology.

A group which many youngsters skip is the sub-adolescent courtship group. Here the child makes his first tentatives at a heterosexual adjustment, and participates in a kind of courtship that is usually limited but emotionally absorbing. In the adolescent courtship group many interesting phenomena appear, some of which have been touched upon in a previous chapter. The transition from the sub-adolescent play group is sometimes an awkward one, especially as the members of one's former group often contrive to embarrass him in his new entanglement. This is the age of bashfulness and all social awkwardness, together with the vivid inner life that goes with it. Booth Tarkington's *Seventeen* is the story of a young man who has just emerged from the play group to go courting.

In these groups the child lives. Those who populate these groups are the real people of earth for him. The activities of these groups are vivid and interesting, and all else is dull by comparison. The loyalties of this world are paramount, and they exclude others. Adults do not enter this world. Most adults are shadowy and unpredictable persons who need only be reckoned with negatively; other adults are able to make themselves useful accessories. No more, for the thing is the game, and the people who matter are the members of the little group.

The primary groups of the young, arising in the interstices of the adult world, may furnish to the young a means of escape from the rules and conventions of that world. Mischief has often this explanation.

One Hallowe'en night I got in touch with two of the toughest boys in my school class. We decided to celebrate in royal fashion. We were in reality a crowd in action, not a gang, because we were not organized and had no program. We began to act. We put a dead chicken in one house only to have it thrown out. It was promptly placed in another house. Then a collection of garbage began. A good twenty gallons was distributed over the porches of the best houses in the town. Then porch swings were broken down and stacked most any place. A huge pumpkin from a back porch made a nice mess on one sidewalk. We kept at this sort of thing for over two hours, going about as noiselessly as possible. I then slipped quietly home and enjoyed a peaceful night's rest. The next day at school the principal made a special trip to our room to tell us of the atrocities of the previous night and said that boys in our room were suspected. Nothing more came of it, and so we gloated privately over our successful venture. That was one time I thoroughly escaped my rôle for a few hours and enjoyed what seemed to be entire freedom. The escape and the ecstasy of it still glow in my memory. Of course it all seems crude now, but then it was the living out for me of a great dream of escape to freedom. (Autobiographical document furnished by a minister's son.)

In the school, those bits of social ritual and rules of conduct known as tradition are passed on in primary groups. They are passed from the elders of the group to the younger, as all tradition—what matter if only a year or so separates elders and juniors? It is seniority in the group that counts. Tradition varies from school to school, but nearly all schools have some articles of tradition after they have been lived in for a while. There is a certain corner in which the big boys play, a seat that they alone may sit upon; there is a story, epic, Homeric, about a fabulous character of a few years before. One article of tradition that is unfailingly transmitted is the so-called school-boy code, which forbids students to tell tales upon one another. We have elsewhere explained that this has its origin in the conflict group morality existing between teachers and students.

A rather complicated folkway in groups of boys, and one whose explanation is not readily apparent, pertains to the informal initiation of a youngster by fighting. It has often been remarked that a newcomer among boys does not have status in the group until he has had a fight. After the fight, the group receives him cordially.

It was in A—— that I made my first boyhood friendship. A certain boy lived next door to us, and the first day we were in town I gave the boy some candy, although I eyed him rather suspiciously. The following day we met in the back yard in our old clothes and had a real fight. After a long struggle I won the battle and I was accepted into the life of the other boys, and from then on we were firm and fast friends. Thus was I taken into the new social group and accepted. The one fight provided my entrée, and after that my status was not questioned. (Ibid.)

One youngster whose parents frequently changed their residence relates that he developed a technique for meeting the problems of the newcomer most expeditiously and with the greatest possible advantage to himself. He would look over the new group carefully, and would select some boy who was a little larger than himself but whom he knew that he would have no difficulty in whipping. He would pick a quarrel with this youngster, and a very satisfactory fight would ensue. After that, his status among his fellows was assured.

The primary group of youngsters impresses some of the taboos of the older group, perhaps a bit more violently than does the adult group itself.

There are several specific incidents in my life here which are worth noting. I had often heard the epithet ——, but I did not know what it meant. One day I thought I would try that out on a fellow, and so I called him that. No sooner were the words out of my mouth than the fellow was on me and I was flat on my back. He pounded me thoroughly and I finally got enough breath to tell him that I would swallow those words. In this manner a meaningless phrase became a specially significant phrase. That phrase simply meant a thorough pounding. (Ibid.)

The boy had stumbled upon a "fighting word." It is important that these "fighting words," as an element of culture, have survived longer in the play group than in the workaday world of adults.

Hazing is sometimes in the tradition, but even when it is not, it appears naturally as a product of primary group life. That is why it resists so successfully the most determined and well-advised attempts to eradicate it. The elders are an in-group; in the primary group of children the elders are those who have been longest in the group. Newcomers are not admitted easily to this closed group. They are for a time regarded with suspicion and distrust. If they must be included in the group, they must submit gracefully to the period of probation and to some ceremonies of initiation. So they reason who maintain the standards of the primary group against the attacks of newcomers. Hazing rests upon this solid rock of human nature. Oddly enough, various kinds of hazing are in force on most faculties, even those most determined to suppress all kinds of hazing among students. The new member is never quite received into the fold. The older members of the faculty always take him at first on probation. He does not really belong. Sometimes this faculty hazing assumes a very definite form. There are many jokes to be played upon newcomers. There are ridiculous stories to be told him, and he must believe them or not. There are rules of decorum and of precedence which new teachers fail to observe at their own cost. In one private school for boys in an isolated community of the Middle West, a definite ceremony has been built up. The new teacher, always male, is never received into the brotherhood until he has joined the Elks. When he joins the Elks, he is well and properly hazed, and after that he belongs.

Hazing has had its apologists who have stated more or less clearly its merits. The most effective and perhaps the most justifiable form of hazing is the system of fagging as it has been developed in the English public schools. It is a most efficient mode of passing on the school ideals in so far as they have been assimilated by the students doing the hazing; it is a method of using the tame elephants to capture the wild ones. It does not in fact usually turn out so, for the faculty feels that an authority conflicting with its own has been set up by the hazers, and hazing does undoubtedly interfere with faculty control. Perhaps the best justification of hazing is that it has some value as a means of socializing overprivileged youngsters; these are at last brought face to face with an authority which wheedling cannot placate or bluffing terrify, and from which there is no appeal. Hazing is a part of a powerful engine making for conformity. It is the nature of the primary group life of school children to produce, by steady pressure, conformed individuals. All arguments that support conformity may therefore be advanced in favor of hazing.

The chief argument against hazing is that the person who hazes lacks the judgment to deal with the cases which he is accustomed to pass upon summarily. This is a valid objection. It is partly overcome by the fact that hazing is borne, in the majority of instances, with the greatest equanimity. It is in fact often ill-considered, but little vocal objection is taken to it, and the hazed one often takes a certain pride in the roughness of the treatment he is subjected to. If, however, a member of the faculty did anything one-tenth as extreme as the tyrant of the playground attempts to do, there would be a great deal of objection. The difference is in the relationship. There is not in the relation of student to student the latent hostility that exists between teacher and student. And the suffering of the hazed one is often balanced by the partisanship of the hazer which operates in his behalf at other times, and it is made bearable by the admiration of the young for those a little less young.

The determination of youngsters to stick to the standards of their own group, and their willingness to suffer any injustice from that group rather than betray it, are often puzzling to adults. Adults are only puzzled because they do not realize how mighty is the force of opinion in the play group or understand that status in that group does not depend upon adult standards. Where loyalties conflict, it is not easy to decide what standards should govern; the stool-pigeon is trustworthy from the adult's point of view but not from that of the insider. And what is humiliation in one group is honor in another. In a life history occurs the following passage: "I received my first licking at school, of which I was alternately very proud and very ashamed, depending upon the group in which I found myself. Among my classmates I was proud of having weathered the storm of a licking. Among my elders I was caused to feel ashamed, because, I suppose, I had violated some educational convention or taboo."

The boundaries of the primary group of children are not coterminous with the school class, and yet certain permanent patterns of relationship appear within the class. A sort of specialized and cumulative leadership grows up through the years of classroom association. A certain little girl becomes the actress of a class, and a teacher who chooses another girl as heroine of a play arouses horror and consternation in the entire group; the complex of attitudes which he stirs up is something like that which the coach arouses when he "benches" an athletic hero. Usually there is some boy who becomes the acknowledged orator of the class, and he habitually represents the class in public relations. There is a politician, who may be the orator or merely a silent boss. There are yet other specializations.

The attempts which members of the faculty have made to organize the primary group life of children and use it for purposes of control have generally been unsuccessful. It is a tempting vision, that of using the primary group sanctions of children, the public opinion of the school, to obtain, painlessly and perfectly, a conformity to the teacher-ordained social code. But somehow the realities of primary group life have always proved elusive. The formal group life of the school, that of classes, of ranks, and of teams, has, with the exception of the teams, failed to take hold. The Boy Scouts, with their nicely graded set of activities, and a set of corresponding distinctions, have done rather well in organizing the primary group life of children. The boys' club, under a suitable leader,[1] is possibly our best weapon for combating juvenile delinquency. But an entirely suitable technique for utilizing the primary group life of children for the inculcation of adult behavior norms has not yet been devised.

Yet nothing would be more desirable than that we should have a strong and well-organized primary group life of youngsters under adult control. The young can be initiated into the social life of the community only by slow stages, and can come to full citizenship only through a nicely graded and continuous progression of social groups that approximate ever more accurately the conditions of adult life. But character is formed in participation, and the groups through which the child passes on his way to adulthood must be such as absorb his interest fully and excite his deepest loyalty. Formal training, however nicely adapted and efficient, can never take the place of experience in the primary group. An analogy suggests itself between the child and the immigrant. Americanization studies have shown that the assimilation of the immigrant proceeds most rapidly when he is received into the group life of the American born, for he then absorbs the definitions of situations indigenous to the American culture and works out his personal problems by adopting a set of social rôles and attitudes not incongruous with the current definitions of the situation.

The barriers which separate the adult, especially an adult who happens to be a teacher, from the primary group life of children, are nearly impenetrable. But there are certain techniques by the use of which the teacher and the adult may obtain provisional standing in the group and perhaps an opportunity to peer through the door of the inner world of children with the consent of the observed. These techniques are well known, but will perhaps bear mention here. Basic to all of them is the attempt to make the members of the group believe that this one adult understands their peculiar customs and point of view. The teacher may, without loss of dignity and with great gain to his understanding, join the group of school children as an ex officio member. The male teacher may knock out fungoes to would-be ballplayers; in so doing he makes himself a great convenience, and he does not enter into definite competition with the youngsters, so that it is possible to keep his distance. A similar technique is that of merely showing interest in the more important business of youngsters, by supporting teams, etc., but it is necessary to remember here that a

[1] Leaders whose influence is entirely wholesome are uncommon.

verbal statement of interest is rarely effective, and that in general the teacher is the more convincing for saying little. Less ethical means of installing one's self in the student group are to join in ridicule or abuse of the school enemy, or to be tolerant of the persecution of the school goat. Some teachers who have the same students year after year attempt to solidify the group with themselves as members by taking a tentative or intolerant attitude toward newcomers among the students; it is an attempt that is more or less successful, but at what cost we do not know. It is important, if the teacher is not to lose his standing in the group, to deprive those whom he punishes of their group standing before proceeding against them. The teacher is by no means always successful in this. What the teacher shall do with this group standing we shall not attempt to say, beyond indicating that the possession of it will make it easier for him to live with his students, providing that he has not lost his standing as a teacher in gaining this primary group rapport, and that if he has it he may, if he is very skillful and very understanding, be able to guide the primary group life of children into wholesome and acceptable channels. It is this latter possibility which is in point here.

It occasionally happens that the conditions of life are so satisfactory at one stage in the development of one's primary group experience that the individual is not willing to pass from that stage to the next. It is a small world, but an interesting one, and he does not want to leave it. The full and satisfactory life of the school hero, surrounded with every distinction and constantly waited upon by obsequious adults and contemporaries ready to do him every homage, is a life that one is loath to relinquish. We find these individuals, sometimes, prolonging their school life by every possible device, and displaying themselves forever after in trailing clouds of prep-school glory. The world of amateur athletics is thickly populated with such individuals. In the adult world, of course, they display no high degree of flexibility. Michael Arlen has invented the term "prefect psychology" to designate the state of mind of those who carry over prep-school personal adjustments and social techniques into adult life.

PROJECTS

1. Study the political process in a self-governing play group. How are decisions arrived at? How is discipline enforced? What is ambition?

2. Study the play group relationships of a precocious child who is considerably ahead of his own age group in school. What problems does his social life present?

3. Make a list of the social groups which have successively been important in your life, and show the importance of each one.

4. Discover by inductive study the moral and ethical principles which have force in a play group of boys.

5. Make a case study of someone who exemplifies "prefect psychology."

6. Study the behavior of a "spoiled" child in his first play group. What effect did this group have upon his personality?

7. List members and ages of the principal play groups in one school. Do these data confirm or disprove the stair-stepping of these groups?

8. Make a case study of a younger brother. How complete is the younger brother's exclusion from the elder brother's play associations, and what is its effect upon the younger brother's personality?

9. Make a case study of a boy who likes to play with younger children.

10. Study the hero worship among younger boys of high-school athletic heroes.

11. Study the fights arising on a playground in a given period. Analyze the social situations leading up to these fights.

12. Write the life history of a congenial group.

13. Study the interplay of attitudes within a clique of high-school girls. Study especially the attitudes of rivals and of girls only partially within the group.

14. Study several chum relationships.

15. Record the behavior of an adolescent or sub-adolescent courtship group.

16. Study initiation ceremonies of a group of boys.

17. Study a group which hazes, and analyze its psychology.

18. Make a study of "fighting words" in a group of boys.

19. Study hazing on a faculty.

SUGGESTED READINGS

(1) Cooley, C. H., *Social Organization,* Chapters III-V.

(2) Krueger, E. T., and Reckless, W. C., *Social Psychology,* Chapter III.

(3) Peters, C. C., *Foundations of Educational Sociology,* Chapter XVI.

(4) Thrasher, F. M., *The Gang.*

(5) Young, Kimball, *Source Book for Social Psychology,* Chapter IV.

Part Four

THE TEACHER-PUPIL RELATIONSHIP

Chapter XIV

TEACHING AS INSTITUTIONALIZED LEADERSHIP

Leadership is the control of one individual over the behavior of others. Every social situation tends to polarize itself in the relationship of leader and led.

Some persons lead because they cannot help it. They lead spontaneously, and perhaps they lead without any awareness of the fact that they are leading. Park has noted that leadership depends upon a psychic set-up of expectancy, upon a certain eager attentiveness focussed upon the leader, and upon a willingness to take a cue from him. Such leadership arises inevitably from the association of unlike persons; it has its roots in the relative mental complexity of the leader which renders him unpredictable to those he leads. The leader must be a little readier to act than his followers, a little more determined to have his own way, a little more ruthless in carrying his projects through; the led must have some faith in the competence of the leader. These are the elementary conditions of personal leadership.

Other persons lead because they have to. A social situation has been set up and its pattern has been determined. The pattern is one which calls for a leader. The pattern governs also what the leader shall do with the led. This is institutional leadership.

Personal leadership arises from the interaction of personalities. It is an effect of personal gradients among the parts of a social whole. Personal interchange is at its height in personal leadership; there are no barriers shutting off one person from communion with another. In institutional leadership, personalities must be strained through the sieve of the social pattern before they can come into contact with each other.

In personal leadership, the properties of the interacting personalities determine the pattern of social interaction. In institutional leadership, personalities are forced to conform to the preexisting pattern; they are pumped up or deflated to make them fit their station. This is not to say that there is no pattern in personal leadership, but that the choice of the pattern and the place of each person in it are determined by the interplay of human forces in the situation.

The relationship of personal leadership arises when the group waits to see what some one person is going to do, feeling that what he does will be something very much to the point, and that it will be such a thing as the others would never think of. Superordination and subordination of this kind is determined by the relative range of personality and the complexity of mental organization of those involved in the situation. The extreme form of such leadership is found in the religious sect with an inspired leader, for then God is the leader, than whom no leader could possibly be more inscrutable or unpredictable.

In institutional leadership the leader has been established by another process, and he steps into a situation already prepared for him. Some sort of formal organization intervenes between the leader and the led. The extreme form of institutional leadership is probably that provided by the hereditary kingship. The king steps into the station made for him by his predecessors. His subjects wait to see what he will do, but, then, he must do what is expected of him, too. The school teacher is another kind of institutional leader.

In personal leadership, social patterns are always more or less in the way; that is why the dynamic leader breaks precedents. Personal leadership is borne more or less gladly, because it conforms to the realities of the situation; if conventionalized fictions come between the leader and the perception of the actual situation, he is an institutional leader. There is a need in human nature for personal leadership.

Institutionalized leadership gains by a clear demarcation of boundary lines and by rigid adherence to them. Personal influence must always be strained through the sieve of formality. Institutional leadership cannot remain institutional save by an insistence upon the lines of demarcation, for there is always a tendency for the human interaction in the situation to transcend those boundary lines. Where the pattern of leadership is predetermined, there must be a continual struggle to keep a more spontaneous kind of leadership, with the same or a different leader, from arising.

Institutional leadership persists because it satisfies a human need for dependence; it makes all a man's difficult decisions for him, and carries him along in a "moral automobile." But institutional leadership, no less than personal leadership, is ever destroyed and ever created anew; it seems likely, too, that because of its more rigid character, leading to a certain amount of inadaptation to the dynamics of present situations, and because of the conflict between institutional and personal leadership, the institutional kind arouses a greater amount of hostility.

But personal factors exist in both kinds of leadership, and patterns exist in both. In personal leadership, the social patterns are carried in personalities. In institutional leadership, the personalities are contained in the pattern—sometimes hampered by it as by a straight-jacket, sometimes expanded and ennobled to fit it.

All leadership proceeds from a mode of defining the situation. Institutional leadership sets up a ready-prepared definition of the situation and adheres to it rigidly. Non-institutionalized leadership defines the situation in terms of policies to be elaborated later, in terms of measures to be improvised according to the demands of the situation. Institutionalized leadership tends to break down under conditions of peculiar strain, and personal leadership, with its continual modification of measures, steps in to take its place. The peace time army can afford to be rigid, but under battle conditions it must improvise, and every subaltern in it must improvise, in order to adapt to the rapidly changing situation. Personal leadership tends to become institutionalized when time has made its forms explicit and usual, and when the mantle of the prophet descends upon his successor.

Some prestige is necessary for all leadership. In personal leadership the prestige attaches to the person. In institutional leadership, the prestige attaches to the office (and is more likely to be associated with a rebellion against the officer as a person).

Prestige depends upon idealization. In personal leadership, the elements of the person are selected out and made to fit into some prestige-carrying pattern. In institutional leadership the pattern is already present, and the individual must be assimilated to that pattern or to none. Social distance is necessary in both kinds of leadership, for prestige is usually an illusion produced by the partial perception of a personality and the fitting into the picture of qualities not incongruous with those perceived. But in institutional leadership the necessity for social distance is greater, since the pattern is more definite, and the chance of the leader's failing to categorize favorably if all his qualities are known is immeasurably increased.

Personal authority is the principle of personal leadership. The authority of the office is the principle of leadership that is relevant to the institution. Personal authority, because it is gladly borne and always in point, is arbitrary but does not seem so. Institutional authority, being subject to strict rules and a long tradition, seems arbitrary but is not. It seems arbitrary because it does not grow out of the situation directly but is imposed from without. It is really the leader that makes the difference; where the leader is determined by social interaction in the situation, his power is not arbitrary. But where the leader is determined otherwise, his power seems arbitrary. In the non-institutional situation the power of the individual depends upon the fact of leadership. In the institution, power goes with a certain official capacity and makes the leader.

The school depends almost entirely upon institutional leadership. Our discussion will be relevant to the kind of institutional leadership found in the school. We shall attempt to describe in detail and to analyze as minutely as possible the personal aspects of this process.

Much of our space will necessarily be devoted to an analysis of the technique of institutional leadership, its problems, solutions for its problems, devices used by persons to work upon each other in the institutional situation, etc. A word may be in order concerning the point of view from which this discussion of institutional leadership is oriented. We do not favor the kind of institutional leadership that is now in vogue in the schools. As between the narrowed and channelized personal interchange which now takes place in the schools, and the broader, freer communion advocated by progressive writers, our preference is for the latter sort of situation. But we feel that both the theory and practice of education have suffered in the past from an overattention to what ought to be and its correlative tendency to disregard what is. When theory is not based upon the existing practice, a great hiatus appears between theory and practice, and the consequence is that the progressiveness of theory does not affect the conservatism of practice. The student teacher learns the most advanced theory of education, and goes out from school with a firm determination to put it into practice. But he finds that this theory gives him little help in dealing with the concrete social situation that faces him. After a few attempts to translate theories into educational practice, he gives up and takes his guidance from conventional sources, from the advice of older teachers, the proverbs of the fraternity, and the commandments of principals. It is this failure of the science of education to deal with actualities that largely accounts for the slow pace of progress in educational practice. Be it ours, then, to try to understand institutional leadership in its present form and to hope that that understanding may lead to its reform.

Underlying our discussion of dominance and subordination in the school is the notion of the school as an institution. There is a certain routinization of the behavior of students and teachers. There is a pattern determining the situation; there is a set of interlocking definitions of the situation. We are discussing the interaction of personalities within that conventionalized situation. We shall discuss various means which teachers use for keeping students in line; this presupposes that there is a line. The ordinary situation of the ordinary classroom is the background of our discussion.

We may generalize a bit further concerning the characteristic features of institutionalized dominance and subordination. Simmel has endeavored to show how subordination is possible as a social arrangement between human beings. The gist of his discussion seems to be that subordination is possible because the relationship is meaningful to the dominant person, and, relatively, not meaningful to the subordinate one. Thus the dominant personality enters into such relationships with his whole personality or with a relatively large segment of it, whereas the subordinate gives but a small part of himself. One man may be ruler over millions, because the one man gives his entire self to the relationship; the millions participate in it but slightly. So by a psychic arrangement within the subordinated and the dominant personalities the permanence of a social structure is made possible.[1]

A certain conflict of interest must always exist between the person who rules and the person who is ruled. And there seems always to be a certain amount of friction between the persons playing those rôles as long as the relationship continues. But it is possible for the relationship to persist; subordinates do not always hate their masters, and inferiors do not always rebel, and this is because the flow of self-feeling in the subordinate is away from the relationship. Sub-

[1] We are conscious of some oversimplification. All of Simmel's three types of subordination are found in the school. Subordination to the teacher is subordination to a person. There appears also subordination to the group. Many teachers attempt to establish subordination to a principle; that is the meaning of "justice" in the school situation. We are discussing principally subordination to a person. The student should consult N. J. Spykman, *The Social Theory of Georg Simmel*, pp. 97-108; Dawson and Geddes, *Introduction to Sociology*, pp. 462-472; Park and Burgess, *Introduction to the Science of Sociology*, pp. 688-703; and Georg Simmel, *Soziologie*, pp. 141-186. The last, in a translation by Small, appeared in the *American Journal of Sociology*, Vol. 2, pp. 172-186.

ordination is bearable because it is meaningless. The self expands in a pleasant situation, and contracts in an unpleasant one. The self grows into a pleasant relationship, and moves away from a relationship in which one feels inferior or thwarted. Subordination in the institution is possible because institutional and non-institutional selves are split off from each other. The whole social order may be seen as a tangle of interlocking social selves. Every man must have some pride, and he must have some relationship in which he really lives. Defeated on one surface of the tetrahedron, he grows into another. When a thousand men come together, each striving to establish an equilibrium of superiority and inferiority in a multitude of activities, each continually altering his participation in those activities and revising from moment to moment the psychic weighting of that participation, each striving to obtain for himself a favorable balance of trade in that coin with which social debts are mostly paid, namely, praise, and each disturbing the equilibrium which every other has worked out, when a thousand men live together, then each man lives a thousand lives.

In terms of this psychic adjustment to the institutional situation, the struggle between master and subordinate goes into a new phase; the same mechanisms seem to operate in all kinds of institutions, in armies, churches, schools, and penitentiaries. The dominant personality strives not only to maintain the relationship, but to maintain and if possible to increase, its meaning. He lives in the relationship, and he expands into it. The subordinate, on the other hand, strives to achieve a psychic reorganization which will reduce the meaning of the relationship to nothing. The subordinate does not live in that relationship, and therefore superiors are not important as persons. This is a process which has many complications. It is important from the standpoint of sociology to remark that groups of superiors and inferiors commonly develop into in-groups. Each of these in-groups has its own life, which tends to be rich and full of meaning, and each has its own standards and its own morality. It is the problem of administration to prevent these in-groups from becoming conflict groups. The system of personal relationships is complicated by the entry of various mechanisms of abnormal psychology which are brought into play by the personal disunity which the complex situation engenders. Thus the subordinate commonly refuses to remain conscious of the actual meaning of the subordinate relationship, and compensates by an unreal phantasy life. The superior, too, must often repress certain elements of his personality, usually tendencies to social responsiveness directed toward his inferiors which might damage his standing in the relationship.

Formality is a compromise, an accommodation, which enables institutional leadership to survive. Formalities, a complicated social ritual and a body of rules and regulations, define once and for all the rights and privileges of all persons involved in the situation. Formality prevents friction by preventing the contact of personalities. Politeness is a device enabling us to get along with persons whom we do not like, more accurately, a device enabling us to get along with persons whether we like them or not.[1] Formality usually relates, on the surface, to the formulae of respect and consideration owed by the inferior to the superior; perhaps a return is exacted, such as the salute, but it may not be, as in the case of the "Sir" which army officers "rate." But formality is not wholly one-sided, for it confers an equal benefit upon the subordinate. It allows him, if he conforms to all external forms, to reduce the psychic weighting of these formulae of respect to nothing if he wishes, to mechanize the ritual of respect as he will, and to live his inner life on another level. We salute the uniform and not the man. And formality protects the inferior from arbitrary exactions of the superior. The social ritual of the Japanese under the Samurai prescribed how many teeth the peasant should show when he smiled in the presence of a noble; it was his privilege, then, to give of himself neither more nor less. It is a failing of the recently elevated to demand too much; this, formality prevents. The art of command is the adjustment of personality to the rôles that are most in conformity with one's station. Authority carries with it both privilege and inhibition; new authority is often irksome to all concerned, but old authority is as proper a thing as an old hat.

The teacher-pupil relationship is a form of institutionalized dominance and subordination. Teacher and pupil confront each other in the school with an original conflict of desires, and however much that conflict may be reduced in amount, or however much it may be hidden, it still remains. The teacher represents the adult group, ever the enemy of the spontaneous life of groups of children. The teacher represents the formal curriculum, and his interest is in imposing that curriculum upon the children in the form of tasks; pupils are much more interested in life in their own world than in the desiccated

[1] G. H. Mead speaks of good manners as a "means of keeping possible bores at a distance," in "National-Mindedness and International-Mindedness," *International Journal of Ethics*, vol. 39, 1929, p. 393.

bits of adult life which teachers have to offer. The teacher represents the established social order in the school, and his interest is in maintaining that order, whereas pupils have only a negative interest in that feudal superstructure. Teacher and pupil confront each other with attitudes from which the underlying hostility can never be altogether removed. Pupils are the material in which teachers are supposed to produce results. Pupils are human beings striving to realize themselves in their own spontaneous manner, striving to produce their own results in their own way. Each of these hostile parties stands in the way of the other; in so far as the aims of either are realized, it is at the sacrifice of the aims of the other.

Authority is on the side of the teacher. The teacher nearly always wins. In fact, he must win, or he cannot remain a teacher. Children, after all, are usually docile, and they certainly are defenceless against the machinery with which the adult world is able to enforce its decisions; the result of the battle is foreordained. Conflict between teachers and students therefore passes to the second level. All the externals of conflict and of authority having been settled, the matter chiefly at issue is the meaning of those externals. Whatever the rules that the teacher lays down, the tendency of the pupils is to empty them of meaning. By mechanization of conformity, by "laughing off" the teacher or hating him out of all existence as a person, by taking refuge in self-initiated activities that are always just beyond the teacher's reach, students attempt to neutralize teacher control. The teacher, however, is striving to read meaning into the rules and regulations, to make standards really standards, to force students really to conform. This is a battle which is not unequal. The power of the teacher to pass rules is not limited, but his power to enforce rules is, and so is his power to control attitudes toward rules.

Rules may be emasculated by attrition through setting up exceptions which at first seem harmless to the established order but when translated into precedent are found to destroy some parts of it altogether. One value of experience in teaching is that it gives the teacher an understanding of precedents. A trivial favor to Johnny Jones becomes a ruinous social principle when it is made a precedent. Or students defeat a rule by taking refuge in some activity just beyond its reach; what the rule secures, then, is not conformity but a different kind of non-conformity. Both teachers and pupils know well what hinges on these struggles over rules and evasions of rules. Johnny goes to the blackboard but he shuffles his feet; he is made to walk briskly but he walks too briskly; he is forced to walk correctly but there is a sullen expression on his face. Many teachers learn to cut through the rules to deal with the mental fact of rebellion; this is a negation of institutionalized leadership and requires a personality strong enough to stand without institutional props.

Most important in making conformity to external rules harmless are habitual adjustments to the inconveniences which teachers can impose upon students. A certain boy is in rebellion against the school authorities; he violates many rules and he devises new offences which are not covered by rules. Penalties do not stop him from breaking rules, for he is used to penalties, used to "walking the bull ring" or staying in after hours, and toughened to beatings. New penalties, likewise, do not stop him long, for he soon becomes accustomed to them as thoroughly as to the old. Likewise, it does little good to devise rules to cover a wider range of contingencies, for the new laws, the new risks, and the new penalties are soon a part of life. A social machine, however finely worked out, can never make a human being go its way rather than his own, and no one can ever be controlled entirely from without.

Dominance and subordination in the schools are usually discussed as "discipline." On the objective side, discipline is a social arrangement whereby one person is able consistently to exert control over the actions of others. Subjectively, discipline is the morale obtaining under institutionalized leadership. It is observable in the social interaction of the persons concerned, and it rests upon psychic arrangements in the minds of those persons. "Discipline" is often used as a value term to denote something regarded as constructive and healthful for the student or something of which the teacher approves.

In the bad old schools, partly as a result of the school curriculum and partly as an outgrowth of a stern ideal of character, an almost Spartan ideal of discipline was in vogue. Children had to do things they did not like because they did not like to do them. This rule had its correlate, of course, in that philosophy of the adult world, a philosophy not, to be just, altogether unproductive, that we should do every day something difficult simply because it was difficult, "to give the will a little gratuitous exercise." When such a philosophy ruled the schools, it was a mere incident of academic routine that if children were forced to do certain things because they did not like to do them, they did not like doing them because they were made to do them. The subtler personal effects of this sort of discipline were not considered. Education consisted of learning things one did not want to know because he did not want to know them. Whatever seemed bad was therefore good and what seemed good was bad. The best rule of school management was to find out what the children were doing and tell them to stop it. This disciplinary ideal must be classified with those other superstitions in our folklore, the belief that medicine is good if it tastes bad and that asafoetida keeps away the evil spirits. There is in fact more to be said for these primitive medical beliefs than for their educational parallels, for bad medicine may work because we think it will and a bag of asafoetida around the neck undoubtedly reduces contagion by eliminating contact. But education that is not in some sense pleasant is not education.

Discipline is partly personal influence and partly the social standing of an office. It is the resultant from the filtering of the teacher's personality through the porous framework of the institution. The larger the pores in the framework, the more personalities come into contact through it, and the more profound and permanent are the effects of social interaction. The more evident the social pattern in the schools, the less are personalities involved.

Discipline is a phenomenon of group life. It depends upon a collective opinion which superiors cause inferiors to form of superiors and of the tasks imposed by superiors. Essentially it depends upon prestige, which is largely a fiction, upon the ability of leaders to capture and hold attention (and by shifting objectives, to maintain the tonus of the relationship), upon formality setting the stage for social interaction, upon social distance which keeps primary group attitudes from eating away at formal relations, upon the reenforcement of respect for superiors by the respect of superiors for each other and upon the reenforcement of the inferior's respect for the superior by the respect which other inferiors pay him. (The maintenance of discipline may depend also, in the long run, upon the establishment of channels for the hostility of subordinates to superiors.) Discipline shows itself, in the group, as a one-way suggestibility.

The techniques used by teachers to maintain this mixed rapport, discipline, may be classified, approximately in the order of their utilization of the institutional and the arbitrary, and inversely to their dependence upon personal influence, as follows: (1) command, (2) punishment, (3) management or the manipulation of personal and group relationships, (4) temper, and (5) appeal.

(1) Institutionalized dominance and subordination appears in its

purest form in the command.[1] A command is a suggestion directed by the superior at the subordinate relating to the behavior of the subordinate. As a suggestion mechanism, it depends for its effectiveness upon the general conditions of suggestibility, upon the inherent suggestibility of the subordinate, upon the one-way rapport between superior and inferior, and upon the personal prestige of the individual from whom the command emanates. The command as such is most effective when most formalized, that is, when given without any personal implications. The presumption is present that the superior is willing to back up the command with all the (unknown) resources of his personality and of the organization of which both the superordinated and the subordinated one are a part. Army officers are accustomed to speak of a voice of command, which is strong and virile, but flat and entirely unemotional, takes obedience for granted, and is formalized as far as possible. On this latter point, note the military custom of mechanizing as many commands as possible. "Attention" means but one thing, and there is but one way of calling for attention. Likewise all commands relating to military maneuvers are completely formalized. There is a tendency for even these bare words to be reduced to their essential parts; thus "Attention" becomes "Tenshun" with an accenting and a drawing out of the first syllable and a sliding over of the last, and "March" becomes symbolized by "Ho."

It seems clear that the reason for a command should never be explained. Although it may be desirable on other grounds to explain it, it should be recognized that the explanation, by introducing an element of doubt concerning the command, or by the suggestion that it might not be obeyed, or by the mere weakening of the stimulus word by bringing it into connection with others, detracts from the force of the command. Certainly a command should never be coupled with a statement of grievance, for that will revive hostility and sometimes induce disrespect for the person weak enough to allow grievances to arise when he is presumed to be in control of the situation; this is an error common among mothers and weak teachers. Likewise a command that is couched in the language of the whine or the complaint operates powerfully to bring about its own frustration, for it calls into being a whole system of disgust reactions which militate against obedience. A plea is often used to back up a command, but

[1] N.B. Commands are often given in the non-institutionalized relations, but these are not formal commands. They proceed from whole personalities, and are directed at whole personalities; it is precisely this which is forbidden in institutional relations.

it seems certain that where this technique enables a person to obtain control it is the plea that does the work and not the command. A threat is commonly attached to a command, and the threat sometimes operates to give force to a command by attaching a fear sanction to it, but the threat detracts from the efficacy of the command as a pure command by presenting the alternative of disobedience, and by calling out the hostile attitudes implicit in the situation of dominant and dominated persons. It is likewise unfortunate to give a command in the form of a question, such as, "Will you shut up?" The giving of a command implies authority, real or theoretical, formal or personal. A command without authority becomes a mere exhortation, which is usually quite meaningless. In actual human relationships an attenuation of authority occurs by its being spread over a field so wide that it cannot hold. Thus a great theoretical but unenforceable authority is congruous with the issuance of exhortations, while the person of more limited authority can give commands.

(2) The sanction enforcing the command is formal punishment. Punishment is a measured pain or inconvenience imposed according to rule by the representative of authority upon those subject to that authority. Punishment is impersonal, unemotional, and proportioned to the offence rather than to the offender, every care being taken, in the pure case, to separate the offender and the offence, and to keep apart the punishment and the person inflicting the punishment. Punishment is usually justified according to a hedonistic theory of discipline. To every infraction of the rules must be attached a penalty just severe enough to make it unattractive. Students will be good because it will pay them to be good. Without embarking upon a theoretical refutation of hedonism, we may remark that punishment often fails to accomplish its purpose, even when the pains connected with it are multiplied far beyond any possible pleasure connected with a violation of the rules, because the causes from which offences come are more deep-seated than the remedies superimposed, so that the only effect of punishment is to enhance mental conflict, or to produce a more complex mental organization. It is not possible by punishment to produce very much effect upon a deep-lying personal hostility, except to increase it, or to deal with an irrational, unconscious attitude of rebellion.

A real value of punishment is that it serves to define the situation. It puts the student in the way of distinguishing clearly the permitted and the not-permitted, the right and the wrong within the complex social situation of the school. If consistently and unvaryingly applied, it tends to set up certain rules as essential limitations to action within the situation, and the student comes in time, unless motivated otherwise to rebellion, to accept those basic limitations and to adapt his behavior to them. A further value of punishment as it takes place in the actual social situation of the school room is that it removes the offender from the group. When the dominance of the teacher is threatened by some act of a student, it is imperative that action of some sort be taken in order to prevent others from copying the behavior and reenforcing each other in their derelictions. It is the use of formal punishment to put an abrupt end to the process of interaction which might ultimately lead to concerted rebellion by removing from the group the one from whom offence first comes. It may be that the individual is punished by some form of banishment, such as sending from the room, sending to the principal's office, suspension, or expulsion; in this case the isolation from the group is physical. If the offender remains physically in the group, the fact that he is under the ban, that he has an ordeal to face, or that he has lost standing through humiliation serves to isolate him from the group psychically and to lessen his influence upon other students. The effect of the punishment on the person isolated is another matter.

It is necessary to distinguish carefully punishment and not-punishment. A good deal of personal influencing that is not punishment is commonly associated with punishment in the schools. Punishment consists merely in the infliction of the pain, inconvenience, or humiliation that constitutes the substantial part of the punishment. Rarely is punishment pure, for it is usually mingled with all sorts of mechanisms of personal and social disapproval, with outbursts of temper, ridicule, threats, and intimidations designed to make the occasion more memorable or to furnish an outlet for the teacher's temper. These features of the actual social situation in which punishment is administered are not punishment, although they are almost invariably associated with it. They are means of exerting influence, and they operate according to the mechanisms of primary group life, which are not the mechanisms of formal relationships. A chief difference of effect is that these primary group influences tend to make the student ultimately become similar to the teacher as he really is, and have a deep influence upon character, constituting training by example and by manipulation of the life situation, while formal punishment is more narrowly concerned with a particular relationship, and does not permit much transmission of actual character traits. The epigram has it that character is caught, not taught; these personal outbursts accompanying punishment allow character to be caught.

Punishment is probably used more often for personal reasons than for reasons inherent in the formal relation; offences, likewise, often arise from the clash of personalities rather than from the formal structure. The usual thing is for the machinery of punishment to be made the means of carrying on the teacher's part of a conflict in which teacher and student become involved but which neither understands. It should be noted that punishment used for personal ends ceases to be punishment and becomes a feud or a struggle for status, an aspect of social life in the school which we have noted elsewhere.

Some further generalizations may be made concerning the use of punishment in the schools. The first of these is that there is in the school very little punishment as strictly defined. It is very difficult to keep punishment impersonal, under conditions of physical intimacy and constant association such as those in which teacher and student are thrown together, and therefore it is hard to keep punishment punishment. When the personal element enters into punishment, an intense hostility is aroused on both sides. The system of punishment is apparently at its best when the entire group, the teacher as well as the student, is regarded as subordinated to a principle; in this case the teacher is not the source and spring of punishment, but the channel through which it comes. If the principle is consistently but not fanatically adhered to, it may help to remove the personal element from punishment almost entirely. The difficulty is in finding a principle. We should note, furthermore, that punishment is bearable in proportion to the social distance of the person inflicting it from the person upon whom it is imposed; hence the advantage for the teacher of belonging frankly to the adult group and the teaching group. Nor can the necessity, for the teacher who punishes, of adhering to the code of fairness, and of treating all students alike, ever be too much emphasized. We should note that the personalities of students and teachers become deeply involved in the struggle over punishment in another way, through the attempt on the part of students to adapt their lives to penalties, making them therefore of little weight, and the opposite struggle of the teachers to find penalties with teeth in them. A new broom sweeps clean and a new penalty hurts, but both deteriorate rapidly. The tolerableness of human life results from its monotony, and any monotony is tolerable. Justice and the ease of human life result rather from completeness of adaptation to the basic conditions of association than from anything intrinsic in those conditions. We should record, however, that the mixture of control by punishment and control by personal influence that is now usual in the schools is one which does not contribute to the healthy development of the personalities of either students or teachers.

(3) A means of control that is important for many teachers we may refer to in the absence of a better name as management. Under this heading we should include all means of getting the teacher's definition of the situation accepted and the teacher's wishes carried out without a direct clash of wills between teacher and student. One of the most important devices to be included under this head is that of indirect suggestion, which many teachers have learned to use most effectively. Indirect suggestions are such suggestions as are carried in stories, fables, anecdotes, and general expressions of attitude toward actual or potential behavior. We should also include under the heading of management the principle of precipitating conflict at the time most advantageous to the teacher, at a time when the opponent, though definitely in the conflict, is unready or in some other way at a disadvantage. The policy most often followed by teachers is that of attempting to precipitate conflict before the student is emotionally ready; this is the policy, to use the slang phrase of teachers, of "getting the jump on them." Many sagacious teachers have also learned to apply this principle with reverse emphasis, to postpone dealing with an angry or rebellious student until his emotions have had an opportunity to cool. Both these empirical principles are apparently based upon a sound psychology; the emotions are of value in a struggle, they have a temporal quality, they cannot be called immediately into play, and they cannot last forever.

Under the heading of management, too, should be included all manipulation of the student in his social relations. Isolation is a powerful weapon. The teacher may ignore a student, or he may state or infer that this person does not really belong to the group, or he may, by curtailment of privileges, actually deprive him, for a time, of his opportunities for association with other youngsters. This is a long lever that makes dreadfully for conformity. The limitations upon it are the limitations of the teacher's ability to manipulate the pupil group and the undesirable effects upon the personality of the student if this technique is used recklessly and successfully. The teacher, again, may attempt to manipulate group alignments so that the ukase of the teacher appears to be backed up by the authority of the student group; a subtle example of this is the use of the first person plural in giving reprimands or rebukes, as, "We don't like that, John," or

"You are disturbing us," or "Can't you see we are busy?" Ridicule is sometimes used as a means of depriving the individual of status before punishing him. The effectiveness of these devices depends upon the effectiveness of the teacher's personality. If the teacher is thoroughly in control, the members of his class may feel flattered at being admitted into partnership with him, and will be carried on by this feeling to form their attitudes after his; but if he is not already in command of the situation, the whole procedure becomes absurd. Likewise, the teacher may attempt to manipulate home and community relationships with reference to himself and his students in such a way as to increase his own prestige. Thus he may cultivate acquaintance with parents, and may, in his dealings with children, refer to talks he has had with parents and attitudes expressed by them in those conversations. A classic device is that of holding the parent's ideals before the child. The teacher says, "Now, John, I know your mother would not want you to do that," or, "John, I know your parents want you to do well in school and grow up to be one of the outstanding men in the community." This device is mostly ineffective. If the relationship of parent to child is meaningful, and the meaning is of a positive nature, the child may resent having his parents dragged in by the heels by someone who has less weight or a different kind of meaning altogether. If the attitude toward the parent is mixed with a considerable rebellion, as it often is, the teacher-pupil relationship will be unduly complicated by the release within it of affects belonging elsewhere in the scheme of life.

There are other devices for playing upon the group alignment of children. Catching the child in one group, teachers attempt to obtain his assent to some general principle that carries over into the school group. If subtly done, this technique may be effective. When it is subtle enough to be effective, it proceeds no further than indirect suggestion, or at most to verbalization of things already in the child's mind. In the unsubtle extreme, it amounts to seizing a favorable opportunity to preach a sermon without receiving backtalk, or to mere posing in the presence of parents. The compartmentalization of the child's mind whereby one set of attitudes comes to expression at one time and another at another time—so that the child is hard and then soft—this too may be played upon. But such suggestions as are offered to a child when he is in a melting mood must be very indirect, else he will build up his defences and be soft no more in the presence of that particular person. Teachers are sometimes able, by long and serious talks, "heart-to-heart" talks, to induce this softened mood in their students and then to preach them a sermon. But if this is done, the teacher must not speak from the teaching rôle, for that will destroy any favorable effect, but as one human being to another. He must also be prepared to accept a resumption of the old relationship when the mellow mood has passed, with reserves restored and no further reference to the incident of communion and no effect traceable except perhaps a slight modification of the general attitude.

(4) Teachers also control by displays of temper. The display of temper is marked by diminution of social distance, by sloughing of social inhibitions and reserves, menacing behavior, and obvious, weakly controlled, or uncontrolled emotion. Control by temper is far down on the scale of social distance and high on that of actual human influence. Passion has become too much for social forms. The ritual has broken down and human personalities have come into contact without the intermission of buffers. It is implicit in the school situation that hates should sometimes run so high that they break through all barriers, and it has also become a part of the code. It is unwritten law that the only emotion a teacher can display is anger, that all else is softness. It should be noted that the technique of control by anger is often mingled with punishment, or confused with it. Strictly speaking, anger destroys punishment as punishment, but the machinery of punishment may be used as a part of the technique of control by anger, and it is probably so employed more often than it is administered without passion.

A person who teaches usually acquires a temper worthy of remark, or, if he is already blessed with such a characteristic, he learns how to use it more effectively. The manner in which this personality change ensues will be elaborated elsewhere, but we may note it briefly here. The strain of a situation created by the behavior of students mounts, in the absence of a technique for neutralizing it, until it becomes intolerable. An outbreak of temper ensues. Perhaps the teacher himself is surprised at the violence of his emotion. (Most new teachers report at least one such experience.) The teacher gains his point. He finds the school room thereafter easier to live in, his students respectful and perhaps even affectionate.[1] He cultivates a rapid-fire, intense temper. He expresses his grievances as they arise without reserve. Or the teacher does not gain his point, in this case he becomes frantic

[1] It seems paradoxical that affection should be won in this way, and yet there is much evidence that it often happens so. The explanation seems to be that the teacher has established leadership, and that students are grateful for the opportunity to be dependent. We must not forget that institutional leadership, for all the conflict that is in it, is real leadership.

and meets the situation with redoubled emotion and with increased energy, perhaps attaining ultimate success. Quickness in organizing anger, enough violence of emotion to carry one through the crisis and to inhibit all disposition to temporize, ability to maintain an angry attitude until the last vestige of rebellion has been crushed, all appear to be requisites of the school-teacher temper. The formation of a technique for expressing anger is important also in that the expression of the teacher's anger enables him to deal with the situation calmly afterwards and to minimize the holding of grudges. The effect of teaching upon the personality is probably to increase the total amount of anger in one's scheme of life, and this is deplorable; but if the emotion is there, it is probably better for the teacher's mental health and for his relations with his students that it should occasionally be expressed. Long-standing grudges, unexplained but persistent hates, are likely to result from strong emotions which remain long unexpressed. It is through these grudges, we should remember, that many teachers become involved in feuds with their students. Even grudges do not always appear to work unfavorably; we should not obscure from ourselves the fact that the dominant motivation of many teachers who are regarded as successful is an underlying antagonism toward students. These are teachers' teachers; they are as popular as a man's man.

The chief utility of anger seems to be in the transmission of taboos. The outburst of temper on the part of the teacher serves to establish very definitely certain things which may not be done. General taboos, pertaining to sex, to honesty, to manners, to cleanliness, or to fair play, may be effectively transmitted in this manner. The effect of these taboos upon the student's personality is not always favorable, but some taboos are necessary, and it should be remembered that the teacher is doing a useful social service when he transmits them. The teacher's own unadjustment, of course, enters here as well as elsewhere to limit his usefulness; it is much to be doubted whether the average spinster school teacher confers a benefit upon her students or upon society when she passes on to them her version of the taboos upon sex. Certain school taboos may also be transmitted through the medium of anger. These relate to the conditions of school life, and especially to the social structure founded upon teacher domination. Ultimately the teacher, by living within the rules and regulations and by being responsible for their enforcement, internalizes them; as a result she is able to use her personal resources for the defence of the established order in the school, and thereby to protect her own peace in the school. The human being becomes the embodiment of institutionalized leadership.

The effectiveness of such control as is to be obtained through the reconditioning of the teacher's temper depends upon the insight which the teacher has into the actualities of the pupil's mind and upon the integration of anger into the teacher's personality. Anger which goes too far defeats its own purpose; it arouses the bitterest hostility on the part of students and community alike. Most pathetic of all is the ineffectual anger of the teacher who never had, or has lost, the ability to control the dynamic social situation of the classroom. Such ineffectual anger, real but helpless, menacing beyond all possibility of making good its threats, makes the teacher fair game, and it becomes the part of valor to torment him. Such anger, interpreted by students as hate, and correctly, furnishes them with a motive for tormenting the teacher and with a means whereby that may be done. There is little escape from such a situation. The teacher hates the students because they torture him. The students hate the teacher because he hates them; therefore they torment him by arousing him to repeated outbursts of ineffectual anger. There is no remedy. Every school man has seen a number of excellent persons goaded almost to insanity by being in such a situation. For many the situation is made worse by reason of economic worries. The effect of such teachers upon students is of course not a favorable one, but these thoroughly inadequate personalities may in fact do less harm than some who are more effective.

(5) The technique of appeal is most often used for dealing with minor infractions of the rules, or, in a more important case, for effecting a change in the general attitude of the student. The appeal is an attempt to manipulate the child by calling into play, usually through verbal reference, some basic attitude or strong trend in his personality which it is thought will be effective in bringing him to conform to the teacher's wishes. An appeal may be direct or indirect, public or private, positive or negative in its nature. A direct appeal is what it purports to be and amounts to an exhortation with special reference to some supposed attitude of the child. An indirect appeal may imply this reference or it may be couched negatively, in the form of a challenge or a shaming reference.

Some of the supposedly dominant attitudes of children to which appeal is made are the parents' ideals, fair play, honesty, chivalry, or self-esteem. A favorite appeal is that to the ideals which the parents, especially the mother, are supposed to entertain concerning the child. "Don't do anything you would be ashamed to have your mother see you do." "I know what your mother would think of that," says the teacher, and the boy is then supposed to be ashamed of himself. Likewise an attempt is made to assimilate the school to the home: "I know you would not act like that in your own home. Why should you do it here?" There are reasons enough why he should, but the child does not know them! The sense of fair play is also called upon to enforce a certain amount of law and order in the school room, sometimes effectively. "Henry," asks the teacher, "do you really think it's fair to treat a smaller boy that way?" If Henry does not think it fair, he may conform to the teacher's wishes. An appeal is likewise made to honesty, usually in the form of praise for certain honest actions, and it is often successful. The self-esteem of the child is of course played upon in all these instances. Sometimes the appeal to self-esteem is even more direct. "I'd be ashamed, a great big boy like you, Leo, to make silly faces like a six year old." Or, "I'm surprised at you. I always thought you were such a gentleman." Women teachers commonly appeal to the sense of chivalry of the male students. In the unsubtle cases, the appeal takes about this form: "Well, just go on, now. I can't do anything with you. I'm just a poor weak woman." Women who know how to capitalize their sex more subtly may be able to do so with a considerable degree of success. Usually such appeals are quite hopeless, as is, for instance, the double-barreled one which assimilates the woman teacher to the mother: "All that I ask is that you show the same respect to me you'd show to your mother. Your mother's a woman, too, and she would understand."

Appeals which are most effective are those which are most delicately made. A frank appeal for help which a teacher makes because he cannot otherwise go on will usually, also, get a favorable response. More than once it has happened that a class which took no prizes for orderliness while the teacher was well and hearty became very cooperative when she sprained her ankle. The challenge, in the hands of a vigorous personality, can accomplish remarkable results. It is sometimes very strong. "You lazy boob, all you do is warm a seat. Do you think you'll ever learn anything? You're the biggest fool in school." When the teacher is vigorous enough to lay down his challenges in such a way that they cannot be avoided, he can often secure very effective control through that technique. It is a technique, however, which induces failure at least as often as success, and the wise teacher will use it soberly and sparingly.

Factors which limit the effectiveness of the technique of appeal are the social distance and antagonism between teacher and student and the lack of a suitable technique on the part of the teacher for discovering the dominant complexes of the student and adapting his procedure so that a real connection between them and the intended appeal can be made. Social distance obstructs appeal because it makes it difficult for the teacher to speak to the child as one human being to another. Antagonism between teacher and student tends to neutralize the effect of an appeal that really hits the mark; after one or more appeals the preexisting antagonism may cause the student to increase the social distance between himself and the teacher. Chiefly important in making the technique of appeal difficult is the utter lack of ability of most teachers in practical character diagnosis; the importance of this is obvious, because one must know what to appeal to before he can attempt to make an appeal; an appeal that goes wrong does more harm than good. Teachers sometimes attempt direct appeals in a very foolish manner and one that disregards wholly the existing attitudes of a child. Teachers commonly do not realize how necessary is a favorable rapport for any such suggestions as those we have been discussing; nor do they understand the technique of getting hold of a person a little at a time, of gradually building up a favorable feeling tone before attempting to make the relationship carry a heavy weight of suggestion. So little do teachers realize what emotional factors are involved in the appeals that they are trying to make that they sometimes do not hesitate to make their most intimate and touching appeals in the presence of a large group.

These are by no means all the techniques used by teachers in the attempt to maintain this mixed rapport which we call discipline. Probably all teachers use all these techniques and more, but with different emphasis and in different degrees. Particularly interesting, but puzzling as yet to the present writer, is the difference between the combinations of techniques used by men and women teachers. A considerably greater latitude seems to be allowed to men. It is thought that an analysis of the techniques used by men teachers would show that they rely more upon command than women teachers. This, however, is complicated by the fact that women teachers usually maintain a greater social distance in their general relations with their students, although their techniques of control are much more intimate in their nature than are the techniques used by men. Again, it seems possible that women can maintain in general a laxer discipline without losing control, and can without damage allow themselves to be imposed upon more frequently than can men.

The effectiveness of all techniques depends upon the personality into which they are organized and upon the teacher's understanding of the student mind. This understanding may be in fact of a very limited sort; it may be entirely limited to the school situation, and may run rather to manipulation than to general understanding, but it is always important. Since the effectiveness of any technique is a personal matter, depending upon the technique plus the total effect of the personality of the teacher using that technique, it will be well to turn to a discussion of those traits which seem to determine the impression which the teacher's personality makes upon his students.

PROJECTS

1. Study the pattern of leadership which arises in a group of college students who, previously unknown to each other, decide to work together on a committee.

2. Study the same pattern on a faculty committee.

3. Make a list of defence mechanisms by which students reduce the meaning of obedience to faculty demands.

4. Make a study of "precedents" established and overthrown in the daily contact between teacher and pupil.

5. Make a historical study of rules, regulations, and precedents in a private school.

6. Study the effect of a new rule, the effort of the faculty to enforce it and to make it meaningful, and the effort of students to destroy its meaning.

7. Analyze the technique of some teacher who attempts to disregard the technical aspects of rules and to deal directly with rebellious attitudes.

8. Study a boy who has become accustomed to punishments.

9. Watch an army officer drill the R.O.T.C. Analyze his technique. Pay particular attention to bearing, voice, formality, etc.

10. Study the disciplinary activities of several teachers and analyze their use of the techniques discussed in the chapter.

11. Report incidents illustrating the definition of the situation through punishment.

12. Describe the techniques followed by a number of teachers in imposing punishments. Analyze the effects of these. Relate to personalities of teachers and students.

13. Relate incidents showing the successful and unsuccessful use of appeals. Relate success or unsuccess to the personalities of the teachers.

14. Relate instances illustrating successful and unsuccessful uses of "management."

15. Make case studies of good and bad teachers, showing their use of temper as a means of control.

16. Study several high-school students carefully with a view to ascertaining what kinds of appeals might most successfully be made to them.

17. Make a number of case studies with a view to comparing the techniques of control of men and women teachers.

SUGGESTED READINGS

(1) Clark, T. A., *Discipline and the Derelict.*

(2) Cooley, C. H., *Human Nature and the Social Order,* Chapters VIII and IX.

(3) Park, R. E., and Burgess, E. W., *An Introduction to the Science of Sociology,* pp. 688-708.

(4) Sorokin, P. A., *The Sociology of Revolution,* Chapter VIII.

(5) Young, Kimball, *Source Book for Social Psychology,* Chapters XX and XXI. (See bibliography.)

(6) Young, Kimball, *Social Psychology,* Chapter XV.

CHAPTER XV

TRAITS DETERMINING THE PRESTIGE OF THE TEACHER

THE realities of control do not reside in the theoretical institutional structure of the school, but in the interaction of personalities that takes place within that structure. We turn, then, to a discussion of the influence of personalities filtered through an institution.

We shall attempt to discover the institutional significance of the personality traits of the teacher. The more important traits known to affect the prestige of the teacher and his ability to control the classroom situation may perhaps be discussed under the following heads: age, social background, physical characteristics, dress, manners, manner, attitude toward students and subject matter, voice, expression of features, tempo of reactions, range of mental personality, and the nature of the organization of the personality (in which are included such factors as complexity, stability, etc.).

Age, as it affects the teacher in his relationship to his students, is not wholly a matter of years. It is rather an affair of social experience, poise, and of the maturity of understanding, judgment, and interests which enter into it. It is, as we have noted elsewhere, a matter of the basic configurations into which one's inner world is organized, and of the portion of the cultural heritage one has absorbed as well as the way in which he has experienced it. (Cf. the discussion of different age and culture levels.) Teachers who are young in this sense, usually young in years as well, commonly suffer from their inability to maintain social distance between themselves and their students.

The natural social distance between adult and child, a distance which gives rise sometimes to mutual misunderstanding amounting to enmity, is at a minimum when, as not infrequently happens in the high schools and colleges, adolescents are taught by late adolescent or post-adolescent teachers. Teachers who are too close to their own adolescent frame of personal organization, and to the social and mental world of the late years of childhood, tend to be caught up in the social interaction of children and involved in their social life. We all tend to live most really and most deeply in the world of our contemporaries, and a high-school boy or girl takes more definite shape as a human being and a considerable personality in the eyes of the post-adolescent teacher than the principal of her high school ever can. The things students say will be noted and remembered because they are understood, but the remarks of the principal will be thought the pointless maunderings of toothless senility, to be laughed off and forgotten in the next moment. Because of the essential similarity of interests of the young teacher and his young students, the social world of the students presents the teacher with an alluring opportunity for that self-realization which is withheld from him in his contacts with the teacher world by reason of his youth, and which is achieved there in a most imperfect fashion at any age. The social situations presented by the life of students must inevitably seem to the young teacher very intriguing, and it will only be by the exercise of the greatest self-control that he will succeed in refraining from entering into them. It is not easy to stand on the sidelines and disapprove and censure, or approve and applaud, when one longs to be in the center of the arena. The young teacher longs for a greater participation. His need is enhanced by the poorness of the opportunities for desirable social life in the community at large.

The teacher, however, who comes to be involved in the social life of students loses all the privileges and exemptions that would accrue to him if he were frankly a member of the teaching group and no other. He must pay in the students' world for the crime of being a teacher and in the teachers' for the sacrilege of being friendly with students. And the attitudes which both teachers and students form toward him are incompatible with further functioning in the teacher rôle. The primary group attitudes which students have toward him lose him the immunity that teachers enjoy for the injustices they put upon children; and when he is called upon to give a reason for his authority, it usually occurs that he cannot answer. Trying to reconcile friendship and authority, he ends by losing both.

The situation which arises when students and teachers live in the same social world is damaging to the teacher in yet another way. The teacher who enters the world of the students does so for the sake of personal self-realization; from this it ensues that though he may be friend and ally to some he will be rival or enemy to others. Rivalry between teacher and student is thus in part a result of a previous entry by the teacher into the students' world. It is also one of the mechanisms whereby the young teacher becomes drawn into that world. The young teacher and student are striving for the same sort of self-expression, they are striving for the same prizes; hence they compete with each other to excel in this or to obtain possession of that. This changes the teacher's rôle from that of the somewhat aloof friend and helper to that of the competitor. Older teachers learn to sublimate their own thwarted wishes in furthering the self-development of others, but almost inevitably the young teacher, since he has not found his place in the world, or has not, as many older teachers do, given up the hope of finding such a place, is concerned with the making of his own career. If that career is not to be made in the students' world, students are nuisances or else mere chessmen, which is perhaps the explanation of the alleged fact that teachers who are young and much in earnest give the lowest marks and take the most ruthless disciplinary action. If that career is thought of as capable of being realized, in part at least, in the students' social world, the teacher ceases to be a helpful elder and becomes a contemporary rival. Enemy morality motivates, as his inexperience makes possible, rebellion against the young teacher.

Young teachers have not yet worked out the problem of their own destiny, having neither achieved that destiny nor yet accepted it as a fact that they have none. They have not found their mates, and often they have not found a permanent vocation. From this unsettlement arise some interesting consequences. There is first the fact, apparently inevitable, that such teachers are more interested in their own achievements than in those of their students, which materially affects the opinion students have of them. The situation of the young teacher who has not yet found himself is distressing in another respect: he is expected to give guidance to others when he has obtained none for himself; it is his duty to give travelling directions in a country whose topography and speech he knows only a little better than do his charges. In smaller communities the situation of young teachers is affected by the attitudes which parents take toward their efforts to find a place in the world. Here the difficulty arises because the parents are older than the teachers and therefore have a different attitude toward life, because the parents have the attitudes of a previous generation, because parents are usually married persons and young teachers are usually not, because parents are rural and teachers have probably been exposed to urban influences, and because the community does not believe that teachers should attempt to find a personal niche in life. These are irreconcilable differences in point of view, and seem to account in large part for the fact that parents so bitterly criticize teachers who insist upon living from Friday to Monday. We are here concerned with the fact that this criticism of teachers by parents, especially if it takes the form of gossip, undermines the standing of the teacher in the eyes of his pupils.

Youth has some advantages, even in the teaching profession. Young teachers are more likely to represent an ideal than are older teachers because they are almost of the current generation and their accomplishments and ambitions have not yet become passé, because they have retained the vigor and attractiveness of youth, because their faces are unfaded and their arms are still strong, and because their predominant interests are still those of adolescence. The ideal which they represent is, relatively, attainable, and it is understandable because only a few years of achievement separate them from students. Because of the physical attractiveness of youth, young teachers are more likely than old ones to become love objects for their students, which gives rise to a rapport which is unsatisfactory, but is often utilized. Young teachers, further, are aided in their contacts with students by a greater understanding, on a quite personal basis, of the problems of youth and of this particular generation—an understanding which arises from their nearness to the problems and the people who have them. This understanding, however, can never be so satisfactory as that of a person who has passed through youth and has solved its problems but has not lost sympathy or contact with the rising generations.

The older teacher more easily secures subordination. He categorizes as one of the elders, becomes a parent substitute and therefore endowed with authority. The older teacher, furthermore, has achieved through age that ossification of the mind and social inflexibility which are of such value in getting one's way with the young (through the channels of institutional leadership). He never becomes involved in the social situations of the young, he never sets up as a rival, and his very inability to solve his own problems in previous years may even operate to make him more interested in the achievements of the young. He achieves vicariously through his students. He can never become involved in the social life of the young because of his age and the social distance that goes with differences in age. He can never be a person to his students because his students are not persons to him; being no person, he has authority, but no influence.

But age is not wholly advantageous. Because of the distance in years between the teacher and student and because of the intervening generations, the difference of experience, of ideals, of standards, and of mores may become so great that teacher and student have no common ground and each is wholly unable to understand what the other is talking about. This occurs the more frequently because teachers, in our culture, being uprooted and deprived of intimate contact with the procession of the generations or the life of particular communities, being regarded not as persons but as agents of cultural diffusion, the sooner lose the bloom of youth themselves or an appreciation of its value to others. School teachers, it has been remarked, lose their mental plasticity prematurely. If they do not completely lose the identifying marks of youth, they learn to preserve a neutral personality and to depend upon the school-teacher stereotype to make them old in the eyes of their students. The very old, of course, lose their ability to maintain authority by reason of the degeneracy of age.

The teacher-pupil relationship seems to realize its best possibilities when the teacher is a young adult, a young adult far enough away from adolescence to have solved his own problems but near enough to be understanding and tolerant, far enough from the students' world never to become a rival and close enough to maintain an interchange of feelings and ideas, far enough removed in age from his students to classify definitely as a member of the adult generation and young enough not to represent a horrible example of what normal young persons do not want to become. This generalization, though based upon a different body of facts, seems to be reenforced by certain studies of gains in teaching efficiency through experience and the passage of years; these studies show the point of maximum efficiency to be reached after about three years of experience. The fact that teaching is a routine job accounts in part for the short period in which learning is possible or necessary, but it would seem that, if the teacher were given an opportunity for a greater degree of personal growth and development, a longer period of increase in teaching ability would result.

The social background of the teacher is readily apparent to students, and it affects the attitude which they have toward him. In every instance the teacher, as the paid agent of cultural diffusion, must represent a level of attainment in certain formal values of education somewhat above the average level of the community. Sometimes these educational values correspond closely to the general cultural and social values of the community. Where they do not so correspond, we must orientate our discussion with reference to the actual values of the community. In the smaller communities there are numerous examples of teachers who should be classified as to family background, early training, and personal cultivation as much superior to the community in which they live. Where this distinction is too great, it interferes with the prestige of the teacher. The teacher is affected, snobbish, conceited, lacks touch with the realities of human life, is "high-hat," and given to "lah-de-dah" ways. Thus in a rural community a young woman teacher was severely criticized for manicuring her finger nails. The man of unusual cultivation is often subjected to criticism on the grounds of unmanliness. In private schools and the high schools of exclusive suburbs the reverse situation is to be found. Children are taught by teachers who have less economic standing and less opportunity to enjoy the so-called good things of life, if they have not less culture, than their parents. Provided that the lack of personal refinement is not so extreme as to lead to disgust reactions on the part of the students, the effect, as regards the maintenance of school authority, is not undesirable. The personalities of the teachers, stabilized, relatively uncomplicated, relatively simple, and direct, produce upon the students who have been reared in homes of much culture an effect of coarse virility, which may in many cases furnish desirable elements to the ultimate make-up of the child's personality. The coarseness of the teachers and the slight value they put upon the amenities constitute a reason for laughing off their contributions, but that does not destroy the power of their personalities or their vigor of speech, or prevent these individuals from exerting a profound and favorable influence upon their students.[1] Dominance seems to be most easily maintained, however, when the teacher, without attaining cultivation which prevents him from being understood by his students or knowing what they are thinking about, represents a level of attainment slightly above that known to his students. The teacher has most prestige when he has attained those things which the parents of the children he teaches would like to attain.

[1] A recent study at Pennsylvania State College shows the following (special technique) correlations between teacher success and father's occupations:

Father's Occupation	*Elementary Teachers*	*High-School Teachers*
Professional men	0.124	0.104
Business men	0.564	0.077
Farmers	0.000	0.361
Artisans	0.281	0.004
Laborers	0.484	0.017

(From "Pre-Training Factors Predictive of Teacher Success," pp. 7-12, doctor's thesis at Pennsylvania State College, 1931, by Harry L. Kriner; unpublished. Abstract published in *Abstracts of Studies in Education*, edited by C. C. Peters and F. T. Struck, School of Education, Pennsylvania State College.)

The above figures seem approximately to bear out our theory. The present writer would suggest that the reason for the smaller correlations for the group of high-school teachers is perhaps the longer period of time spent in training, emancipating them more completely from the social backgrounds of the parents, and the fact that a more select group survives the longer training period.

Certain empirical generalizations may be offered with regard to the effect upon students of physical characteristics of teachers. The physical appearance of the teacher is important, but because of the different meanings attached to different traits when they are incorporated into different personalities it becomes very difficult to reach anything further than the most tentative conclusions concerning particular traits. The problem is further complicated by the fact that men and women differ widely. Size, the appearance of health and strength, stamina, some strength, and the absence of ridiculous characteristics are apparently important for both men and women, but they are important in slightly different ways, so that it will be necessary to discuss them separately. For men, size and the appearance of strength are apparently the most important physical characteristics. The man below the average in size, or perhaps the man not apparently above the average, is at a handicap in dealing with children of high-school age. The small man apparently fails as a disciplinarian for two reasons: one, the fact that he appears somehow ridiculous to his students, and the other that he is very likely to have a feeling of inferiority that makes him either timid and unassertive or causes him to look for trouble. The reason why the small man is ridiculous, unless he be indeed a homunculus, is not easy to find, but we do know that the ridiculous element is there. It has often been remarked that the absurd person of the stage is nearly always a very small or a very fat man. Perhaps the essential absurdity lies in the contrast between the exaggerated claims which such men make upon our attention and consideration and their real importance when they are judged, as men must always be judged by many people much of the time, in terms of their size. The physical insignificance of the small teacher contrasts sharply with his institutional importance, and therefore he is funny. Any physical trait other than size which appears ridiculous will hinder the teacher in his attempt to maintain dominance over his students. Effeminacy of features, or lack of physical force, may in this sense handicap a man.

Height is apparently the most important element in size. What its influence is remains something of a mystery, but it is assuredly true that much of dominance and subordination is in terms of looking up and looking down, especially as between members of the same sex. Breadth of shoulder is also important, and in a more obvious manner. The set of the jaw, the pitch, inflection, and the intonation of the voice, and the expression of the eyes have a real significance. The appearance of strength is more important than the actual strength of the teacher; actual strength may be considered occasionally, but it is considered less than the mere appearance. Among business people the handclasp is recognized as of extreme importance; dominance and subordination, as well as those first impressions of strength, vigor, and cordiality, are decided in terms of the strength of the grip. Important in the handclasp are the strength and the vigor of shaking, both of which are utterly spoiled if they appear self-conscious. (Handshaking is probably of very little importance for the teacher.)

It is not easy to explain how the size and strength of the man teacher influence the attitudes which students have toward him. An explanation which has possibly been overworked in the past is that the large man makes a good leader because he is an attention-getting object merely by virtue of his size. One is inclined to reject the hypothesis that size helps the man teacher because he appears able to master his students physically, but the possibility deserves consideration. This sort of thing could be important as a subconscious hangover of physical domination. A consideration of the negative cases almost forces one to conclude that size and strength are a part of our masculine ideal, perhaps derived from the early image of the father, and that the large, strong man has prestige because he conforms to the ideal. Of some importance, too, is the fact that the large man is easily distinguishable from students. That the prestige of the large man has a subrational basis seems sure because of the fact that the prestige persists even when the appearance of strength and competence is shown to be fallacious. One generalization that may be made with a considerable feeling of safety is that the adjustments of personality that go with satisfactory size are at least as important in determining teaching efficiency as is size itself. The relatively great stability, the high margin of equanimity, self-assurance, and freedom from rivalry with students that go with size do much to make large men fortunate in their relations with students. This belief is further corroborated by the fact that small men have occasionally found it possible to substitute personality adjustments for conspicuous size.

An even more puzzling topic is the relation of the physique of women to their prestige among students. Size is apparently of less importance for women because it is not definitely a part of the feminine ideal and because women teachers maintain a kind of rapport further removed from any conceivable resort to physical strength than that of men. Extremely small women, however, are definitely at a disadvantage in holding the attention and maintaining the respect of high-school classes. For different reasons, extremely large women are likewise at a disadvantage; the reasons here are that large women have inferiority feelings analogous to those of small men, and that large size, especially if it is the size of corpulence, is much more likely to be ridiculous in a woman than in a man. Apparently bulk is still an advantage for women teachers. It seems also that women are more likely to succeed in teaching who have a rather large dash of the masculine in their physical make-up and behavior; that this is a circumstance laden with danger for their feminine students is a conclusion that seems obvious. Analysis of the rôle of physical characteristics of successful teachers forces us to conclude that for women, as well as for men, the influence of these traits upon the general personal organization is probably more important than are the traits themselves. One frame of personal organization which is often connected with certain physical qualities is that which leads students to look upon the teacher as a real or potential love object. The personality make-up is that which gives the teacher a lowered threshold for coquettish interplay with her students. Generalization is again difficult, but it seems that rapport based upon sexual attraction is short-lived and unstable, likely to be easily metamorphosed into definite courtship or active sex antagonism.

The dress of the teacher is thought to affect his prestige noticeably. All extremes are therefore usually avoided by those familiar with teacher tradition. Men teachers are usually quite conservative in dress, running to the middle-aged styles and the undistinguished colors. It seems the rule that men teachers pay relatively little attention to dress. Perhaps this is because dress has chiefly a negative value for them; they can lose prestige through dress, through extreme slovenliness or dandyism, but they can gain none; clothes are therefore a requirement to be slighted if possible. There is a very explicit tradition concerning the dress of the woman teacher. Almost every reader, in fact, will find himself calling up some definite visual image of the dress of the typical school mistress. Even more than men, women teachers must dress conservatively. As do the men, they dress for utility and not for display, but this characteristic is more noticeable in their case because standards of dress for women are different. Whereas other women dress to emphasize feminine characteristics, women teachers dress to obscure them. From the larger point of view it is regrettable that in time they lose either their interest in dressing for display or their ability to dress sex-consciously, and it is a fact that may have something to do with the general unmarriageability of school teachers. But from the point of view of the schools, the demure dress of women is possibly a very good thing. Occasionally, however, there appear in the schools women who by the quiet good taste of their apparel are able to gain the respect and admiration of all their students. In such cases, dress is an asset. Women who gain prestige by dress are much more numerous than men.

The manners of the teacher are chiefly important as they cause him to categorize favorably or unfavorably on the matter of his social background. This we have elsewhere discussed. This is not all, however, for manners, especially decorous, even courtly, manners are important means of maintaining social distance. In addition, good manners suggest that the teacher respects students and argue powerfully for respect for him.

A different matter, but an allied one—no play on words, at any rate—is manner. Manner, too, conveys an impression as to social background. Perhaps it conveys a truer impression than do manners. Manners are in decay. (It has been truly said that the members of certain younger sets have no manners but a manner.) Manners, too, may be more convincingly imitated in the synthetic varieties than a manner may. But to give a favorable impression of one's presumed social background is by no means the chief function of manner. When we speak of a manner we refer to a total impression of the personality, an impression to be thought of as largely a by-product of the person's habits of social expression. In the manner there is always an element of self-consciousness. Manner is demeanor rather than simple behavior. Certain manners which are easily recognized are: the competent manner, the efficient manner, the arrogant manner, the modest manner, the timid manner, the fault-finding manner, the brusque manner, etc. To analyze the effect of each of these manners upon the classroom life of student and teacher would be long, perhaps it is enough to remark that each manner has its own meaning in the school. One deserving of special attention is what is popularly known as the classroom manner, a manner supposed to be acquired by teachers in the classroom and carried over into life outside. The classroom manner is dry, authoritative, and runs to didactic inflections; it represents an admirable adaptation to teaching conditions.

Mannerisms represent the breakdown of the manner, the point where it fails to convince, or where it becomes so obviously artificial as to hold an element of the ridiculous. Mannerisms have no little importance in the social life of the school room. Mannerisms are personal peculiarities, usually considered ridiculous, and sometimes characterizing the person sharply. Usually they are compensatory in their nature. A person who has adopted a manner which he cannot quite carry may give expression to the other side of his personality in occasional gestures, which have deep personal significance as expressing the less visible side of an ambivalence. Or a person conscious of a weakness may fall into some mannerism in his attempt to remedy the weakness or to conceal it from others. Nervous teachers fall into many mannerisms of gesture, which either serve as releases of unconscious tension or are intended to fortify them in the eyes of their class. Mannerisms may appear otherwise, as a sort of expression of a general attitude; the cynical man learns to shrug his shoulders cynically. It is difficult to generalize about mannerisms because they may mean anything. As a rule they have, as we have remarked, great personal significance. Students learn these mannerisms quickly and learn also to judge accurately of their significance, at least as regards themselves. They learn, of course, to mimic the mannerisms of the teacher, which helps to make life more bearable for them and only in the extreme case less bearable for the teacher. Pupils also acquire a certain kind of control over their teachers by a knowledge of their mannerisms. When the teacher says, "Don't," but does not change his facial expression, he is merely enforcing discipline, and the consequences may not be disastrous if, after a discreet interval, the offence is repeated. But when he says, "Don't" in exactly the same tone of voice, but follows that with a setting of the mouth so firm that little wrinkles appear on each side of it, it is no time for temporizing. Thus mannerisms, by making communication more complete than either teacher or pupil realizes or intends, may serve a very useful purpose in the classroom. The social interaction of teachers and pupils becomes stereotyped, and patterns recur; the mannerisms and expressions of the teacher (sometimes those of students as well) are likewise stereotyped and incorporated into this social interaction. The result is a complication of the processes of social interchange by an increase in the knowledge of all parties of what the others are going to do; the game becomes a chess game that depends upon the opponent's making the best possible play. Mannerisms may, in this manner, add something to the teacher's actual effectiveness by making his meaning clearer, but they do not add anything to his prestige.

Of vast importance in determining the opinion students hold of teachers is the attitude which those teachers have toward students and the subject matter they are attempting to impart to students. The attitudes which teachers may have and those which they may correspondingly evoke in their students branch off into such an infinity of social processes that we shall here be able to do no more than to mention certain type attitudes and indicate their effects. The advantage is seemingly with the teacher whose attitude toward his students is respectful, earnest, as friendly as possible and as little hostile as may be, impartial, and relatively unyielding. Definite personal interest in the student there should be, but it creates fewer problems if it is formalized and restricted. Let us take up each of these phases of the teacher's attitudes toward his students in turn. Respect of the teacher for the personalities of students is something of a *sine qua non* of any real respect for the teacher. The teacher must accept the students for what they are, and as far as possible for what they think they are, for students are very quick to detect and to resent a belittling attitude. What is perhaps even more important, a teacher must respect the reserves of his students. It follows likewise that the teacher must be quite earnest and sincere in his dealings with students. What they do in earnest, he must take earnestly. What is an earnest business to them must be one to him. Friendliness and hostility must both be strained through the channels of the institution. Unyieldingness and impartiality are also indispensable attributes of the teacher's attitude toward his students. The unyieldingness is necessary in that the teacher must maintain a consistent pose and a consistent and unvarying definition of the situation; the reasoning by which one may establish the necessity for impartiality is not more obscure: the teacher must be impartial because it is the code, and because the favored ones will take advantage of their special position and perhaps both favored and unfavored will rebel against the nepotism. An impartial application of all the school laws requires that the teacher have a respect for the established order somewhat in excess of his respect for his students (subordination to a principle).

Whether the teacher meets his students and the problems they present courageously or whether he fears that contact is a question upon which students soon make up their minds. Writers upon the practical aspects of teaching have repeatedly emphasized the quality of courage as one of the necessary requisites of the good teacher. That these writers are saying something very true there seems no doubt, but one is inclined to wonder what kind of courage they have in mind. Physical courage is not always necessary in the teacher, though its lack, if it is ever discovered, may disqualify an individual as a teacher. Nor is it correct to say merely that "moral courage'' is requisite, for few teachers, even the most successful, have distinguished themselves in that direction; few of them would take up a ruinous course of action because they think it right. With respect to moral courage, teachers are probably little better and certainly no worse than the rest of the community. Nor is the frantic desperate courage of the teacher who is failing and knows that he is failing of any very great value. What is perhaps in point is that the teacher must have an institutionalized courage, which is in its best form merely a patient willingness to face out all the little unpleasantnesses that arise as incidents of the relation of teacher to students. Institutionalized courage is supported by an institutional temper. Both of these traits of character are apparent in the effect they have upon the teacher's attitude toward students.

The teacher's insight into students in the institutionalized situation, his understanding of the boy in school and of the conditions affecting the collective opinion of the group of boys and girls in the school room, is a determinant of prestige both directly and indirectly, but chiefly indirectly in that it affects the teacher's attitudes toward students. What is wanted is not the exact measurements of the clinical psychologist, for these measurements do not help much when one has a whole class to instruct, and to keep in order, nor the complete comprehension of a functioning personality which the novelist and the psychiatrist strive to attain. It is sufficient for the narrower purpose of the school if the teacher has institutional insight, if he knows his way about in the social world of the school room. It would be better if he knew more, if he knew something, at least, of the learning now built up about problem children; it would be better if he knew a great deal about human nature in general. But institutional insight, an understanding of the social interaction of the school and the classroom, is absolutely necessary, and that is what this book is about.

We hear of teachers who have ''a sense of proportion,'' and of less fortunate colleagues who have none. What is meant by a sense of proportion is a degree of understanding of the mental sets and contexts of students. The teacher who has this kind of insight knows how far he can go, and he does not, by pushing the wrong button, evoke an inappropriate mental set from his students. The habitual mental set of students is one which takes learning seriously, and is disposed to be greatly pleasured by even a little learning. This habitual set takes grades and examinations seriously, and resents an unseemly lack of interest on the part of the teacher. Probably, this mental set takes the teacher seriously, but it is disposed to resent any tendency of the teacher to exceed his authority. The teacher who gives an unauthorized command or encroaches upon a regularly scheduled vacation lacks a sense of proportion. We may illustrate our point further by briefly considering classroom humor. Teachers who are "socially hard of hearing" never learn to use humor properly. A danger of humor, improperly used, a danger of humor that is not labelled as humor, a danger of good humor, therefore, is that it predisposes students to interpret the teacher's remarks in a humorous context. If directed at students in a belittling way, it arouses hot resentment. Humor has a use in alleviating antagonism and securing friendly rapport; one moment the teacher is teaching, but when that begins to be boresome, he makes a gesture of coming from behind his desk, sitting on the benches with his students, and joking about the teacher. But this device must be used with care. That is what we mean by institutional insight.

Institutional insight and institutional courage are indispensable qualifications, and the attitude of the teacher toward his students shows students at once whether he has them or not. The teacher whom students like and admire above all others is the teacher who knows what it is all about, and boldly demands his rights, all of them, but no more, the while he insists upon the amount and kind of subordination that is correct within the institutional situation.[1] On the college level a certain amount of intellectual courage is also necessary, a sort of faith in the authoritativeness of one's own mental processes, and text-slaves and teachers who are afraid to answer simple questions fail for the lack of it.

Similar generalizations may be made concerning the attitude of the teacher toward the subject matter which it is his business to impart. The teacher must be quite in earnest about his subject. He must take the business seriously, for it is impossible for young persons to realize that something may be important for them which is not important for their grown-up teacher. The cavalier attitude toward subject matter, however much the part of sense for the teacher

[1] An eighth-grade student compared two teachers in this manner: "Miss W.'s fine. We all liked her. She told you. She'd yell at you anywhere. I don't like Miss J. so well. Aw, she gives us candy." This reflects no masochism, but the reaction to contact with, first, a vigorous, tonic personality, and, second, a less adequate personality, the contact, in both cases, taking place through the pores of an institution. The situation might be different outside the institution, yet this boy's statement expresses a fundamental need of human nature, the need for leadership, and his affection for the vigorous teacher is merely the gratitude which attaches to the person who, within the bounds of the situation, is able to furnish leadership.

as a member of the larger world, must inevitably kill whatever interest students would otherwise have in it. Tradition requires that the teacher should be both earnest and enthusiastic over his subject; the commandment to earnestness is more easily met than that to enthusiasm. Long teaching experience in one subject works both for and against the success of the teacher who wishes to preserve these valuable attitudes. A person who is concerned over a period of years with passing on some particular subject, who is regarded as a success or branded as a failure accordingly as his students develop proficiency in that subject or fail to develop it, magnifies the importance of the subject. But it is hard to see how loss of enthusiasm can be avoided; that is part of the fundamental difficulty of being a teacher, that one must go on doing things that have lost their appeal because one has done them so many times. The advantage here, as in some other respects, is with the teacher who has not too high an intelligence, for it is the less intelligent teacher who has least difficulty in keeping himself convinced of the fundamental importance of his work and in retaining his enthusiasm over the obvious. Some of the stupid ones, indeed, take a keen delight in its annual rediscovery. Rationalization and the compartmentalization of the mind help some teachers to preserve their balance and enthusiasm. A continuation of reading and research in one's field keeps one from forgetting that an academic subject is really a live phase of human thought and not merely a set of facts and figures to be memorized by sophomores; one who takes this way out fights off the boredom of specialism by taking on more specialism. For the teacher who insists upon evaluating his instruction and his subject correctly, and upon preserving a general human perspective, the best refuge from ennui is in the personalities of his students, from whose development he may take such satisfaction as the institutional setting allows.

Perhaps the most important single characteristic of the teacher in determining the long-time relationship of student and teacher is his voice. Other characteristics of the teacher may, when students have grown accustomed to them, fade into the margins of perception, but the voice, continually active, carries the burden of instruction, and it must therefore stay near the center of attention. Important elements in the total impression of the voice are its pitch, its volume, and its intonation. The lower-pitched voices have in general a more impressive and a more soothing effect, and they are more likely to be associated with a volume which is adequate for school-room purposes and is yet relatively effortless. The intonations of the voice are apparently most important in their unconscious betrayal of the teacher's state of mind and his character. Thus from the succession of tones in which a statement is made we can tell whether a teacher really means what he is saying and is quite sure that there will be no argument about it, whether he means it and thinks that there may arise some discussion, whether he is trying to convince himself, whether he is trying to bluff someone else, etc. These interpretations children make without analysis or without realizing that they are subtle interpretations, but they make them. This is one phase of social life in the school which has apparently escaped the attention of students of education altogether. When we follow out this hypothesis we find that it helps to explain some of the otherwise surprising successes of students in character interpretation. For instance, a superintendent after long and careful study employs a teacher who will, he thinks, be satisfactory in all respects, including his ability to discipline. He has had satisfactory preparation, and he knows his subject. From the interview the superintendent gains the impression that he is intelligent, alert, and competent. His references show some years of apparently successful experience. For all the superintendent can tell he is a most capable classroom personality. But in two days, in at most a week, his students have located all his weak points, and a great teacher-baiting holiday is in process. How do they do it? Very likely through those intuitive judgments which, from their own point of view, they make very accurately. And the pitch and the intonation of the voice have not a little to do with those judgments.

There are recognizable types of good and bad voices for classroom purposes. One of the worst of the bad voices is that called effeminate when it is found in a man; really it is infantile. This voice places the individual at once as a person who has not outgrown his infantile habit of dependence upon the decisions of others. This voice, chiefly through its use of rising instead of falling inflections, fails to give an impression of finality of decision. It characterizes the individual deeply, as they vaguely realize who seize upon such voices as points of mimicry or takeoff. In any pronounced form, this voice by itself is fatal to the teacher, and it almost goes without saying that it is more quickly fatal in the man than in the woman. It is fatal because, strangely enough, it arouses resentment. Seemingly even the most equable and conformed individuals resent any form of domination by a person lacking authority and self-reliance. "Why," asks the high-school student, with an indignation that we cannot say is entirely unfounded, "Why should I have to mind a guy like that?"

Another voice which is most unfortunate in its effects is that with emotional overtones. By emotional overtones we mean to denote that emotion is somewhere in the voice, and is recognizable, roughly, as an emotion of one particular sort. These are, of course, not overtones in the musical sense. They are most commonly tones of fear or of hatred, or of bravado covering fear and hatred, as in the blustery voice. An overtone of affection is sometimes found. The voice tinged with emotion is apparently damaging to the teacher because it shows that he is emotionally involved in classroom situations, and it tends to call out in others a corresponding involvement of segments of the personality which should not be in play in the institutional situation. If the emotion that comes out is mainly fear, this makes the teacher a tempting mark for teasing. If the overtone is one of hatred, the voice invites an emotional response of like character. Bluster is an invitation to all hardy spirits to call the blustering one's bluff. If, as often happens, bluster is accompanied by dire threats, it metamorphoses those threats into definite challenges which more rebellious students find it difficult to avoid taking up. Bluster, of course, impresses some students, the more timid ones who rarely make trouble anyhow; but it creates more problems than it solves. The voice with an overtone of affection does not always produce bad results if the affection which comes out is sincere, tempered, and dignified, but it results unfortunately if there is in it the slightest trace of soppiness, sentimentality, or favoritism.

Peculiarly unfortunate is the voice which we may refer to for want of a better name as the voice of strain. A person under a tension is likely to speak with pressure on his vocal chords. This manner of speaking causes the tones of the voice to be flattened out, imparting an effect of shrillness, an effect which is usually enhanced by a raising of the pitch. In addition to this shrillness, this voice usually acquires a rasping quality. Sometimes it has a nasal twang. In fine, the effect of strain seems to be a distortion of the voice not unlike that produced by a poorly adjusted amplifier. The overtones of nervousness and fear are unmistakable. It has often been noted that students in the classes of teachers whose voices are strained show more evidences of restlessness and unease than they do under the influence of teachers who labor under less tension. If a student has himself the slightest tendency to nervous instability, it will be enhanced by the influence of a nervous teacher. In addition, the nervous tones of the teacher are sooner or later correctly interpreted as coming out of a want of confidence in his ability to control the school situation, and that factor makes likewise for a failure of the teacher to hold his class.

A better voice, unquestionably, from the standpoint of the necessities of the school room, is the dry, impersonal, and didactic voice which teachers usually fall into the habit of using. Apparently it is produced by continuous exposition. Exposition is itself dry and impersonal, and since it is rather the teacher's function to tell people things than to raise questions or to invite them to wonder, the teacher's whole personality comes to be cast into that form of discourse. The dryness of the teaching voice is increased by the necessity for many repetitions of facts which were never very meaningful to the teacher, and from which all vestige of meaning has long since been drained out. The didactic voice is the voice of authority and the voice of ennui. There is in it no emotion, no wonder, no question, and no argument. It imparts facts. There enters likewise into the classroom voice the impersonality of the voice of command. The voice of command is also in large part a product of the social experience of the person who must continually order others about. This tone of voice goes with a formalization of all social relationships and a stereotyping of the words of command. Probably more desirable from the human point of view, certainly much rarer and less attainable by the average teacher, is that tone of voice which is completely human, completely personal, and entirely relaxed. In any case, as schools are at present constituted, such a voice needs to be coupled with a personal organization which interposes great social distance between the teacher and the student. In actual teaching personalities, there are of course all combinations of these qualities of voice, ranging from the completely desiccated and didactic through the quizzical, the urbane, and the bland to the entirely direct and personal.

Those who live by controlling others must take thought even of their laughter. There are some teachers who think that they should never smile. They may be right, for where the moral order is frankly imposed upon students from without they will welcome any show of relaxation on the part of the imposing agent as an opportunity to break through. Teachers who never smile, however, lose an opportunity to gain status as human beings, for the thought that after all "Old So-and-So" has a sense of humor or "knows how to take a joke'' is one which makes students less inimical and teacher domination less unbearable. Sometimes teachers compromise by acknowledging the ridiculous with the grim smile, which does not simply mean, "I am a fellow human being and like you I find some things amusing,'' but says rather, "I am of course the teacher. But I am willing to admit that this is amusing. But do not forget that I am still the teacher.'' As for laughing aloud, that is for many teachers entirely out of the question. When they do laugh audibly, it is usually not from amusement but from a realization that certain situations must be recognized by laughter. The bitter laugh is sometimes found in teachers. Students can recognize it for what it is, but since they have rarely suffered the sort of personal frustration which is likely to be the lot of teachers, they do not understand and they do not sympathize; teachers therefore lose status rather than gain by it. The taunting laugh directed at particular students is usually resented. Laughter which is quite free and unrestrained may help much to establish a favorable rapport between teachers and students, provided that the teacher has a technique for making the transition from the light to the serious mood, and provided that he knows what he ought to laugh at.

In all social situations the expression of the face and eyes of the persons concerned is one of the most important facts. The expression of the face sets the stage for all social interaction, it very largely determines how all statements are to be taken and gives completer meanings to all words and declarations. It is regrettable that the mental and social sciences have discovered so little about the basic expressions or their influence upon the attitudes of others. In the absence of laboratory findings on the subject, we must again offer our empirical generalizations, frankly only approximations of the truth, but worth whatever they are worth. There is in the social life of human beings not under institutional conditions a complex interchange of personal attitudes as mirrored in the face, and, correspondingly, a considerable appearance of spontaneity of expression. And most of the interaction of human beings is relevant to this interplay of attitudes and gestures rather than to overt acts. But the teacher, who must play certain rôles a large part of the time, must sacrifice something of his spontaneity, and develop facial expressions corresponding to his rôles rather than to his feelings.

The better to keep their secret thoughts secret, and the better, therefore, to maintain the consistent pose of the teacher, some teachers adopt an impassive expression of the face. This mask-like countenance, this poker face, drops over their features when they enter the school room; and from then on they are, or they fancy themselves to be, inscrutable. The mouth is set in a straight line; perhaps it is tightly pressed. It is disturbed but little when speaking, which has a part in the close-clipped, dry enunciation of the teacher. The facial muscles are quite inactive. With some teachers they are relaxed. With others they are set in some pattern which is not inconsistent with the teaching attitude or which is easy for the particular teacher to maintain. Thus the expression sometimes is one of sternness, sometimes it is bland, sometimes vacuous. The muscles around the eyes have also to be ironed out or set in some particular pattern; usually the pattern adopted is one of general disapproval. Glassy eyes, protruding eyes, or eyes which for other reasons fail to give the ordinary clues to internal states are here an apparent advantage. The impression of the entire countenance is wooden, mask-like, usually vacuous as well. It is slightly stern and forbidding, it is the expression of one prissily concerned with the negative virtues. The French have an expression *l'air pion*, the under-teacher look. It may be worth while to point out that the impassive teacher face is an attempt to make the school in fact what it always is taken to be in the theoretical treatments of it, a place where learning goes on quite unattended by any by-products of human life or personal influence. The impassive face is considered by some teachers an aid in the imparting of subject matter as well as in the maintenance of discipline, for the teacher whose face is inscrutable gives no cues to his students while they are reciting, and it needs therefore a greater mastery of subject matter before students can essay a satisfactory recitation. This psychology seems flawless.

Probably all teachers adopt the impassive countenance to a greater or a less degree. Seemingly some such influence of a dominant rôle is inevitable in every relationship where one person must control, manipulate, or fend off others. The impassive face comes because it is a necessity of the situation. It is the face of social distance. The impassive countenance is sometimes colored by other expressions, such as the cynical or the sneering appearance. Cynicism probably does not contribute to the prestige which a teacher enjoys, since it is mostly wasted upon persons young enough to attend school; but it does not always detract markedly from the respect which a teacher gains, if it has not a personal object. The sneering countenance, however, with its implied personal derogation, its air of belittling, distrust, and antagonism, is greatly resented.

The control which teachers attempt to exert over their facial expressions by no means stops here. They must be able upon occasion to assume more cheerful expressions. For these purposes some teachers have worked out a synthetic smile. It is used for parents when they call at school, when speaking to parents of children, for children in the presence of parents, and upon certain occasions of state. It is a rather broad smile which appears upon the face suddenly, without the customary prolegomena of that expression of amusement. As suddenly it disappears, as if it had been conjured into nothingness. The artificial smile is usually identifiable as such. The absence of a preliminary stage is one element which gives it away. The smile of real amusement either spreads slowly over the face or, after a momentary pause in which it threatens to break out, suddenly seizes possession of the face. The smile of recognition has likewise a preliminary; so has usually the smile of response. A smile that is not artificial, too, usually leaves a trace upon the face when it has gone, but the school-teacher smile disappears miraculously. It makes one think of the performance of one of those rather poor stage magicians who pass their hands over their faces and meet you with a changed countenance. There are other defects in the willed smile which betray its artificiality. There is, for instance, the fact that often the upper lip does not break as it does in the spontaneous smile. The attempt by teachers to maintain friendly relations with their students and patrons through the use of this "public relations representative" helps to account for the feeling among parents and students that teachers are not real human beings. Unless the performance is much more convincing than it usually is, it adds nothing to the teacher's prestige, and it may, by contributing to the general failure of the teacher's personality to convince, detract considerably from his standing.

A recognizable variant is the wan smile. This is the smile one uses when he feels that he ought to smile or that the occasion deserves a smile, or when he is slightly amused, but is in no case quite ready to let go completely for fear of starting a riot. It shows some real feeling, or a fairly convincing feeling that one has the feeling, plus the hope that everything will "go off smoothly," that is that a disturbance will not immediately break out, and some fear that things will not go off smoothly. This is the smile that the high-school principal puts on on alumni day. The principal has written some quite cordial letters inviting the alumni to return for the occasion as guests of the school. (Is it characteristic of teachers to have a greater facility on paper than otherwise?) The alumni secretary has written enthusiastic letters inviting them to "come back and renew their student days, come back and have a whooping good time." The principal has read these letters with misgivings. The alumni have returned. The principal is afraid that they are going to follow the suggestion of the alumni secretary. He is mindful of other occasions when certain events took place which gave him no pleasure. Yet the occasion calls for a smile. He does the best he can. The result is the wan smile. This is likewise used in the classroom. It is one of the reasons why the teacher fails to register with students as a real and forceful human being. We have mentioned the grim smile. In this there is no artificiality, but the frankly ambivalent expression of both amusement and the desire to maintain order. It shows real amusement, or real friendliness, seeping through strong barriers. It does not break down the barriers, but it permits real communication in spite of them. This compromise of authority and friendliness is for many teachers, for all those who have not learned how to get the classroom situation back under their control at once after they have allowed it to take its own natural course for a while, the best compromise for classroom purposes. It allows students to see that one has a sense of humor, or that he is friendly, but it does not open the gates.

It follows from the above discussion that teachers profit from a certain facility in acting. It is necessary for a teacher to control the mood of a group. Necessarily, that mood must shift from moment to moment. The teacher's face must give the signal that the mood of the group has now changed, and that a different definition of the situation holds. Therefore it is desirable that a teacher should have certain easily recognizable expressions to serve as signposts. As a result of this necessity, the subtler nuances of expression sometimes become lost, but that is probably not, from the point of view of the classroom, a disadvantage.

The personality traits which we have hitherto discussed in their relation to the prestige which the teacher builds up among his students may be thought of as components of personality. Without splitting hairs, it seems possible to distinguish another set of qualities which arise out of the manner in which those components of personality are organized, out of their interrelation in the ensemble of personality. These may be thought of as qualities of the personality as a whole. Some of these qualities of the entire personality will be found to be even more important than the traits which go to make up personality. We have had to note again and again that the meaning of particular traits was in terms of the entire personality; when we discuss the qualities of the total personality we are at least a step nearer the ultimate reality of personal interaction. Certain of the qualities of the total personality which seem worth our attention at the present time are the tempo and range of personality, the complexity of personal organization, and the stability of personality.

The tempo of the teacher's personality conditions the relation of dominance and subordination as established between student and teacher. It seems altogether advantageous if the teacher has a more rapid intellectual tempo than his students. When there is a struggle for mastery, the race is usually to the swift; the opposite is a doctrine that is heartening but not true. The person who thinks more rapidly than his opponent can always manage to be a few moves ahead of him, and he can be preparing to check contrary moves before his opponent has thought of making them. This presupposes that the terrain is equally familiar to both antagonists, which is not true in the case of the student and the teacher. The teacher has always been over the same ground many times before, and he may make up for a relative slowness of mental reaction by knowing all the landmarks. If it is not associated with nervous instability, the ability to mobilize emotional resources rapidly is also an advantage to the teacher. When associated with quicker thinking, this is an advantage of much importance. The person who thinks quickly and feels quickly can bewilder his opponent with a succession of unanticipated reactions, he can anticipate moves and check them before the antagonist has had a chance to mobilize his resources. These generalizations seem to hold whether it is a question of constellating the attention of another or of beating him into submission. If, however, rapidity of emotional reaction is obtained at the cost of mental integration, if it is obtained through dissociation or compartmentalization, it probably, in the long run, ceases to be an advantage.

Foremost of the subtler determinants of dominance and subordination is the range of mental personality. This is a figurative expression, but it is a figure which seems apt for the summing up of certain aspects of personality. Personalities vary in the number of their interests, in the amount of knowledge and wisdom they encompass, in the number of facets which they display to other people, in the number of group contacts; they have both breadth and depth. These aspects of personality are included in the range of mental personality.

If other factors remain constant it is nearly always possible for the person of wide interests to maintain an ascendency over the person whose interests are narrow. The exception occurs, of course, where the person of more narrow interests has compactly organized his personality about the few interests that he has and has closed his mind to other possibilities. Perhaps this ought not to be the situation in the schools. The teacher is dealing with continually expanding personalities and is in a position to enjoy favorable recognition for his ability and accomplishments in diverse lines. Personal ascendency of the teacher based upon breadth of interests is ideal. Not only does it encourage students to widen the range of their own interests more rapidly, but it raises the inherent conflict of teacher and pupil to another level of emulation, and puts it into terms bearable for both teacher and student. Instead of an overt clash of personalities arising from a struggle concerning dead subject matter, the conflict becomes merely a competition between the wider and the narrower interests of the student. A wide range of interests is usually associated with a wide range of favorable group contacts. The personal authority of the teacher is much strengthened by wide group membership, especially if he receives favorable recognition. In college communities, particularly, even a man's colleagues do not judge him by their own standards, but by the reputation which he has acquired in his field of specialization. It is thus peculiarly unfortunate that so many avenues of personal growth and expansion are closed to the teacher.

The amount of knowledge and wisdom of the teacher of course affects his prestige directly in that students judge from it his general competence or incompetence. It also affects his prestige in a quite irrational way, and when one considers the strength of the mechanism involved, one wonders why the influence of teachers is not usually greater than it is. The teacher has an opportunity to acquire the prestige of a person who leads others into a world to them unknown, and this unfailingly conditions dominance and subordination. The questions which appear too puzzling to students have long since ceased to hold any complexity to the teacher; what students labor over for days he can answer in a moment. Where the teacher in fact assumes the rôle of guide and helper, where he introduces his students to a new world which gradually unfolds and takes shape, his prestige is enormous. But the teacher does not often assume that rôle, for usually he must drill his students into a false and unnecessary mastery of fundamentals (but one never masters fundamentals until one understands something else besides); he must impose upon students knowledge in which they have no interest. It will be to the lasting credit of those educators who have championed the project method and other enlightened modes of teaching if they succeed in devising means whereby the student can be brought to do systematic work without sacrificing his interest, for they will also have solved, possibly without a complete recognition of all that is involved, some of the most puzzling social problems of teaching. We should remark further that the situation in the schools at present is less favorable than it might otherwise be because the curriculum is unadapted to the needs of the average student, so that the teacher is forced to take his students into intellectual territory which they have no desire to visit.

The depth as well as the breadth of the teacher's interests will influence the attitudes of students toward him. Teaching does not require a deep mastery of any subject, and it may in fact put the premium rather upon a many-sided facility than upon complete and productive mastery of any one thing; but even students have ways of detecting the fraud and discounting the dilettante, and ways of distinguishing the genuine enthusiast from the spurious. All this is not to say that the advantage, in the actual social situation of the average school, does not lie with the happy and unthinking sort of extroversion which sincerely experiences broad and shallow enthusiasms.

Through dissociation there is sometimes produced a many-faceted personality which gives the appearance of having a great range. The large number of sides which teachers of this sort show to the world results from the fact that they are not at one with themselves. They have split off certain segments of their personalities, and they have segregated certain others from all contact with each other; from the strain inherent in this sort of organization and the psychic structures which they have worked out to buttress it there results a factitious and delusive appearance of great range of personality. Complete integration is not always useful in the school room, and it would be folly to demand that the mental hygiene of teachers should be vastly in advance of that of the community in which they live, but it ought to be worth noting that whatever prestige the teacher gains from this frame of personal organization is unstable and costly both to himself and others.

Another aspect of personality which is of vast importance in determining dominance and subordination is its comparative complexity.

Generally speaking, the adult personality exceeds in complexity that of the younger person. The adult has met the dilemmas of youth and has resolved them by translating them into dilemmas of a higher order. The complexity of the adult who has achieved a worth-while life organization may therefore be thought of as including the complexity of younger persons following the same general course of development; the advantage in terms of dominance and subordination is manifestly with the person who has achieved the more complex mental organization. A difference in ability to dominate the situation arises here in terms of understanding. The more complex personality, since it can comprehend and understand all the mental states of the more simple one, can control it, but the simpler personality cannot understand the more complex one, and therefore it can wage no successful battle with it over the issue of control. The teacher has, and should have, the advantage of unpredictability. Students do not know what his next move will be; they do not know what he is thinking, or why; they are ignorant of what he is thinking of them, and they do not know whether he is going to tell them or not. But the teacher knows what the students are going to do, what they are thinking, and what they think of him, and why; he is therefore greatly advantaged in the struggle for mastery. This is a practical psychology which school men use everywhere; it is boiled down in the bit of practical wisdom which asserts that "you have to keep them guessing." Here again we are thinking of one kind of complexity only, of the complexity of organization rather than disorganization, of the complexity that grows out of complete integration rather than out of the failure to deal with all one's fundamental impulses. The complexity of disorganization, though it has its advantages in particular situations, is on the whole probably a handicap. What it gains through unpredictability, it loses through lack of unanimity in action; what it gains through occasional neurotic brilliance or neurotic vigor, it loses through lack of stability.

If the teacher has a margin of superiority over his students in the respects which we have mentioned, there should arise between him and his students the relationship of the container and the contained.[1] The teacher, having the more complex personality, a greater

[1] For this concept we are indebted to the psychiatrist, Jung. As Jung has developed the concept, this is a relationship which arises chiefly between husband and wife, though the concept may be applied to other relationships as well. On the basis of the differences in ranges of mental personality (Jung's phrase), and differences in tempo, arises a discrepancy between persons such that the personality of one of them is apparently completely contained in the other. The contained one is wholly bound up in the relationship, and his attention and

range of interests, and a more complex insight into the nature of human life, may be able to constellate the attention of his students completely, at least during school hours; he may be able to contain them. If so, the dominance of the teacher has been completely transformed into personal ascendency, and a form of ascendency that is easily borne; the teacher no longer controls because he is the teacher, but exerts influence because of what he is. This is silken domination. Because of the limitations imposed by the institutional situation, because of personal lacks in teachers and defects in their training, this form of leadership is rare.

Upon the stability inherent in the frame of personal organization worked out by the teacher hinges much. We think of stability as including a relatively high margin of equanimity, perhaps of imperturbability, and the ability to follow a settled course of action without undue temptation to deviation. Stability is one of the great factors conditioning dominance and subordination in general and the authority of the teacher over his students in particular. Stability is important not merely as the opposite of instability, but from certain qualities of its own. Instability, of course, has a negative value in the struggle for ascendency. The unstable teacher makes inconsistent demands upon his students, and he therefore finds himself in conflict with himself for the control of his class. Some of the disadvantages of this procedure may be avoided, as we have elsewhere described, by establishing complementary definitions of the situation and making transitions from one to the other very clear. But this is in fact a device which is best employed by a stable person, for the unstable one cannot even maintain consistency in his definition of inherently inconsistent situations. To employ this device successfully requires rather the ability to follow out two or three settled policies and to keep them separate than the inability to follow any. The unstable teacher, however, can establish no clear definition of the situation, for the good reason that he cannot himself decide what he wants to do or what he wants others to do. When a teacher is not

interest are entirely centered in the container. The contained one finds the relationship completely satisfactory, except for his lack of security. But the container is not so completely held, and often wishes to get away from the relationship. Jung thinks of the container as surpassing the contained in range of personality usually as a result of what we have called the complexity of disorganization. For a more complete discussion of the concept *see* Jung, C. G., "Marriage as a Psychological Relationship," in Keyserling, Hermann Alexander, *The Book of Marriage*, pp. 354 ff., Harcourt, Brace and Co., New York, 1926. For our own comment upon the concept *see* Waller, Willard, *The Old Love and the New*, pp. 163-169, Horace Liveright, New York, 1930.

fairly clear in his own mind what demands to make of his students, to expect them to show any great concern over the state of his mind would be asking too much of human nature.

It seems a generalization of some value that we always adjust to the stable elements of our environment. This means that we adjust to the stable person as a part of our social environment. In any situation we focus our attention upon the aspects of it which are capable of being manipulated. It is the moving parts of a machine that catch our eye. It is the remediable ills of human life that excite our ire, and therefore the best argument of the conservative is that it has always been so. Stable things we accept. There was no need of the proverb, for we endure what we cannot cure because we cannot see it, or cannot see it long, or cannot get excited about it.

Likewise we accept the stable person as one of the unchangeable elements of life, perhaps regrettable, but there. He cannot be changed, and effort directed at him is effort wasted. Directly we lose interest in reforming the person who does not waver; it takes a very high-pressure salesman or a very stupid one to keep on trying to sell a man who gives no faint indication of yielding. Likewise the very stability of the unchanging person gives us control of him, a control which does not, however, challenge the fact of his domination. "That's just his way," we say. It may not be a way that pleases us, but it is a settled way and we accept it. His ways are ways that compel us to adjust to him, and put it altogether out of the question that he should adjust to us, but when we have learned his ways and adjusted our behavior to them, we have a harmless control over him, a control analogous to that which man has over those parts of the physical universe whose processes he understands but cannot manipulate. In this manner we can adjust even to a settled and stable instability.

The stable teacher defines classroom situations once and for all. He does not deviate and he does not often alter his policy. When he makes a rule, he enforces it; those questionings of self and of motives which torture others do not bother him. When he punishes, he does not relent. When he assigns a task, he sees that it is completed. His policy works not only because he establishes a clear-cut definition of the situation, but because he himself becomes incorporated in the situation as one of its changeless components. Here we find one reason why the weak teachers are the system builders, why they are the ones who put into effect the largest number of institutional devices. Weak teachers are system builders in part because system building makes them weak. It is the unstable who are weak. It is the unstable who cannot wait for the values which time can give to any established order, just as, in another sphere of life, it is the unstable who cannot wait for the values which time can give to any marriage. From this, the rapid shifting from one system of school discipline to another; from the shifting comes defeat.

The control of the stable person is operative on a number of different levels of social interaction. Control sometimes goes to the person who is physically immobile. Part of the struggle for domination can be stated as a struggle to determine who shall move from his place and who shall, therefore, adjust his behavior to that of the other person. One mechanism of control is to establish one's self in a particular spot and to make all others come to him. This same mechanism is employed on a different level by those who cultivate inaccessibility. Examples of the operation of this mechanism are not hard to find. In the familiar classroom situation, one person has a piece of paper to give to another. They are, let us say, ten steps apart. When it has been decided who is to take those ten steps, part of the problem of domination has been solved. The person who takes the steps takes the responsibility for the joint activity. This is how it comes about that the principle of least interest often determines dominance in cooperative activity: The person less interested in the activity controls it. He who dislodges himself from his place and meets the other person upon his own terms must make the adjustment, whereas the other person merely agrees to let him make the adjustment. A parallel is the proverb that in every love affair there is one who loves and one who allows himself to be loved. This is a principle not new to the world in general.

The whole life of the classroom revolves about the stable teacher, who may thus in a perfectly effortless fashion, and often without the least knowledge of how he does it, secure dominance. He is there, changeless, immitigable. When students wish to consult him, they go to him. When they have papers to show him, they take them to him. The immobility of the teacher symbolically argues that it is not the teacher's job to educate, but only to help the student educate himself. He has defined the classroom situation clearly and finally, and there is no doubt that his definition will persist. The stability of such a teacher may be, indeed, the stability of phlegm. Stability is likely to be found in a character in which some of the subtler personal attributes are lacking, somewhat more likely, perhaps, than in persons who have achieved a great and varied sophistication. The simpler forms of character organization are the most useful for the teacher. Those who have observed the high degree of success of the highly stable, relatively simple personalities in teaching have sometimes been inclined to argue that fools were the best teachers. What may rather be argued is that there are personal qualities of more value than mere intelligence, and that stability is one of them. Some teachers who are successful in maintaining discipline because of their stability do not in fact accomplish very notable results in passing on knowledge to their students. They are nevertheless known as successful and reliable teachers, for they can keep order. And students like them, as a rule, for they need some stable and secure persons in their lives.

The stability of the strong character should never be confused with the obstinacy of the weak. There are teachers of this latter description who are conscious of their weakness and who nightly resolve on the morrow to be stronger. "Tomorrow," they say, "Tomorrow I will be firm." Usually the resolution does no harm, for it is forgotten in the first excitement of the next day's confusion, and the harassed teacher does not attempt to be firm on that day more than on any of the others because he is still at a loss as to what to be firm about. But in some instances he actually carries out his resolution and suffers from it more than he previously had from his policy of irresolution. He makes a rash and ill-considered decision and chooses that as the point upon which to establish his firmness. He chooses his course, and he persists in it though he learns that it is wrong; he clings to it the more frantically the more obvious the insanity of his policy becomes. The effect upon students is merely to stir up all the latent hostility in the situation. Students very quickly learn to regard such privileges as they are accustomed to take in the classroom as rights. Who indeed can say what is and what is not right in an arbitrary system? When the teacher revokes those privileges, and does it in a tactless and arbitrary manner, the only reaction of the students is one of resentment, nor does it soon penetrate into the students' minds that the teacher is really cultivating the respectable quality of firmness, that he is not simply being tyrannical. This impression is usually enhanced by the total want of judgment with which these overnight despots enforce their decrees. The pitiable feature of it all is that, if the weak teacher has really let his students get out of hand, it will take him some months to establish himself as a firm character and a disciplinarian, and his strength is usually insufficient for such a struggle. The next week will see both him and his students back in the same old rut.

Superintendents, observing the weakness of a particular teacher, commonly advise him to cultivate a greater firmness in his dealings with students. In other cases, teachers themselves become aware of this crucial fault in their teaching and resolve to correct it forthwith. It is, however, much to be doubted whether stability of character can be attained by a mere resolution or whether it can be imposed upon another personality through exhortations. Desirable stability is not self-conscious and synthetic. Stability of the sort we are here discussing arises naturally out of good mental hygiene and a thorough knowledge of what one is about. A teacher may set himself the task of learning from his experience what the important things are that go on in the classroom, or a superintendent may attempt the laborious task of giving him some insight into the intricacies of this social interaction, and from this a stability based upon a grasp of fundamentals may be born; but much more than a good resolution is needed. Resolution without insight is little better than irresolution without insight, and if the irresolution is established it is better left alone. There are, of course, some cases in which a teacher possesses all the needed traits except some knowledge as to a desirable social technique for dealing with students; a school superviser who steps in in such a case will probably not be wasting his time. Further, if the day ever comes when the importance of psychiatric work with teachers is realized, it will be possible for qualified persons to increase the stability of teachers' characters by resolving their mental conflicts, thereby making them at once better disciplinarians and more wholesome influences upon their students.

In the meantime, those supervisors who counsel stability must at least be given credit for correct diagnosis. The teacher must seek first a stable domination, and such other things as friendliness and cordiality may be added to it. Contrast the pleasant domination of a good teacher with the vacillating command of a weak one. The good teacher can afford to be pleasant and good-humored; he may even dare, because he has the situation in hand and knows what means to take to restore the balance, to introduce moments of relaxation and amusing interlude. But as a commander he never exposes his subjects to the pain of any mental conflict concerning his commandments, and they are grateful to him because he always orders them to do the right thing and does not permit them to think. His prestige—which is the greater because he has weeded out of his personality those traits which are not consistent with the prestige-carrying image—makes his commands acceptable, even welcome. He is strict, because pleasant working conditions for his students demand strictness; but he is evenly strict, and he is strict without being unpleasant. It is the strictness of high tonicity, vibrant, and somewhat inspiring.

All these factors contribute, contrariwise, to the unpleasant feeling tone which pervades the relationship of the inept teacher to his students. The teacher is judged on the basis of those qualities which affect his official relations, and the personality of the successful teacher may be less well integrated and less attractive—perhaps, in matters that do not concern the school, less stable—than that of the unsuccessful teacher. Many who fail as teachers have more merit as persons than most of those who succeed, and some of the most valuable human qualities of successful teachers are sacrificed to their academic success. But so long as we have a system which aligns personalities in this particular pattern, we must have teachers who get results according to the rules.

It seems possible by way of an aside to evaluate certain educational theories and classroom devices in terms of the principle established above, that control usually goes to the person who remains motionless while the life of others revolves around him, or, on the higher level, that control of a situation is most easily achieved by the person who demands that others adjust to him. Various writers on educational practice have advocated on what seem to be good grounds various policies which involve a large amount of motion in the classroom and study hall by the teacher, or the assumption by the teacher of much responsibility for giving help to students or for educating students. It is argued that teachers should distribute and collect papers in order to avoid the confusion of having students help themselves or crowd about the teacher's desk. Confusion is a very real problem for the classroom teacher, but it should be remembered that the teacher who moves from his place may create confusion as well as prevent it. The best solution seems to be some such sort of monitorial system as Bagley suggests, which avoids the chief evils of the other alternatives.

The essential idea of some of the newer educational theories seems to be to put as much as possible of the responsibility for the process of education upon the shoulders of the teacher. The teacher must be ready with help at every difficult stage. He must watch, supervise, and explain. He must drill. He must kindle enthusiasm. Yet every hardened veteran of the classroom knows that the real problem is to get students to take the responsibility for their own education. Young teachers commonly start out with an ambition to be high-powered teachers. They explain vigorously, drill long and patiently, help their students to get their lessons and help them to recite. This is the ideal of educational practice that has been drilled into them. Gradually they become aware of the fact that their efforts are wasted. Their students do not prepare their lessons because they know that the teacher will help them to recite. Canny students even learn how to get these teachers to work out the answers to examination questions for them. In time the young teacher learns that the educational principle of most value is that every person must educate himself. The amount of responsibility which the teacher can bear is limited in any case, but the situation is further complicated by the fact that the teacher loses something of his control of the classroom when he takes too many of the burdens of adjustment upon himself. The best relation, ideally as well as institutionally, seems to be that in which the teacher, mostly at rest and active only in emergencies, serves as mentor and guide through the intricacies of the curriculum but does not do the students' work for them. A clever colleague once characterized his rôle as one of "masterful inactivity."

PROJECTS

1. Investigate the relationship of a very young teacher to his students. Sound out his attitudes toward students and attitudes of students toward him. Compare with similar information concerning an older teacher. Interpret your results.
2. Describe the social world of the very young teacher, paying attention to the relative significance of different relationships, and to the imaginative weighting of projected and wished-for contacts. Ask young teachers to introspect upon the subject.
3. Describe the relationship of a very young teacher to his students of opposite sex.
4. Make observations over a period of months upon a teacher who allows himself to become involved in the social life of students.
5. Make observations upon the rivalry mechanism which enters into the relationship of the young teacher to his students.
6. Make extended observations to determine exactly when "enemy morality" arises between students and a particular teacher. Base your conclusions upon observation of behavior, but use introspective evidence of students and teachers to obtain clues.
7. Make a case study of a teacher whose deficiency in the social graces interferes with his teaching efficiency.
8. Make a case study of a man of vigorous, coarse personality who has marked influence upon students.
9. Make case studies of very small teachers. Note devices by which they

attempt to compensate for lack of size. Probe into attitudes of students toward them. Analyze and interpret.

10. Make extended observations to establish the truth or falsity of the generalizations in the text concerning the physical characteristics of teachers in their relation to student attitudes.

11. Rate a number of teachers in the matter of dress and compare with ratings of teaching efficiency.

12. Describe the dress habits of a group of successful teachers. Find out their attitudes toward dress.

13. Make observations upon good teachers who have good manners and upon good teachers who have bad manners. Compare and analyze.

14. Compare a number of teachers as to manner. Give definite incidents. Analyze manner in relations to teaching efficiency.

15. List the mannerisms of a group of teachers. What meaning have these mannerisms in terms of personal adjustment and teaching efficiency?

16. Collect instances showing the bearing of teachers' mannerisms upon social interaction in the classroom.

17. Discover by observation typical attitudes of teachers toward students and subject matter and the interaction of students and teachers.

18. Relate instances to show the exact meaning of "institutional courage," and "institutional insight."

19. Analyze the classroom voices of your own teachers. Interpret in terms of your own attitudes.

20. Analyze the laughter of teacher and students in a particular class for the light it sheds upon the rapport between teacher and student.

21. Compare a group of successful teachers with a group of unsuccessful teachers with regard to measurable traits. Analyze and interpret results.

22. Analyze the classroom techniques of teachers who have and others who have not adopted the mask-like expression.

23. Make observations upon the behavior of the principal of a small high school on some gala occasion.

24. Analyze the techniques used by a number of teachers for signalling to a class that the group alignment has been changed from humor to serious study.

25. Rate a group of teachers on the range of their interests and teaching efficiency. Superimpose the two curves.

26. Make case studies of pairs of persons between whom exists the relationship of container and contained.

27. Work out and analyze the mechanisms by which stable persons force other persons to adjust to them.

28. Study a teacher who continually devises new social schemes to secure discipline, a "system builder." Analyze his personality and his relationship to his students.

29. Record the new decisions and resolutions of a teacher who is having disciplinary difficulties.

30. Make careful observations and record incidents in order to determine exactly what "firmness" is.

SUGGESTED READINGS

(1) Emerson, R. W., *Representative Men.*

(2) Gowin, E. B., *The Executive and His Control of Men,* Chapter III.

(3) Miller, G. F., *Letters From a Hard-Boiled Teacher to His Half-Baked Son.*

(4) Waples, D., *Problems in Classroom Method,* Part II, Sections III and VI.

Chapter XVI

VARIETIES OF PRESTIGE AND OF DISREPUTE

Prestige is what makes the leader different from anybody else. It is not a real quality, but a consequence of the way in which those who are under his sway think about a particular leader.

Prestige is carried by social images to which the leader is assimilated. Flesh-and-blood humans do not conform to these prestige-carrying patterns, but are made over into them by the dream-work of idealization. The leader is always made over in the minds of his followers. What fits the pattern they have decided upon for him is kept. What does not fit is thrown away. So it occurs that every man's leader is a man after his own heart, and no man lives in a universe populated by heroes who exceed him in complexity of mental organization. Prestige is a quality of the whole arising from the way in which the parts of the hero are fitted together.

In unrestricted social life, the varieties of prestige-carrying images are infinite. In the institution they are fewer, because only certain types of images can sift through the institutional network. Within every institution certain typical images are the usual carriers of prestige or its opposite.

We leave aside the questions of the origin of social images, of their relation to the imagined qualities they carry, and of their effect upon the contact human beings have with each other. We turn now to a consideration of certain social images to which school teachers are assimilated. These images are configurations, or patterns, into which the teacher's personality is organized in the child's mind. Some of the images existed before the teacher came into the life of the particular youngster; these were superimposed upon the teacher from the early experience of the child, particularly his experience of his parents, and relevant attitudes were transposed with the images. Other images appear to have been manufactured on the spot from the materials at hand. It is our purpose here to be thoroughly inductive, and to present descriptions of these organizations of ideas and attitudes rather than interpretations of them. That important and unsolved problems of theory are connected with the social image is clear, but we have not here the space, nor do we presume the ability, to make any contributions to them.

Let us consider first those social images whose value to the teacher is a positive one. Some images which carry prestige when the teacher is assimilated to them are: (1) the parent substitute, (2) the image of the cultural or social ideal, (3) the image of the officer and the gentleman, (4) the image of the patriarch, (5) the image of the kindly adult, and (6) the image of the love object. These images are not always clearly distinguishable, but we can roughly classify teachers as deriving prestige from one or more of the images just noted.

When the child assimilates his teacher to one of his parents, attitudes are transferred from teacher to parent. Men and women teachers acquire meaning for the child, in so far as they do acquire meaning, in terms of the parent to whom they are assimilated. The man teacher, as in after life the employer, the doctor, and the priest, among others, is assimilated to the father image. If the father is feared, the teacher is feared with a fear that emanates from no personal experience of him. If the father is hated, the teacher is royally hated, since he may be made to serve as a convenient outlet for a father hatred which the child may not wish to admit to himself. The woman teacher is frequently assimilated to the mother. If the attitude toward the mother is one of unalloyed affection, then the attitude of the child toward his teacher will tend to reproduce the same undivided pattern. If the mother is thought of as a thwarting agent, the child will clearly see the thwarting activities of the teacher and will treat her accordingly. Women teachers, especially in the early grades, find it a very convenient technique to play the part of the mother to their pupils, and apparently there are no very serious objections to it. Women teachers are also occasionally assimilated to the father image.

The discussion of the cultural or social ideal as a prestige-carrying image has been anticipated in the discussion of the social background of the teacher. Social classes exist in all societies, and the admiration of each class for those above is one of the fundamental social facts. A teacher enjoys prestige derived from this source if he manages to categorize as a member of the upper classes. Students may dislike a teacher who manifestly does not belong to their own group, but they hold him none the less in awe. In the rural districts, where learning is not widely diffused, the school teacher is often held in near reverence because he is a learned man, but to be accurate we must remark that this attitude is not wholly a matter of class feeling, being in part produced by the superstitious veneration of the unlettered for one who knows the esoteric lore of books. The native American teacher has great prestige in immigrant districts because he was born in this country, and this seems a purer case of respect for the cultural ideal than the former example. In the slums, also, pupils who have had experience only of slatternly and dirty women will often venerate and well-nigh worship their clean and well-dressed teacher. It may be argued that prestige due to the supposed superiority of one social class over another is not to be had in a democratic society, but this is not true. Because of the great social mobility of American society both parents and teachers set much store by a person who embodies upper-class qualities, and whom they can use as a model of imitation. Lower-class parents and lower-class students tend to see the problems of the upper-class teachers in terms of their own daily dilemmas, and to judge these teachers by their own unreal standards of what ladies and gentlemen ought to be; many amusing situations and some tragic ones arise from this fact, but on the whole the masses judge fairly both the person and his qualities, and appropriate only those qualities, as they respect only those persons, that may be of some use to them.

Some teachers acquire prestige quite like that of the army officer. We may therefore speak of them as conforming to the image of the officer and the gentleman. The prestige of the officer has a long tradition behind it, and it usually assumes a definite form. The officer is a member of the ruling group, as such different from enlisted men and set off from them as the members of self-conscious ruling groups always are set off from those they rule. The officer represents the dominant group; he must cast his personality into that mold whenever he is in the presence of members of the subordinate group. The officer is made of finer clay than men, certainly of different clay. He wears better clothes than the enlisted man, and different clothes. His clothes are different to distinguish him from the men and they are better to help him maintain his prestige. Neatness is required of enlisted men, but the officer must attain in this respect an unbelievable perfection; who is not immaculate is no officer. The officer must live like a gentleman. He must stop in a good hotel. He must eat in the better restaurants. He must smoke expensive cigarettes. He must travel on the Pullman. He carries no packages. He engages in gentlemanly sports and avocations. He does not consort with women to whom privates have access. He can go to the head of a queue but he cannot shine his own shoes. The officer never slops over. Certain ceremonies of respect are due him. All these things serve to mark the officer off from the men. Very important are the things the officer cannot do. It is what one does not do that determines whether he is a gentleman or not. As James puts it, "To ignore, to disdain to consider, to overlook, are the essence of the 'gentleman.'" One who is an officer and a gentleman is distinguished from all others by a certain kind of poise, a characteristic "seeking-avoiding balance," an inhibition of action and reservation of opinion which enables the individual to preserve the integrity of his personality in crisis situations. The person who most lacks this poise is the diffuse and poorly balanced extrovert.

Likewise a teacher who is erect, a little stiff, who dresses with a quiet good taste and is scrupulously neat, who takes the respect paid him as his right, who is always the poised and inhibited member of the ruling class, who uses the technique of command skillfully and always keeps his distance—a teacher of this sort acquires a prestige which is the first cousin of the prestige of the army officer. Because of the almost complete cessation of human intercourse which this prestige requires, it is perhaps unfortunate for the school room, but it is nevertheless important in the schools as they are.

Prestige of a special sort usually attaches to the patriarch in the schools. This is prestige derived from association with the father image, in all probability, but it is prestige which not uncommonly exceeds the prestige of the father image (perhaps because it is less ambivalent than the prestige of the real father). The typical case seems to be that of the elderly man who takes a fatherly interest in all his students, controls by influence only, applauds achievement but does not always insist upon details, and excites the liveliest affection in all his students. It may be that he teaches with unparalleled incompetence, but his students hear him gladly and always insist that they have learned much from him. His very foibles, his very weaknesses, his inability to be severe, his willingness to be sidetracked from the lesson, and his absent-mindedness on examination day are great points in his favor. These elder teachers play a very important rôle in the impressment of mores, and it could easily be argued that they choose the better part, that what they lose in academic efficiency they gain in personal influence. Many a school system contains such a patriarch, but there is rarely room for more than one in any system. Colleges and universities develop a cult about the school patriarch. His sayings, even the bitter ones, his anecdotes, his whimsies, his kind deeds, and the memory of his face and voice are passed down reverently from one generation to the next. It is noteworthy that age alone does not make a patriarch. It is rather certain personal qualities which make one known and remembered as "the old man," and by no means all old men have those qualities. There are naturally many more persons who have certain elements of patriarchal effectiveness than persons who conform to the pure type. The pure type is relatively rare, and is therefore, for our purpose, not very important, but the patriarchal rapport is not rare. Witness the number of teachers of whom students speak, jestingly but not without respect, as "the old man." Even those teachers with a mixed form of the patriarchal rapport are very important to students, for they furnish them an opportunity to express symbolically their emotions toward their own fathers. Even women teachers are sometimes known to embody a mixed form of patriarchal authority.

Another important image sometimes imposed upon the teacher, or formed about his personality, is that of the kindly and understanding adult. The image has certain overtones from either the father or the mother. If the home life of the child is happy, the kindly teacher may derive elements of prestige from both parents. Sometimes, however, especially where the child's relationship with his parents is not fortunate, the kindly teacher becomes very important without such reenforcement. In such a case the teacher becomes emotionally significant simply because we grow into a relationship that is pleasant and satisfying and away from one that is not. Usually the understanding and kindly adult is the praising adult as well. It is part of the technique of a certain kind of social work to find something that the child can do well and then to praise him for it. This involves giving the child the impression that one understands him and appreciates his real qualities. Slightly different is the rapport established by the sympathetic adult. This is the adult who attempts to win the child's confidence, to listen to the story of his troubles, and endeavors to let the child know that he realizes the nature of his difficulties and feels with him in them. This rapport is likely to be very strong on account of the transference mechanism. Because it is so very strong it is a little dangerous for the child, who is then unduly susceptible to any injury which the teacher, as a teacher, might work upon him.

The whole matter of control by praise is puzzling and a bit paradoxical. Where it is wisely carried on, it may result in the most happy relations between students and teachers. Where it is unwisely applied it is absurdly ineffective and ultimately very damaging to the student. Praise must always be merited, and it must always be discreet, else all standards disappear. Cheap praise both offends and disappoints, and it breaks down the distinction between good and bad performances. Praise must always be measured; it must not resort to superlatives, for superlatives give the comfortable but deadening sense of a goal attained. Such praise as is used must open the way to development and not close it. Praise must always be sincere, for otherwise it is very difficult to make it seem sincere, and if it does not seem sincere it fails to hearten. Praise as a means of control must be adapted to particular students. It is a device to be used frequently but only on a fitting occasion rather than an unvaried policy. Control by a rapport based upon sympathy likewise calls for delicate distinctions. Sympathy, to be of value, must not be the facile emotionalism of a fool, but the measured feeling of somebody who completely understands. One of the uses of understanding is to know when one is being imposed upon.

The category of the love object is one which may have either positive or negative value for the teacher. To make one's self a love object to students is a technique which has its greatest utility in the first few grades of school. Teachers of primary grades may apparently control their students most easily and most pleasantly by making themselves acceptable mother substitutes. This rapport is rapidly replaced, for the majority of students, by the traditional order of dominance and subordination with social distance, but for a few years more the teacher may retain her position as a love object in spite of the interposition of distance, shaping up then as a resplendent goddess to be worshipped from afar off. Even in high school, women teachers sometimes profit by going to some pains to categorize favorably as women; subtle adaptations of dress and manner may allow them to do this without losing their effectiveness in the teaching rôle. They must, of course, surround themselves with sufficient distance to remain far off and mysterious. This rapport is often of great utility in the management of high-school boys, whose idealism and chivalry may be utilized by such a technique when they would rebel at more obvious attempts to exploit them. One of the most important values of prestige as a love object comes from an abnormality of sex life, from the homosexual crushes which high-school girls, particularly, conceive for their women teachers. Women willing to play upon these girls of the Schwarmerei age have no difficulty in obtaining a following in any high school.

The disrepute into which teachers fall, the hatred which they beget, and the contempt which they sometimes arouse, may likewise be thought of as the product of certain personal configurations into which they fit. We turn now to a consideration of the more common of the unfavorable categories.

One of these is the easy mark. There are some teachers who can be put upon; they are easy marks. From the easy mark a student can get a good grade without working for it, or he can commit an offence in his presence and remain unpunished, or he can offer him a personal affront without harm, or get off from an imposed punishment with a flimsy excuse or a half-hearted apology. Sometimes personal qualities of the highest value may make a teacher an easy mark; excessive amiability may make him suffer too many affronts or be too charitable, a highly sympathetic nature may betray him to impostors, or a keen sense of human values may make it difficult for him to administer routine discipline to the children fed into the hopper of the educational system. Or it may be a trait of a different nature that betrays him, a lack of courage which he tries to hide beneath a pose of good nature, a lack of mentality which enables students easily to hoodwink him, or a lack of understanding of juvenile social life which prevents him from knowing what it is all about. Whatever the cause, the results are the same; students do not respect and they quite possibly hate such a teacher. The catastrophe is perhaps not so complete in cases of the first sort as in those of the second, for teachers who fail by reason of their virtues may have other virtues to redeem them, or compensating vices. Perhaps the worst case is that of the person who lacks courage to face the barbarism of young persons in school, for his attempt to mask his fear beneath an amiable exterior never quite succeeds and he is ultimately found out.

To the young teacher, one of the most disillusioning discoveries that he makes about the social realities of school life is that teachers are often made to suffer for their virtues. In a common-sense world, it would seem that amiable and sympathetic teachers, teachers who try to apply the golden rule in the school room, would have a high reputation in the eyes of their students. But they rarely do, and they never do in the orthodox school unless they are able to form some sort of compromise between friendliness and dignity. It is painful to see fellow teachers whom one knows to be persons of unusual qualities in disrepute with students because of those qualities, painful to see them suffer because they are genial and sympathetic, painful to see the evidences of disrespect and hatred which students give them. The young teacher casts about for a reason. It is not easy to find. Part of the answer may be made by reference to the general disrespect which young persons in our culture have for a person who impresses them as "soft," and this explanation has particular weight because of the traditional patterns of social interaction in the school; the teacher's personality must be a little hard if it is to survive the strain of the hard situation in which the teacher is placed. A related principle is that the competence of teachers is judged by reference to other teachers, and a teacher who does not do as others do, or as others would obviously like to do, is judged incompetent. Since most teachers are strict, one who is not strict does not know his business; either he does not know that he ought to be strict or he does not know how to be strict. In either case he is incompetent. He who would be good to students must first "sell them the idea." The definition of the situation is so clear in most classrooms, in terms of dominance and subordination, strictness, mutual antagonism, offences and punishment, that it is not possible for any but a most unusual teacher to adjust his relations with students to any other pattern. For a teacher who shows other traces of incompetence, this is probably a sufficient explanation of his disrepute.

The experienced teacher has a ready explanation for the failure of her good-natured colleague. Miss Jones fails "because she doesn't make those students respect her." Apparently this is a true explanation, but it still leaves some important questions unanswered. Why is it necessary to force students to "respect" the teacher, in the sense that her colleague, who has in mind a definitely institutional sort of respect, means? Why is it ever necessary for a teacher to "make students respect her"? Why do students not respect the pleasant Miss Jones rather than her cross and bad-tempered colleagues? These are puzzling questions, and one can never be quite sure that he has worked out a satisfactory answer to them. Something may be gained by going back on Miss Jones's steps and trying to discover what, by reason of her extreme equability, she did or failed to do that made the difference.

One important fact is that she failed to establish any boundary between teacher rights and pupil rights; she failed to establish a clear definition of the situation.[1] As a result, her students from day to day kept extending the boundaries of their own rights and privileges at the expense of those of Miss Jones. In the absence of a rigid definition of the situation, a definition is worked out by the

[1] For a discussion of the definition of the situation in the school see below, pp. 292 ff.

interaction of human forces; it is natural, then, that students should extend their activities until they come into contact with the real boundaries of the situation. Older persons sometimes learn not to impose upon good nature, for they have internalized the rule; but young persons have rarely attained to this moral delicacy. A further important fact is that there is here a motivation for imposing upon Miss Jones, a hostile motivation which prompts students to see just how far they can push things with her. This is not hostility toward Miss Jones, not personal hostility—not yet. It is the hostility which most students feel for most teachers. Miss Jones is pilloried for the misdeeds of all her students' other teachers. The activities of her students continue to push this good-natured teacher into a corner; they will push her as far as she will go. It is now a process beyond her control and more or less beyond the control of students; they are bound up in the process because they are involved in a rivalry to see who shall go furthest. Ultimately, whatever her good nature, whatever her phlegm, a point is reached where she feels the situation to be unbearable. She makes a stand. If she tries the technique of appeal, her appeals fail because she has no personal standing, and she becomes pitiable and somewhat odious. If she tries to command, she fails and makes herself ridiculous. By this time something has happened to her equanimity, and she has decided to fight. She enforces her commands with punishments. She defends her position desperately. Now the students begin to hate her. They hate her as they do not hate the teachers who have been strict from the first. Her stand has come too late, and the things which she is punishing now have become established as the rights of the students in her classes. Has she not permitted them on previous days? The precedent is against her. She must use more punishments than other teachers in order to enforce her points; her students will feel that it is unjust that they should be made to suffer for her incompetence. Have they not already decided that she is incompetent? She must use stronger punishments than other teachers; she must punish right and left; sometimes she imposes quite unreasonable penalties; she never dares relax. It is thought that she hates students, that her previous good nature was an illusion. Soon students hate her; they hate her so much that no penalties will be sufficient to restore her authority. That is the end.

The above may be regarded as a natural historical account of the life of the good-natured teacher. It is a process observable over and over again in any school system. With different classes, it is often repeated several times over with the same teacher, for the amiable are often slow to learn. The process has many variants, but the same general outline seems to underlie them all. Especially does the above pattern come out sharp and clear in the case of the teacher whose good nature with students is coupled with a considerable regard for their good opinion and some effort to be popular with them, popular as a person rather than as a teacher, for a chasm yawns between these two types of popularity. In some cases the teacher, after a long struggle, or through the use of heroic means, wins his struggle to establish domination. More often some sort of compromise arrangement is reached whereby the relation is enabled to continue, although it never becomes satisfactory to either side. If the teacher repeats the process in his second year, it is not likely to be so extreme. Many cases, however, are so extreme that the teacher, however well trained and skillful in instruction, is without value for the ordinary school system, and has to be dropped in the middle of the year or relieved of many of his duties.

The experienced teacher who has learned "how to make those students respect him" is involved in no such situation as that which centers about the teacher who is too good-natured or the teacher who wants to be popular. He at once sets up a rigid definition of the situation in terms of his own dominance. If he sets it up quickly enough and firmly enough, it is never questioned afterwards. Such minor threats as are made upon his dignity he is able to repel easily. It costs him, to be sure, something in the way of initial unpleasantness. He has to accept the disrepute which goes with being a school teacher, and there may be, early in the year, some pretty definite evidence that his students find him unpleasant and some less definite evidence that some of them dislike him. But if he has established his dominance so that it is not again questioned, the hatred toward him never really becomes personal. And, what is even more to the point, the absence of friction between personalities leaves the way clear for real friendliness to grow up within the known boundaries of the situation. Primary group attitudes spring up which make the situation human and bearable. Often such a strict teacher wins the liking of his students after the initial hate has passed away and his dominance has been softened by habit and acquaintance. Of him the students say, "He is strict and he puts up with no nonsense. But he knows his business and I guess he's not such a bad old fellow after all." In the "after all" is something significant. Earlier impressions are contradicted by later ones, with both the teacher who begins by being popular and the one who begins by being unpopular; the latter is in a better position because it is human nature to react excessively to such contradictions, to be more bitter over a quarrel with a friend than over a quarrel with an indifferent person, and to be more grateful for friendly advances from an enemy than for like advances from a friend. From this fact arises the practical wisdom of superintendents who advise their teachers to "come down on them pretty hard at first, because it is better to relax after a while than to tighten up." All very good if one knows how to "come down on them."

Nor is our explanation of the disrepute of the amiable yet complete. It will never be complete, for we must leave it suspended from certain paradoxical generalizations about human nature, for it is a true fact, and one not easy for the optimist to accept or the scientist to understand, that throughout the whole of human life the qualities of amiable persons are held at a low valuation. It is contrary to common sense, but it is true. Perhaps the reason is that those who fail to make themselves felt are not considered as persons, for which reason their favors, being taken as a matter of course, get no thanks, and they themselves get no love.[1] The meaning of good temper, then, is in bad temper. From a realization of this fact and an attempt to compensate for it, as well as the notion that it is not fair to impose upon good nature, arises the terrible wrath of some good-natured men. Some teachers, indeed, knowing themselves to be afflicted with the vice of laxity, try to establish themselves in the minds of students as persons who are usually quite easy but merciless when aroused. It is not at all a bad arrangement, for it permits them to be aroused rarely.

It is less difficult to account for the ill repute of teachers of the sort next to be described, for they represent a type of human being that has little standing in any group. This is the type of the egregious ass, or the nincompoop. We use these terms with a perfect awareness that they lack that exactness which terms should have which make any pretension to scientific accuracy, but since we are speaking of social types, and looking at them from the outside through the eyes of others, and since this is exactly what we think of such persons as

[1] Cf. the following statement from Park and Burgess, *Introduction to the Science of Sociology*, p. 574: "In general, we may say that competition determines the position of the individual in the community; conflict fixes his place in society. Location, position, ecological interdependence—these are the characteristics of the community: Status, subordination and super-ordination, control—these are the distinctive marks of a society."

being, the value terms will have to stand. The ass is usually a person of rather low intellectual power, though he need not show any defect of intelligence in the usual sense of the term; his lack is rather on the side of mental flexibility. The ass has little social sense, practically no awareness of the meaning of his activities or those of others in group life, no "sense of proportion." Most of all does he lack a true conception of his own place in the group; his exaggerated idea of his own value distorts all his perception of others. The ass is out of touch, and he makes the most amazing blunders in that subtle interchange of human reactions which makes up our life. His humor is humor relished almost entirely by himself, if it is relished at all. There is a certain laugh, a forced giggle, in the upper register of the voice, given with a rising inflection rather than the usual falling inflection of laughter, often coupled with a shaking of the head or other evidence of enjoyment, evoked by situations which others do not think of as funny, indulged in with a total disregard of what others may be thinking of him—this laugh we think of as asinine, and we know that the man who laughs that way is an ass. Or it may appear merely as an overloud laugh over a joke in which others do not participate. It has a correlate in a fairly well identifiable smile. What effect such a personality has upon students may well be left to the imagination. When the revolt begins, he rarely has personal force enough to meet the situation vigorously, and he attempts to meet it with piteous but unmoving appeals. It is difficult to be sympathetic with such a person, however pathetic his plight may be. It is especially difficult for the young.[1]

Another type of teacher who frequently gets into trouble is the one who is known to be incompetent, either in subject matter or in the disciplining of classes. In smaller systems, and occasionally in the larger ones, it commonly occurs that teachers are called upon at the last minute to teach subjects in which they have not adequate preparation, so that sometimes the most well-meaning instructors are put into situations where they are incompetent. There are others, of course, who feel that they can teach any subject by keeping a few minutes ahead of their classes, an opinion which obtains some support from certain alleged authorities on educational method. The situations in which incompetent instructors are put, and the shifts to which they resort in order to maintain their prestige, are sometimes ludicrous. There was the case of the foreign language teacher who was called

[1] See Somerset Maugham's description of an irresistibly comic, though tragic, character in *The Moon and Sixpence*.

upon to teach English. His students, suspecting the inadequacy of his grasp of the subject, laid a trap for him. In the day's lesson there occurred an *-ing* form o: an English verb. "Professor Smith," came the question, "is this word *going* a gerund or a participle as it is used here?" The professor was completely baffled, but did not desire to admit it. Quickly he thought of a way out. "Well," he said, "there's some question. I would not want to settle that arbitrarily for you. That wouldn't be democratic. Let's take a vote on it. How many say it's a gerund? One, two, three, four, five. Is your hand up or not, Nelson? Now Johnson, if you don't stop making those silly faces I shall have to send you from the room. Now how many say it's a participle? How many say this form of *going* is a participle? Oh, easily the majority. How many? Ten. Yes, easily the majority. Well, it is a participle. Now don't laugh, *I'll stick you every one.* It's a participle." First-year Latin is sometimes taught by teachers commandeered for the purpose without reference to their preparation for the task. One person who struggled through a year of teaching Latin without having studied it previously reported that he had been able to get quite satisfactory results by his "answer-your-own-questions-method." This meant that when a question was asked or a dispute arose the teacher refused to be called into it, but forced the entire class to look through their books until they found something relevant. If there was a dispute, that suited him all the better, for he was the debating coach, and besides it helped to pass the class hour. The discipline of this teacher was not good, but he ascribed his failure in that respect to his policy of "being human" with his students rather than to his incompetence. Either factor, in his case, would have been sufficient to account for difficulty in discipline. A defect in preparation which becomes obvious to students is fatal to a teacher's prestige, although it goes without saying that such a defect must be extreme before students can become aware of it. Further, if a teacher's inability to discipline his classes becomes obvious, he also categorizes as an incompetent.

Another kind of disrepute into which the teacher falls is that of the tyrant. The teacher ideal of the stricter sort of school is probably that of the benevolent despot, as that phrase is used by some school men. But a benevolent despot knows how far to push his domination, and he knows how to relax it. The martinet, put in the same position, knows neither of these things; he requires too great a perfection, he attempts to maintain too complete a domination, and he uses methods too vigorous for his purpose. The following excerpt will perhaps make this clear.

In the private school in which I taught there were two divisions, known as the upper and the lower schools. Military organization is difficult enough among boys of high-school age, but in the lower school it had frankly been given up as an almost impossible job. Some of the lower-school boys were quite young, ranging down to a nominal ten years of age. The smaller boys, barely liberated from the nursery, had not reached an age at which it seemed reasonable to expect of them the extreme self-control required for a strictly military unit. There were other difficulties inherent in the situation: the boys were so badly assorted as to size that a uniform step was practically impossible, their parents would not have approved of a rigidly military system for them, many of them were too small to wear a uniform satisfactorily and much too young to be expected to have spotless uniforms, and many of the teachers were youngsters who had had no military experience. On the whole, it was a reasonable arrangement by which the lower school was not expected to maintain the same military standards as the upper school. They wore a uniform, and they marched in a body in a quasi-military formation, but otherwise the control of them was a friendly, firm, paternalistic domination. The military forms were present, but it was impossible to take them seriously.

Then came Captain N. to take charge of the military system of the lower school. He was a Scandinavian, with that devotion to duty and utter lack of a sense of proportion which is not unknown among those of that nativity. He was a war veteran, who had achieved no more than moderate success in the army. Nevertheless, the military idea had got into his blood. He was more military than any bona fide officer, and more officer-like than any West Pointer. He was, in fact, a perfect martinet. It was his job to take charge of the military system of the lower school. He never had complete charge of the discipline, of course, but he was responsible for the military machine. What followed was the natural result of the fact that he took his duties very seriously. Other men there had been who in his position had done their duties conscientiously, but they had never been so vigilant and so unremitting; they had some sense of the humor of it all, and one felt that they were not above smiling about it on occasion. But Captain N. did not feel that way about it, and he worked out a *reductio ad absurdum* of the military idea.

Grimly he set about his task of whipping the lower school into shape. He demanded and tried to get from his ten-year-olds a perfection which could reasonably have been expected only of mature men and soldiers. He was on the heels of the boys when they fell out of step, as the smaller boys must inevitably do because of the shortness of their legs; he boxed their ears for talking and scolded them for standing unsteadily in ranks. He imposed penalties for spots on clothes; he made the small boys march in and out of the dining room in the most rigidly military fashion. He was everywhere with his sharp voice and his terrifying manner, trying to reproduce the spirit of the United States Army among children still damp behind the ears. He was in deadly earnest, and apparently he never smiled about his task. He may have known that what he was trying to do was hopeless, but it is a safe bet that he did not realize that it was silly.

The first effect of this military enthusiasm was a real improvement in the appearance and probably also in the morale of the lower school. For this, Captain N. received the plaudits of the faculty, especially of the administrators. He was a bit forward for a new man, and he took himself too seriously, but he "was doing a good job." At the height of his popularity he had the lower school clicking its heels in a very acceptable small-boy imitation of the army, and he had a considerable following among the faculty. At one time he had enough influence on the faculty to induce several members of the faculty, including at least one whose appearance in uniform had never been anything for the school to be proud of, to order made-to-measure puttees through him and to submit to his instructions concerning their conditioning and care.

Slowly Captain N.'s system went to pieces. One noticed that the number of penalties he imposed, of cases of discipline referred to authorities, increased somewhat. One noticed that the number of minor punishments, of cuffings, shakings, thumpings, and scoldings, increased greatly. Apparently Captain N. had whipped the lower school into shape and now he was whipping it out of shape again.

Then the members of the faculty began to find his everlasting "pep talks" concerning discipline in the mess hall and on the way in and out quite boring, later unbearable. The school was usually treated to one of these after each meal. Faculty members were supposed to remain in their seats in the mess hall until both schools had marched out of the room. Captain N. fell into the habit of making a short address on military amenities. After the upper school had left the hall, when the lower school had been called to the uncomfortable dining room position of attention, with arms crossed and held stiffly in front of them, Captain N. would arise and go to the front of the hall for his short speech. It was about as follows:

"Now I want the lower school to get up now and march out briskly, without any of this silly business, and without looking so foolish. Table One, right here, should march out first, and then table Two should fall in right behind. I want you all to keep step. It's a shame the way some of you can't tell your left foot from the right. You ought to be old enough by now to tell one foot from the other. Stand erect and swing your arms slightly as you march. And there's altogether too much noise when you get up from your chairs. There ought to be just one noise when everybody gets up and puts back his chair at the same time. After that, come to the position of attention, with your thumbs even with the seam of your trousers. Now let's see you do it right. All right. Lower school, Rise!"

During this harangue the faculty, upper school as well as lower school, sat quite still and remained silent. But they were anxious to be off about their business, at morning and at noon for a short smoke and a little relaxation before beginning the grind, and in the evening to get away. So they came to resent the man, with his airs and his inspirational lectures. The upper-school men resented also his unspoken but plain belief that the administration of that school was inefficient, that if he had it, he could make a real military machine of it, that the lower school, for all its handicaps, was a better organization. Faculty hostility toward Captain N. grew rather rapidly as a result of certain disputes which he had concerning jurisdiction, the ordinary private-school quarrels, which are rarely fatal for others, but were very deadly for him since few persons liked him anyhow. The faculty sympathized somewhat with the boys who were subjected to his browbeating tactics, and that received attention, too. All in all, the faculty felt that Captain N., far from becoming an important person in the school, was very fortunate to be allowed to finish out the year.

The words of a person who talks much are little considered; those of persons who speak little have a scarcity value which makes them heeded. Especially is this true of teachers and of all persons who must live by ordering others about. Explanations of commands detract from their force, and completeness of personal expression, by filling in all the gaps in the picture of a personality, makes idealization difficult and therefore detracts from prestige. Especially does excessive loquacity operate to a teacher's discredit if he attempts to discipline by a flow of words, or mingles humor and discipline, or talks so much that he becomes ridiculous. There is no more incompetent teacher than the fool who talks too much, and talks rot. This type of disrepute is well illustrated by the following excerpts from a case study:

Soon after I began teaching in the private school which I have mentioned, the school decided to change its policy by incorporating a regular evening study hall into its program. Previously the boys had been studying in their rooms under the supervision of the teacher who happened to be in charge of the barracks that evening. It was thought that by instituting a regular evening study hall, to last two hours, it would be possible to insure more continuous application to studies. Students who were able to maintain a satisfactory scholastic standing were to be exempt, and it was thought that this would be an added inducement.

It was plain that whoever was in charge of the evening study hall would have a difficult job. The boys were not used to it, and they would probably resent the study hall as cruel and unusual. It was certainly contrary to custom. There would be problems of lighting, ventilation, supervision of the boys during intermission, etc. There was the added difficulty that the study hall would be heavily weighted with the irresponsible and the rebellious, all the good students having been excused. Apparently no member of the regular faculty wanted the job, nor was there one whose duties were light enough to permit him to take the study hall as a regular thing. It was rather a delicate matter, for anyone who took the job would have to be paid extra, and this was contrary to the school policy up to that time. All in all, it was thought best to employ an outside man.

The school authorities took much thought and employed the most unsuitable person in the world for the post. Not that anyone was to be blamed for employing R. Bysshe Bauer, for he could have sold crucifixes to the Ku Klux Klan, or cork hats to the Eskimo. Himself he could sell in any capacity whatsoever. He was a man in his middle thirties, a teacher of commercial subjects in a city high school, and he was conducting a business which kept him poor. He agreed to take charge of the evening study hall, and gave one the impression that he knew all the tricks. In spite of what happened later, one had to concede that he probably did.

Bauer was a rather large man but soft. His size was not impressive because of his disgusting obesity. He dressed poorly. He may have chosen his clothes well and paid a good price for them, but he used them so hard and gave them so little attention that he presented a very bad appearance. His face was often dirty, and it is possible that he did not bathe frequently, for he exuded a very unpleasant odor when he had been out in the rain. But he had a brilliant, rapid-fire mind, and a magnificent power of self-expression. He talked in a rapid monotone. His words seemed to come out under pressure and to tumble over each other in their haste to get themselves said. For all that, he chose his words well, and his rapid sentences often summed up amazingly keen observations of men and affairs and human nature in general. Pregnant remarks worthy of a Bacon or a Voltaire were mingled in his speech with the coarse ribaldry of the gutter snipe. Apparently he had a high homosexual component, for the female sex seemed utterly meaningless to him on any but the grossest and lowest level, and he frequently joked concerning homosexuality. Bauer was perpetually in financial difficulties, but he was always going to be rich soon. He was involved in a hundred speculations, and none of them turned out well. He borrowed from everyone he met. He netted a great deal more through his borrowings from the people in our school than through his earnings, and one suspected him at times of cultivating the school connection for that purpose. When trying to negotiate a loan, he had a most affable manner, and he seemed perfectly sincere in his determination to pay back all at the agreed time. But when he was unable or unwilling to repay he seemed very callous and cynical about it. The person had taken his chance on the repayment of the loan; it was a business transaction, and after all business was business. If the other person lost his money that was no affair of Bauer's. He had other things to worry about. This is far from a pleasant picture of the man, but it is far from complete. No mere objective description could convey an adequate impression of his spirit. He was an indomitable optimist, always raging with enthusiasm for some new project, imbued with a mental and moral vitality that would have served as motivation for a thousand adventurers. And when he got off some bit of trenchant wit, and followed it with his odd little chuckle, he was the most amiable and humorous creature in the world.

Another man and I occupied a first-floor room at that time, and Bauer formed a habit of dropping into our room every evening before and after study hall. He would come in puffing, his honest Teutonic face aglow from exercise—he had walked two blocks. He sat down and removed his glasses, the pince-nez variety, and massaged the sides of his nose. Sometimes he seemed quite tired, as well he might, for he had taught a full day and had worked in his office in the afternoon. And occasionally, quite shamefaced, he asked permission to lie down on the bed for a few minutes of rest; but usually he asked nothing better than to sit with us and talk.

Then for fifteen minutes he would pour out upon us a flood of talk that would have shamed any of the famous conversationalists of history, acute analyses, pointed jokes, epigrams, rodomontade, bluster, lies, self-revelation of the frankest and most obscene sort. He was an interesting man, and he had none of the inhibitions of the gentleman. It was good for me to know Bauer, for I felt that he was a worse teacher than I was, and a much more intelligent man.

Though I was at the time far from shrewd in such matters, I began to suspect that the evening study hall was not going off well under Bauer's guidance. It was evident that in his conversations with boys on his way to study hall, and even when he met them in the office over some matter of discipline, he was adopting a tone of great familiarity. Frequently one would find him in the center of a group of boys engaged in rowdy conversation with them, his voice louder than any of the others. His conversation with boys was scarcely less Rabelaisian than with the teachers. One noticed also that the boys came back to their rooms much elevated after evening study hall, with every appearance of having had a good time. It was something which I noticed particularly on those evenings when I was in charge of the barracks.

Bauer had no dignity, no official dignity as a teacher and no personal dignity. Apparently he revolted at the thought that one had to maintain dignity with students or anyone else; he was a person, and his personal expression was far more important to him than his ability to discipline students. He even rebelled against any attempt of others to confer dignity upon him. The instructors in the school, as is usual in military schools, were known as "Captain," a paper dignity, but one which was fitting in the military organization. Some of the more conformed boys, anxious to be right and to avoid giving any possible offence, began to address Bauer as "Captain Bauer," although he was not in uniform. He put a stop to that decisively. "I'm not a captain," he confided in his genial, cynical way. "So-and-So's a captain, and so is Such-and-Such over there. But I'm not a captain. I wouldn't try to palm myself off on you as a Captain. I'm just a top sergeant. I'm just plain old Sergeant Bauer, and you needn't salute me or anything." Later he told me that he had thought the whole matter out carefully, realizing that his position as an outsider was a difficult one, and that he thought that be could fit into the system as a top sergeant but not as a captain. I was sure that he had just thought of the answer on the spur of the moment.

Bauer could not be serious, not wholly serious, even in his attempts to discipline students. He always seemed to be attempting to make a joke of the offence and the penalty as well. It was his idea, as he explained it to me, that by being jocular about the procedure he could make the machinery of formal punishment less unpleasant to his students. Sometimes his humor took the form of sarcastic, written reports. He reported one boy for "General disorderly behavior and throwing various and sundry missiles and projectiles across the room." The other men of the faculty felt that it was desirable to exchange as few words as possible with students concerning these formal reports of misbehavior, and it was in fact a rule of the school that a student could not begin a conversation concerning such a report without the permission of the instructor. But not so Bauer. He felt that he ought to argue the boys down on every point, and he used all his verbal resources for tripping up his opponent and talking him out of his opinion. He always won a verbal victory, but one wondered how sound it was. I later came to the conclusion that Bauer was a coward, and that on that account he did not attempt to control by commanding students, but rather tried to argue and joke them into good behavior. He could not directly assert his authority, for he was afraid to do that, but he could outargue any man in the world. Perhaps he hoped that his students would not resent his authority if he placed it upon this basis of sweet reasonableness.

One evening I paid a visit to Bauer in his study hall. I arrived at about the middle of the two-hour period, just before the evening intermission. The whole building was filled with the noise of a study hall in uproar, voices, the noise of desks and chairs, laughter, jeers, catcalls, etc. I stood just back of the doorway to observe the show. Over on one side of the room two of the larger boys were having a friendly little tussle. I understood at once how it had occurred that those seats had been broken recently. Numerous conversations were going on; they were quite open. Desks were opened and slammed frequently and insistently. A boy who wished to return a book to another boy at the side of the room stood up and threw it to him. Bauer attempted to reprimand him for this disorderly behavior, but the boy insisted that he was just returning the book, answered in the tones of outraged innocence, and faced Mr. Bauer down. Meanwhile a boy threw a penny, then another boy threw a penny, and then the penny-pitching began in earnest. Bauer stood in front of the room, darting eagle-like glances here and there, but entirely without effect. He was a little excited, if one could judge from his flushed face, but he still contrived to smile. It was time for intermission, and he began to make a little speech:

"Now we're going to have a ten-minute intermission and I want all of you fellows to be back here in exactly ten minutes from now. Look at your watches and verify that. I've warned you and you are responsible. If you have no watch, stay here and look at the clock. But just a minute, now, I have one or two things I want to say to you before you go. Now you've had a good time this first hour and when you come back I want you to dig in and study. You know I enjoy a good joke. I enjoy it even when I seem to be the butt of it, and I'm telling you, fellows, that's the test of a real humorist. But you fellows have fooled around too much and I'll have to take some action if you don't stop. None of you will have your lessons for tomorrow. Not that I care about that, but I'll get the blame, and that's where I come in. I don't want to have to take action. I don't want to have to turn people into the office. I don't want to make a lot of you walk the bull ring, and I don't see why I should if you fellows will just be a little reasonable about this. I was a youngster once myself, strange as it may seem, and I remember how it was. I'm not going to report you if I can help it. If everybody will just be reasonable, now, there won't be any need for anything of the sort. I don't think it ought to be necessary to maintain a rigid military discipline in this study hall. You boys have it hard enough being under strict discipline during the day and it would hardly be fair to expect the same thing of you at night. So I'm going to do my very best to treat you right. Now you've had your little jokes, and once in a while I'll have mine with you. But let's do away with the nonsense for the rest of the evening. All right, now you can have your ten-minute intermission. You know that it is only supposed to be five minutes, but I realize that you need some relaxation. Ha! Ha! So I am just going to make that a ten-minute intermission. All right."

A terrific din. Yells, "But you've talked three minutes already." "Well, all right, then, ten minutes from now."

The subject of the above case history obviously had many strong points, both as a teacher and a personality, but failed because of his even more obvious defects, and because his personality was peculiarly ill adapted to that sort of teaching which requires the subordination of one person to another. The factors involved in the case seem apparent enough. When a command is lost in a flood of words, its force is lost. When the talkativeness of the teacher wells out of an urge for social expression, so that it is self-revelatory talkativeness, the relationship between teacher and student breaks down by reason of a lack of social distance. When the excessive talk comes out of a feeling that it is necessary to explain disciplinary action to a student, it betrays an underlying fear of the loss of the student's good will (a lack of institutional courage), a fear strong enough to blot out utterly the common-sense realization that when a student is punished for a manifest and red-handed dereliction he knows well enough why he is being punished. And when the teacher is worried about the imposition of penalties, his students know that they have really the upper hand. The technique of arguing down objections, and of cajoling refractory boys into good behavior, does not work. Nor does it help to joke about a penalty, for such humor is rarely relished by the person punished; the punishment is a very serious thing to him. It is difficult to reconcile the two aims of humor and of discipline.

Another type of teacher who rarely fails to obtain the disrespect of his classes is the weakling. The weakling may be intelligent, and he is quite possibly well prepared for his job on the intellectual side. He is almost certain to be on the positive side of the moral ledger, and he is frequently a pietist. But he lacks sufficient physical stamina to win the respect of students as a physical object. And there is some subtle lack in his moral make-up which prevents him from standing out against the opinion of the student group and makes it difficult for him to face unpleasant situations with the unpleasantness which can solve them. He lacks the hostility reactions which one needs for success in the ordinary school. He cannot fight. It is worthy of remark that a sadistic strain in the teacher's make-up is a useful aid in securing subordination from students, especially if it is balanced by a certain amount of friendliness and a strong sense of justice and organized into a personality deserving of respect on other grounds. Sometimes this is what the weakling lacks, but it does not seem too cynical to suggest that this element is not so often entirely lacking as inhibited by fear.

When I was in high school we used to have great fun with an odd character who taught us commercial Spanish. He was a man of about medium height, very slender and wispy. His eyes were a washed-out blue, watery and without fire or sparkle. His mouth was a beautiful Cupid's bow, delicately modeled in an expression of exquisite, sweet weakness. His face was thin without being in the least sharp, and his body was almost cadaverous. He had a voice of which he was somewhat proud, but it was a womanish voice and somewhat nasal. Altogether he was a pitiable rather than an attractive picture, friendly, polite, obliging, good-natured, conscientious—but hardly anybody really liked him. He was a would-be preacher, and the religious activities carried on as a sideline about the high school gave him just the opportunity he wanted. He had charge of the Hi-Y, and he seemed very enthusiastic about all that it offered. He used it as a channel for his long, silly speeches. He was a bear on purity, and he used to enjoy talking about it. He had one speech in particular which it delighted him to give; it was his prepared address, something about Sir Galahad. In it was much pathos, more bathos, and the stuff of human tears. When we overcame our contempt for the fellow, we felt sorry for him because of the dull, hard life he had. But that was rare.

The other members of the faculty used his classes as a dumping ground for their more stupid and intractable students. He welcomed all and sundry, for he was building up a department. And he made sure that everybody got a good grade who attended class. His judgment was also slightly influenced by one's behavior in class. His classes were in continual confusion. Everybody talked as he pleased, and recited, or read another book, or wrote letters, as the mood struck him. Mr. B. rarely said anything about the disorder, and he seldom upbraided anyone about not preparing a lesson. Sometimes he ventured a mild remonstrance; once or twice he became quite hard with some of the less dangerous fellows. One picture I will never forget—his way of calling a class to order. He had a little bell on his desk; no other teacher had one or felt the need. Trying to look unconcerned, but succeeding only in looking foolish, he would stand in front of his class with a severe expression on his face and hammer on the bell with a book. This seemed to us the essence of the ludicrous. (Life history document.)

The flirtatious teacher also gets into disrepute. Sex, as we have shown elsewhere, is much in evidence throughout the whole of school life, and it is unavoidably present in the attitudes which students and teachers have toward each other. A highly sublimated sort of sex appeal is sometimes made the basis of favorable rapport, but it is a rapport which may, with its emphasis slightly askew, degenerate rapidly. This is the case with the flirtatious teacher. The flirt is the man or woman teacher who is frankly open to the charms of students of opposite sex. Where teachers usually attempt to exclude such matters from their relations with students, these teachers attempt to bring them into play. Sometimes they wish to exploit their students sexually by means of their authority, but more often they merely open themselves to exploitation by students whose charms they appreciate. Sometimes the sexual motivation toward students is conscious and ruthless. In other cases it is never recognized for what it is, or, as in the case of young women teachers, it is merely a by-product of their whole social training up to that point. In any case, an attitude of the teacher which lays him open to frankly sexual interchange with students is one which has damaging effects upon his control of his classes. It makes nepotism unavoidable, and on those grounds it is hotly resented by those in the class who receive no favors. Where there is a marked age difference between students and teacher, any pronounced sex interest on the part of the teacher will seem depraved or ridiculous, although an older person may on occasion disguise a strong sexual interest in a particular student as a fatherly or motherly interest. Where there is only a slight age difference between student and teacher, the worst effect, for the teacher, of establishing a love relation with one of his students is that it involves him in the student world. It is, further, likely to involve him in an unfavorable manner.

Our most important point concerning the love relation in the schools may be stated in quite general terms. The rapport of the love relation is quite incompatible with dominance and subordination as it is established in the schools. Further, the love relation, even in its incipient stages, is incompatible with the maintenance of such social distance as is expected of the teacher. The sexual motivation of the student (or the teacher) prompts him continually to attempt to break down barriers; if the student succeeds in his attempt, the teacher loses standing, and if he does not succeed he becomes troublesome and bitter. It is a failure to reckon with this mechanism which accounts for much of the trouble which women teachers have with girls in the age of crushes. It might be pointed out also that the flirtatious teacher loses standing in the school and the community because of his violation of that principle of morality which holds that those who stand in an authority relation should not exploit that relation for personal reasons. This is a very strong taboo indeed, and has led in some cases to violence or indignity on the part of townsmen toward the teacher who failed to respect it. It is perhaps vaguely realized that the flirtatious teacher violates the special ethics of the image relations, that morality which requires that those who stand in relations which have special force because of their emotional reenforcement from other sources, as teachers, preachers, lawyers, doctors (especially psychiatrists), and priests, should not exploit that rapport for any purpose of their own.

Another type of disrepute into which the teacher falls is that of the caricature. Apparently it is of the nature of the teacher as an occupational type to get out of touch with the community of men in general, and to develop his own special way of life without much thought of the world that is not the school. When this process of specialization has gone on for a long time, the teacher may develop into a caricature of the occupational type. Now the occupational type of the teacher is, as we shall see, usually developed by way of an adaptation to the conditions of teaching, but when the teacher has passed a certain point in the development of occupational traits he becomes so completely out of touch with human beings in general that even his teaching is handicapped. Then he has become a caricature, and the caricature is ridiculous. It is not only ridiculous in itself, but it tends to make all other teachers ridiculous because of their similarity to it in some essential qualities.

A teacher who comes to be much hated is the bully. The bully attempts to keep his students under control by keeping them in a constant state of fear. He badgers students, threatens them, lords it over them, keeps them in fear by sudden displays of anger, and uses the social technique of one who is determined to have his way by unpleasant means if possible. His is the institutional variety of quarrelsomeness. The bully speaks in a badgering or blustery tone of voice, one that suggests that he is already angry and that he is likely if at all irritated to become much more angry, which may convey the idea that this teacher never did care very much about students anyway, and is now at the end of his patience with them. This voice may be shrill and sharp, though it is not so in the typical case; it is more likely to be full and fuzzy, as if a number of ragged edges of emotion adhered to it. The classroom manner of many teachers is built upon this bullying technique as a basis. The following story will perhaps illustrate some of the typical behavior which we think of as going to make up the bullying personality.

Inadvertently we sat a little straighter in our chairs when we heard our teacher's step in the hall. He was a rough man, and bad-tempered, and we never knew where his temper was going to break out next. This morning he paused in the doorway and looked us all over before entering. There was on his face not the shadow of a smile, and that expression which left no doubt in any of our minds that he was not happy over the thought of having to spend the hour with us. We had the impression that he did not like us and would not regret an opportunity to punish us. The suspense was heightened as he looked over the class. He walked into the room; slowly, deliberately, and with a slight swagger he made his way toward his desk. He looked at a little boy in the back row. "Johnson," he said in that deadly way he had, "I told you to write our yesterday's lesson four times. Where is it?"

"It's on your desk, sir," said the small boy in a very small voice.

"Well, it had better be. Where did we stop yesterday? You tell us, Jones, that's all you can do. We've got to make some use of you."

"Page 96, line 7," said Jones, apparently not offended.

"Sir," said the teacher.

"Yes, sir," answered Jones, mechanically.

We turned to the lesson. "All right, Jones, try to translate the first sentence."

Jones began, "When the lights were turned on . . ."

"Oh, Lord, no, no, nonono! Sit down. Shut up. That will do from you. *Prima luce* does not mean when the lights were on. Why did I ever call on such a dumbbell as you. I'll never be able to teach you anything. You're too smug and too conceited. Why don't you ever get next to yourself? Palmer! All right, Palmer!"

"I'm afraid I can't today, sir."

"Why not?"

"I don't understand that sentence," said Palmer, in desperation.

"Ha, ha. I know that trick. Translate the next sentence."

"I can't, sir."

"Well, then, translate any sentence in the assignment. You can't?" His voice raised, and we knew that the storm was going to break. His voice filled the room. "Now, listen here, Palmer. I'm damned good and tired of the way you act anyhow. All you do in this class is take up a chair." He walked up to Palmer's chair and began to shake his fist in his face. "I want you to know that I'm tired of your damned nonsense." Exhausted, he sank back into his chair. (Fictionized case study.)

This is a method of teaching which tends to wear itself out. The loud voice and dire threats with which the school year begins tend to lose their force unless they are followed by a yet louder voice and more blood-curdling threats in the near future, and there is an easily attained limit to this process. It has the further disadvantage that it puts a nervous strain upon both students and teacher which, though it may be a spur to the dull and a challenge to the idle, is an obstacle to achievement for many students. Further, it is a method which will make a teacher hated, unless it is in the folkways, and even then if the teacher is not able to balance it by some pleasant traits of character.

But it should be stated emphatically that the bully often gets by, and that his students often develop a real affection for him. He gets results from students whom other teachers have given up. And he has at least the psychological advantage of the initiative, he "has the jump on his students." Sometimes it even gets abroad that he is a rough old codger but he has a heart of gold and "would give you the shirt off his back if he thought you needed it." This, it may be said, is often true of teachers whose classroom personality is most definitely given over to bullying, and it helps them to obtain forgiveness. It is said that boys will take any abuse from a man whom they consider just and from a man who, "away down under," likes them. But perhaps the most important point in the bully's favor is that he has color and that he gives his small but discriminating public a good show.

There are some teachers who have ego-gratifying devices which interfere with their teaching efficiency. They find in the classroom an opportunity to cultivate expansive moments, and they manipulate their teaching procedure with a view to squeezing from it as many such moments as possible. The list of ego-swelling poses, of tricks which give the teacher that pleasant feeling of being somehow a very remarkable fellow, of sayings which are thought to make others wonder and admire—this list is literally endless. Pride everywhere betrays men into a fall, and it betrays other men, perhaps, as consistently as teachers, but the teacher is in a position of unusual temptation. He has the attention of a large group, and it is his job to keep that attention constellated upon himself. To expand his personality to include the entire group, and yet to refrain from using the expanded contact as a means of gratifying his private wishes, to include other personalities within the control of one's own and yet to exclude the interior self, in a word, to dominate impersonally, is a truly great achievement, and it is not so amazing that the teacher usually lacks this extraordinary grace as that he ever has it.

The pride-fulfilling devices of teachers do not always affect their student relationships unfavorably, and these devices are, in fact, useful if they do not pass certain bounds or bring the teacher into direct conflict with his students. Self-dramatization is effective if it includes relatively little of self and drives home important elements of subject matter; it is difficult to tell when it becomes a vice. A habit of trying to say things well is a good habit, and students are usually grateful for a teacher who has it. But a teacher who says things well may go out of his way to find things to say well, and once he has started he may range further and further afield in his search for epigrams. In the extreme case, he becomes "one who says smart things smartly," a "wise-cracker." Somewhere he has crossed the invisible line that separates good practice from bad. This is but one example. There are other ego-gratifying mechanisms which injure only the teacher himself; an example of this is a certain brilliant, ultra-sophisticated teacher of English who, in the apt phrase of a colleague, "has so many poses to keep before the public that he never has time for anything else." Many teachers whose rapport with students is excellent are accustomed to nourish their self-feelings at the expense of their colleagues, particularly of underlings, and the devices they employ are uncountable.

We are here concerned with a particular variety of disrepute into which teachers fall if they allow their ego-feelings to obtrude themselves too obviously into their transactions with students. Two different mechanisms are involved in these cases: first, that the individuals involved become ridiculous because they make ridiculous claims upon the students' respect, either by priding themselves upon ridiculous things or by gross exaggeration of their own merits; secondly, that they attempt to gratify their own self-feelings by making an attack upon students, and receive, as a general thing, repayment in kind. Animosity aroused by some direct attack usually supplies the motive for caricature of the sort first mentioned, and if there is no such animosity the inherently ridiculous claims of the teacher may pass unchallenged. The following story illustrates the disrepute of the teacher who too obviously uses his authority as a teacher as a means of ego gratification:

"I am James Weatherford Robinson. I see you are the new man in our department. Starting out as assistant-instructor, are you? Well, I did the same twenty years ago. You have a long, weary road ahead of you, but what one man has done another can, I always say. Of course, you have much to learn. But there are magnificent opportunities here. As for me, I have at present a very satisfactory position, and a fine income. I am a full professor, insurance statistics, you know, and I draw a nice salary from that. In addition I get many fat fees from insurance companies for one little job and another. I have a very fine thing of it indeed. Now let me see, what did you say your name was?"

"Watkins."

"All right, Mr. Hawkins, I'll remember you."

"I'm sorry, the name is Watkins. W-a-t-k-i-n-s."

"Oh, yes, to be sure, to be sure, to be shewer! Do you have your doctor's degree, Watkins?"

"No, Dr. Robinson. I'm sorry to say I haven't."

"Well, you'll have to get it one of these days. Drop everything else till you do. Never get anywhere in this line of work till you do. Well, see you again, Hawkins. My office is just down the hall. Name's on the door, of course. James Weatherford Robinson. See you again some time."

"I hope so, Dr. Robinson," I said politely.

Dr. James Weatherford Robinson made an exit. I sat down in my chair to put in order the array of impressions this amazing man had left.

He was big and he had a florid face. His manner was expansive, his gestures large. He smiled often. He had several gold teeth that showed when he smiled. His voice was rather poor, high-pitched, but hoarse. He had been smoking a very opulent-looking cigar. He had a stomach, and he wore it proudly. His eyes were of that peculiar staring kind which I had never been able to diagnose; no glint of humor or responsiveness was in them. I thought I had seen a war medal on his vest. I was sure I had seen something glistening under his coat.

In the years that followed I was to learn much about James Weatherford Robinson. For the present I thought that I liked him. Halfway I understood him. Now I wonder, I asked myself, why he told me about his income? "A fine income," he had said. And all that stuff about my degree. Everybody had been telling me that. He was the sixth, and I had been here only a week. Well, they were right.

I wondered where Dr. Robinson got his degree. I found a catalogue. After much hunting, I found his name. I was puzzled to see that no Ph.D. was listed, only an M.A., taken twenty years before from a second-rate institution.

I was very tactful with James Weatherford Robinson. I did not allow him to learn that I knew that he did not have a doctor's degree. He did a great many things for me, and I was profoundly grateful to him, only a little the less grateful because I knew that these favors had been won from him by my own tact, by seeming to sympathize with him in his struggle against his many enemies on the faculty, by seeming to be impressed by all his stories. I had for him, perhaps, that sort of gratitude long ago defined as the lively expectation of favors to be received.

Robinson had, indeed, many enemies on the faculty. There were many who felt that he had at one time or another been too lordly in his dealings with them. Others resented the fact of his large earnings, and registered official complaints against him on the grounds that he neglected his school work for his outside activities. These charges were not proved. What was proved, however, was that his frequent references to his income were most unwise. Faculty members told and retold an old story that Robinson had once tried to pass himself off as a veritable doctor of philosophy. He was also accused of having stolen another man's course.

Robinson, I learned, had many students. He had also many friends among the students, and he had been known to go to great lengths to help students out of trouble. Nevertheless, students hated him.

"His course," said one student, "is a course on Why I Am a Great Man. I registered for it once, and went a couple of times. The first hour he talked about himself and what a great fellow he was. He leaned over the rostrum and showed us his four medals. One was a war medal, for bravery. Another was for marksmanship. Another was for a prize essay. The fourth was for high-school track. He tried to make us think they were all war medals. I heard the real story from someone in the class, and then one day, long after, I got up close to him and looked at his medals closely and I found out it was true.

"Well, I suffered through the first hour. My impulse was to drop the course at once. But I said to myself, 'It can't be as bad as that all the time, and I need that course to round out my schedule. So I'll stick around just a little while longer and see how things turn out.' I did, and the next day he told us all about his outside connections, and how much money he made from them. He leaned back, stuck his thumbs in his vest, and said, 'I just teach for the fun of it. The money I get for teaching is a very small part of my income, a very small part, indeed. It really costs me money to teach, because I could make so much more working outside.' I dropped the course after the second hour."

"I finished Robinson's course," said another student. "But it was very unpleasant. He was always bulldozing and personal. He would call over the roll and come to a foreign name and say, 'Here's one. S-c-e-m-a-n-k-o-w-i-t-z. Now I don't want to have to sneeze every day; just have to call you Simmons, I guess.' There was a fellow named Dolittle. Of course he told him he would have to do more than that. His delight was to catch somebody unprepared. If he did, he was very sarcastic and unpleasant. Pulled out his grade book and ostentatiously marked down a zero. Then he would tell the fellow how poorly he was doing and how hard he would have to work to pass the course. He would ask the boy where he was from and when he told him he would say, sneeringly, 'I thought so.' He used to amuse himself by getting some dumb-bell up for questioning—he always made us stand up to recite—and questioning him until he was confused. Then he would laugh. He was really unbearable."

"But didn't the students ever try to get back at him?"

"Oh, yes. Especially the class I was in. It was right after the war and we didn't stand for it meekly by any means. We guyed him about his medals, and when he finally got wise to the fact that we were guying him he was sore. The class got away from him entirely. It was in an uproar most of the time. He'd stalk up and down in front of the class and threaten us with what he would do to us, and when he turned his back to write something on the board we'd all give him the Bronx cheer. Then he would turn around and rave some more. We didn't learn anything, and he flunked a lot of us, but the school paper raised a row about it, said it was his inefficiency that caused it, and he had to let most of the fellows through after all. They say that he would have lost his job that time if it hadn't been for his outside connections. That part of his line isn't a bluff, by the way. That was several years ago, but he's still the school joke. As he goes down the walk all the students call out, 'Hello, Professor Robinson,' just to get him going, and he always waves and throws up his arm. It's a riot. And every once in a while there's a little piece in the paper about 'The Almighty,' or 'The Man With the Iron Chest.' That's him."

"But why do students continue to elect his course?"

"Well, it's hard to say. He's unpleasant. He's vindictive. He's unfair. He's a hard marker. But it's a good course, and usually he makes things interesting. There are so many professors who are dull. Robinson's an ass, but he's rarely dull. And he's so nasty that you enjoy trying to get ahead of him. And he's so serious and so naïve about it that it's fun to razz him. We have lots of good laughs without his knowing why."

Said Professor Robinson, "Watkins, you must deliver the goods: That is the secret of my success, if you'll pardon a personal reference. You must make good. I have lots of students because I have a good course. I deliver the goods. I work hard in the classroom. Many a boy has come up to me, just as he was handing in his final examination, and said that it was the most interesting course he ever had. I'm telling you the truth; many of them have said that. They get me out to their fraternities and have me talk about myself. They like me. I feel it. They like me in spite of the fact that I work them hard and mark them low. When I go down the sidewalk, more students speak to me than to any other teacher on the campus. That's really so, Watkins." (Fictional.)

The ego mechanisms of the above character are sufficiently clear to pass without extended comment. Such behavior is to be seen in thousands of classrooms. It is incredibly difficult for the teacher to ascertain when he crosses the line and becomes ridiculous. The moral obtuseness with which such teachers pursue their egotic aims is remarkable, the more so since it is so often coupled with neurotic keenness in ferreting out remote implications of status. The psychology of the inferiority complex seems to be the necessary background for the understanding of these cases. The underlying sense of inadequacy is in them, and compensatory behavior and the basic life lie. Such is the egotist.

Ego involvements of the sort under discussion are to be found in other cases which we have mentioned. They are basic in the martinet, the bully, and the over-talkative teacher, but it seemed best to illustrate them by a special selection. It is heartening to reflect that this type has its opposite, that there are many teachers who tread warily among the feelings of students and colleagues. They walk softly, as the saying is, and they go far. They have learned how to disarm, which is a special technique and one requiring much practice—a very long art.

This completes our presentation of the varieties of prestige and disrepute which attach to the teacher. Most of these have been illustrated by cases drawn from actual life and as faithfully portrayed as circumstances would permit. Some readers will object, as they have every right to do, that these cases are not typical. Teachers who represent these behavior mechanisms in such extreme form are in fact rare, and these cases are therefore statistically atypical. But they illustrate common mechanisms and it seems to have served the purposes of exposition to use them. The alert reader will also recall that we are here dealing with social images, which are by definition distortions of impressions of persons; we are dealing quite frankly with illusion, and not with reality. We have therefore filtered most of these cases through the minds of students, and have been less concerned with what these persons really were than with what others thought they were. This is not the place for a discussion of the various kinds of selves, and it should be clear enough that this procedure is justifiable. We have been concerned with one kind of social self, and our studies do not preclude that these same persons, seen from another vantage point than that of students or colleagues, might appear to wear different faces.

Ordinary teachers rarely exemplify any of these types in unmixed form. The successful teacher is usually experienced by his students with overtones of two or three of the prestige-carrying images, and has quite possibly some things in his personality which suggest the images of negative value. The attitudes of students toward the best of teachers are in most instances ambivalent, and the net effect of the teacher's personality depends upon the relative weight of counterpoised attitudes, or upon arrangements which allow both sorts of attitudes to be expressed. It would be misleading, of course, to explain student attitudes toward teachers entirely on the basis of these social images, for there are many other images, and there is always, in addition, something of the uniquely personal which enters into the impression which the teacher makes upon the pupil. But when this that is uniquely personal creeps in, it is because the institution cannot keep it out, and the interaction which then arises no longer pertains to those illusions of prestige and disrepute upon which rests the institutional leadership that teachers practice. Teachers are shapes seen in a fog, and students have fog-bound attitudes toward them; the shapes are human and occasionally personal, and yet the most significant thing is that they are seen in a fog. The analysis of the teacher into personal and institutional elements is a task which cannot fail to challenge the research worker of the future.

PROJECTS

1. Make case studies of persons exemplifying all the kinds of prestige and disrepute mentioned in the book.

2. Make case studies of successful teachers. How far can they be interpreted in terms of our categories? What further categories do you suggest?

3. Probe into the attitudes of students toward particular teachers as a means of seeing whether teacher prestige conforms to these categories or not. List favorable and unfavorable comments, and classify.

4. Study the teaching personalities of a number of older men who do not classify as "patriarchs."

5. Relate instances showing the difficult situation in which the teacher becomes involved if she allows herself to become a love object to her students. Analyze and interpret.

6. Make extended observations upon teachers who fear students.

7. Write the life history of a too good-natured teacher, in one particular school. Was the experience repeated?

8. Analyze student attitudes toward a competent but over-strict teacher.

9. Study carefully some teacher who has become a caricature. Analyze and interpret.

10. Analyze the student relationships of a teacher whose ego demands interfere with his efficiency.

SUGGESTED READINGS

(1) Burrow, Trigant, "Social Images Vs. Reality," *Journal of Abnormal and Social Psychology,* Vol. XIX, pp. 230-235.

(2) Carlyle, T., *Heroes and Hero-Worship.*

(3) Finney, Ross L., "The Unconscious Social Mind," *Journal of Applied Sociology,* 1926, Vol. X, pp. 357-367.

(4) Le Bon, G., *The Crowd: A Study of the Popular Mind,* Part II, Chapter III.

(5) Leopold, L., *Prestige, A Psychological Study of Social Estimates.*

(6) Michels, R., *Political Parties,* pp. 64-68.

(7) Overstreet, H. A., *Influencing Human Behavior,* Chapters I, II, and IV.

(8) Petersen, J., and David, Q. J., *The Psychology of Handling Men in the Army.*

(9) Webster, H., *Primitive Individual Ascendency,* Publications of the American Sociological Society, 1918, Vol. XII, pp. 46-60.

Chapter XVII

SOCIAL DISTANCE; BUFFER PHRASES

Social distance is characteristic of the personal entanglements of teachers and students. It is a necessity where the subordination of one person to another is required, for distance makes possible that recession of feeling without which the authority of another is not tolerable. Students would hate teachers more than they do if it were not for the fact that distance between the teacher and his students makes the teacher relatively meaningless as a person.

A certain social distance is necessary even where students and teachers have made the transition from secondary group contacts to primary group contacts, where long use has metamorphosed a categorical into a personal contact. For the only primary group attitudes which are compatible with dominance and subordination are those which grow up within the relationship itself. All primary group attitudes established on a purely personal basis, without the one party insisting upon or the other accepting the authority of the teacher, are likely to come into conflict with the school-room relationship. But if the primary group attitudes spring up within the situation as defined in terms of dominance and subordination they do not cause the teacher's authority to be questioned. Primary group attitudes born of experience on the playground may indeed enhance the prestige of the teacher; if the teacher performs favorably in any respect, they may enhance it much; in other cases a situation of contradiction and reenforcement is established. But it should be borne in mind that the intimate association of teachers and students in play, whereby primary group attitudes sometimes arise to humanize the teacher-pupil relation, is possible only by virtue of the acceptance of social distance.

Between adult and child is an irreducible social distance that seems at times an impassable gulf. The distance arises from the fact that the adult has absorbed the heritage of the group, and represents therefore in some sense the man plus the wisdom of all his ancestors, whereas the child is much more the natural and uncultivated man, and from the fact that the adult has found his place in the world and the child has not. The distance arising from these facts is but little diminished when the adult is in revolt against the group heritage which he has assimilated or when he is not satisfied with the place which he has attained in the world. To the natural distance between adult and child is added a greater distance when the adult is a teacher and the child is a student, and this distance arises mainly from the fact that the teacher must give orders to the child; they cannot know each other, for we can never know a person at whom we only peer through institutional bars. Formality arises in the teacher-pupil relationship as a means of maintaining social distance, which in its turn is a means to discipline.

Almost every teacher has certain favorite means whereby he maintains the necessary distance between himself and his students. These means are usually a part of the teacher's personality, and are a function of his general social adjustment, so that they are applied without any awareness of their effect, or with only a vague realization that "one must keep one's place." They are, for all that, none the less effective. Most important of the means whereby distance is maintained, and most closely connected with the teacher's personality, is that classroom procedure which defines the situation in an impersonal manner and excludes possibilities of spontaneous human interaction. This is the dry, matter-of-fact, formal procedure of the classroom, a human intercourse which gives nothing and asks nothing of personalities, but is always directed at the highly intellectualized matter to be studied. Spontaneous human intercourse is often inconsequential and meandering; it goes first here and then there as the various attitudes of persons are called out and in turn call out relevant attitudes of others, but classroom intercourse must always more or less follow the custom, the outline, and the book. If it is rarely interesting, it is bearable because it is impersonal. If it is rarely inspired, it is not so often silly and absurd as it would be if it followed the whims of human beings who are absurd and silly. It is an intercourse which gives nothing of the self and reveals nothing of it but contrariwise does not demand anything of it. The teacher questions, the pupils answer. The pupils question, the teacher answers. The teacher assigns tasks, the pupils do them. The pupils do lessons, the teacher criticizes. Occasionally there comes a temptation to wander from the path beaten deep by the generations; the teacher, mindful of the course of study, brings the class back to the matter in hand for the day. This is the most effective and the most painless means by which the teacher maintains social distance between himself and his charges. As shoptalk has it, "he lets them know that he means business."

For many teachers a business-like teaching manner is all that is required to fend off possible advances from students which might lead to a diminution of the social distance between teacher and student. Other teachers have worked out, not wholly consciously, techniques by which approaches may be discouraged and the teacher protected from intimate contact with students. A favored technique is to answer all statements regarded as improper for a teacher to receive from students in a cold voice and in words distinctly non-committal. Teacher and student are talking in a friendly but still distant way; the student is moved to a burst of confidence and he remarks, "I sure was out on a swell date last night." The teacher answers, "How interesting," and passes on to another subject. Or a student comes to a teacher with a complaint about another teacher. The teacher answers, "I feel quite sure Mr. So-and-So is competent to run his classes." The tone is dry, uninterested, and disapproving. There is likewise a look which betokens social distance, and reminds the offender of the difference in the formal positions of the persons concerned. In a moment of friendliness and familiarity, the student lays his hand upon the teacher's shoulder. Turning, retracting his head, and gently disengaging himself from the contact, the teacher remarks in a frigid manner, "Oh, yes, Mr. Jackson." Or a student assumes in class a bit too relaxed a position, or seems slightly too free with his opinions, and the teacher looks at him coldly and at once looks away. The favorite technique of college teachers who wish to discourage expression of student opinions is to listen to such expressions politely, and then to say, "Hum! Yes! Are there any other contributions?" accompanying the words with a bored look and a slight but evident straining to be polite. It should be noted too that the look of animosity with which teachers occasionally quell students who are guilty of misconduct is a look which asserts the existence of an immense social distance, a look which says, "You are a very low form of creation. Between you and me there is no human bond. The distance is so great that I can look at you with the most unrestrained animosity."

There are many other techniques which are used for the purpose of reestablishing social distance. One is the interposition of a command or a fault-finding assertion in a situation which the teacher believes is becoming too intimate. The teacher has unbent somewhat and the student is alarmingly at ease. Gently the teacher reminds him of the formal relationship. "Now, John, I want you to have that Latin lesson tomorrow." Or the teacher says, with friendly roughness, "Now don't let me hear any more bad reports from you," or, "Now see to it that you keep up your record, or I'll be right after you.'' Less adroitly, she says, ''These papers show that you have not been applying yourself, John. I'm afraid you are a very careless boy.'' A certain college professor who often unbends in private saves himself partially from a carryover of familiarity by referring at the end of the conference to school matters and taking the opportunity to deliver certain teacher-orientated bits of advice and criticism. It is a technique which represents an excellent compromise between intimacy and authority. It is friendliness without a complete abdication of distance and the authoritative rôle. If the familiarity which the student is displaying is of a sort more dangerous, and there are no desirable attitudes to be carried over from the situation, the teacher sometimes uses tactics less polite. She says, ''Please don't lean over my desk when you are talking to me,'' or, ''Stand up straight. Don't slop over so; now what is it you came up here to say?'' In other cases where there is nothing of value to be preserved from the situation, the teacher meets some bit of self-revelation on the part of the student with the definite statement that he is not interested and a reminder of the strictly business relationship existing between the two.

Perhaps every teacher develops a different technique for meeting the situations called forth by his personality in the situation in which he must meet his students and instruct them. There are some interesting instances of such devices in fiction. One of the best of these is in *Chimes.*

The women were not as a rule pretty or even attractive. Clavercin had determined from the start to keep the reactions of the classroom and the office as sexless as possible. It was not difficult in the majority of cases, for the women were plain and not always tidy. Sometimes a woman would linger after class, and when the others had drifted away would try to bring something into play other than the objective, the impersonal matter between student and instructor. Clavercin had a way of assembling his books and papers while dryly restating the question that effectively suppressed this personal appeal and quickly he found that he had gained a reputation for being "stiff," even "snobbish." An incredible story went the round of the campus to the effect that Professor Clavercin had asked his women students not to bow to him outside his classroom because he did not wish to have social relations with them. Mrs. Crandall reported this tale to him with much amusement.[1]

Students in their turn have ways of fending off undue advances from teachers. The young have their reserves which they rarely cast

[1] Herrick, Robert. *Chimes,* p. 58. (Reprinted by permission of The Macmillan Company.) (Cf. p. 42 for our discussion of *Chimes.*)

off in the presence of their elders, and likewise the subordinate has an inner life into which only his equals can penetrate. Defences of the young against the teacher's curiosity and occasional yearning to be accepted by students consist mainly in treating the teacher as a teacher and refusing to consider him otherwise. Many a teacher attempting to make his classes personal has felt the disgust of certain reserved members of his classes, and not a few have been called to order by some quiet and respectful student who wanted to ask a question about the lesson. The respect of students disciplines the teacher. It is important for the teacher to know that social distance, unless it is to be quite destructive of the self-respect of the subordinated person, must always have two sides. If the teacher is to maintain his own reserves he must respect those of his students.

But it is not enough for teachers to know how to keep their students at a distance. They must know how to control the impact of their personalities upon students (and the impact of students' personalities upon themselves) in such a way as to avoid giving unnecessary hurt to the sensitive, to obviate antagonism, to arouse the interest of students, and to draw them into the social process in which learning takes place. We turn to an analysis of the mechanisms, revolving around the use of set phrases, and conventionalized verbal formulae, by which these social manipulations are accomplished.

Persons engaged in certain kinds of salesmanship are coached in the proper use of what are known as buffer phrases. These are phrases to be used when an objection has been made to the program one is trying to promote, or when a question has been raised that one does not care to answer or is not prepared to answer at that time. The buffer phrases which are then interjected into the conversation are phrases which seem to have come in quite naturally, but which enable the salesman to gain time to think or to divert the attention of the person from the point he was making. Everyone uses phrases in this way to gain time, or he uses noises made with his voice for that purpose, but buffer phrases enable one to think for a second while he appears to be taking up the conversation where the other person left off. Phrases which can be used to gain time are such expressions as the following: "Well, now I'll tell you about that, Mrs. Jones," "Well, Mr. Smith, it's this way," "It's just like this, Mr. Hopper," "You see, Mr. Johnson, it's this way," etc. Phrases which can be used to gain time and also to divert attention from the issue, or to postpone its consideration until it is forgotten or taken up in a different connection are such as the following: "Now that is a good point, Mr.

Jones, and I am very glad indeed that you brought that up . . .", "I was coming to that, Mrs. Smith," or, "We'll come to that in just another minute, Mrs. Smith."

Teachers are not under the same sort of pressure as the salesman, but they often have need of buffer phrases. On occasion, teachers learn to apply all these devices and many more. Probably it is better, and certainly it is more honest, for the teacher who is perplexed to take time to think, and if he thinks of no adequate answer, to confess his ignorance frankly and promise to remedy it. But not all teachers are temperamentally constituted to wait five seconds between the time a question is put and the time when they begin to answer it, and as they require rapid-fire answers of others they likewise require them of themselves; further, the social situation of the classroom does not always permit of deliberation, and many teachers do not feel that it ever permits a frank confession of ignorance. Therefore teachers use buffer phrases to gain time and to conceal ignorance. They use all the phrases mentioned above, and in addition they have some of their own which have a great ring of verisimilitude. They say, "Let us not anticipate, John. That will come a little later in the course." "Now when I get through talking I think you will understand that all right." "I think we had better stick to the lesson, John. Now what were the issues in the presidential campaign of 1832?"

There are other sorts of phrases which are used in a similar manner but which do not merit so cynical a presentation. They are sometimes used to gain time, too, but the time which they seemingly waste is required for transition, and beneath their apparent waste is a real achievement in maintaining a friendly tone and avoiding antagonistic rapport. They are buffer phrases because they are rather artificially interjected into the conversation, and because they postpone the actual statement of the teacher's opinion or enable him to hide his actual attitude. But the dissembling in them is the dissembling of one who chooses to reveal himself gradually in order to be the more fairly evaluated, and the time that such words waste is time that is needed for the other person to change his mind. Artificial they are, certainly, but an artificiality of speech that enables another to retire gracefully from an erroneous position is justifiable. Getting along with people is mainly saving their faces.

In the simplest case, the teacher uses certain quite formalized and artificial phrases to crystallize the interest of the student and to gain a further rapport with him. One says, "That's a very good point, and I am glad you brought that up. It deserves serious consideration." In a discipline such as sociology, it is often possible to reply with perfect honesty to a student question in this wise: "Yes, Mr. Jones, that is a good question, and I am glad it occurs to you because it shows that you are doing some thinking of your own. It is one of the great unsolved questions of human nature (or of social organization). I imagine that many of us in this line of work have been puzzled by it at one time or another. Now my opinion is . . . (directly contrary to that of the student)."

If one wishes to go further with such a technique, and to take advantage of the opportunity thus afforded to impart information, advance an argument, or instill a favorable attitude, he may use the question as a means of catching hold of the student. This is done through the use of the technique of persuasion. One says, as above, "Yes, Mr. Jones, that is a good question. It covers an important point, etc. Your question seems to reflect a certain point of view, which I believe could be stated in this way . . . Now that is a very tenable point of view, and one for which many arguments may be advanced. It is vastly superior to the unenlightened attitude which holds that . . . At one time I was strongly committed to your present point of view. Many able students of society still think that way. Their arguments are very convincing, and I believe that those arguments are perfectly sound as far as they go. The principal arguments are . . . Those are excellent arguments, and I can see how they convince many persons. To me, they seem to fall down, or to fail to be entirely convincing, because they leave out of consideration certain other important matters (or certain facts, or certain emphases indicated by modern researches). But a few years ago we all believed that (feeblemindedness was a principal cause of crime). It seemed reasonable, and it looked as if it were true. But So-and-So came along and proved conclusively that, according to the army tests, there was the same percentage of feeblemindedness in the general population as was revealed by the same tests in the prisons. The inference from that, you see, is pretty unmistakable, if we are to believe that the tests really test intelligence, which they may not do. . . . This conclusion was corroborated by other investigations which showed the same result. Now we are almost forced to believe that we must look elsewhere for the fundamental cause of crime."

This is the technique of persuasion, which strives to convince without argument. In an argument the principle of bipolarity operates, whereby the persons opposed become more convinced of the correctness of their own opinion the longer the argument lasts. That is why the story about the Democrat and the Republican who argued for sixteen hours about politics and at the end of the time found that their positions were completely reversed, so that the Democrat was a Republican and the Republican was a Democrat, is a funny story. When we persuade, we do not allow a discussion to become an argument. One using the technique of persuasion avoids committing the other person to a point of view, because he avoids identifying himself with the opposite point of view. Or, one commits the other person to a series of successive compromises which end by reversing his position. It makes the reversal of opinion, however, dependent upon the attainment of a higher synthesis of thought and attitude, and makes the person convinced feel that the volte face came out of his own attitudes and enables him to hide from himself the fact that his conversion was really brought about by another. This is the same idea as is expressed in the principle of salesmanship which recommends that the salesman should enable a customer who has advanced an objection to back out gracefully. A further parallel between teaching practice and salesmanship may be found in the use that both can make of objections. Objections are used by clever salesmen to draw their victim into the situation, so that he can be sold, and to open his mind to a volley of arguments which he has no time to evaluate because of their number. The teacher, without resorting to the chicane of the salesman, may utilize the objections of the student to arouse interest and to obtain a more complete emotional participation in the life of the classroom. Objections are valuable to the teacher, as to the salesman, in another way also, because of the inference of the person who states a definite objection that if that objection were but removed he would find it possible to accept the other person's point of view.

This line of reflection brings up the subject of foolish questions. A realization of the value, for the teacher, of questions fairly met and intelligently answered has prompted some writers to say that there are no foolish questions. Probably it is good for teachers to be told that there are no foolish questions, for more of them err by considering serious questions foolish than by taking foolish questions seriously. Most questions, moreover, are honest in that they reveal a real perplexity or spring out of a real interest of the student, and in so far as they are honest they should be given an honest answer. Sometimes they are poorly phrased, but a teacher will gain more by trying to understand them than by brushing them aside because of technical defects in wording. The questions may not be as much to the point, from the teacher's point of view, as questions would be which the teacher could ask about the same subject, but the fact that a question is asked shows that it is important in the student's mental context. We apprehend the universe by facing and resolving a succession of dilemmas; our adult dilemmas grow out of our infantile dilemmas by slow gradations. We must take these dilemmas in their turn, and this is precisely what the intelligent answering of student questions enables the teacher to do. It should be remembered, too, that nothing kills student interest so quickly and so completely as a failure of the teacher to meet and deal with honest questions, or any evidence of disrespect for student contributions. When this occurs, it is the more regrettable because it usually happens to the more alert and self-active members of a class.

But there are, to be sure, foolish questions. Every teacher has heard them, and it is folly to argue otherwise. There are questions which reveal a failure to prepare the daily lesson, questions intended to divert the teacher's attention or to kill time, questions reflecting a total and irremediable failure to comprehend subject matter, questions intended to impress the teacher, questions intended to amuse the class, questions intended to trip up the teacher, questions intended to show up the teacher, questions asked merely because the person asking them wants to say something. A wag has remarked that college students ask questions for three reasons, to show how much they know, to show up the instructor, and to find out something. Two of these varieties would have to be treated as foolish. It should be noted that there are many more foolish questions in the established disciplines than in those not so well worked out. In mathematics and Latin, for example, subject matter is well worked out, and the teacher is under considerable pressure to get a certain amount of work done, but this is not true in sociology or the various arts and sciences of business administration.

Every variety of foolish question has to be treated differently. Every sort of answer to every sort of question starts a process of personal interaction which may be projected into infinity. The problem of the manner in which such questions may best be answered is complicated, and an exposition of possibilities would be extremely long. A general principle of value is that every such question must be answered in a way which does not involve the teacher in an undesirable social interaction, interferes as little as possible with the teacher-directed process, sets up no alternative process, and if possible draws the student back into the teacher-directed social process of the classroom. To take but one example, students often ask questions in order that they may score off the teacher as humorists; if they succeed, they will repeat the action, and a social process will be initiated in which the student attacks the teacher and the teacher defends, suffers, or wards off the attacks. The process may last for years. A different process is initiated if the teacher attempts a retort in kind, as teachers are so often tempted to do. Rarely does such a retort "squelch" the student more than momentarily. More often the student thinks of the retort as an invitation to join in a contest of repartee, and enters gleefully into the game. The battle of wit is on, and the remarks become ever more pointed and more personal, and they constitute more and more an attack upon the teacher's dignity. Until one morning when the teacher has a headache he loses his temper and punishes the student for being "fresh." The next day the teacher feels better and the process begins all over again. Many experienced teachers feel that it is better to ignore these barbed shafts of student humor whenever possible. Thus they remain aloof from student-initiated social life and refuse to be drawn into such contests as we have mentioned. No doubt this is the best general practice, but in such cases a contest sometimes arises out of the student's determination that the teacher shall recognize him as a wit and the teacher's determination not to recognize him. (One such instance is described below. See p. 344.)

What the teacher needs is some gesture of finality which will put an end to such a process. Sometimes formal punishment serves this purpose, but it is always expensive, and it can only be used for more serious cases. A better means is some remark or gesture which shows that the teacher understands fully what is afoot, is not gulled by any pretence, intends to retain control of the situation, and will meet any definite challenge to his authority.

But we must return to our consideration of concrete devices for securing and maintaining the proper group alignment and the proper combination of social distance and involvement in the social situation. There are certain classroom tricks which ill-prepared and lazy teachers sometimes employ, but they are scarcely worthy of our attention. There is that barrister's trick, the trick of the person who has a limited time in which to speak and but one good point to make, the trick of wasting time until the last five minutes and then presenting that one good point with much gusto, leaving the audience to regret that one did not have the time to develop one's arguments further. And there is that favorite trick of all personally inadequate and poorly prepared teachers everywhere; to avoid questions which might prove embarrassing, lecture. But our major concern is not with these.

A point of some importance concerning the didactic manner is that it is one that throws out grappling hooks to draw the other person near and to hold him without possibility of escape until the teacher can take possession of his mind and deposit therein a cargo of useful information. Would you know what the mechanism is which the teacher employs? We have illustrated it already. The teacher learns to throw out little questions and hints which put the other person in a receptive mood or place him under social compulsion to listen, and those are his grappling irons. The butcher and the teacher were discussing mackerel. The butcher was busy, and the teacher was not quite certain that he would remain to hear all his story. Perhaps it would be necessary to make sure.

"Do you know how they fish for mackerel?" asked the teacher.

"No," said the butcher, showing only a polite interest.

"Well," said the teacher, "I'll tell you. I have fished for mackerel. You go out . . ."

That is how teachers fish for men. That is one of the mechanisms which they employ to make it easier to cram knowledge down the throats of others. First a question that elicits interest or commits the person to a statement that he wants to know. In the latter form it would be, for the above example, "Would you like to know how they fish for mackerel?" The indicated answer is "Yes." An impasse is reached if the other person says, "No," or if he says, "Yes, I know how they fish for mackerel. You go out in a little boat . . ." But nobody ever answers "No" and few care to take the teacher's information out of his mouth. When the answer has been given, the teacher goes on to tell his story; he has been invited to tell it. But really it is a technique of forcing others to listen.

Another form of this technique utilizes the *believe it or not* kind of interest as a means of drawing students into the social interaction of the classroom. There is a parade before the circus. An interesting fact (even if not very directly related to the subject of the lesson) is displayed in order to excite the curiosity of the class at the beginning of the hour. "Do you know," asks the English teacher, "that *forlorn hope* really means a desperate band?" Her students, who are used to her tricks, listen with mild interest. She continues, "I quote from *A Dictionary of Modern English Usage,* by H. W. Fowler, a book with which all of you who aspire to use English with discrimination should become familiar. Dr. Fowler says, concerning forlorn hope: 'Forlorn hope is not an abstract phrase transferred by metaphor to a storming party, but has that concrete sense in its own right, and only gets the abstract sense of desperate chance, etc., by misunderstanding. *Hope* is not the English word, but is a misspelling of the Dutch *hoop* (equivalent to) English *heap*; the forlorn hope is the devoted or lost band, those who sacrifice themselves in leading the attack. The spelling of *hope* once fixed, the mistake was inevitable; but it is well to keep the original meaning in mind.' "

With a slight break she continues, "Now, let's see, we were discussing changes in the use of words, weren't we? That makes an excellent starting point for today's lesson." Such teachers have learned to cram themselves full of interesting bits of information which serve to inspire curiosity in the uninitiated.

PROJECTS

1. Make comparative observations upon teachers who form friendships with students early in the school year and upon teachers who establish such intimacies later. By this means test the generalization that primary group attitudes which spring up within the institutional situation of dominance and subordination are less fatal to the teacher's authority than primary group attitudes which arise before this definition of the situation is established.

2. Record the fluctuations of social distance in a classroom during the course of a single day. What incidents seem interpretable as attempts of students to diminish social distance? Observe carefully the behavior of the teacher when this distance is threatened. Present your analysis to the teacher observed and record his reactions.

3. Compare the classroom procedure of two teachers of the same subject, the one a highly formal teacher and the other informal. Evaluate the learning product in these two classes.

4. Record the devices used by teachers to "squelch" students who obtrude too much of their personalities into the classroom.

5. Study the use of students' first names by teachers. Analyze in terms of social distance. Does faculty practice affect student usage?

6. Study attacks made by teachers upon the reserves of students, and means used by students to restore distance.

7. Make extended observations upon the technique of a successful life-insurance salesman. Note his use of buffer phrases and his manner of turning objections to his own advantage. Analyze and interpret.

8. Make observations similar to those above upon a successful school teacher. Trace differences and parallels.

9. List the reactions of a number of teachers when they are asked to answer difficult questions. Are these reactions stereotyped?

10. Analyze the classroom situation revolving about a teacher who believes that "there are no foolish questions." Compare with the situation in the classroom of a teacher who handles such questions impatiently. Evaluate the learning product in each case.

11. Employ the technique of persuasion in convincing a fellow student of some proposition in which he does not believe. Record the conversation.

12. Observe the course of an ordinary argument on politics or religion. Contrast argument and persuasion by means of sociological analysis.

13. Observe the devices by which persons usually considered disarming avoid arguments.

14. Give examples of grappling-hook devices used by teachers, clergymen, salesmen, and others.

SUGGESTED READINGS

(1) Bogardus, E. S., "The Personality Clash and Social Distance," *Journal of Applied Sociology,* Vol. XI, No. 2, pp. 166-174.

(2) Dawson, C. A., and Gettys, W. E., *An Introduction to Sociology,* pp. 307-311.

(3) Macpherson, W., *The Psychology of Persuasion.*

(4) Park, R. E., and Burgess, E. W., *An Introduction to the Science of Sociology,* Chapter V.

(5) Park, R. E., "The Concept of Social Distance," *Journal of Applied Sociology,* Vol. VIII, No. 6, pp. 339-344.

(6) Poole, W. C., "Distance in Sociology," *The American Journal of Sociology,* Vol. XXXIII, pp. 99-104.

Chapter XVIII

THE DEFINITION OF THE SITUATION

One of the sociological concepts most useful for the understanding of the life of human beings in and about the school is that of the definition of the situation. This concept we owe to W. I. Thomas. Although loosely defined, it is a valuable concept because it designates certain real aspects of psychic and social life, and explains phenomena otherwise without significance.

Strictly speaking, the definition of the situation is a process. It is the process in which the individual explores the behavior possibilities of a situation, marking out particularly the limitations which the situation imposes upon his behavior, with the final result that the individual forms an attitude toward the situation, or, more exactly, in the situation. In another sense, however, we use the phrase, *the definition of the situation,* to denote the actual concrete situation as it has been defined, or to denote certain psychic products of group life which are left as residua from the definition of many situations. Many persons living together in a common group life for many overlapping generations have mapped out clearly the limitations of behavior inherent in the social situations most common in their culture. From their experience has arisen a consensus concerning what is and what is not thinkable in those situations. From these situations as they have been defined have been generalized certain group products which have in turn become important conditions of life in that group. We may refer to these group products as definitions of situations. When we take an abstracting attitude toward these group products we may think of them as folkways, mores, taboos, collective representations, group attitudes, laws, etc. But all these things affect the individual only as they are incorporated into the situations of his life; they affect him by virtue of the fact that while he is working out his attitude toward the situations of his own life he is influenced by certain preexisting definitions of situations; they affect him only in so far as he becomes aware of and assimilates those preexisting definitions of situations. Those group products that we know as folkways, mores, etc., are preconditions and necessary elements of the definition of the situation which the individual works out for himself.

From a slightly different point of view further looseness of expression appears. Actually the definition of the situation, as a process by which the individual explores and feels out through behavior and thought the behavior possibilities of a situation, is a process most intimately subjective, and one that must be worked out anew in the mind of every human being. But because one person can greatly affect the definition of the situation which another arrives at, we are accustomed to say that one person defines a situation for another. The attitudes of others are in fact the most important limitations upon the behavior of any one person, and they are also the most important inducements to any particular action. The attitudes of others are dynamic elements in the undefined situation which presents itself to any individual, and as a result of those attitudes the individual may come to define the situation in one way and not in another. Therefore we may say that one person defines a situation for another.

Before proceeding further with our elaboration of this concept we turn to Thomas for a statement of his views:

> Preliminary to any self-determined act of behavior there is always a stage of examination and deliberation which we may call *the definition of the situation.* And actually not only concrete acts are dependent upon the definition of the situation, but gradually a whole life-policy and the personality of the individual himself follow from a series of such definitions. . . .
>
> The family is the smallest social unit and the primary defining agency. As soon as the child has free motion and begins to pull, tear, meddle, and prowl, the parents begin to define the situation through speech and other signs and pressures: "Be quiet," "Sit up straight," "Blow your nose," "Mind your mother," "Be kind to sister," etc. This is the real significance of Wordsworth's phrase, "Shades of the prison house begin to close upon the growing child." His wishes and activities begin to be inhibited, and gradually, by definitions within the family, by playmates, in the school, in the Sunday School, in the community, through reading, by formal instruction, by informal signs of approval and disapproval, the growing member learns the code of his society.[1]

This behavioristic account of the process of the definition of the situation seems essentially correct. One might venture to change its emphasis in two ways: (1) by substituting for its atomistic conception a more explicit statement of the fact that every situation affecting the individual is organized into some kind of totality, usually a wholly unambiguous totality, and (2) by allowing for the self-activity, often

[1] Thomas, W. I., *The Unadjusted Girl*, pp. 42 ff. (Reprinted by permission of Little, Brown, & Company.)

the intelligent self-activity, of the individual who is learning the definition of a situation.

There is, indeed, a place for self-activity in a possible behavioristic account of the definition of the situation. The individual facing a situation with a relatively rigid social framework makes a large number of incipient attempts to adjust; those not adapted to his purpose fail and are eliminated; those which are adapted persist and are at length assembled into the individual's final adjustment. But it is submitted that this is not an altogether truthful account of the manner in which a definition of a situation is arrived at; intelligence enters into the process, and there ensues a dynamic reorganization of the parts of the situation into a pattern. In short, it is submitted that a Gestaltist account of the process of the definition of the situation is in some respects superior to the behavioristic account.

It is clear that the definitions of situations which the child must learn are in fact a part of culture, and are carried by the group and imposed upon the child through group activity. When we turn our attention more narrowly to the subjective activity of the individual who is working out a definition of a situation, or, if one prefers, is assimilating the definition of a situation which his group is imposing upon him, we find that the process resolves itself into certain other elements. Elements implicit in the process of the definition of the situation are:

(1) The configuration in which it is perceived.
(2) The aspect of the situation toward which action is directed.
(3) The attitude or activity which comes out of the interaction between individual and situation and the organization of himself which the individual effects with regard to the situation.

Much of the importance of the definition of the situation in human affairs arises from the configurational element involved in the process. When a situation has once been seen in a particular configuration, it tends to be seen in that configuration ever after, and it is very difficult to see it in any other. The configuration first established may be said to inhibit the formation of other configurations. The changelessness of custom arises in part from the fact that we cannot see those alternatives of behavior which are contrary to the folkways of our group; we have organized the situation, and ourselves with reference to it, in another configuration. As configurations differ in their stability, we find some definitions of situations which are easily resolved, whereas others are stubborn and resistant to change. The extraordinary rigidity of certain cultures may thus arise from the fact that they are organized into stable configurations. Further, as an important element of intelligence is the ability to blast the units of configurations loose from their context and to recombine them in different patterns, we find the intelligent ever the (relatively) emancipated. From this configurational element, too, arises in part our well-known lack of ability to discover many things which are close to us; the things we do not see appear in our vision, but with the arrangement of foreground and background or of wholes and subwholes such that they do not take shape as definite entities.

The aspect of the situation toward which action is directed is also a factor of importance. We direct our attention toward that which is in the foreground, and we overlook that which is in the background of the situation as it is organized into a particular configuration. The foreground tends to be, in a configuration which makes up the definition of a situation, the point of least resistance. We direct our attention and our action toward that which can be changed, and we do not attempt to alter changeless things. Only so, of course, can we realize ourselves at all, and that law of attention is also a law of mental hygiene. The attitude or activity which comes out of the situation is the third element which we have noted. We think of the attitude as behavior or incipient behavior resulting from the organization of the situation in the individual's mind and the concurrent organization of the individual with reference to the situation.

The process by which the individual works out a definition of the situation, or an attitude toward a situation, seems to conform closely to Kohler's concept of closure, which is defined as follows: "In every process which issues at all in an end-situation, independent of time (although it is possible to apply this to events occurring in time), the mode of distribution [of energy] shifts in the direction of a minimum of configurative energy."[1] The attitude inheres in the definition of the situation as "the answer sticks in the question." "Questions demanding thought arouse configurational processes which are incomplete and call for closure. The answer thus 'sticks' in the question. A good question and a good answer are not matters of chance: they fit each other as the key and the lock. Once the form suggested by the question is apprehended, there is a sudden *Einschnappen*; the inner bond appears, baring the structure, and the configuration is

[1] Quoted by Helson, Harry, *The Psychology of Gestalt*, p. 45.

completed."[1] In a manner exactly analogous the attitude is interlocked with the definition of the situation.

The social rôle, like the definition of the situation, appears in the mind by a sudden Einschnappen. In a simple society, one always prays, or one always gets drunk on certain occasions, but it sometimes happens in our more complicated life that an individual enters a new group quite uncertain as to which of these he will be called upon to do. Who has not, when faced with a novel situation, felt an unease and a sensation of gawky discomfort, and who has not felt these suddenly dissipated by a flashing awareness of his rôle? The problem of social adjustment is the problem of finding a rôle. The definition of the situation determines one's rôle and sets up the delimitations of his self-feelings. The rôle appears in the social situation, as the attitude in any situation, in accordance with configurational processes conforming to the concept of closure.

Personality develops through the growth of adaptations to a finely graded series of definitions of situations. (From discontinuity and discordance in the definitions of situations presented to the individual arise most of our mental conflicts.) The evolution of situations, and of definitions of situations, goes from simple to complex, with occasional breakdowns (in which complex wholes, of which the structure may or may not have been perceived at one time, break up into simpler units) apparently determined by the laws of attention. Within existing situations, too, there may be a growth of structure attended by a corresponding refinement of adaptation. In accordance with general principles of configurational change, human situations advance from chaotic and confused groups of elements with a minimum of structuration to more and more complex and clearly organized structures.

Without embarking upon any more extended discussion of the concept of the definition of the situation as an important bit of social theory, we may remark that this concept becomes important in our interpretation of the social life of the school in a number of different ways. First, the school may be viewed as an agency for imposing preformed definitions of situations. Education, as has been truly said, is the art of imposing upon the young; it is the art of imposing upon the young the definitions of situations current and accepted in the group which maintains the schools. The school is thus a gigantic agency of social control. It is part of its function to transmit to the

[1] Helson, *op. cit.*, p. 54.

young the attitudes of the elders, which it does by presenting to them social situations as the elders have defined them.

Again, and this is our major concern at this point, the social life of the schools may be seen as a mass of situations to be defined by or for the persons involved in them. The many and various social situations of school life may be defined, as it seems, in three ways:

(1) Spontaneously by students or teachers, or by students and teachers.
(2) By teachers, chiefly with reference to standards current in society outside the school or current in the teacher group.
(3) By students, chiefly with reference to standards current outside the school.

From the fact that situations may be defined in different ways and by different groups arises a conflict of definitions of situations, and we may see the whole process of personal and group conflict which centers about the school as a conflict of contradictory definitions of situations. The fundamental problem of school discipline may be stated as the struggle of students and teachers to establish their own definitions of situations in the life of the school.

We see many undefined situations confronting the individual in the school. The new teacher confronts a situation wholly undefined, and he has very little idea as to the details of the definition that would be desirable from his own point of view. The experienced teacher who faces a new class faces an undefined situation, and it is part of his job to impose his definition of the situation upon the class quickly, before any alternatives have had an opportunity to be considered. The child in school for the first time also faces a situation with whose definition he is not familiar, and it is sometimes long before he can understand what is expected of him in school.

It may be well to consider in detail the process by which some of these persons work out satisfactory definitions of school situations, impose those definitions upon others, or adjust to the definitions put forward by others. Many teachers have learned that it pays to spare themselves no unpleasantness in order to establish and make secure their dominance in the first few days and weeks of school. They exert themselves particularly to define the situation as one in which the teacher is dominant. Until this definition of the situation is accepted, there will be some conflict between teacher and student, and some hostility of students toward the teacher; the problem will be more severe in a school that has previously been poorly disciplined. Until his definition of the situation is thoroughly established in the minds of his students, the teacher cannot relax. After the first few weeks in which conflict over the definition of the situation has been severe, the hostility toward the teacher dies down; this is in most cases owing to the operation of two factors: use and acceptance of the situation makes teacher domination bearable to the students, and the teacher relaxes his grip slightly, just enough to give friendly attitudes a chance to spring up within the situation. But these friendly attitudes must always spring up within the situation as defined in terms of teacher domination; if they spring up outside it, they conflict with it and operate to overthrow the so painfully established social order. The following is a description of the technique employed by one teacher who adhered to the policy we have just outlined.

Each of the four schools I have worked in had a "hard name." One had "run a teacher off." Another had told their last teacher to mind her own business. A third had taken the tires from the principal's car and hidden them. The fourth had locked the principal in the classroom. I got my first school because I was the only man teacher available in the county, and the district wanted some one who they thought could "handle the kids." The others I got on the reputation I made at the first school for being a "handler."

Of course I wanted to make good in each place—partly for my own future good, partly because everyone expected me to make good. Perhaps I sensed the perilous equilibrium situation in the school. Anyway, my desire for success, the fact that I am a small man, and the feeling that if the teacher isn't the boss he'll be run out or have a hard year ahead of him, made me attack the discipline problem with especial vigor. I was afraid, yes, desperately afraid each time I went to a new school. It wasn't so much the children that I feared or the problems ahead of me, but the whole new situation frightened me. So I thought and worried a lot just before the first day of school, and when that first day finally came, I went at things almost savagely, almost fiercely, as a man in a trap fighting for his life.

Outside of getting studies started as quickly as possible I did little the first four days of the first week. I just stood around getting the lay of the land. The students were beginning to think I was a washout as a principal. But by Friday of that first week I had gathered enough material to grind my ax on, and I went on the warpath. For the four or five weeks following I was meaner than h—. Nothing the students in my classes did in the way of studying and preparing lessons suited me. I scolded them if I found a *t* uncrossed or a paper not folded straight. I made them do much work over, made them stay after school, gave them poor grades—did anything to be disagreeable.

"Now listen here," I used to say, "there are several people in this class who don't seem to be here for business. Now I'd just as soon you folks wouldn't come back to class any more. You'll eventually get put out of the class anyway. No, I don't care at all to have that kind of students in my classes, and they don't usually stay long either.

"And by the way, some of these same people don't seem to be in school for business either. I'd advise *you* not to come to school if that's the way you feel. There'll be no monkey work this year. We're all here for business. Old Man Bishop and not Mr. Nelson is running things here this year, and we're not going to be bothered with such people at all. We absolutely will not fool with you. I'd advise you to get out of here right now.

"Of course we're not trying to drive any one away, but we just won't put up with you. If you don't change your attitude toward school, it'll just be here's your hat and books. Home you go. We don't want you around. If you feel different by tomorrow, come back; if you don't, stay home."

Always after such an initial tirade, the pupils, especially the big boys, would look as if they would like to say, "Whew! So hot, for a little man." They never did, however; if they had, my story would have been entirely different. As to discipline, I contested almost everything of any consequence that happened during those first few weeks. I bawled them out mercilessly, sarcastically, and impersonally. I usually made a big boy or two cry with my sharp tongue and cuffed a fellow or so whom I caught in the act. I was bold, brazen, and despotic, and I never understood why they bore with me. I often wondered what I should do if all, or even one, would not obey me when I ordered. Of course I would have sent him home, but suppose he wouldn't have gone. I never answered the question in my own mind nor had an occasion where I had to solve the problem in practice. I'm afraid my system built on bluff would have broken down at that point, for I should not have whipped a girl, and I could not have whipped some of the larger boys.

I never was unreasonable or personal to any great extent, however, and I never acted without an excuse for action; but give me an excuse and my action followed swiftly and directly on the heels of the misdemeanor. I usually kept a big distance between myself and the students during school hours. Thus I gave the school plenty to talk about and think about over the first week-end of the academic year and for several week-ends following. They thought me the meanest, the worst-tempered, the most mentally unbalanced slave driver who had ever set foot in their school building. They would have liked to do a lot of things to me if they had dared, but my persistence had worn down their resistance. Besides, they were never sure how I'd take a thing or what I'd do next. After I had thus undefined and redefined the situation for them, I would slacken up gradually until, toward the beginning of the second semester, at which time the situation became quite democratic, democratic with this background of control. About Christmas time it was rumored in the neighborhood that I wasn't such a bad fellow after all. At the end of the year almost everyone was asking me back. (Life history document of a school teacher.)

The above may serve as an illustration of the technique about which we have been talking. There is no question, however, that this teacher injected too much unpleasantness into the process and that he was far too excited to get the best results. The ideal use of this technique depends upon a stable personality which makes uniform demands, assumes that other persons will conform to them, seeks no unpleasantness and avoids none, but has sufficient insight into the social life of the school room to differentiate between situations that call for unpleasant methods and those which do not.

Likewise the child in school for the first time, or in a new school, or a new grade, meets situations for which his previous experience furnishes him with no adequate definition. He then either works out a definition in collaboration with his fellows or he accepts the definition of the situation which the teacher offers. How this occurred in one instance is interestingly told in the following document:

Cousin Frances sits with the circle of kindergarten students. It is her first day of school. Thus far all has gone well, and Miss Lamb, the teacher, has made the little girl feel quite at ease. From the first moment that Frances entered Miss Lamb's room, the whole new situation which she found herself a part of—the whole of her new surroundings—and the whole of her past experience carried within her own little personage—have been conditioning or modifying her behavior. Of this fact Frances is partly conscious and partly unconscious. As Frances looks about the circle, she spies Dale, the boy who lives next door. Dale sitting nearby is the situation or object presented. She defines the situation as she has defined it many times before. Here is Dale whom she often plays with and talks to. The situation defined, the attitude that she will play with him and talk to him now arises. . . . She goes toward him and begins a conversation. But her progress is hesitating and her speech subdued due to her new environment. At this point the teacher intervenes. Evidently Frances has defined the situation wrongly. A crisis—a minor one—is at hand.

"What shall I do?" says Frances to herself. "No one has ever stopped me from playing and talking with Dale before. How shall I act toward this intruder, called the teacher, who thus interferes with the way I am used to doing things? Shall I cry, or shall I smile, or shall I be angry?"

. . . Thinking that perhaps this is the way things usually happen in school, she decides to return to her little red chair. This she does without unnecessary ado.

Miss Lamb then proceeds to talk to Frances. She says school is a place where everyone has work to do, and that each must stay in his place and keep quiet so that he and everyone else can get their work done. And Miss Lamb is glad, too, that Frances decided not to bother anyone and returned to her own seat. Thus the teacher tried to re-define the situation for Frances and set up a counter-attitude which will change the habit of action or behavior.

A few days later the same thing confronts Frances. But now she finds herself possessed of her own definition and its attitude and Miss Lamb's definition and its attitude. She compromises, and instead of going to Dale and talking, she merely talks to him in a low voice, without leaving her place. This time the teacher—and the pupils—decide that if Frances is going to keep them from their work, she will have to sit apart from the group. Here is another minor crisis with a similar re-definition of the situation calling up the same counter-attitude.

Frances now passes to the stage where she whispers to Dale, and more crises interjected by Miss Lamb are necessary to fix the new definition and the new attitude. Finally a major crisis comes when as a result of Frances' whispering the whole class must do its work over. The unsocialness of her conduct drives home the school definition and fixes her concurrent attitude. Then after a time when Frances has several times refused herself the luxury of whispering and the attitude of prohibition has become integrated with the habit of prohibition, the process passes from the realm of consciousness to that of unconsciousness. . . . The school conduct of Frances is good and she knows it as such and keeps it thus. In her own eyes and the eyes of others, she is a "good girl" at school. (From *The Social Aspect of Classroom Teachers' Problems,* unpublished manuscript, Kenneth McGill.)

It is axiomatic among school men that the first day of school, or the first meeting of a class, is all-important in determining the success or failure of the school year. A realization of this fact has led certain school men to lay down rigid rules for the conduct of classes on the first day of school. Bagley, whose work along this line is classic, has given us a set of directions for the first day, which, if closely followed, will present the child with a situation whose boundaries are quite clearly indicated and quite firmly held, so that acceptance of the teacher's definition of the situation is almost inevitable. Bagley asserts that "It is generally agreed among school men that, the sooner the regular routine is established, the better will be the results." He believes that it is best "to make the very first day thoroughly rigorous in all its details." He gives minute instructions concerning preparations for the first day, most of them relating to making ready physical conditions for carrying on school and to the teaching plans which the teacher must prepare in advance. The teacher must examine his room, find out what pupils he is likely to have, make sure that blackboards are clean, that chalk, and erasers are present, and that books, paper, pencils, pens, ink, etc., are on hand in sufficient quantities. Bagley then states certain rules concerning the conduct of school on the first day. Since nearly all his suggestions have some implications as to the relationship established between the teacher and his students, they will be quoted *in extenso.*

1. Be on hand early.

2. See that the classroom is in good condition; floors clean, desks dusted, wardrobes ready for use. Do not complain to principal or janitor unless conditions are intolerable. Remedy matters yourself.

3. See that the chalk and erasers are distributed at the blackboard, or in readiness for distribution by monitors to be appointed. In any case, be sure that these necessary materials are on hand and in condition to be used—chalk boxes open, erasers cleaned, etc.

4. Place upon the blackboard whatever work you have provided for your earliest classes. Your program will doubtless indicate arithmetic as one of the earliest forms of seat work. Have examples upon the blackboard in sufficient number to provide arithmetic for all classes.

5. Pupils who arrive early should be greeted pleasantly and directed to take seats. Many successful teachers require pupils arriving before the "first bell" to observe the same decorum that they would observe during the regular session, so long as they remain in the school room rather than upon the playground. Whether you adopt this policy or not, it is well on the first morning to check any tendency to run about the room or to pass from seat to seat.

6. It is good policy always to enlist the aid of pupils in helping you about the routine preparatory to the real school work. On the first morning, they may, at your direction, distribute the chalk and erasers, slips of paper for the names of the pupils, the pencils, etc.

7. Everything should be in readiness when the bell rings and the lines come in. The teacher should direct the pupils to take seats regularly in the different rows in the order of their entering the room. After this preliminary seating, changes may be immediately made if desired. If there are two classes, and if one has already been in the room—as will be the case wherever the promotions are semi-annual—let the older pupils take the seats occupied the preceding term. If all or most of the pupils are new, let them take seats as suggested as speedily as possible, making temporary changes where necessary to accommodate pupils to different sizes of seats and desks. This should occupy but a brief period.

8. Place into immediate application your prearranged plan for disposing of the hats and wraps. If they are to be collected, appoint the first or the last pupil in each row as a monitor for this purpose. Give clear, distinct directions, and enforce these directions rigidly from the outset. If the wraps

are to be left in the wardrobe as the pupils pass in, have the lines file out and return to the room according to your plan, depositing their wraps as they pass. The manner in which you handle this, the very first bit of routine, will have a large share in determining the first impression that you leave with your students.

9. When this has been accomplished, the time is opportune for your opening remarks, if you wish to make any. Let these be brief, clear-cut, and devoid of threats, cant, or platitudes. Especially guard against "soft-soapiness." A song is also in place if you can select one which is familiar to all the pupils, and lead it well yourself. Devotional exercises are in place unless prohibited by law, ruling, or public sentiment.

10. After these preliminaries direct each pupil to write his name upon the slip of paper handed to him. Have the first pupil in each row collect the slips, placing his own at the bottom of the bundle, and the others in order. As the slips of each row are brought to you, place a rubber-band about them and then arrange the bundles across your desk in the order of the rows. You will then be able, with a minimum of trouble, to find the name of any pupil by reference to the slips belonging to his row.

11. All this should occupy but a brief period of time—certainly not more than twenty minutes—and from this time on, in a two-class or three-class room, the regular program should be adhered to. Assign work to the more advanced class, if there are two, or to all but the lowest class, if there are more than two. The first recitation should begin with this. If the pupils are to come forward to occupy a recitation bench, give explicit directions for the passing of lines, and explain the signals that you propose to use. It will probably be necessary to give two or three drills upon this before the movement to the bench and back to the seats satisfies you. The first day's work may very well be devoted in part to such drills, but always save time for some serious work. If the class passes to the blackboard, drill it several times in the prearranged movement of lines.

12. [Relates to classification of ungraded schools.]

13. Stop all work a few minutes before recess time to drill pupils upon the passing of lines. In a large graded school it will be necessary to know how all the lines pass to the playground in order that you may assemble your pupils in the proper place. This should be one of the matters learned beforehand by consultation with the principal or with other teachers.

14. Appoint monitors to distribute pens, tablets, copy-books, etc., just prior to the first periods when these materials are used. Distribute the monitorial functions among as many pupils as possible, holding each strictly responsible from the first for the efficiency of his service. Devote some time during the first day to drilling the monitors in these duties. Let them pass and collect the materials again and again, until they can do the work with celerity, dispatch, and good order. If you propose to use this monitorial service as a reward of good standing, let the pupils know this at the start,

stating that changes will be made at the beginning of the second week or month, as the case may be.[1]

Perhaps the thing which most impresses one who is familiar with a different philosophy of school management is the extreme rigidity of the social order which Bagley would see fit to set up in the schools. But one is struck, too, with the extreme practicality of the discussion, and this impression is increased by the reflection that thousands of teachers and prospective teachers have profited in the past from a study of Bagley. Bagley has stated clearly and succinctly the rules of thumb which school men have worked out for the starting procedure in schools of the more rigid sort. These rules of thumb are correct as far as they go, and Bagley's remains the classic statement of them. They have more meaning, however, when we think of them as going together to make up a procedure for the definition of the social situation in the school, a procedure for working out and imposing upon students a particular definition of the situation in which the student does almost nothing on his own initiative and in which the teacher is completely dominant.

The teacher who follows Bagley's suggestions presents the child with a situation in no respect equivocal, a situation completely worked out and prearranged, a situation which the student has no option but to accept. The teacher has thought of everything, and there is neither need nor opportunity for the pupil to work out any arrangements of his own. One notes that, throughout Bagley's discussion, the emphasis is upon a preorganization of school life so thorough that no opportunity is given for spontaneous organization by the students, from which disorder might result. The classroom is always a new social world, an arbitrary and artificial social world, but the pupil is given the impression that he is entering a changeless society. He must conform.

Particular rules are perhaps deserving of further comment. The meaning of the suggestions concerning preparation of the school room on the physical side, and the assembling of materials for school work, is plainly to prevent improvisation by students, which is not regarded as desirable. It is suggested that many teachers require pupils arriving before the first bell to take their seats at once and to observe school-room decorum, and that those who consider this excessively stern should at any rate check any tendency to run about the room or to pass from seat to seat. This prevents the spontaneous definition

[1] Bagley, W. C., *Classroom Management*, pp. 25-28. (Reprinted by permission of The Macmillan Company.)

of the situation which children might work out on the spur of the moment from becoming established before school opens. The drill upon routine matters serves two purposes: it impresses the school situation, with its rules and its restrictions and its mechanized routine, firmly upon the student's mind; and it gives the teacher an opportunity to establish his domination by giving directions about matters over which conflict is not likely to arise. The monitorial system which Bagley recommends has another function, that of aligning certain students favorably with respect to the teacher; the drill upon the functions of the monitors is again a means of impressing the teacher's definition of the situation upon the student's mind. (As we have elsewhere noted, the use of monitors allows the teacher to remain immobile, and therefore to remain in command of the situation more easily.)

In certain places in the discussion quoted above, the attitudes of the professional teacher crop out undisguised. ". . . the time is opportune for your opening remarks, if you wish to make any. Let these be brief, clear-cut, and devoid of threats, cant, or platitudes. Especially guard against *soft-soapiness.*" There speaks the teacher! Intercourse between teacher and student must be limited to the matter in hand; the teacher must not say anything which would involve him in a human interaction with his pupils. Bagley here demonstrates his thorough understanding of life within the institution of the school; it is better if the teacher takes the classroom situation for granted and defines the situation from that standpoint by words and deeds relevant to that orientation; and a verbalization of any of the principles upon which the classroom rapport is based would be very difficult and dangerous; a correct statement would antagonize students unduly, and a faulty statement would set up a conflicting definition of the situation. Undoubtedly this is excellent advice for one who wishes to keep a well-regimented school room, but one feels that it is the sort of advice which ought to be given regretfully. To the professional teacher, there is no occasion for regret in the fact that neither teacher nor pupil can express his whole self in the classroom; it is all to the good that teachers speak little, crisply, and without tenderness. But from the larger point of view this may have regrettable consequences for teachers and students alike.

Bagley would probably be the first to admit that all definite rules have limited utility. Teachers differ, and the sort of rapport which one finds workable may be quite impossible for another. The teacher who regiments his students in the older way might not make a good

Morrison plan teacher, nor should a teacher whose effectiveness depends upon good nature and stability ever attempt to increase his effectiveness by adding to his accomplishments the fault-finding technique. Better, then, than to suggest specific techniques as always useful, and better than to attempt to develop like character traits in all teachers, would it be to attempt to give teachers a complete understanding of the social processes centering about school life, and to leave to each one the task of working out that technique which will help him most in carrying on the particular sort of education which he considers desirable.

But it is never enough to define the situation clearly on the first day of school. If the teacher is to retain control of the school-room social life, he must renew his definition of the situation from moment to moment and adapt his technique to the developing occasion. Bagley, in common with many other writers, suggests that as much of this school-room activity as possible should be routinized and mechanized. According to this theory, the teacher must so order the first day that everything goes as he has planned and no opportunity is given for even a moment of spontaneous life in which a definition of the situation contrary to that of the teacher can be worked out, and thereafter he must crystallize as much of this procedure as possible into routine. Thus from one year to the next the teacher maintains his absolute unvarying control and children never slip from his fingers.

It never happens, however, that the situation can be so clearly defined and classroom procedure so rigidly routinized that no disorder, that is, no definition of the situation spontaneously arrived at by students in opposition to the definition of the situation put forward by the teacher, can ever arise. Life has a way of finding breaches in the fences that we put around it (and this is one of the arguments for a more plastic technique of maintaining discipline). When these conflicting definitions of the situation confront the teacher, the teacher must consistently renew his own definition of the situation, using whatever technique he has found most satisfactory for himself. The conflict of definitions of situation may involve the teacher in personal conflict, or it may be resolved in other ways. Bagley, discussing the quality of persistence as an attribute of the teacher, has incidentally described the technique by which the stern disciplinarian maintains his initial definition of the situation. It is a technique of persistence, consistency, and persistence with redoubled effort. (All of these depend upon an initial stability of character.) We quote:

In creating a condition of order in the classroom, it is essential that every rule laid down be adhered to rigidly, unremittingly. The acme of good discipline is reached when the conditions of order are preserved automatically, without thought or judgment on the pupils' part. In other words, a classroom that is well disciplined has the conditions of good order reduced to habit. But the law of habit-building operates here with unrelenting certainty. To make the conditions of order automatic, every slightest exception must immediately be noted and corrected. At first, some allowance should be made for forgetfulness on the part of the pupils; that is, an exception to an established rule should be corrected by brief admonition. But this must not be permitted to continue. "I didn't think" cannot be condoned more than once. It is the business of education to train pupils to "think" about the matters that require thought; and pupils who habitually forget to obey rules should have their memory stimulated by something more effective than an admonition. The teacher who must constantly warn pupils and correct them for the same misdeeds over and over again is not an efficient disciplinarian.

The vital import of this principle cannot be too strongly emphasized. It is a byword that more teachers fail through inability to "discipline" successfully than through any other one cause. And failure to discipline is most commonly due to lack of persistence. The teacher lays down a rule. The pupils break it once or twice to test the teacher, or perhaps they break it through forgetfulness. The experienced teacher gives the pupil the benefit of the doubt in such cases once and once only. But the young and inexperienced teacher keeps on with admonitions which become increasingly ineffective the longer they are employed; or, what is far worse, he neglects to note a lapse from the established rule. That insidious Rip Van Winkleism, "This time will not count," is the rock upon which many a teacher's prospects are wrecked.

"What shall I do?" the young teacher will surely ask in this connection; "What shall I do when I have tried every device that I can think of and still fail?" There is no explicit formula that will cover each specific case, but one general suggestion may be given: *Get order.* Drop everything else, if necessary, until order is secured. Stretch your authority to the breaking point if you can do nothing else. Pile penalty upon penalty for misdemeanors, and let the "sting" of each penalty be double that of its predecessor. Tire out the recalcitrants if you can gain your end in no other way. Remember that your success in your life work depends upon your success in this one feature of that work more thoroughly than it depends upon anything else. You have the law back of you, you have intelligent public sentiment back of you. Or, if the law be slow and halting, and public sentiment other than intelligent, you have on your side right, justice, and the accumulated experience of generations of teachers.[1]

[1] Bagley, W. C., *Classroom Management*, pp. 95-97. (Reprinted by permission of The Macmillan Company.)

There is much sound sense in this passage, as in everything of Bagley. It may serve as the ideal statement of those sterner teachers who pin their faith to repression by force. There is much excellent advice, also, for teachers who lack institutional courage or experience, and many such have no doubt profited by Bagley's exhortations. But it is good advice only because advice is only advice, and should neither be taken nor given literally. The teacher who followed it literally would soon find himself up against an impasse. It is not literally possible to increase penalties for every misdemeanor. Nor is it ever possible, in the concrete human situation, to take official cognizance of every breach of rules. One may question whether it is worse as a matter of practice for a teacher to suffer a rule to lapse by seeming to forget it than for him to meet its breaches with ineffectual admonitions and penalties.

We become aware how far we have travelled along the road toward the humanization of education when we contrast the arbitrary mode of maintaining the definition of the situation described by Bagley with the one which would be recommended on the basis of modern psychology and the experience of the more advanced modern schools. The stern disciplinarian knew only one tune; he played it softly at first and then he played it more loudly; we know some variations now. Nor are we quite so sure as Bagley was that the character training which is always one of the aims of education is to be effected by denial of choice and the imposition of good habits from without. We should pin our faith to that subtler control which comes from insight into the character of the person to be controlled, and should try to inculcate in him desirable general attitudes rather than specific habits. Nor do we think, now, that the "acme of good discipline is attained when the conditions of order are preserved automatically, without thought or judgment on the pupil's part." When we did think that, persistence with redoubled effort was the keynote of school policy; now the cardinal point of policy is persistence with an effort revised and corrected by growing understanding and insight. And though good order might well be habitual and largely unconscious we should not want good order attained without thought or judgment on the pupil's part.

The newer order of school discipline, still rare, it should be said, makes greater demands upon the teacher than did the old. It requires a greater imagination, a greater understanding, and a more fluid and adaptable technique. To be sure, the demands of enlightened discipline may cost the teacher less than it would cost her to maintain a

Prussian organization; the teacher's personality was warped under the old system as thoroughly as the student's, the strong teacher's character no less, though differently, than that of the weak teacher who broke her heart trying to maintain an order that was, for her, impossible. But whereas a simple technique for defining the situation was sufficient for the highly regimented school, a complicated technique is required for a school that tries to maintain a more flexible life.

In the orthodox school, old style, the interaction of definitions of situations was about as follows. The teacher definition of the situation, a definition in terms of a rigid social order and teacher domination of all social life, was established at the start. It was a definition that sought to be inclusive, and to leave nothing for improvisation. There was little opportunity for student definitions to arise. But such definitions did arise, for human life can never be forced to conform altogether to the demands of a rigid social order. When they arose they were dealt with in accordance with a thoroughgoing policy of repression. The pupil definition of the situation was wiped out, supposedly, as completely as if it had never been, and the teacher definition of the situation was reestablished, or extended to fit the new situation. This regimen for students was supposed to be character forming. The unyielding social order made it necessary that students should form a set of "good" habits, and it was supposed that they would carry these throughout life.

That was the older technique as it was supposed to work out. In the actual human situation of the classroom, it rarely resulted so fortunately. Pupils inevitably attempted to establish their own social order independently of teachers, and a lethal conflict sprang up between the teacher-directed social process and the social process which students pushed forward. The social order which the teacher worked out in advance and attempted to establish could never be quite complete; the rules could not cover everything. In the interstices of the social order there sprang up spontaneous life of students. There was always a loophole, and life always found the loophole. When a student definition was established in one of the neglected corners of the social order, the teacher had to pass a rule in order to cover that phase of the school situation. But the more numerous the rules, the more hair-splitting there is about where they do and where they do not apply; where there are many regulations there are sure to be "regulation lawyers." There is thus an inevitable conflict between those who tear holes in the dikes and those who try to patch them up. The conflict that always arose between the teacher definitions and the pupil definitions which grew up in the interstices of the teacher-planned social order was made more severe by the fact that the students never quite accepted the teacher-ordained social order as one of the unalterable facts of life. The teacher order could never be established without at least a minimum of unpleasantness. There was always the chance that this irreducible unpleasantness might grow to enmity through the conflict over the pupil order which grew up in the interstices of the social structure and the attempt to extend the teacher's authority to cover it. This conflict easily became so severe that a conflict group relation was established between teacher and students. Where there are conflict groups, the morality of the conflict group governs. The essence of conflict group morality is that injuries to persons belonging to the opposition are considered meritorious, and friendly rapport with such persons treasonable.

In the light of this analysis of the effect of the rigid social order upon students, it is necessary to evaluate quite differently the character-building features of rigid discipline. In the first place, it seems clear from modern psychology that habits cannot rest upon nothing, that if they are to persist and to assume a real importance in the personal organization of the individual they must have a basis in his general attitudinal set, i.e., they must be hooked up to something deeply ingrained in his make-up. The technique of character formation through the building of habits does not allow for any such connections. When such connections are made, as they sometimes are, and as they always must be if the character-building program is to succeed, it is entirely a matter of accident. A character builder who succeeds only by accident is no very efficient character builder. But the situation was, in fact, in the school of the old sort, even worse than that, for the conflict between teacher and student actually gave to those habits which were connected with the teacher-constructed social order a negative emotional value. Thus the value of those habits which the school laid so much stress upon establishing was more than neutralized by the negative emotional weighting which those habits acquired, and by their contrariety to the general, underlying attitudinal set of the individual. Sometimes, indeed, and by no means infrequently, the process worked for good, and rebellious pupils acquired by antithesis desirable attitudes from teachers whom they hated. But these instances must have been few when compared with the cases in which students, by struggling against the established order in the school and attempting to circumvent its representatives, acquired law-breaking attitudes which they were to carry throughout life.

The new schools may perhaps lay claim to a much more rational utilization of the social process. We shall do well to be sceptical, for the history of man's attempts to devise institutions for making over human nature according to specification is a history of almost uniform failure. Schemes have been devised in ignorance of the actual causal mechanisms which they set into operation, and they have failed to produce the specified qualities in men because their theory was never sound. But it does seem possible on the basis of social experiments of the past quarter of a century to say that schools in which teacher domination is less rigorous and flows out of personal leadership rather than from an institutionalized social and autocratic order have much more fortunate effects upon human personalities than did schools of the more despotic type.

The social process in the newer sort of school is more flexible and more spontaneous. It calls for a working out by teacher and students together of a definition of the situation in terms of the needs and desires of all concerned. And this is no changeless definition of the situation which is worked out, and no rigid social order which it produces, but an evolving situation which is continually defined and redefined in terms of the attitudes and interests of the group as spontaneously functioning. The teacher dominates by leadership, and is able to direct the attention and the energies of the classroom group into certain channels. This process is facilitated by the fact that pupils already have a favorable attitudinal set toward the acquisition of such knowledge as is really necessary for participation in the social life of their group. There must still be an exclusion of frivolous or otherwise aberrant definitions of situations, but so far as possible this must be a process in which the group rather than the teacher, or the group through the teacher, seems to discipline the individual. The advantage from the standpoint of character evolution is that there is normal development from participation in a gradually expanding group life rather than a distortion of personality from the antagonistic social life centered around the problem of teacher domination. It must be admitted that this may be an idealized and unduly optimistic statement of the situation, and that the process often takes a different form even in the most enlightened of the newer schools. It must be admitted, too, that such schools frequently fail to uphold academic standards and that they sometimes fail to develop children's character favorably by reason of neglecting to impose standards of achievement. But the general practice in the past quarter of a century has moved markedly away from the more rigid type of school discipline, and much has been accomplished without lowering of standards.

Whatever the type of discipline which he tries to build up, and whatever the sort of social order which the teacher tries to establish in the school, the teacher has need of a number of techniques for defining the situation. The same techniques, with different emphases, are apparently used by all kinds of teachers. Some of the more important devices for defining the situation or maintaining an existent definition are the following: routinization, punishment, express statement, ritual, personal influence resulting from the involvement of the teacher in classroom situations, and personal influence derived from understanding and the use of psychological mechanisms. Routinization has already been discussed.

The favorite device of the teacher attempting to maintain strict discipline in the older sense is punishment. Punishment separates out certain kinds of behavior as reprehensible, and imposes certain unpleasantnesses upon those guilty of such behavior. When punishment is successful, it defines the situation by imposing a taboo upon certain aberrant behavior. The empirical psychologists who conduct the schools think of punishment as a deterrent to undesirable behavior on a hedonistic basis. The penalty, as in the older criminology, must be made just sufficient to outweigh any pleasure which those to be controlled might take in tabooed behavior. It would be possible to work out a theoretical justification of punishment in terms of behavioristic psychology as negative conditioning. The difficulty here, as in the hedonistic theory of behavior and its control, is that the behavior itself often springs from attitudes which are not affected by punishment. There is a further difficulty, too, in that punishment often gives rise to countervailing attitudes which more than outweigh the punishment itself as a determinant of behavior. Experienced teachers, however, know that punishment does sometimes work, that it is called for in the dynamic social situation of the school. The value which it has seems to arise from the fact that it marks out certain behavior as taboo.

Another technique by which the situation is often defined is that of express statement. The teacher says, "We do this in our school," or "We do not do that in our class." This technique often suffices for the verbal imposition of a taboo or to mark out a change in the situation. Almost every teacher who has to succeed some weak or easy-going or popular teacher in the control of a school or class finds that he has to resort to some such device as this to make clear the transition from the control of the other person to his own domination. Students say, "But Mr. So-and-so let us keep our books open in class," and the teacher replies, "It's not old Man Nelson you are dealing with this year. It's Old Smith, and that's another story altogether."

Ritual is often used as a means of establishing a definition of the situation and keeping it established without change. Thus certain formalities in the relation of student and teacher are ritualized in order that no variants in those formalities may arise and in order that the attitudinal sets involved in the formalities may be carried over into other aspects of the relationship. This is one of the benefits of that mechanization of routine which Bagley advocates. In another use of ritual, formalized attitudes are taken or expressed with the hope that they may become internal. (See the chapter on ceremony.)

When the teacher becomes identified with the formal social organization of the school, his personal influence is likely to be almost wholly directed at the maintenance of that social order. The social order of the school has become a part of the teacher's expanded social self, and he lives and breathes in and through it. Thus it may happen that all the teacher's personal influence, composed of all the subtle and unconsidered personal emanations and psychic irradiations that come from him, his earnestness, his character, and his personal force, seems to be concerned with the maintenance of the teacher's definition of the situation. The temper of the teacher, to be specific, is nearly always metamorphosed into an instrument for maintaining teacher domination. As the new teacher becomes familiar with all the intricacies of the social situation of the classroom as students and teachers come to define it, he learns to become angry when any action of a student gives the slightest indication that the student is trying to define the situation in an unorthodox manner. This is the institutionalized temper.

In our discussion of the techniques used by teachers for defining the situation we should not fail to reckon with the possibility of a technique based upon a different kind of personal influence. This would be a technique not based upon the earnestness with which the teacher identifies himself with the moral order of the school room but upon his personal qualities plus an understanding of the social process in the school and of the characterological trends of his students. It is a technique already practiced in its simpler forms by teachers who have a high common-sense knowledge of human nature, and with more sophistication but perhaps less judgment by those teachers whose psychological and psychiatric training has made them aware of suggestion mechanisms and inferiority complexes.

We have already indicated that students become aware of many of the definitions of situations current in their culture as a direct or indirect result of their social experience in the schools. We have implied, as well, that one of the most important functions of the school is to transmit to young persons an awareness of these definitions of situations. That is, indeed, the central task of character education —to lead the young so to perceive and so to range themselves for action with reference to the social situations current in our culture that the result will be in accord with social policy. This is a task for which the actual social situations of school life should be utilized, for it is difficult to impose definitions of situations at long range through either the assigning of lessons or the reading of lectures. The social life of children has been utilized all too little, school authorities preferring to suppress that social life as frivolous or worse and to impose character traits by exhortation or other sleight of hand. Certain definitions of situations, however, do become clear to the child while he is in school, and it is perhaps worth while to consider these briefly.

The definition of the situation which teachers are at most pains to impose is that concerning the school life of the child, especially so far as it concerns his relation to his teachers. Since we have discussed this at such length, we shall say no more about it here except to state that this definition of the situation, so laboriously built up by teachers and so deeply impressed upon the child, is one which rarely finds a parallel in adult life, and that it is therefore wasted as a training for life. Subordination to the teacher does not prepare the child for anything, because there will be no teachers where he is going.

A type definition of the situation which grows more spontaneously out of the life of children, and which therefore more often has a parallel in life outside the institution, concerns sportmanship and fair play. The spirit of fair play or sportsmanship is often quite strongly inculcated in children who play competitive games. Perhaps it is the result of those endless arguments and interminable jourings of young boys who are learning to play games. It is a very limited spirit of fair play which boys develop in the unguided interaction of the play group. It is a fair play, usually, which does not necessarily apply to an individual who is not a member of the group; it does not hold for a member of another gang or for a teacher or a member of the opposite sex. It is an honesty which does not condemn a sharp trick. But, within its limitations, this is a definition of the situation concerning which the boy's attitude is sharp and clear. With boys in a private school, or in some other groups where much is made of competitive athletics, sportsmanship comes to be something of a religion; it is the one moral principle which boys can understand.

Since the most important value in our culture is property, it is only natural that the school child should absorb certain taboos concerning property and its use while yet in school. It is one of the situations most sharply defined for the child. One of the few situations (perhaps the only one) in which students and teachers can cooperate whole-heartedly in defence of the social order is that created by the presence of a thief in their midst. Much more rarely, and always more uncertainly, students work out certain taboos concerning personal honesty. There are in fact many features of school life which make rather for the development of personal dishonesty. There is the school situation which calls for a respect to the teacher which is quite contrary, often, to the child's actual feeling and to the attitudes which he expresses outside of school. There is the rigid marking system, with its emphasis on grades and its invitation to cheat, and this feature of the situation is made worse by the enemy morality which holds between teachers and students. Under such circumstances, cheating can come to be a fascinating game, and one which the student loses no status by playing; it often happens that students do not outgrow this conception even when they enter college. When the main thing is the amassing of a certain number of meaningless credits, what does it matter, after all, by what method they are acquired? There is, too, a deep-lying discrepancy between the precepts which teachers give out to students and the ingrowing personal dishonesty of teachers who say things for hire that they do not believe.

Certain definitions of the situation with regard to sexual functions are very much a part of school life. One of the definitions which it is most important to impose upon children is the heterosexual definition of the situation. This is sometimes done, and in a natural and spontaneous way. Teachers who arrange for a cross sex interchange of valentines on Valentine Day are thus doing something to manipulate the social process in the correct direction. In a monosexual group, it is sometimes necessary to impose taboos in a drastic manner. When certain definitely sexual ties began to appear in a group of boys as a result of the assumption of feminine rôles by some of them in a minstrel show, a virile man teacher was able by means of a downright speech to define clearly what expressions of affection were and what were not proper in a group of boys, with the result that the homosexual interchange became much less open and in most cases disappeared entirely. Teachers are also concerned with imposing the taboos of conventional morality upon their charges. The taboo of chastity is imposed upon girls with unrelenting severity. There is evidence that the virginity of their female charges is a matter over which women teachers exercise themselves greatly.[1] As a result partly of this feeling, and partly of the feeling that "puppy-love" is a silly and bootless emotion, and one not in accord with the ideal of academic achievement, many teachers ridicule or punish all students who take an obvious interest in members of the opposite sex.

PROJECTS

1. Minutely observe the behavior of a successful teacher in taking charge of a new class. Describe and analyze particular acts in terms of the definition of the situation.

2. Study likewise the technique of a less competent teacher. Analyze carefully and compare with the above.

3. Describe the behavior (over several days) of a critic teacher "breaking in" a new practice teacher.

4. Study the techniques employed by skillful teachers in restoring order when some extraordinary incident has disrupted classroom routine.

5. By inquiry among students and teachers investigate the question whether teachers should permit students to argue about grades. Interpret your results in terms of the definition of the situation.

6. Investigate pupil-originated definitions of situations and teacher techniques for meeting them in a grade-school classroom during a single week.

7. Relate some single incident which seemed to change the tone of an entire class. Analyze and interpret.

8. Study the course of student attitudes toward a teacher who begins by being strict and later relaxes. Compare with a similar study of a teacher who begins by being lax and later tightens up. Analyze and interpret.

9. Observe classroom incidents which mark a crisis in teacher domination, situations in which the teacher must "do something" or lose control. Observe successful and unsuccessful attempts to meet these situations. Interpret.

[1] Of a group of about seventy-five short papers written by women teachers upon subjects to be chosen by themselves, about one quarter concerned the experiences of some girl who departed from the conventional morality. This would seem to be a strong indication that this is, for women teachers, one of the central problems of school life.

10. Write the history of certain "character-building" programs in a particular school.

11. Tell the story of a crisis produced by a thief in the school. Interpret.

12. Investigate the process by which students form judgments concerning teachers. Describe the process of "trying out the teacher." How far is this conscious? Does it involve penetration of the teacher's unconscious motives?

13. Describe some case in which the tone of a school was changed by a single event. (Quoted from Clow.)

14. Describe some case in which the attitude of a class seemed to be determined by a single member. (Quoted from Clow.)

15. Describe some instance in which the standing of a teacher in a community was changed by a single incident. (Quoted from Clow.)

SUGGESTED READINGS

(1) ALMACK, J. C., and LANG, A. R., *The Beginning Teacher,* Chapters IV, V, and VI.

(2) BAGLEY, W. C., *Classroom Management.*

(3) BAGLEY, W. C., *School Discipline.*

(4) HELSON, HARRY, *The Psychology of Gestalt,* pp. 45-54.

(5) MONROE, WALTER S., *Directing Learning in the High School,* Chapter XI.

(6) THOMAS, W. I., *The Unadjusted Girl,* pp. 42 ff. (See also YOUNG, KIMBALL, *Source Book for Social Psychology,* pp. 47-53; THOMAS, W. I., and ZNANIECKI, FLORIAN, *The Polish Peasant in Europe and America.*)

(7) THOMAS, W. I., *The Behavior Pattern and the Situation,* Publications of the American Sociological Society, Vol. XXII, pp. 1-13.

Chapter XIX

ATTITUDES AND RÔLES IN CLASSROOM SITUATIONS

The attitude is a tendency to act produced in the dynamic interaction between the individual and his environment. When a situation is defined we know what our attitude toward it is. Further, we seek to define a situation by taking an attitude toward it. The search for an attitude is a search for a definition of the situation. Most of the situations in which human beings are involved are predominantly social, and the attitudes worked out in those situations may be called social attitudes. Our discussion will therefore be concerned in the main with social attitudes, or such attitudes as persons take toward situations in which other persons are involved as factors of primary importance. It is especially true of the situations centering about the school that they are predominantly social, and the failure to take cognizance of this fact may account for the fact that many writers on subjects educational have missed the point and that programs of educational reform have never turned out as they should.

But there are certain non-social reactions, certain attitudes into which social influences enter only indirectly, and we shall attend to these first. Very important in the list of non-social attitudes of teachers and students are their reflex reactions to the physical conditions of the classroom or the school. Lighting conditions, ventilation, odors, noises, and the construction of the classroom are known to have a direct influence upon the attitudes of teachers and students; the influence which they have is rarely translated directly into action; certainly it is never expressed in action for which the social situation does not also furnish a motivation, or for which it does not supply a pattern; but it is an influence worthy of remark. Teachers have often thought that children were more restless on rainy, uncomfortable days than on others; Dexter has tried to measure these weather influences and he has concluded that this common-sense generalization of teachers rests upon solid fact. Teachers who have kept study halls and who have a sensitive ear for the shuffling of feet will not find it difficult to agree. Smells are also important determinants of social attitudes. Other non-social causes within the person operate to influence his attitudes; the wickedness of students is partly a matter of the teacher's digestion, and in schools where written report sheets are kept it is possible to tell when the teacher suffers from his migraine. We have no wish to fall into the error of using any of these factors to explain social behavior directly, and we certainly do not wish to give aid or comfort to that numerous party who avoid all social problems by referring them to physical conditions thought to underlie them. It is merely necessary to note that these reflex reactions to physical conditions are important elements in the total situation. Perhaps they are far from being most important elements. If it is on a rainy day that the insurrection against a bad teacher finally comes, that is an important fact, but not nearly so important as the fact that he is a bad teacher. Rain falling upon the students of good and bad teachers alike may make them all alike restless, but the restlessness will be translated into quite different sorts of social behavior.

Certain general attitudes of a slightly different class need also to be discussed under this heading. These are the attitudes taken toward subject matter. Although attitudes coming out of the social situation in which the child is involved are paramount in determining the attitude toward subject matter, the attitude itself must be impersonal so far as the subject matter is impersonal. Thus a child applies himself to his work because he loves his teacher, or because he wants to surpass a rival, or as a refuge from the life about him, or, as a compensation for an inferiority complex, to gain esoteric lore which will distinguish him from his fellows, or because he wishes to please his parents. These are all social attitudes. But when he turns to the subject matter of his courses in school, the child's attitude must be impersonal. The orientation which he then assumes with reference to the theoretical situation confronting him is usually that which can be called the memorizing attitude or the problem-solving attitude or the recalling attitude. More rarely there is an attitude of trying to understand the inner mysteries of things. (It is, of course, quite possible for the student to have a personal attitude toward subject matter that is personal, as that of history may be.) These are attitudes of extreme importance in determining the child's success in the assimilation of subject matter. The psychology of the school men sometimes errs by considering them changeless functions rather than attitudes dynamically evolved in connection with concrete subject matter. Perhaps educational measurements do not measure the efficiency of mental functions but the effect of attitudes! We may gain something by a study of the social attitudes determining these non-social attitudes, but this is a subject largely untouched. It is thought by most school men that the social system most conducive to a favorable attitude of students toward subject matter is a system of rigid ranking based upon numerical grades, with two classes, the failures and the successes, clearly marked off, and subclasses within each group. Because the desired attitude is not in fact engendered in a satisfactorily large number of students, an attempt is made to patch up this social structure by importing other and extraneous inducements into it. Hence all the futile patter about motivation.

Social attitudes are attitudes directed at situations in which other persons are factors of primary importance. Social attitudes are more numerous and more important than non-social attitudes, and social attitudes always condition, where they do not control, the expression of non-social attitudes. Faris has noted that it is possible to distinguish conscious and unconscious attitudes, group and individual attitudes, and latent and kinetic attitudes. We may identify all these attitudes as actually present in school-room situations. The exploration of the unconscious attitudes of students and teachers is a task that has as yet hardly been attempted, but it is a work that promises rich rewards for all investigators. Certainly the unconscious attitudes of teachers influence students as deeply as their more conscious thoughts. It is partly by virtue of their penetration into the teacher's unverbalized attitudes that children are such good practical psychologists. They judge by the teacher's general behavior, and unconscious attitudes are likely to show themselves more plainly in that general behavior than in the teacher's conscious thoughts. Even where the teacher's unconscious attitude is not clearly grasped, it frequently influences the child's situation in such a way that the child develops an attitude that corresponds to it either by way of reenforcement or by way of opposition. Group attitudes, as distinguished from individual attitudes, are present in the school room under the guise of prejudice or in the form of collective representations. Latent attitudes are those which are not in themselves demands for activity; they are lesser habit systems at the service of the greater, and more demanding, kinetic attitudes. The ability to write is a latent attitude, whereas the desire to smoke is a kinetic attitude. It is perhaps enlightening to reflect that the formal task of the school is the inculcation upon children of certain skills which should be classed as latent attitudes, the ability to read, write, and figure, and that the greatest enemy to this regimen is the child's kinetic attitudes, his spontaneous interest in play, in fighting, and in love.

A further distinction is that between social attitudes which arise out of primary group situations and those which arise from secondary group relations. As we have shown elsewhere, primary groups are those intimate, face to face, personal groups in which members participate with little reserve; secondary groups permit or demand of their members only a segmental participation. The school situation, and especially that part of it which arises out of the relation of teachers to students, is one which gives rise to a peculiar melange of primary and secondary group relationships and attitudes. It is not possible for the relationship to stabilize itself on the basis of either primary group attitudes or secondary group attitudes alone, so that arrangements arise whereby mixed attitudes come to expression, or complementary, even antithetical, attitudes come to expression at different times. We have analyzed elsewhere the softening of the authoritative attitude, a secondary group attitude in its inception, by the slow growth of friendliness, a friendliness not opposed to the acceptance of authority; we have also called attention to the failure of many teachers ever to establish secondary group attitudes when primary group attitudes are prior to them in time. Secondary group attitudes may be softened by the subsequent growth of primary group attitudes within that structure, but the opposite process is psychologically more expensive, and it is rarely possible.

Many, if not most, social attitudes partake of the nature of rôles. A rôle is a social attitude reflected back upon the individual either actually or in his imagination. It is an attitude to which has been added a realization of an attitude of another which it evokes in that other. (It may in fact be chained to a whole configuration of mutually interlocking attitudes.) Since this concept of the social rôle will be very important in the interpretation which we shall make of life in the school, it will perhaps be worth our while to essay an extended discussion of it.

That much of human nature is to be understood as the playing of rôles the poets have always known.

> All the world's a stage,
> And all the men and women merely players,
> They have their exits and their entrances,
> And one man in his time plays many parts

said Shakespeare, doubting reality.

For the scientist, however, the rôle is not important as a symbol of unreality and the mark of disparity between men's deeds and the estimates they put upon them; it is not so much important in that connection as in emphasizing the reality of behavior oriented by a knowledge of the attitudes of others.

One group of sociologists have considered the concept of the social rôle as of such central significance for the understanding of human nature that they have based their conception of personality upon it. Park and Burgess define personality as "The sum and organization of those traits which determine the rôle of the individual in the group." This definition is sometimes altered to read: "Personality is the sum and organization of all the rôles one plays in all the groups to which he belongs." This definition is important because it brings clearly to the fore the dramatic element in human behavior, and emphasizes the fact that social behavior falls naturally into certain units which may be called parts, or rôles.

The rôle arises from that bipolar organization of the field of consciousness in which self and others, real or imagined, are given over against each other in experience. The action of the individual thus comes to be oriented with reference to an entire situation of which the supposed attitude of that other is a part. Thus when one behaves in a social situation of this sort, he behaves self-consciously—to some extent he plays a part. This behavior is always different from what it would be if another were not present, and it was therefore with a correct intuition that Spencer made modifications in the behavior of one individual as a result of the presence of another the basis of his theory of social control.

The rôle appears as the organization of the individual with reference to an entire situation; it is the response of the individual to the entire situation as it has taken shape in his mind. Some insight (correct or incorrect) into the attitudes of others is implied. The insight may be entirely fallacious, or it may be incomplete, but to play a rôle is to regulate one's behavior by the imagined judgments of others. In more complicated cases there may appear interlocking rôles of two or more persons for the completion of which many interconnected acts are required. (The nature of the social act is to be directed at a responding object.) Or there may appear in the life of a group a network of rôles so extended in time, so complicated in their interconnections and so subtle in the influences which they exert upon each other that the keenest analyst must despair of making out more than the basic outline of the picture.

The rôle inheres in the social situation as the non-social attitude inheres in the more general sort of situation. Both are contingent upon the working out of a definition of the situation. When the diverse elements of a social situation are seen in a configuration, and the various tensions which the situation arouses in the individual are at length synthesized, there is a moment when the proper rôle appears. When we are confronted with the life of a new group, the first impressions are chaotic and incomplete. But when we make out the sense of that group life, when we become cognizant of the definition of the situation, we are able to assume a rôle. When the proper rôle is found, uneasiness disappears.

The patness of a rôle, its propriety or impropriety, depends upon its acceptability. One individual never, except in the most primitive and biological sense, responds directly to another; he responds rather to a more or less veracious imagined construct of that other. The ideal fitting together of human personalities depends upon a correspondence between the rôles which a person considers himself to be playing and the rôles which another fancies him to be playing. Complete contact is attained when the individual's conception of his rôle corresponds exactly to the imagined construct others have of him. Let us suppose two individuals, *A* and *B*, to be brought together in a social situation. With reference to *A*, it is important to know his conception of *B* and his conception of his own rôle with reference to *B*. Both of these persons conform to (the immediate social) reality if they conform to each other. When it is an individual and group that are involved, a rôle is acceptable to the group when it conforms to group standards, i.e., the folkways and mores of the group and the basic definitions of situations upon which group life rests; the rôle is acceptable to the individual if it conforms to his conception of his rôle.

From disparity between rôles and group standards arise the phenomena of conflict between the individual and the group. From a failure of the rôle assigned in group life to conform to the individual's conception of his rôle arise mental conflict and neurotic behavior. The inferiority complex forms about an inacceptable rôle, together with the attempt to get away from it, a negative identification mechanism. For few of us do the rôles we ideally play actually conform to reality. Rarely does our own conception of our behavior coincide with the conception of others, and to the extent that it does not so coincide, we live by fictions rather than rôles. A fiction is a rôle falsified or distorted so that it no longer even approximates the conception which others have of it. To some extent, we all live by fictions. And a sorry world it would be if the poet had had his wish. If one morning we should awake to find that we had the power to see ourselves as others see us, perhaps few of us would care to finish out that day alive. Every man, says Adler, has his own basic life-lie that helps to make existence tolerable. But a life organization that depends upon fictions to too great a degree is unhealthful and leads to a sort of social suicide. In extreme cases the fiction may often be detected by the fact that the individual is given to frequent and extreme changes in his conception of his rôle without any perceptible changes in his overt behavior.

Once a rôle has been accepted, it is internalized and made meaningful by a process of dynamic elaboration. In the drama of life every man writes his own lines and revises them from moment to moment. The check on this process is conformity to the reality principle. As a rôle is made meaningful, it comes to be itself one of the aims of existence, one of the criteria by which other possible rôles are judged. (This process may be seen as equal and opposite to that other process by which ends become means, and it cooperates with that process to restore the balance of nature.) A rôle which has thus been internalized may become one of the chief drives of the personality. Not only does such a rôle sink in toward the centrum of the personality; it also flowers out. It is supplemented by all manner of arrangements, habits, and tested social techniques which enable the individual to make the most of the rôle.

But an individual may either accept or reject a rôle which a group offers him. In case he rejects it, if the rôle continues to be assigned, the formula of rejection is subject to a like elaboration. The subjective side of such an elaborated rejection is the inferiority complex.

A point which has perhaps been anticipated in this discussion is that rôles may be either conscious or unconscious. Long-established rôles are removed from the center of consciousness by mechanisms of habit formation; such rôles tend to be accepted as matter of course, while attention is transferred to the newly elaborated details or to newer rôles in accordance with the long-established one. A difficulty in the introspective interpretation of behavior is that behavior often arises from the following out of rôles which have been so long established and have sunk so deeply into the foundations of the personality that it is no longer possible for consciousness to take account of them. Otherwise unconscious rôles may arise from an organization of behavior into which the individual has no insight or only partial insight, but which nevertheless becomes an important part of the personality. (Thus identification, for some of the psychoanalytic writers, is unconsciously taking the rôle of another.) Or a rôle of some importance may become unconscious through its repudiation by the forces in control of consciousness, through the action of the psychoanalytic mechanism of repression, and this is apparently the more common case.

Writers on social psychology have attached considerable theoretical importance to the concept of the social rôle. The playing of rôles and the acquisition of behavior patterns is thought to be a central process in the development of personality. One becomes conscious of his own personality by becoming aware of the attitudes of others toward him; he acquires a rôle and becomes a person because he is treated as a person. One then becomes conscious of others as embodying rôles, and he incorporates into his own personality the rôles of those others, a process which accounts for much of imitation. Of the importance of this mechanism of the accretion and internalization of rôles in the growth of personality there seems no doubt; behaviorists and psychoanalysts alike have attached much importance to these identification mechanisms.

The concept of the social rôle is particularly fruitful for the understanding of social life in schools. As an artificial social order the school is hard put to it to sustain, through the teacher, its correlative artificial rôles, and to keep the conventional rôles of teachers and students from being crowded out of existence by spontaneous rôles which would be dangerous for the established order. It seems worth while to analyze both the conventional and spontaneous rôles of students and teachers.

The central rôle of the teacher in his professional capacity is his executive rôle. The teacher is the representative of the established order; as such he must be ever ready to force conformity and to enforce discipline. The teacher represents the established order of business; it is therefore his to call the class back from tempting divagations to the more or less boresome routine of acquiring skills and information. The teacher is the representative of authority, and his is *par excellence* the dogmatic position. These are the components of the teacher's rôle as such. It is a rôle which demands an inflexibility of personality far surpassing that exacted or even allowed by most occupations. As might be expected, it has far-reaching effects upon the personality, and it receives both internal and external elaboration. The details of the carrying of authority are worked out with minute perfection; the teacher's voice and the expression of his face are formalized and forced to conform to the necessities of the authority rôle. Likewise, there is an internal adaptation to the conditions of teaching such that the teacher's personal dignity depends upon the teacher rôle; one comes to think of himself not only as a teacher but as *the teacher.*

Though the teacher rôle as such is inflexible, it is supportable either for the individual teacher or his students only by virtue of a rapid alternation with it of supplementary or even contradictory rôles. Thus one softens the incidence of his authority by allowing certain indications of a dignified personal interest, of a kindliness with reserve, to seep through his countenance. One alternates the rôles of the kindly adult, the mildly amused adult, and the fatherly individual with the teaching rôle. This alternation, and this rôle which is ever the same for all the alternation, may perhaps become clearer if we take an example. The following account of the activities of one section of one day has been furnished by a teacher skilled in introspection:

I looked forward with some dread to the beginning of a school day. Teaching meant hours of boredom spent in making smug youngsters learn things they didn't want to learn. Therefore I shaved off the last possible second from my time for going to school.

This morning I left home at eight-forty-five, neither more nor less reluctantly than usual. Once I was out of doors, my school-teacher conscience began to get in its work, and I hurried because I did not want to be late. Every day at this time I resolved to start a minute or so earlier on the next day, but I was never able to remember the resolution on the next day. At the corner I met Jack B., a student in my first class of the day. I wondered whether I should wait for him or continue my walk to school alone. It was necessary to be friendly, but it was also necessary to keep one's distance. He quickened his step and gave me no choice. The greeting was a little troublesome. I was never sure I got it right. "Good morning, Jack," I said, using a tone of voice that I thought combined excellently the desired semicordiality, dignity, and reserve. I was perhaps a shade friendlier than I should otherwise have been because of the boy's show of friendliness.

"Good morning, professor. How are you today?"

"Rotten," I answered. He laughed, for my chronic ill humor was correctly evaluated as something of a pose, and it was therefore amusing.

We fell in step. I hesitated to start a conversation. I felt cynical and defeated beside Jack's young freshness. I was conscious of the discrepancy between my drooping shoulders and his square ones. I felt very old. I liked Jack, for he was a fine, straightforward boy, but I was never altogether at ease with him. No doubt he felt the same way about me, but I must admit that he showed it less.

"Do you think Dempsey has a chance to come back?" he asked.

I pondered a while. It was part of my pose to know the inside history of such matters. "Naw, he hasn't got a chance. They couldn't even get suckers to attend the fight if it weren't for the old ballyhoo." Thus I emphatically, who knew nothing about it whatever. I began to expand. I felt quite friendly toward this boy who had asked my judgment. But I guarded myself, and checked the flow of speech, for I knew that a half hour later I might call upon this boy in class and find him unprepared. I did not want to be inhibited when that occurred. I remembered that on the week previous I had condemned Jack to spend three afternoons in the make-up study hall, and that he had not taken these penalties with the best grace in the world. I wondered whether he were thinking of that punishment now. Apparently he held no grudge. What had he told his parents about me? Perhaps there was no harm in being friendly, in letting the boy see that I could be human outside the classroom. He went blithely on with the conversation,

"Say, I sure saw a swell movie Saturday night. Doug Fairbanks in 'The Mark of Zorro.' Y'oughta see it."

I began to be a little angry. Decidedly this was going too far. Suggesting that I should go to a movie! And Douglas Fairbanks indeed! But it would not do to show my feelings too plainly. Coldly I said, "Thanks. I don't care much for movies, and less for Douglas Fairbanks."

The boy drew back. My tone had been altogether too chilling. Suddenly I felt sorry for him. After all, he was only trying to be friendly. Perhaps I could mitigate this blow by joking with him a little. I went on, "Oh, of course, when I was your age, gallivanting around and breaking hearts, I suppose I did like those romantic things." I smiled, and tried to look some twenty years older than I was. I must give the impression, of course, that all these things were definitely in the past. It would not do for him to begin joking me. It soon became evident that he had no intention of doing so. He was too completely teased himself and enjoyed it altogether too much to try to turn the tables on me.

He gave a little laugh that showed that he was embarrassed and quite pleased with himself. "No, it's not that. I haven't any girl," he said.

"No? Then who is that little girl that's supposed to be eating her heart out for you? It seems to me I saw the two of you the other day and that you seemed to know each other very well. Of course, it may have been your cousin."

The boy was overcome, and there seemed no point in pressing my advantage any further.

I felt quite friendly now. The realization came suddenly that this boy was winning me over against my will. Would he try to take advantage of this little friendly interlude? Well, what if he did? I could show him soon enough that I drew a line between what went on in school and what took place outside. We chatted pleasantly, exchanged some old and feeble jokes, and went on to school together. For the first time, I felt quite free from constraint.

We came to school and I decided to enter the front office. I did not want to seem too intimate with this boy. Some of the other teachers might look askance at me if they saw the two of us come in together. I took leave of him gruffly, "I'll see you in a few minutes, I guess. Ha! Ha!" I thought that would show Jack that I would be ready for anything that might come up. Jack smiled but he was not amused.

A few minutes of relaxation. But I remained on guard just the same. I greeted some friends absent-mindedly and some persons with whom relations were temporarily strained with elaborate politeness. There was a note in my mailbox. One of my students was convalescing from a recent illness, and he thought that he would be able to make up some of his work if he knew what the assignments were. I sat down at the secretary's desk and wrote. I made some show of consulting my classbook, in which was absolutely nothing that pertained to the matter, and not very much pertaining to any other matter. But I carried it because it seemed to contribute a little something to my teaching prestige. I felt very important as I wrote, and was reasonably sure that I made a very convincing picture of the efficient and conscientious teacher.

"Well, I guess that will fix him for a little while," I said.

I knew that it was useless, that it was the last that I should hear of the matter until the boy returned to school, and that it was absolutely unknown that a "Seventy student" should prepare back work in the hospital. The secretary thanked me politely. But there was a quizzical look somewhere in her face that made me wonder what she really thought. I left the office and started toward class.

Classes had already passed. One or two belated students were scurrying for their classrooms. Let them hurry; I didn't have to hurry. I was the teacher. Sedately I climbed the stairs. I paused outside the door of my classroom. What a babble! I should have to speak to them about that. In a moment it would be hushed. What if it did not hush? Perish the thought! There had been a time when I could not be quite so sure. I put the thought aside. Striving to appear perfunctory, uninterested, and quite unaware of my own importance, I stepped through the door. Rubber heels were a disadvantage in some ways. They did not announce your coming. I did not want to be one of these sneaking teachers, and I'd rather have a bell on me than always be catching students doing things they shouldn't. Perhaps the next pair of shoes . . . But still the other kind of heels did disturb a class dreadfully. Thus my professional thoughts.

Three or four boys saw me. I stood framed in the doorway. I had heard somewhere that actors did that. It constellated attention upon one to stand with a frame about him. The rest of the class saw me.

"Shhhhhh."

I knew. They were trying to curry favor by this show of respect. Slowly I looked over the class. I stared mildly at each person in turn, a little longer upon enemies and suspects than upon others. I moved slowly. I had learned that it was best to be deliberate. It gave them time to settle down and I could then call their attention to the lesson by slow stages. Of course the text-books said one should jump right in and start pounding, but I didn't believe that got as much activity from students as my methods did. After all, pupil activity was the thing. I sat down. I adjusted myself in the seat. I was in no hurry. Let no one think that I was nervous. I was bored. I could outwait them all. I opened my book. The suspense heightened. I spoke for the first time.

I barked out a question, "Where did we leave off yesterday, Henry?"

I knew. But I wanted Henry to tell. It was part of our regular daily ritual, and the members of my class knew as well as I that it was just a little game. But woe to Henry if he could not tell!

Glibly he answered, "Page 146, line 20."

"Humph." I turned to the page.

"All right, Translate. . . ." I looked around for a victim. There was Jack. I had an idea that he was not prepared. I might as well meet that issue now. "Translate, Jack."

"I'm sorry, sir. I'm not prepared today."

"What?" I raised my voice. I was going to give him what for. Going to see "The Mark of Zorro?" instead of studying his Latin! I looked at him. Oh, well, after all he was a good kid. With a sigh and a gesture of helplessness I indicated to the class my despair of ever being able to do anything with Jack. Relieved, he slumped down in his seat. "You could at least sit up," I said, naggingly. The over-acted despair was not yet out of my voice. I held my head in my hands, still acting out discouragement.

"Well, who can translate the first sentence?"

Half a dozen hands went up. Ivan was gesticulating wildly. He was very anxious to be called upon. That meant that he had only prepared the first sentence. Very well, I should call upon him for the second sentence and enjoy his discomfiture. Strange, that little play had happened so many times before, but Ivan could not catch on. Very well, I should stage it once more. Charles, a quiet boy and a clever one, was looking out the window. I wondered whether he was doing that with a thought-out plan. I decided to call on Charles; I called his name. I watched him narrowly, but tried not to let him see. A very faint smile played over his lips. He was eager to begin.

"Never mind, Charles."

He was very disappointed, I gave him a look that said, "Caught you, didn't I?" I smiled somewhat sardonically. Charles smiled back. There was resignation in his smile, and some admiration. After all, it was a game.

"You show them how to translate the first sentence, Harold." Harold was the worst Latin student in the world. He had never been known to translate a sentence correctly. But he was brave. He read it first in Latin. He read beautifully. Then came the translation.

"Cæsar—Labienus—mumble jumble—Horsemen—mountain—mumble battle."

"Oh. Lord!" Again the comic despair. "Where's the verb?"

"I don't know, sir." Harold might not remember any Latin but he never forgot the sir.

I had an inspiration. Carefully I explained it to Harold, "Now, Harold, I listened carefully to your sentence. I believe that on the whole it was correct. But wait, I cannot let that splendid performance pass by without speaking of it in words of the highest praise. I will go so far as to say that it sounded to me like one of the best translations it has ever been my pleasure to listen to. Yes, sir, man and boy, I have had more years of experience with the Latin tongue than you have had years of life, but I never, positively, never, never in my born days, heard a translation that equalled yours. But you spoke in such a low tone of voice that I am afraid the rest of the class missed it. Would you mind, Harold, for the sake of the rest of the class who will otherwise remain in ignorance of what a good Latin translation is, would you mind repeating your rendition of that sentence, the first sentence of the lesson, and the only one to which we have today attended?"

Harold complied, but resentment was in his eyes.

"Splendid," I said. "Perfect. Exactly right. Now Maurice, I hope you have attended carefully, for I am going to ask you to translate that same sentence, not, you understand, not that Harold didn't do it perfectly, but because I wish to see whether you followed him or not."

Maurice was the best student in the class. He translated. I paid little attention. Maurice could be trusted. Harold proceeded to think of more important things, probably what he would like to do to me some time.

"Fine." I was grateful to Maurice for being such a good student. Sometimes he presumed upon that unspoken gratitude, but not often.

"Now Charles, the second sentence."

Charles looked sheepish. I taunted him. With exaggerated wonder, "Well, now, isn't that strange. You don't know the second sentence. Well, now, isn't that just too bad. You seemed to know the first one so well that I decided that you must know the entire lesson and thought it would be wiser to call upon you later. I'm very sorry. Quite unintentional I assure you." Charles hung his head. I was having fun this morning.

"Well, Ivan. You translate."

Ivan did. As he finished, he began to smile. I appeared not to notice. "Go on, Ivan, go on. I didn't tell you to stop. You did that sentence so well that I'm going to give you a chance to recite the whole lesson." Blandly I urged him on. But Ivan could do no more.

"Well, Ivan," I conceded, "it nearly worked."

More translating, but mostly routine now. Midway of the hour. This is the day for the lesson in composition.

"All right. I'll take those composition papers."

Much shifting and folding of papers. I went from student to student. One or two turned in no papers. I glared at each of these and made imaginary notations in my book. One boy hastily wrote something on a sheet of paper and folded the paper. I saw him from the corner of my eye. When I came to him I seized his paper, opened it, and found that he had merely written the English of the first two sentences. In a rage I glared at him. I started to speak but was unable to find words strong enough to express my feelings. I tried again. With an obvious effort, I controlled myself and pronounced judgment.

"For that your presence at loafers' study hall will be required for one week. Harold and Ivan will report for one day only. And the next time you're going to be smart, Thurston, don't try it out on me."

The students passed to the board in an orderly fashion, and soon began to write. I had a few moments of rest while I gazed out of the window and thought of other things.

Then I went the rounds of the class, correcting the first two or three sentences of each student, and berating them individually and collectively for their stupidity.

I heard a little noise outside the door. The principal! And another man with him. A parent, of course. They came in.

"Just go right on with your work, professor, we're looking the place over and we just came in here for a little while."

The atmosphere changed. Chalk clicked upon the blackboard more methodically. My manner changed. I became patient, fatherly, efficient.

I went the rounds of the class, stopping by each student to point out mistakes. This I did a little more thoroughly and much more calmly than before. No beratings now. Only explanation and a little benignant exhortation.

Poor Harold had made little progress. He was patiently looking up words in the vocabulary and writing them down. I wondered whether the visitor knew any Latin. I gave Harold a little lecture on Latin composition.

"Well, you have not got very far have you. I'm afraid you will have to erase all that now and start over. Now listen to me and I will tell you again some of the important things to remember when translating. Find the subject of the English sentence. Sometimes it is a good idea to diagram the English sentence. Anyhow, find the subject. Translate the subject. Put it in the nominative case. Find the verb. Find the number, person, tense, mood, voice of the verb. Translate the verb. Be sure you have the correct principal parts of the verb. Be sure it agrees with the subject in person and number. Has the sentence a direct object? If it has, translate that. Put it in the accusative case. Has it an indirect object? Put it in the dative. Has it any adjectives? Make them agree with the noun they modify. Has it any prepositional phrases? Be sure you get the correct preposition and the proper case to go with it."

Harold was somewhat mystified at receiving so much attention. Perhaps he was not mystified. Perhaps he saw through it all. At any rate he was polite. "Yes, sir. Thank you, sir."

Harold had not understood a word. But I had to deal with him somehow. It wasn't that I wanted to pose. But there he stood and I could not ignore him in front of a parent. And it might be equally bad to write his sentence for him, for then the persons watching would think me easy, something which I certainly was not. I knew the principal would privately inform the man (against the possibility that his own boy might sometime be in one of my classes) that I had the reputation of being something of a Tartar, and that he guessed that I sometimes got after them pretty hard. And anyhow parents didn't understand; I had never been a parent but then most parents had never been teachers, so that made it even. And it didn't do to show parents things they would never understand. Besides, I did not want to fly into an infantile rage in the presence of a strange adult. That was all very well for boys, and it was not embarrassing in the presence of fellow teachers, but one hesitates to make a fool of himself in the presence of a real grown-up. (Fictionized life history document.)

The kaleidoscopic shiftings of rôles apparent in this case history could doubtless be paralleled in many others. The essential rôle, however, remains. It may be sharpened, or softened, or it may for the moment be laid aside, but the teacher is always conscious of it, and he will not allow any rôle really to interfere with it. It is also significant to note the disappearance of the juvenile antics when other adults appeared on the scene, and the resultant limitation of the teaching to the essential teaching rôle, which was itself somewhat embroidered for the benefit of the audience. One should distinguish carefully rôles played by teachers for the benefit of students and those played for the edification of persons outside the situation, as other teachers and parents.

There is a greater variety among the rôles customarily played by students, and not all of them are obviously centered around any one point. In the primary group life of children, students often play rôles quite at variance with those which they find it necessary to assume when a teacher is present. Thus school children are often like those men who, aggressively obscene in the society of men, become reticent and refined in the presence of women. Rôles which recur in almost every play group are those of the leader, the clown, the bully, the goat, the trusted member of the gang (by contrast with marginal member, or the candidate for membership), etc. There is a tendency for these rôles to be carried into the school room, but each one is subjected to some metamorphosis, and sharp breaks, as we have remarked, are always possible. Thus the leader may remain a leader, but he must adapt his leadership to the (usually) superior force of the teacher, which he may do through alliance, opposition, rivalry, or other means. The clown is still a clown, but his buffoonery must be disguised, it may become covert, or it may adopt a mien of innocence and pose as blundering stupidity. The trusted member of the gang, the loyal one, may play no such rôle with reference to the teacher. It is his to avoid any entangling alliances between himself and the teacher. The goat receives the teacher's protection, and perhaps becomes all the more a goat for having it. Many rôles which the student frequently plays with reference to the teacher are rare or entirely non-existent in the play group. Such are: the good boy, the bad boy, the teacher's helper, the teacher's representative, the sychophant, the stool-pigeon, etc. It is noteworthy that certain children acquire recognized prescriptive rights in particular rôles.

The teacher, following out his customary rôle, attempts to delimit the social interaction of the classroom. He strives to canalize the attention of students and to make it work upon subject matter. The perfect picture of the normal interaction of personalities in the classroom is that of teacher and pupils playing their customary rôles, of the teacher exerting pressure first at one point and then at another in order that attention may be concentrated on routine business. "Pay attention now," says the teacher. "Just listen to this." "What do you think George Washington said when his father asked him who chopped down the cherry tree?" "Who can tell us the story of the Boston Tea Party?" Thus the teacher continually strives to evoke in students the attitudinal set which we call "attention," the attitude toward subject matter from which ensues "the phenomenal definition of the contour and inner articulateness of a perceived configuration." The attention of students tends to wander from cut-and-dried subject matter. As attention wanders, the scope of social interaction broadens. The teacher brings it back in a manner very similar to that of a dog driving a herd of sheep. Normally the teacher is able to prevail over the tendency to wander and to call back attention to the subject of discussion. Sometimes no effort can prevail, as on the last day of school before a vacation, or the day before a big game, when the attitudinal set of the children is firmly held by something much more alluring than Beowulf or the binomial theorem; and sometimes attention is diverted to the struggle of personalities rather than to subject matter; this will certainly be true if the problem of discipline remains unsettled, or if the teacher makes too much of discipline. (That is another reason for the feeling of school men that "the less said about discipline the better.") This is the degeneracy of the normal social process of the school.

The teacher may use the assigning of rôles for the control of students. Whether they will or no, teachers use identification mechanisms, and a teacher who does not understand the subtle processes involved is very likely to invoke the gods of suggestion to his own hurt. (The identification mechanism, clearly conscious, self-conscious in fact, where it is imposed by one person upon another may be regarded as a special case of suggestion; it is the suggestion of a rôle.)

Identification mechanisms which are most frequently used with any awareness of their nature are positive identification mechanisms. Positive identification mechanisms are those assigned rôles with which the individual identifies himself positively and which he lives out with a feeling of pleasure. Their weight depends upon the psychic value of the rôle and the significance of the relationship in which it arises. One's reaction to a rôle may of course be either positive or negative, but it is always significant if the group is significant. One grows into the rôles to which one reacts positively; he expands through them, and elaborates them. One grows away from the rôle to which he reacts negatively, and he elaborates his defences against the rôle. All human life may be seen as a shifting tangle of social rôles, and from this point of view it appears as a complex, interweaving pattern like a Persian rug that has come to life.

The technique by which positive identification mechanisms are employed requires usually two steps: first, to establish the relationship as significant, so that an assigned rôle may be taken seriously; and second, to assign the rôle. One is more likely to accept suggestions from friends than from enemies, and one is much influenced by the prestige of the suggestion agent. It is desirable that a rôle which one wishes to assign to another have some basis in fact, so that it may be acceptable to the other and credible to him. The technique of the visiting teachers, as Mary Buell Sayles and others have expounded it, seems to be based very largely upon this mechanism. First they establish a friendly rapport with their subject; then they select that person's best quality or most notable accomplishment and praise him for it. The result is often that the entire personality is then reorganized about the one rôle into which the individual grows. It would be tedious to give many examples, and it is unnecessary, inasmuch as the technique has been so ably expounded and with such a wealth of illustration in the publications of the Commonwealth Fund. This technique is also important in the scheme of life of private schools; it plays a large part in their ceremonies, and in the social gradations which reflect their systems of rewards and punishments. Where athletics plays an important part in school life, it often happens that a boy first receives favorable recognition for some quality which he displays on the athletic field, and that he then reorganizes his personality around that new rôle. Thus a rebellious Jewish boy was metamorphosed into a pillar of society when one of his mentors praised him publicly as a "fighter." Teachers have been using these identification mechanisms for a long time; it is a very old policy to make the work of the monitor seem rather a privilege than a task.

Commonly, however, teachers use suggestion mechanisms in such a way as to imperil their own control of the student group. When a relationship of hostility exists between students and teachers, favorable recognition from the teacher acts as a negative identification mechanism, and unfavorable recognition acts positively. To some extent this was the case with "Crazy Andy."[1] In other cases, the unfavorable notice from the teacher is more than counterbalanced by the favorable recognition one receives from students, so that a like reversal comes about. Typical of such cases is the following:

> My very worst teacher taught me most about teaching school. I was a very well-behaved child in school, even under this weak teacher. But there was one regulation that none of us ever even thought of observing, because it was contrary to tradition and in our opinion unjust. That was the rule forbidding talking and moving about the room during recess. In common with the rest of the boys in the grade, I talked and laughed at recess time. One day the teacher observed us all from the back door. When school reopened he made a little speech and announced to the school that he had always thought me a good boy, but that he had seen me at recess time, and had then decided that I was a bad boy. I got the feeling from his words and from the admiring glances of the other children that I was a desperate ruffian, and I can still remember the little swagger that I put into my walk as long as that man was my teacher. I did many things thereafter to confirm him in his opinion of me.

There is a limit to the use of identification mechanisms in the school as it is actually constituted. This is set by the social distance between teacher and student, which makes the process difficult, and by the necessity of adjusting the ego demands of students and teacher to each other, an adjustment which is made more difficult because of the tendency of expanding social rôles to bring human beings into conflict with each other. Favorable recognition, if it leads to a failure of the student to adjust his personality to the teacher, may make a boy or girl a very difficult case. The teacher who has bred

[1] See p. 340.

this quality in him may perhaps still be able to live with him, but it often happens that the expansion of the ego involved in living out a favorable rôle may lead a student to disregard utterly the rights of other students, whereupon it becomes necessary for the teacher to "take him down a peg."

This "taking a boy down a peg" is a deflation of the ego which comes from forcing upon a person the rôle which is truly his in a situation and depriving him of some rôle, usually more flattering to himself, which he has been living out. Undoubtedly this technique, used wisely, has a place, though it should be contrary to teaching morality for a teacher to use it merely for the gratification of his own ego demands. A legitimate and very clever use of this technique was the following:

A psychiatrist who has had remarkably good success in establishing rapport with sub-adolescent delinquent boys ascribed a large part of his success to a technique he had developed for this purpose. He invariably began his interview with a physical examination; that established him as a doctor (which marked him off at once from employees of the court) and put him on an intimate footing with the boy, since he demanded that the boy strip for the examination. As a further measure, he sometimes had his secretary, a woman, assist in the process. He reassured the boy from time to time, "It's all right. You're just a little boy and it's all right. Now Miss So-and-So is my secretary and she has to be here to take notes and to help me. And you're just a little boy and it's all right." This technique was sufficient to pierce almost any boy's armor. In extreme cases he did not return the boy's clothes immediately, but continued the interview while the boy remained naked. He remarked that it was very difficult for a small boy to remain defiant when he hadn't any clothes.

Negative identification mechanisms are habitually used by many teachers, usually without any realization of their psychological nature. The epithet is a negative identification mechanism, and it prompts the student to reverse the epithet and otherwise to prove the teacher wrong. (In *All Quiet on the Western Front*, the school-master Kantorek's former pupil has an opportunity to reverse the situation, and to tell him that he is "Quite, quite inadequate, Kantorek." This may serve to show how the epithet really takes hold.) So likewise the challenge, "This is too hard for you," often elicits a better response from a certain kind of student than "This is a very interesting point." But since the negative identification mechanism depends for success on the student's proving the teacher wrong, it is often costly to the teacher's prestige. It may also, by aggravating inferiority feelings, do vast and irreparable injury to the student.

PROJECTS

1. Make a case study of a boy who likes Latin. Carefully analyze the complex of motives behind this taste.

2. Similarly investigate the background of a violent distaste for some school subject.

3. Write the life history of a school child in terms of acceptable and unacceptable rôles.

4. Write an introspective account of the alternation of rôles during a day of teaching. If possible compare with an objective account prepared by another observer.

5. Describe and analyze the rôles habitually played by the members of a small class in the upper grades or high school.

6. Make a case study of a boy or girl whose personality was markedly changed as a result of acquiring some new rôle.

7. Select a teacher who praises students frequently, but apparently judiciously, and attempt to ascertain by inquiry among his students what his effect upon their personalities is.

8. Sit in the classroom of a teacher who uses the challenging technique. Make a list of students challenged. Find out by inquiry outside of class what these students thought of when the challenges were issued.

9. Make a list of ten teachers who use positive and ten who use negative identification mechanisms. Have some other person rate them in teaching efficiency (either on a scale of points or a ranking basis). What do your results show?

10. Study the behavior of a teacher and a student when the teacher is "taking the student down a peg." Describe the behavior minutely, and analyze the social attitudes and rôles involved.

11. Study the alternations of attention, distraction, head movements, eye movements, and apparent outgo of affectional responses in a teacher with a class of thirty. List all of these you can, and show by a seating chart how they are distributed over the class. Compare the results with a similar study of a teacher with a smaller class.

SUGGESTED READINGS

(1) Faris, Ellsworth, "The Concept of Social Attitudes," *Journal of Applied Sociology,* 1925, Vol. IX, pp. 404-409.

(2) Faris, Ellsworth, *The Nature of Human Nature,* Publications of the American Sociological Society, Vol. XX, 1926.

(3) Sayles, Mary Buell, *Three Problem Children.*

(4) Sayles, Mary Buell, *The Problem Child at Home.*

(5) SAYLES, MARY BUELL, *The Problem Child in School.*

(6) WHITLEY, ROBERT L., "Interviewing the Problem Boy," *Journal of Educational Sociology,* Vol. V, No. 2, October, 1931, pp. 89-101; No. 3, November, 1931, pp. 140-152.

CHAPTER XX

FOCAL POINTS OF STUDENT-TEACHER ANTAGONISM

THE teacher, exerting pressure, now here, now there, keeps her class together and keeps all its members moving in the same direction. Normally, by darting from one part of the class to another, she controls the classroom situation easily. But sometimes she does not prevail, and she finds that at every point where she attempts to exert pressure she meets determined resistance. The classroom interaction then becomes a struggle of personalities.

That struggle of personalities may become a feud.[1] In the feud all the latent enmity of teachers and students is unmasked, and teacher and students meet and hate with no social buffer between them. The students' attacks upon the teacher have reduced him to desperation, and he is ready to make his last, agonized stand. The teacher's attacks upon the class, usually undiscriminating and ill advised, have transformed it into a conflict group. The feud involves the whole personalities of students and teachers, and it engages their entire attention. The feud is usually cyclic, moving from incident to incident. Behavior in the dramatic incidents is explicable psychologically as due to summation; it is possible because of the accumulation of tension as a result of intervening incidents. But the major incidents may themselves be ranged in a series; the entire process moves toward a particular point. An excellent description of a feud is the following:

[1] E. K. Wickman has stated the psychology of the schoolroom feud as follows (*Children's Behavior and Teachers' Attitudes*, pp. 161-162; A Commonwealth Fund publication):

"The frustrated individual requires satisfaction in order to secure release from the tension and state of discontent which has been aroused. This satisfaction is usually achieved by attack upon the object that has produced the irritation. The frustrating object in the case of behavior problems in the classroom is the child who has misbehaved. Only when satisfaction is obtained can the teacher restore her equilibrium. Unfortunately, children do not always grant this satisfaction to the teacher. They, too, are human and react to frustrations. In this way a series of frustrations and retaliations, attacks, and counterattacks is often initiated which not infrequently runs the course of an entire school term."

Excellent as this statement is, it stands in need of some supplementation from the sociological point of view. Simmel considers the motivation of the feud to be "the peculiar phenomenon of social hatred, that is, of hatred toward a member of a group, not from personal motives, but because he threatens the existence of the group." (Reprinted by permission of The Commonwealth Fund, Division of Publications.)

The bell rang after first home room period and we all filed into Miss Anderson's room. She was to teach us English and Vocational Readings. Pete, being the largest of the group, also was the leader, so this very first morning he began round one, by throwing kernels of corn which he had in his pockets. Miss Anderson's red hair didn't belie the old adage, "Red hair, fiery temper," and it didn't take her long to run to the back of the room and grab him by the collar and send him from the room. She led him out, and while she was gone the group inside snickered and the snickering didn't stop even after the teacher came in again. She looked about, but, seeing that all of us were laughing, she realized that she could do nothing about it unless she threatened us in some way. The consequence was that we all stayed twenty minutes after school, which gave us an additional twenty minutes to put things over on her.

Raymond and Lee were two pals, and would hatch out schemes to put into play as soon as class opened. Ray advanced from rear to front seat the first week so Lee was left alone, but not for long. His idea was to be as mean as Raymond had been and to get a front seat too. He began by following Miss Anderson around the room asking for a new pencil, a piece of paper, a pocket-knife, a pen-point or a drink. She, thinking to hurt him, usually refused, whereas if she hadn't Lee would soon have run out of ideas. But the very fact that she wouldn't let him have his way gave him a chance to keep after her. She would walk around the room at a break-neck speed and he'd follow, talking continuously and she, holding both hands to her ears, would screech back like a hoot-owl, not knowing at whom she was screeching, until the class was in a fit of laughter. "Go away! Go away! I don't want to listen to you!" Lee never did go away, and knowing that she would soon tire out she suddenly turned on him and, eyes popping, almost frothing at the mouth, she would angrily stammer out several broken phrases, and Lee, realizing he had got the best of her, would take his seat. She had always sat down at her desk after such a scene, and stared over the top of the heads of the class, which was now settled and quietly at work. Such scenes went on for a solid week before Lee won his point. Yes, that front seat had been meant for him in the first place, only Miss Anderson hadn't been big enough to give it to him.

Now Lee, Raymond and Pete were seated in a perfect triangle, center back seat for Pete, and two outside front seats for Lee and Ray. The arrangement was in the boys' favor, so much so that it was obvious even to the rest of the students.

I had been sent to the cloakroom one day for "misbehaving," and it was cold, so that I had to keep active to keep warm. The electric light was my first plaything, and after I found that snapping the light off and on created no disturbance from the inside, I decided to misplace the wraps. After I had changed gloves from one pocket to another and all the boys' caps were under the girls' coats and some of them in the overshoes, I was again out of work. About that time Pete began a whistling tune of his own and I decided to join him, but began a little too late. Pete, ready for action, began again, and as soon as the teacher had run to the back of the room Lee began in front. She gave Pete one icicle look, and dashed up to Lee's desk, not knowing that he really did it. It was Ray's turn now, so I heard a sharp whistle, hurried footsteps and "Stop that now. Do you hear me?" I didn't wait for Ray's answer, but rounding my lips I whistled as loud as I could. There was a moment of dead silence. What was happening inside I didn't know, but once again I heard quick footsteps coming closer, and then Pete's deep voice, "Miss Anderson, there's a robin out in the hall." This was enough for me, for I realized that I was in for something. Instead of sneaking down to the other end of the hall as any normal human being would have done, I stayed where I was, curious to see the outcome, for in my mind I vividly pictured "Crazy Andie" sputtering and spitting at the same time. Roller towels at that time had not been put in the schools, but she certainly was in need of one. Just then her shaky, waspy figure appeared in the doorway and with two outstretched hands she sprang against me, being careful to have a sound footing, as though afraid I had been expecting her quick and powerful bump, and had stabilized my own footing accordingly. With a sudden jerk, I turned myself about and went sliding on down to the other end of the hallway. I was less interested in what she was saying than in keeping my balance, but I faintly heard her cracked voice above the shouts and laughter inside the room, as she shouted, "Get out of *my* hall, get out of my hall!" It sounded very much like a cry for help!

I walked down stairs and went outside, walked around the building, and after composing myself I came back up again. I was wondering how I'd meet her again. I could picture icy stares from her if I walked in on her class again, but decided it was best. No telling when the principal might come along and catch me in the hall!

For several minutes I stood before the door—I couldn't enter this door, for I'd have to walk all the way up the aisle to get to my seat. That would never do, for I'd create all over again the upheaval I'd just created a few minutes before. I walked in the front door, passed the teacher's desk, and, sitting down at my own desk, I took up my book and began to study. I didn't look up at anyone so all went well.

For some time I was quite the goody-goody child, and the queer part about it to me seemed to be that the teacher, of all persons, was taking a real liking to me; I realized one day, to my great surprise, that I had gradually become the teacher's pet. The class didn't seem to mind, because underneath all this outer coating I was still as mischievous as ever, but I erased the blackboards, passed out papers, took slips to the office, etc., all of which I hadn't asked to do.

So it happened that one day I was studying and was not fully conscious of the tug of war going on about me between teacher and pupils. My head was close down to my desk and I was reading when someone's poppy eyes stared from below me into my face, and before I realized whose face it was

I recognized the jaggy voice as she hoarsely whispered (loud enough for all to hear), "Betty, go down and call Miss ——— (the principal). Tell her to come up immediately." I got up, looked all about me, and walked from the room, being followed closely by Miss Anderson. As soon as we got to the hallway she said to me, "Don't call Miss ———. Just go down and come back up again." I went and came, and as I entered the room, she stopped the recitation, which was now well under way, the class having quieted to meet the principal when she came. Miss Anderson looked at me with a very unsteady glance, and forced herself to stammer, "Is she coming?" "Yes, she'll come," was all I said. This was too much for the class to let go by without getting even with me. The result was that the class organized itself against me, and try as I would I could not break the hard shell which coated the group, so I was left alone to stay on the teacher's side. It wasn't quite so easy for me to erase the blackboard and pass out papers from now on, so I looked all about me for a chance to get a break with the gang. The chance came one day in this form:

I was passing papers when Lee said, "Betty, give me a few extra ones. I want to play a trick on the teacher. Of course I refused but when I passed out papers I passed out a number of extras to his row so he took as many as he wanted from the pile before he passed it back. I anxiously waited for the so-called trick, and it happened that a piece of folded paper came up from the back and as it progressed forward each child picked it up, opened it, snickered, and threw it up to the fellow in front, and then turned and whispered a few hurried sentences to his neighbor. It came up to my chair and I opened it, read it, and found this:

STUNG!

I folded it again, and threw it up to the teacher's desk. One of her peculiarities was picking up scraps of paper on her hourly round about the room, and taking them to the waste basket. Often she even took unused sheets, crumpled them nervously and on her way past the basket dropped them in.

She got up, walked past her desk and picked up the paper. All eyes were on her but none met hers when she looked suspiciously over the group. Everyone was busily preparing his lesson. But many heads behind the backs of the books were turned to their neighbors who were trying to be sober but couldn't.

I was the first person to meet her eyes, and, looking at me rather surprisedly, as if she really hadn't expected it from me, she grinned ironically and said aloud, "But it didn't hurt." I couldn't help smiling, and before I could again put on a sober face she stood at my desk, and with her eyes piercing me through and through, she boldly asserted, "You did this."

"I did not!"

"Yes, you did! Let me see your notebook!" She looked at my notebook, and, finding no evidence, she went on.

"I still think you did it."

"If you do, you better think again."

It was too much for me, but I couldn't prove I hadn't so she said, "Do you know who did it? Tell me! If you know who did it and tell me you know, I won't ask you who it is."

"Yes, I do know who did it."

She walked to the front of the room and sat on a high stool on which she always perched herself whenever she, in a hoot-owl fashion, wanted to get a bird's eye view of the class.

No one in the room made a noise, and finally she called me up before her. She was still sitting on the stool. I stood before her ready for a lecture, but I was disappointed, for this is what she began with, "Do you like school, since you came back?"

"Yes."

"Are you going to high school?"

"I hope to."

"That's fine. I hope you can, too."

All the time she was stroking my blue silk tie down the front of my dress, and I, almost ready to laugh in her face, turned to go back to my seat, but hadn't gone two feet before she cried, "Come here! Come here!"

I did.

She was now at a loss for a goading beginning so finally she said, "What do you curl your hair with, Betty?"

"Nothing, it's naturally curly."

"Oh, it is? It's beautiful, and I think you're a very nice girl, but I don't think you spoke very nicely to me just then, do you?"

"I'm sorry, Miss Anderson." The "I'm sorry" was just a defence of my own, for I experienced no regret whatsoever. . . .

My report card came to me with a row of beautiful red D's. (Autobiographical document supplied by a college student.)

This represents but a cross-section of a feud, but it will serve to illustrate its psychological atmosphere. It is also interesting as an exhibit of the comprehension of complex group alignments by a naïve observer. It is noteworthy that some teachers find themselves year after year engaged in feuds with their students. They have learned to experience the school situation as calling for hostile behavior, and their personalities are such that they beget hostility in students. Such an one was obviously the teacher described above.

Poised and well-balanced teachers learn to avoid feuds. (Being well balanced is the best insurance against them.) Sometimes they avoid them by crushing them ruthlessly at the start, that is, by going at once from the earliest to the latest stage and solving the situation before permanent hostility has had a chance to develop. A special technique has been developed by some teachers for crushing rebellious individuals. It consists in getting the individual in a position where he cannot talk back and breaking him through the pressure of the situation, by exposing him to a large number of commands, relevant and irrelevant, strong suggestions, embarrassing questions (to which an answer is required), etc. Other teachers are able to transform the situation in which a feud starts into one in which a friendly rapport exists. A policy which usually works is that of refusing to recognize as of any importance at all the behavior of a student from which a feud might result. This policy usually works, and it enables a teacher to avoid many conflicts, but there are cases where the teacher's very holding off becomes the matter at issue in the feud. Such a case was the following:

I Am Worried About Delbert

Six bright red heads in the same class—that does not often happen! What bright color spots! Half are straight haired and half are wavy, no, that boy's head is beautifully curly. The new class is busy making out book and enrollment cards. Perched on her laboratory stool the teacher is surveying the new material before her in the shape of thirty boys and girls fresh from their long summer holiday. Glancing over the registration cards she encounters many familiar surnames, probably brothers or sisters of former pupils. These names bring up a host of recollections, most of them reminiscent of happy and pleasant classroom associations, some of situations fraught with great perplexities, others of miserable mistakes, lack of understanding and unfortunate failures in handling troublesome pupils.

The inventory partially completed, the teacher glances up to detect traces of family resemblance. The room is quiet, everyone is on his good behavior—best behavior. The resolutions to make this year "the best ever" are still in working order. How restful and peaceful this unnatural quiet is. Would it might continue, but why ask for the impossible! Continue? There's one over there doing his best to begin the inevitable disruption likewise of order and day dreaming. It's the boy with the curly red haid. He is furtively watching the teacher for an opportunity "to do his little stunt." The teacher is both attentive and amused. Doesn't the red-haired lad know that the teacher has experienced this identical scene of the first day over and over again; doesn't he realize that diverse and various efforts on the part of new pupils to "try the teacher" are an old, old story to her?

Here is the opportune moment. Without waiting for the teacher to acknowledge his waving hand he asks in a high tenor, "You haven't told us your name, is it Miss, or Mrs.?" Without a change of expression the teacher writes her name on the board while the class looks up to locate the voice and to watch the teacher's reaction, but failing to see anything amiss they resume their work.

Having spent his ammunition and being disappointed in the result the boy was well behaved for a few days. He was, however, gathering material and watching his chance for another attack—of that the teacher felt certain. She sensed rather than saw any overt signs of the next attack. The lad under discussion was a little above the average student in intelligence as his written work soon showed. He enjoyed monopolizing the recitation, and in discussion insisted upon addressing himself to the teacher rather than to the class. His chief joy was to introduce extraneous matter, and, when the teacher finally stepped in to bring the discussion back to its main issues, he remonstrated with her in quite a dramatic fashion, which she, however, entirely ignored.

The effect of this situation on the class was most peculiar. The pupils seemed to take no sides, but sat back as if to say, "This is your affair, we're neutral. What are you going to do about it?"

Feeling that she could cope with the situation, the teacher decided to do nothing drastic, but frequently to disregard the boy's waving hand and thus limit him in his means of conspicuous self-expression. Of course she could not "squelch" him entirely, but always keenly aware of his constant desire to "jump over the traces" through some spectacular act or clever remark, the teacher either forestalled him in his little plans or feigned utter and complete density to the point of his oft-times witty remarks. The class continued to pay little attention to the bout between pupil and teacher.

With no outlet in the classroom for his desire to make himself conspicuous, Delbert, for so the red-haired lad was called, tried to create an impression by reaching the laboratory just as the tardy bell rang. He entered very importantly, left arm loaded with books, brief-case in right hand and a bulging notebook filled with closely typed sheets protruding "from under" his right shoulder. Very deliberately he took his seat, glancing about the room with a quite detached air to note any impression he may have created.

Matters ran their usual course, with the teacher always secretly on the alert to thwart Delbert's constant desire to make himself obvious. Recently, however, these objectionable symptoms had somewhat abated, so that the teacher was beginning to take heart—trying to convince herself that her methods were getting results. But one day the long-sought opportunity arrived. The class had been discussing diets when Delbert volunteered the information that he had recently lost fifty pounds through dieting. Here was valuable information in the shape of first-hand (personal) experience that hardly could be ignored. The teacher thinking that she had the situation fairly well in hand gave him the floor and let him tell his story, which he did very well, making a valuable contribution to the discussion. . . . But that's only the half of it. What effect did this free hand have on Delbert? The delight of being in the limelight, brief as it was, proved most intoxicating to him, and he was determined not to relinquish one inch of the ground he had so laboriously gained. He held onto his vantage point like grim death for the ensuing weeks. In self-defence the teacher had to increase her vigilance in order to bring to naught all Delbert's attempts to distinguish himself through his wit. But now this seemed to have a marked influence for the worse on Delbert. He apparently lost interest in his work, neglected his assignments, and failed miserably in his six weeks' test. This brought things to a pass. The office authorities called the boy to account for his low class standing. The matter was then taken up by the assistant principal with the boy's "favorite teacher," whom he was "helping" in a commercial course and whose aid and cooperation were earnestly solicited. She understood the peculiar make-up of the boy and had obtained some excellent results in her class work. This "favorite teacher" sought the first teacher and gave her some valuable hints and information concerning Delbert's character and abilities as she had diagnosed them. The grades went out on Thursday, and Friday after school Delbert appeared with the remark that he had never during his high-school career received a failing slip, and from his actions it was patent that he took it for granted that if he completed all his back work and passed his test the teacher would revoke her former estimate of his standing and issue him a new grade. Monday morning all required work was completed and by Monday night the examination had been successfully passed. The teacher, who did not believe in iron-clad rules especially when she saw that they stood in the way of a pupil's progress or improvement, was more than glad to do what she could to help the boy on his feet. But after the new grade was properly recorded and the self-satisfied chap had left the room, she realized that she had made a mistake in this particular instance and one which would cause her considerable trouble in her future dealings with Delbert. His superior air on leaving seemed to announce triumphantly, "I knew I would make you realize my true worth, my unsuspected ability. You have let down the bars once and I'll expect you to do the same on subsequent issues if the occasion arises."

That the boy had the ability there was no doubt. From several different sources the teacher learned of his great success at organization. She was frequently reminded of his good work as business manager of the Junior Play Ticket Campaign and his efficient management of several other business projects.

One day, induced by the constant requests of the class, "Let Delbert read his paper," the teacher asked the lad to give his report, hoping that the knowledge that the class had a little confidence in him might arouse the boy's pride and help him to get a better hold on himself. Not so, however, for it wasn't the class Delbert was trying to impress, but the teacher. His theme was well worked out and skillfully handled and was much enjoyed and appreciated by the class, much to the satisfaction of Delbert. After the recitation he was more than ever pleased with himself, and his performance. He lingered after class and remarked, "You weren't going to let me read that paper. I knew you didn't want me to read it; but now you're glad for you realize that I have talent. Oh, I'm going to be an actor and write plays too. That's my ambition. Some day when you see me a success you'll be sorry you treated me the way you do!" and with that he pirouetted out of the door.

Things went on indifferently well with Delbert after that. The teacher in several after-school conferences tried to get "under his skin" by attempting to show him the need of actors' having a good education, especially if their province was also to include that of playwright. But as for any positive signs of improvement, her efforts failed to bring forth any. She still had to resort to her tactics of holding him in leash, but this was now becoming harder and harder. The boy, chaffing under the ever-increasing check, grew sullen, or sat staring at the teacher with an injured air during the greater part of a double period. Realizing the uselessness of trying to get him to work when in such a mood, the teacher simply ignored him, and since he sat at the back his peculiar conduct neither attracted attention nor distracted the attention of the normal pupils.

Meanwhile Delbert's attitude toward his work grew more or less indifferent. He did his lessons spasmodically, always trying to cajole himself and his teacher into believing "I have the ability—I can do it when I am ready—No use to bother with such trifles every day." Naturally his grades and class standing suffered accordingly, and toward the end of the year his making his credit was very doubtful.

About this time the teacher was asked to serve as one of the judges of a preliminary program for stunt night—Joy Night. Here she had the opportunity of seeing Delbert in his true element and in all his glory. Not satisfied with his mop of bright red hair he had donned a glorious wig whose long red ringlets enveloped his head like an aura. He was attired in a fluffy, billowy dress of orchid chiffon, short in front and set off by a huge ostrich feather fan of dainty pink and white. A gauzy scarf of softly blending shade draped his bare shoulders and neck. Although his "get up" à la Julian Eltinge was excellent, his skit fell short of any real merit because of his great reliance upon his wit and native ability along closely allied lines. The judges therefore did not pass favorably upon his stunt. So here was another side to the lad. He had talent, but his colossal conceit seemed to block his progress both in his avocation and in his school work.

While the teacher was getting ready to have another session with the boy regarding his unfortunate and thwarting attitude toward his work and himself the crisis so long postponed and avoided by the teacher became imminent, more threatening day by day.

Delbert had always shirked and avoided all disagreeable tasks pertaining to cleaning up the laboratory. This particular day he was asked to take the dissected material, carefully wrapped, to the engine room where it was to be burned. But Delbert demurred. He wanted to refuse, but everyone began to voice his opinion by advising him, "Aw! Go on and take it. Beat it!" Sensing the disapproval in the air, Delbert changed tactics and began to plead, "How can you insist that I carry this revolting material to the engine house? It hurts my esthetic sensibilities. Don't you appreciate my ability, my artistic temperament? Don't any of these have any effect on you?" The teacher was adamant and pointed toward the door. Delbert, with tray poised above his head, started for the door, but turned and reenforced his original supplication with further pleading. The teacher ignored both him and his persistence. Again he made for the door, but returning a third time, threw himself to his knees and with hands uplifted besought the teacher to reconsider her impossible errand.

This was too much for both pupils and teacher. While the room was convulsed with laughter Delbert with his tray of meat scraps disappeared.

Unfortunately, Delbert interpreted this laughter episode as a tribute to his clever acting. He failed to see the tinge of ridicule in it. Now according to him all the bars were down, all ground so carefully contested during the semester was lost. "Aha," he thought, "the teacher has at last acknowledged me as a wit. From now on she's in my hands."

The end soon came, for things had reached an impossible stage. Two days later Delbert's usually sullen and injured air had been metamorphosed by his triumph into insolence. He flatly refused to prepare his work during the study period, whereupon the teacher asked him to go to the principal's office, which he also refused to do. A note was sent to the principal requesting the boy's removal from class, and within ten minutes the desired transfer was made. So much for Delbert. . . .

Of course the teacher disliked acknowledging her inability to help and hold the boy; she hated to admit that she had failed utterly. Where lay the mistake in her analysis of the situation or in her treatment of the boy? She tried to give him the benefit of the doubt; she believed him sincere in his protests and protestations, and she therefore avoided forcing the issue. Perhaps therein lay the difficulty.

In subsequent talks with Delbert's other teachers it was learned that he had conducted himself in like fashion in other classes. Delbert's record for the semester showed two failures, and two barely passing grades. The extent of his utter indifference to school work is indicated by his failure to return any of his textbooks, even though he knew he would be charged with them upon his return to school.

The night of his ejection from class the teacher found the following note in her box: "I have invoked the wrath of the gods upon your head! Beware!" (Autobiographical document supplied by a high-school teacher.)

A complicating factor which the above teacher missed at the time was the fact that this boy was homosexual. (This conclusion was verified by independent investigation.) If he had been a normal boy with normal standing in the group, the teacher's hold upon her class would have been imperilled by her failure to deal with him sooner. Short of such a thorough overhauling as he might receive from a psychiatrist, it seems that little might have been done for the boy in any case. The teacher might have "squelched" him, whereupon, as she correctly observed, he would have lost interest in her course all the sooner. Ultimately she had to take vigorous action, and for a time she had to pursue the policy of walling him off from the rest of the class as a non-learner and a disturbing element (a desperate means but one which teachers are often forced to use). It seems that the only possible solution to her problem would have been to take vigorous action at the start. The teacher would thereby have saved her own face and no greater harm would have been done to the boy than was done ultimately.

This case suggests also certain reflections about the wit and humor which spring from the teacher-pupil relationship. This is a topic of the first importance, and it is unfortunate that our materials do not permit us to give it more than cursory treatment. This wit is nearly always tendency wit, that is, it has a personal object, and it expresses a definite animus. It is typical of the humor which springs up between antagonistic groups. Novelists often picture the teacher as dealing in a heavy-handed, coarse sarcasm, and this sort of thing is, we must confess, all too common in the schools. Students express their hostility by clever take-offs, by plays upon names, by jokes on the teacher, etc. The drab background of the social interaction of the school, and the tension under which both teacher and student labor, make things seem funny that would not otherwise be so, and thus it happens that school jokes are not usually very good jokes. And that the laughter of students over the teacher's jokes, even the poor ones and those of which they are themselves the butt, is servile, proving rather that they are subordinated than that the teacher is a wit, seems certain. The use of humor in the school is not necessarily that of a weapon; humor may serve to relieve tension by giving antagonism harmless expression, or it may serve as a technique of conciliation.

Feuds do not always have a long life. They may lead in summatory fashion to some crisis which terminates them; there is a "showdown," and that ends the feud, or ushers in a new phase of it. The interaction of personalities in the feud grows more and more extreme, and the social arrangements which permit its continuance grow more and more unworkable; at length there is a crisis in which each individual mobilizes and releases all his energies, perhaps calls other persons to his aid; in the end the chaos of unbridled forces resolves into a new definition of the situation. Each person emerges from the crisis with new attitudes. Faris says, "A crisis is to be found just in those situations where existing attitudes fail to apply and where existing objects fail to satisfy expectations.'' Since teachers are usually superior to students in social resources, it is usually teachers who attempt to force a ''showdown,'' while students avoid it. Nearly every teacher can tell some story of a crisis successfully met. The following account is typical:

George P. was a tough boy. He made trouble in his grade room. He made trouble on the playground. He made trouble in town.

Once or twice he was reported to me, and I, as superintendent, had to straighten him out. Since these were minor matters, I administered routine discipline only. He submitted, but told others that I had better not try to whip him, because he would resist.

Finally a more serious offence arose, and he knew that a real row was pending. I called him into the office, and told him the charge. He bristled immediately.

"You aren't going to whip me, are you?"

"Why, yes, George, that is exactly what I am going to do."

Very deliberately I turned to the desk and got out my strap. He waited, standing. When I walked toward him, he "put up his dukes." I laughed at him, and asked him, "What kind of a pose is this? Do you think you're Jack Dempsey or Gene Tunney? Wait till I get my camera and take your picture."

"You're not going to whip me."

"Now don't make me laugh. Always clowning. Bend over."

He "assumed the angle," and I whipped him.

The next day his father stopped me on the street.

"What do you mean by whipping my boy George?"

"Mr. P., your boy broke the school rules, and when he does that he must take the consequences."

"Well, suppose I lick you?"

"You'll need help, Mr. P. When you are ready to try, just let me know. I am busy. Good-bye."

After that, George P. was a very good boy in school, and we became good friends. (Interview with a school superintendent.)

One cannot refrain from comment on the successful use of humor in the above case. Obviously it was ridicule, plus the calm determination of the older man, that decided the issue.

Feuds often move in summatory fashion toward such a crisis, and are often metamorphosed in crisis. Hostility is cumulative in the feud situation, and piles up like static electricity at several points, constellating equal and opposite charges at other points; crisis is like an electric storm which sweeps away these charges. Grudges accumulate and change the meaning of the situation; in the crisis these hostile attitudes are expressed. After the crisis the situation seems different because the subjective charges of hatred have disappeared, and it is different because it has been differently defined.

Interesting mechanisms of conciliation may be identified in the social process of the classroom. Simmel has characterized conciliation as "a purely subjective method of avoiding struggle." He says further, "The state of mind which makes conciliation possible is an elementary attitude which, entirely apart from objective grounds, seeks to end struggle, just as, on the other hand, a disposition to quarrel, even without any real occasion, promotes struggle." The tendency to conciliation is "a factor quite distinct from weakness, or good fellowship, from social morality or fellow feeling." Whereas the essence of compromise is a face-saving formula which does not affect the attitudinal basis of conflict except indirectly by changing its situational roots, conciliation strikes directly at the attitudes from which conflict arises. Conciliation is most often simply a show of friendly attitudes, and it produces its results by evoking similar attitudes in others. Subjective it may be, but conciliation must show itself somehow, and to the present writer it seems to show itself principally in irrelevant concession. Two boys are conversing in a large class. The teacher notices, overlooks; the conversation continues, and the teacher begins to be visibly annoyed. One of the boys raises his hand and asks a pertinent question. The teacher is mollified, and struggle is averted. The teacher has given a low grade to a young woman who values her work highly. She stares at him balefully. He pauses, asks her a question and smiles. She answers, but she is still angry. Soon he asks her another question, and smiles. The attention gratifies her. The young woman ceases to be angry. A clever disciplinarian who was called upon to take charge of a disorderly study hall made a speech which began, "Now first of all, boys, I'm for you." The technique of conciliation seems to be that of making harmless and irrelevant concessions. Teachers have particular need of a conciliatory technique because they are often not in a position to compromise on fundamentals.

It does not seem extreme to say that those brilliant social philosophers who have developed the sociology of conflict might have found adequate material for their discussions without leaving their own classrooms. Nearly all the classic concepts apply to life in the school room, war, feud, litigation, conflict of ideals, victory, conciliation, compromise, conversion, accommodation, and assimilation. Not all these conflicts are visible to the naked eye, not visible, at least, as conflicts, but it is the part of the sociologist to learn to see the invisible world of social contexts.

It will be difficult for many teachers to accept this point of view, because the notion of conflict between teacher and pupil violates their conception of a relationship which they know to be fundamentally constructive. For these, there is an answer in the classic philosophy of conflict. For conflict is a constructive process, and creates as much as it destroys. And conflict unifies as well as it divides; it is one of the greatest group-making factors. Our most meaningful relations are often characterized by antagonistic cooperation. Conflict preserves relations which might otherwise become intolerable. Conflict, further, is a means to peace. Conflict is an essential part of the dialectic of personal growth. It could be argued that conflict in the schools is the feature of school life which best prepares students for facing life outside. What we need in the schools is not to do away with conflict, but to establish the most beneficial kind of conflict.

As teachers and students become familiar with the whole network of social processes in the school, they acquire insight into them, and the whole set of processes is thereby immensely complicated. That is one reason why the inexperienced teacher is at a disadvantage; his students, familiar with the terrain, are actually capable of a more complicated adjustment to the situation than he is. But teachers soon learn what it is all about, or they fail in teaching, and for this reason it is usually from the teacher that the impetus for the further complication of the school situation comes. In the typical case this operates as follows: The teacher, being familiar with the entire configuration, recognizes at once the gestures that foretell an attack, a tentative rapprochement or alliance, an attempt to deceive him, an attempt at humor, a feud, a disorderly outbreak, or any of the other thousand and one things that can happen in school. He bases his own response to the situation upon his awareness of its meaning as an early stage of a long and complicated social process, not only upon what students have done, but upon what they are going to do as well. He acts usually to frustrate, or divert, or to redirect the process. Students acquire a kindred sort of insight. Both teachers and students thus tend to foreshorten the personal interaction between them to a mere conversation of gestures; each bases his action not only upon the completed acts of the other, but also upon his incipient acts as seen in the light of experience. It is noteworthy that each utilizes his knowledge of these gestures according to his own basic conception of the nature of the social situation in the school. To some extent, also, the amount and nature of this insight are limited by one's basic orientation; thus a clever high-school principal may acquire a limited insight which will enable him to be extremely dexterous in manipulation, but if he has no grasp of the ends of education his efforts will have no point beyond his own personal advancement. To sum up, insight foreshortens the social process of the school, adds depth to it, complicates it somewhat, and increases its tempo.

PROJECTS

1. Write a detailed history of a feud between a teacher and a student, or between a teacher and a group of students.

2. Study the personality of a teacher who becomes involved in feuds with students. Analyze her social technique with students in order to learn why these feuds start.

3. Enumerate the devices by which several well-balanced teachers avoid becoming involved in feuds.

4. Describe a situation in which a teacher adopted a policy of treating some student as if he did not belong to the class, of "walling him off" from the rest of the class. Analyze the personal interaction in such a situation.

5. Collect examples of teacher wit. Analyze carefully. Classify teachers known to you according to their characteristic humor. Correlate with teaching efficiency.

6. Note the next ten things that make you laugh in a classroom. Analyze the reasons for your laughter.

7. Rank several teachers in tediousness. Note for each of these teachers five things that have made you laugh in his classroom. Interpret your results. Work out a technique for rating teachers according to the things which their students consider funny.

8. Study "giggling spells" of school girls, and formulate a theory as to their causation and control.

9. Tell the story of a "showdown" and the consequent redefinition of the situation.

10. Tell the story of an unsuccessful attempt by a teacher to precipitate a "showdown."

11. Give instances of correct interpretations of "anticipatory sets," and show how this affects the school-room social process.

SUGGESTED READINGS

(1) Dawson, C. A., and Gettys, W. E., *An Introduction to Sociology*, Chapters VIII, IX, X, and XI.

(2) Low, Barbara, *Psychoanalysis and Education*.

(3) Park, R. E., and Burgess, E. W., *An Introduction to the Science of Sociology,* Chapters IX and X.

(4) Staloup, B. F., "The Sociological Approach to Methods of Teaching and Learning," *The Journal of Educational Sociology,* Vol. V, No. 1, pp. 26-35.

(5) Wickman, E. K., *Children's Behavior and Teachers' Attitudes.*

Chapter XXI

THE BATTLE OF THE REQUIREMENTS

It is only because teachers wish to force students to learn that any unpleasantness ever arises to mar their relationship. We have defined the school as the place where people meet for the purpose of giving and receiving instruction. If this process were unforced, if students could be allowed to learn only what interested them, to learn in their own way, and to learn no more and no better than it pleased them to do, if good order were not considered a necessary condition of learning, if teachers did not have to be taskmasters, but merely helpers and friends, then life would be sweet in the school room.

These, however, are all conditions contrary to fact. The conditions of mass instruction and of book instruction make it necessary that learning be forced. Students must learn many things that they do not wish to learn, and they must over-learn *ad nauseam* even the things that originally interested them. Teachers must be taskmasters. Teachers must keep the classroom quiet in order that students may study. The requirement system is a system for forcing students to learn; certain tasks are laid out, students are graded numerically on the manner in which they perform these tasks; advancement in the social machine, and ultimately liberation from it, depend upon the accumulation of satisfactory grades for tasks performed. Students and teachers are at cross purposes with regard to the amount of work that shall be done for each unit of "credit," and with regard to the grade that shall be given to each performance.

A basic assumption is that human knowledge can be divided into subjects, and that these subjects can be parcelled out in nicely graded courses. Each course consists of a certain number of facts, and of these facts the student must acquire a specified minimum number if he is doing satisfactory work in the course. Or a course may consist of a certain number of practicums which confer, on the average, a given degree of skill. Proficiency is tested by oral or written examinations, which are "graded." Courses are geared to the average man. When the number of facts included in a course, and particularly when the minimum number required for a "passing" grade, is large, academic standards are high. When the minimum is low, or the requirements are often relaxed, standards are said to be low. In general, standards are high in proportion to the amount of a specified kind of achievement which they exact from students.

It is possible to criticize all this, and the job has often been done. Such is not our present purpose. Education must have a content, and students must somehow be induced to assimilate it. The methods employed are imperfect; they often fail of their end, and they are wasteful of time and human personality. But teachers have put much thought upon them, and the methods have improved. Our purpose is not to criticize or to evaluate, but to trace the involvement of personality in academic standards. We are constrained to note, however, that this minute subdivision of subject matter is not possible for all human knowledge, and perhaps not for the most important human knowledge; it is possible only for the knowledge peculiar to schools.[1] Further, the division of knowledge into subjects, and the subdivision of subjects into courses, must seem arbitrary to anyone who is not involved in the schools; and the system of grades upon performance must often seem even to the most experienced teacher to rest upon nothing at all.

The necessity of organizing subject matter into courses, of determining in advance the exact number of facts which the student must learn in order to "pass" the course, has affected the content of education. Clow has put it well:

> Take the current discussion of the school curriculum, for example. Latin and algebra hold their place, not so much because school authorities revere the old, as because these old studies satisfy the first requirement of the classroom teacher, namely, a carefully graded course of work, in which definite assignments can be made and the attainments of the pupils graded according to uniform standards. These requirements are especially insistent with the teacher who has many and large classes to handle. Take again the criticism of the normal schools that they tend away from the pedagogical aspects of the common branches and toward advanced work in language, mathematics, history and science. Now it is not necessary to ascribe this tendency to the wish of the normal schools to ape the colleges, or to any other ignoble aim. It is simply due to the fact that the professional aspects of the common branches, like most of the courses in education everywhere, have not yet been standardized so as to conform to the above requirements of the classroom teacher, and perhaps never can be; the straight academic work

[1] We are pleased to note certain forward-looking experiments which attempt to break down the division of subject matter into courses, and the division of the day into recitation periods. We regard these experiments as hopeful because a great part of the effective ignorance of the world derives, as we all know, from the compartmentalization of knowledge.

goes better and the students like it better, because it has been put into shape to be taught.[1]

Dead matter makes the best courses. It can be taught best, and learned best, within the learning situation peculiar to school. Bulk, too, is essential. Most teachers would rather teach big books than small ones, for the ultimate tragedy of the classroom teacher is to run out of something to teach.

Teachers display an extravagant devotion to academic standards. The complex of attitudes centered around standards and the attempt to uphold them often comes to be the dominant trend in the teacher's personality. In the mental universe of teacherdom, academic learning is the supreme value, and life revolves around it. All persons are judged upon the basis of past or present classroom achievement. No knowledge is of any account save that which can be built into a course and roofed over with an examination. The only effort worth the making is the struggle for the improvement of learning. It is this mania for classroom perfection which most deeply characterizes the teacher.

The explanation of this peculiar attitude of teachers will involve a number of factors. There is the psychological factor of habit, and of the values that go with it. Teachers habitually instruct and examine, and they attempt to broaden and deepen student assimilation of subject matter. On the basis of simple habit, therefore, it is possible to account for some of the emotional values that attach to instruction, and for a large part of the body of rationalizations that cluster about the process of teaching.

A further psychological factor is the distortion of perspective which comes from overlong preoccupation with the subject matter of school courses. One who attends much to the wisdom that is in books, and is little concerned with the unverbalized and unverbalizable rules of thumb by which people live, must usually overrate book-learning. This distortion of perspective is most likely to occur if a teacher has specialized in some one subject. It does not seem too much to say that perhaps the academic specialist is always a little mad.

The psychological effect of specialism is enhanced by certain developments on the social plane. Teachers of certain subjects form cults about their specialisms, and reenforce each other in their devotion to the super-mundane values of their subjects. Each cult has its own tradition and its own shibboleths. "The classics stand for prompt-

[1] Clow, F. C., *Principles of Sociology with Educational Applications*; p. 365. (Reprinted by permission of The Macmillan Company.)

ness." "The ability to think, gentlemen, the ability to think—" The effectiveness of these shibboleths depends upon emotional participation in the values upon which they are based. "This book is certain to do great harm to sociology in the eyes of some," says the reviewer of a recent book. So he renders accurately and tersely an appeal which never entirely fails of its effect among the sociologists, although it would likely leave the great majority of psychologists, political scientists, and economists unmoved.

Further, the teacher becomes devoted to standards because his extended personality becomes involved in the standards of his courses. The respect of students toward the teacher greatly depends upon the teacher's strictness of grading, for students, too, have learned to judge teachers institutionally. And the teacher's standing among his fellows—consequently his advancement—depend upon his doing his part in the struggle to "raise the level of scholastic achievement."

Most important in determining the attitude of the teacher toward standards is the fact that students and teachers are organized into separate groups and that these groups are in conflict over academic standards. A teacher's value in the teacher group depends upon unswerving loyalty to the ideal of the group. Shamefully enough, it may depend upon the wounds inflicted upon the enemy, and many a worthless teacher yet commands a certain respect because of the amount of red ink upon his report cards. The teacher group demands loyalty, of course, not only because the group is in conflict with another group, but because its members are always more or less in competition with each other for the favor of students. A further element in the explanation of the meaning of standards to teachers is that their exaggerated devotion is a means of compensating for an underlying desire to compete unfairly by relaxing standards. This kind of motivation is usually very obvious in university groups. All these things contribute to make a hero of the teacher "who carries the fight to them," and every teacher wants to be thought a person who always fights his battles on the enemy's ground.

The folk talk of teachers shows what the maintenance of academic standards means to them. A group of teachers assemble in an off moment. Their talk is random—fitful. Marlow's little daughter has the measles. Brownley has a new car. Someone drags in the topic of standards.

"These fellows are all whiners. If you flunk them they won't take their medicine. I flunked Harrison; and if anybody ever deserved to fail he did. He came around with a hard-luck tale, and I told him I couldn't think of changing his grade. He said he would be dropped from school. I promised to see the dean and do what I could for him. I persuaded the dean not to drop him. Now the boy won't even speak to me."

The others have listened impatiently, for each one has an experience to tell. The most excited one has eyes that shine with eagerness to communicate.

"Why, I even had a fellow offer me money once. He read his name on the board and was so surprised that he came out to the house to ask me whether it was really true. He admitted he deserved it, but said it would ruin his life, break his father's heart, and all that rot. He asked me, out of mercy, to change his grade. I asked him what kind of academic standards that would be. When he still kept on talking, I went inside and shut the door in his face."

"That's right. Never let them into the house or they'll stay all day."

"Well, the next morning he came around again, right at the beginning of my office hour. He began the same sort of story and then he looked around and changed his tune. I forget just how he put it. He asked me 'how much it would be worth to me to change his grade.' As soon as I realized what he was driving at, I arose in a towering rage and ordered him out of the office. I guess that's what I should have done in the first place."

A colleague has been ready with his story for some time. He bursts out: "One fellow came in and asked me to put down in writing all the reasons for his failing. I put them down, and he took it to the committee and they let him stay in school, giving him a deferred grade or something like that. It was one of those marginal cases. He failed because of a final exam in which he made fifty-nine."

"Surely you don't have any final exam grades of fifty-nine?"

"My assistant marked the paper."

Rarely is a contrary opinion voiced, for these men, dissenters themselves from many of the codes of the greater society, will tolerate no variance in their own group. Teachers who are suspected of not upholding the academic tradition strive pitifully to win the approval of their fellows. The giver of a "pipe course" in history came one day into the office of a more respectable colleague.

"Well," he said, "I've just had to take a stand with some of my folks. I've given 'em the iron heel. A couple of girls handed in identical papers, and when I asked them about it they said it was all right because they had worked them out together. I told them I didn't doubt their word, but I couldn't let that get started. So they've each got to take those two books and work out an eight-page term paper. Some of the others haven't handed in their papers yet. I told them, 'No papers; no grade.' That brought 'em to time."

Such conversations are especially frequent at examination time and the end of the semester. They have two principal functions, the relief of the inner tensions of teachers, and the maintenance of the morale of the teaching group. There have been abuses enough to excuse, if not to justify, the rigid stand of the profession. (Record of conversations.)

Most students take academic requirements for granted the greater part of the time, and seriously attempt to measure up to them. The social machinery which forces students to perform the tasks which teachers assign is very powerful: the authority of the teacher, the rank of the student in the class, and the pressure of the home and other conforming agencies. When the student, however, does not wish to do as he is told, or cannot do the work assigned, he falls into rebellion. It is this undertone of rebellion—directed mostly at standards and grades, or at discipline necessitated by standards—which most writers upon the schools have missed, and which, since they have failed to comprehend it, has frustrated their projected reforms.

Rebellion and animosity flame into unpleasantness when student and teacher disagree over grades. Open argument is more likely to occur in colleges than in secondary or elementary schools, but it is found everywhere. Teachers need, for their protection in a situation which would otherwise be very wasteful of their emotional resources, techniques for avoiding or swiftly terminating arguments about grades. It is likely that neither argument nor persuasion will be very effective, for a student who writes a poor paper is probably unable to understand that such a paper is not a good paper, and besides he is emotionally biased. There is also something to be lost by argument, for argument usually proceeds in summatory fashion to greater and greater emotional heights, and leaves teacher and student more at odds than before. There is something to be said for allowing the student to express his grievance, and that is an excellent procedure if the teacher has sufficient poise to carry it through without allowing himself to become argumentative. The customary procedure is to interpose a certain formality into such discussions. An administrative device, intended merely to strengthen the teacher's authority, is to permit no changes of grades once the grades have been filed. It is regarded as poor policy among teachers to change grades in any case, since to change a single grade multiplies the number of complaints, and, perhaps, embitters them.

Students upon whom the pressure becomes severe may resort to cribbing, cheating, plagiarism, and other devices to beat the game. Cribbing is regarded as a matter of vast importance in most universities. There is a debate of long standing as to whether more students cheat in order to pass a course or in order to get a high grade. Certainly a large percentage of any student body cribs occasionally, and another group cribs habitually. A student investigation in an eastern university estimated the number of those cribbing in certain courses as comprising a third of the class.

Teachers think of cheating in examinations as a moral issue. Sometimes they go to great pains to explain their point of view to their classes. Their classes are composed of young persons of high moral character, and yet cribbing continues. One is forced to conclude that there is a conflict of moralities. Teacher morality, backed by the less interested larger group, forbids cheating at examinations. Student morality does not forbid it. This student morality which does not forbid cheating holds even for students who refuse to cheat, for not even those students who for their own reasons are "honest" will cooperate with teachers in detecting cheaters. In one university there arose a "code of dishonor," which required any student to render assistance to another if he safely could. The code of dishonor thus forced every man to do violence to his own interest. Recognizing this conflict of moral standards, we must differently evaluate the moral aspects of the cribbing problem.

Teachers tend to think of rules against cheating as of a code of penal law. If there is laxity, what is required is a sterner set of rules, and more severe punishment. A famous eastern university supplies examination booklets to students. On the front cover is printed the following set of rules:

THE CONDUCT OF WRITTEN EXAMS

Rule 1. Students shall sit in alternate seats in direct line from the front to the rear of the room. Left-handed students shall be moved to the aisle furthest on the right-hand side of the room facing the rear.

Rule 2. Students shall not write on the examination question sheet. All extra writing (e.g., calculations, scratch work, etc.) must be in the same quiz book in which the examination is being written.

Rule 3. All note-books, books, and papers not properly pertaining to the examination shall be placed on the floor underneath the seat or in such places as the person in charge of the examination shall determine.

Rule 4. All examination books and questions shall be placed on the arm of the chair to the right of the student, with nothing whatsoever on the arm to the left.

Rule 5. No talking between students shall be permitted for any reason. This includes requests for erasers, pencils, the time of day, etc. This rule applies until all students have left the examination room.

When examinations are held in the above school, it is the custom to assemble as many proctors as can conveniently be called. Cases of cribbing are punished ruthlessly and invariably by a court of inquisitorial procedure. Yet, there is an inordinate amount of cribbing in this institution. Can it be that the system is wrong?

It seems to the writer that such a system is absurd. Not only does it insult the self-respect of students by its basic assumption that every one of them is dishonest, and can only be kept honest by constant watching, but it actually increases cribbing. This it does by making cribbing an interesting game. The more teacher precaution is multiplied, the greater the ingenuity that the student must display in order to crib, and cribbing becomes not only excusable but heroic. Human ingenuity cannot devise precautions that human ingenuity cannot circumvent; it becomes a game for both students and teachers. Students boast of "getting away with it," and tell how. Teachers preen themselves on their ability as detectives; men who are doctors of philosophy and the authors of learned works gloat over a couple of sniveling sophomores.

Since the basic theory is wrong, there is no remedy but in proceeding on a new theory. Perhaps it would be well to realize that human beings tend to help one another, and to organize academic work upon a group rather than an individual basis. Perhaps examinations stand in need of humanization anyhow. Doubtless the standards would suffer by such a change, but human life would not suffer. Nor would any valuable sort of learning be likely to suffer, for the learning product which is assured by examinations is of the lowest and basest sort. Examinations favor parrot learning, for the most part; and parrot learning is undesirable not only because it is useless but also because the psittaceous habit of mind inhibits deeper learning.

For most teachers, however, the suggestion that we do away with examinations altogether will seem very much like an invitation to set themselves adrift on an uncharted sea without sail or rudder. A less extreme remedy, and one which has often functioned well, is the honor system of examinations the so-called honor system being, in effect, in most instances, merely student self-government. To put such a system into operation there is required a technique for resolving the conflicting moralities of students and teachers and substituting a compromise morality. To make the honor system work it is essential to build and organize an effective public opinion among students; this will be speedily destroyed if tests, requirements, and grades are not such as students consider altogether fair. Honor systems have often been made to work well for a short time, but have commonly foundered after a few years, perhaps because teachers and administrators did not realize the necessity of continuing effort.

To make an honor system continue to work in a high school or college, it is necessary to effect the conversion of every teacher and every student who enters the system. No better example of the influence of interlocking attitudes in an institution can be imagined. The freshman class brings with it the traditional mental set of students toward tests and examinations, and, unless there is a campaign of conversion equivalent in length and intensity to the original movement for the honor system, the green invasion will triumph and will establish the older attitudes which made proctoring inevitable. The teacher who intends to use the honor system must bore deep into the sociology of conversion.

There are other devices which may be used to get a better grade than the merits of one's written work would dictate. Students in one university are much interested in two practices which they call "chiselling," and "handshaking." Handshaking is the milder of these, and it consists merely of trying to establish a personal relationship with the instructor, with a view, perhaps, to influencing his grading. Chiselling is similar, but more extreme, and more definitely unfair. It comprises all kinds of bluffing, flattery, and sycophancy, and any sort of device which will make the student stand out in the instructor's eyes. Where classes are large and competition for grades is keen, students may display astonishing ingenuity in the invention of schemes which will bring them to the instructor's attention as persons and fix them in his memory. One student who had always made high grades without really acquiring a corresponding amount of knowledge was asked how he did it. He replied, "Well, I'd sit in the class every hour and take in everything that was said, and then, just before the hour broke up, I'd ask the instructor a thumping good question." He chose his time well, and his instructors were undoubtedly grateful for the last-minute fillip that he gave to the waning discussion.

A student informant has supplied the following examples of chiselling, the one relatively blunt and inexpert, the other quite adroit.

The women are accused of being handshakers, and although I do not in the least doubt that they are I feel that the men are just as efficient at this old custom. But entirely different techniques are used, and I am inclined to think that that of the women will prove much more effective in the long run.

Here are examples of both systems which I have seen within the last week. I had a problem due in chemistry and had forgotten to take it up to the instructor during class. So I took it to his office about four o'clock in the evening. In the office was not only the instructor but one very good-looking blonde coed from the class. She was asking the instructor all kinds of questions concerning the course and wondering how chemists can possibly remember so much and wishing she was as clever as a chemist (our esteemed instructor no doubt being the chemist in question), and it wasn't long until she began wondering if she was going to pass the course. About that time I gave up, threw in my papers and left, giving her a clear field although I am sure she was getting along very well with me there. The next day she was telling how she chiselled the Prof., and she feels sure she is going to get an A out of the course. Perhaps she will. Who knows!

On Tuesday I took a final in mathematics. It was very long and tedious and since I really knew something about the course I was spending a lot of time on that final. The instructor didn't seem to be in any particular hurry, and soon there were but two students and the instructor left in the room. The other student, a senior graduating in the spring, is behind in grade points. He came directly out and told the instructor about it and asked for a break. He may get grade points or he may not. He didn't brag about his chiselling.

It is worth while to add that in the above university the student taboo upon handshaking and chiselling is so strong as to interfere seriously with normal friendly relations between students and teachers. It is likely that such a taboo exists in most schools, and that it induces a certain selection of social types among the students whom teachers ordinarily come to know, so that many teachers who think they know the student mind really know only one limited segment of it.

The best chisellers are those who chisel without knowing it, or who begin by not knowing it, and only gradually make their technique conscious. Overdependent persons become teacher's pets without intending to do so, and Wickman has made the reasons for this sufficiently clear. Alert and responsive students also begin to chisel without knowing it, but many of them perfect their technique by making it conscious. The social psychological background of this kind of chiselling is interesting. To understand how it operates one must first realize that exposition is a social process, a fact which would change educational theory considerably if its significance were properly evaluated. One does not explain to empty air; one explains to people. One explains, one exposes, one narrates, and one watches the audience narrowly to observe the effect. There is an interplay of gestures which keeps the process moving; the crowd makes the orator. Now the teacher engaged in the social process of exposition has need for an occasional gesture of assent. Most students are unresponsive because only a small part of their personalities becomes involved in the classroom interaction. But in every class are a few individuals to whom the teacher can look for those signs which enable him to go on. At appropriate places these individuals respond in the appropriate way. They signify that they understand, that they agree or do not agree, that they appreciate the joke, that they know what is coming. Such students must always have a higher personal value to the teacher than their unresponsive contemporaries. It sometimes happens that responsive students, from long and attentive scrutiny of the teacher's face, learn what power they can wield over him. Then their chiselling becomes conscious.

Academic requirements, grades, and examinations set teachers and students at one another's throats. This hostility would partially disappear if either side could realize how much the other is caught in the system. "The system" is of course nothing rigid, but a dialectical process in which what appears the free behavior of the one side constitutes the determining social set-up for the behavior of the other side. A teacher is adjudged effective, and wins the enduring respect of students as well as that of his fellow adults—for we must remember that teaching is real leadership—according as he forces students to learn. He must therefore hew to the requirements. The student is adjudged intelligent, cooperative, and diligent in proportion to the numbers on his report cards; he must at any cost get grades. Neither party has anything to gain by railing at the other, and both are equally unfree. Yet nothing we have said should be taken as indicating that there are not many teachers who are well aware of the defects of academic instruction. There are many teachers who are intellectually emancipated from standards. But neither teacher nor student can ever be more than partially emancipated while the general framework of the educational system remains what it now is. A bewildering conflict arises between the partially emancipated teacher and his students. The following story submitted by a professor of philosophy illustrates some of these points:

I have been trying very hard of late years to meet my students on a common human basis, disregarding as far as possible the authority of the teacher in my dealings with them, and playing the rôle of the fellow human being and a living exponent of philosophy rather than that of a teacher of philosophy. I find that academic requirements have consistently stood in my way. The most troublesome thing of all was the business of examinations and grades.

Hating the silly rigmarole as I do, I have tried to make it automatic and meaningless to myself and my students. As to myself, I have succeeded quite well, but not so well with the students. I have found that students are keenly interested in grades and the game of examinations, and I have frequently been recalled to the (to me) puerile matter by realistically minded students. Occasionally I have found myself in bitter conflict with individual students over the question whether I was a human being with a message as a human being, or a teacher whose primary function was to help students to get through examinations and obtain credits and grades.

I have no sympathy with the teaching point of view which regards a college course as consisting of so many facts, which insists that these facts be learned, and regards the business of learning them as the most serious and important part of the student's life. I have preferred to believe that my students and I alike were trying to understand certain aspects of the world and man, and that my function was to cooperate with students in working out an understanding of the problems of philosophy. I have tried to lead my classes to discuss and to think about these problems. I have tried to get them to wonder. I have wanted to help them to have questions and to find answers for their questions.

I tried to make examinations automatic, and I referred to them in class no more often than I had to. Nor in my classes did I ever attempt to point my students for an examination. The examinations came at stated intervals. I gave them, graded the papers, and returned them. That was all. Students could find the correct answers in the textbook or in their class notes. I did not want to hear about them. Here I know that my attitude was similar to that of some others who had a similar conception of the nature of teaching. My former teacher, Professor J., was driving at the same thing. He, too, wanted to help people to understand. He drew no social line between students and himself. He never turned his class into a quiz-section. He gave an examination at the end of his course, and before giving it he used to say, "The papers will be graded and turned back to you. Say anything you want to say about the grades, because I should not like you to feel unduly repressed. But don't say it to me. I am not interested. Strong men have wept in my office when talking about their grades, but I remained unmoved." I was not aware of imitating Professor J., but it seems that I have fallen into his attitude.

I think but infrequently of examinations, and I heartily dislike talking about them. I split them off from my part of the course, the reasoning together of myself and my students, as completely as possible. In class, I try to avoid parroting the text, or repeating salient points of an assignment as possible examination material. What I want is to answer students' questions. Therefore I make much of a classroom procedure in which students question the instructor. It is no use; the questions usually concern in some way the academic requirements. I have fallen into the habit of making some such announcement as this to my classes:

"I want to answer your questions in this course. Our progress in our mutual enterprise of working out an understanding of human life will be greatly facilitated if we can use these points of perplexity as the starting points of our discussion. I promise you that I will regard no question as foolish and that I will not refuse an honest answer to any honest question.

"But for our better understanding of each other, I ought to say that I will not contract to answer any questions which fall into any of the following three categories: First, questions to which I do not know the answer. They will be many, but I have done my best, and I cannot help it if I remain ignorant. Secondly, I will not answer any questions which are already answered in your text. You can read. Thirdly, I will answer no questions that pertain to jockeying for position for the examinations. Examinations are a necessary evil, and I shall have to give examinations to test your mastery of subject matter, especially your mastery of the textbook. But our progress in this class will be advanced not at all by protracted discussions of examinations, or attempts to maneuver each other into unfavorable positions relative to them.

"That leaves questions of a general intellectual nature, and any questions relating to your understanding of the subject matter of the course. There ought to be many of those."

But there never were many of those. When they came, I encouraged them, and as the term wore on, I found that spontaneous discussions arose more frequently. Mostly, however, there was a dearth of student questions and student contributions. But if I ever relaxed my taboo on questions concerning requirements, or concerning examinations, there would be a flood of questions. At the meeting before an examination, some bold student would sometimes venture to ask a question about the coming test. If I did not answer it, he was likely to resent it. If I answered it there would be many more, calling for information concerning the type of questions, whether I would ask them to know this, would I summarize that. Plenty of questions then! Textbook questions, which I did not want to answer because my students could, after all, read. Devil and the deep blue sea questions, which I could not answer because no one could answer them. "Do you want us to know all these details?" Jockeying for position questions: "Do you really think examinations are fair tests of a student's ability?" etc. The hour would be spent in a fruitless discussion of the examination.

There was some demand for various aids to study, outlines, schedules, etc. These I put off easily. My main difficulty was with the examinations themselves. If a student came into my office a day or so before a scheduled examination, I knew that he was going to ask me to tell him what he should study in preparation for the examination, or how he should study it.

Sometimes there was an attempt at definite imposition. One young man requested a special afternoon appointment. He was planning to cut my eight o'clock on Tuesday, and he wanted me to take an hour to tell him what I was going to say that might bear on the examination at eight o'clock Thursday.

After the examination the same pitiful game continued. Students would come up with an answer on their lips, and want to know whether that was the right answer. Or they would come in for lengthy and very serious conferences concerning their grades.

I was a little bit hostile, and I make no doubt that my students resented that. I realize that if I could have taken the whole business very seriously, if I could have brought myself to sit down with them and gravely discuss their chances of success or failure in the coming ordeal, if I could have made a game of examinations and pointed my students for them, if I could have done these things, students might have liked me better. But I was convinced, and I still feel that this belief is sound, that teaching people to pass examinations results only in their being able to pass examinations. It was that that I was trying to get away from. The truth was that I was not interested in the grade that any student made, though I was tremendously concerned about whether or not students profited from my course in their general understanding of the problems of philosophy.

I realize that the students were more realistic in all this than I. I kept trying to imagine that the relation between us was that of master and disciple, that our contact was a general human one, that the matter at issue was the transmission of understanding. My students knew better. I was the dispenser of grades, and the custodian of the credits. If in trying to exert a friendly influence for sweetness and light, I failed to be a benevolent helper in the struggle for a diploma, or a no more than ordinarily unreasonable opponent, they were perhaps justified in resenting it. I realize also that the students were as utterly trapped as I. It was worse for the stupid, for they had a bitterly difficult time in fulfilling even my very moderate course requirements. But even the brilliant ones had good reason to be concerned over their grades, and to conceive of their association with me in terms of marks and credits rather than in terms of understanding. (Life history document.)

The conflict that appears in the above story is a conflict between institutional and non-institutional leadership. In the social interaction of the school, the teacher usually represents the patterned, conventional leadership, and stands for achievement within the institutional framework. Students are usually concerned with breaking down this framework. But in college the situation is frequently reversed, with the teacher attempting to transcend the academic definition of the situation, while students, thoroughly assimilated to the pattern, strive to confine the teacher to the conventional channels of interchange. The reason of this is sufficiently clear: The social situation of the school puts pressure upon students to make them interested in getting grades, not in getting wisdom. There is about every college and high school a mass of unwieldy and brittle social machinery which works to this end. The dean's office sets up standards and demands reports on grades; the fraternity demands grades; the honorary society demands grades; the athletic department demands grades. But these institutional devices do not promote much real learning. The teacher, a minor cog in the great social machine, can do little else but move when and as the machine moves. In conformity to the institutional regimen, also, the teacher will find his greatest happiness in his relations with his students. He must accept, with whatever grace he can, the social situation of giving and receiving grades and credits; he must alternately set up barriers for students to pass, taking them very seriously and talking about them, not unpleasantly but determinedly, and then come over on the side of the students and help them to get past the barriers he has himself set up.

There are teachers who take this part of their work very seriously, who think of approaching examinations as an ordeal by fire for them and their students. They struggle mightily to prepare their students for any type of examination they may choose to give them. They struggle mightily to prepare an examination which will adequately test the achievements of all students and will yet give a proper scatter of grades. When the day of the test at length arrives, it finds the teacher still suffering more than his students. This is precisely what the alignment of human forces within the institutional situation requires if students and teachers are to live together happily.

The social life of a whole little world revolves about the issue of tests and requirements. The canniness of teachers is largely concerned with this. The specific requirement, once it is set up, hardens like concrete into a changeless moral order. The usual rapidly becomes the right. That is why teachers are so concerned when a little loophole appears in the social framework they have built; they know that this little evasion or exemption, this seemingly harmless little privilege, will soon be translated into prescriptive right. Experienced teachers have learned to evaluate precedents. As requirements are social arrangements which human beings depend upon, they are hardened into right; as they are barriers that stand in people's way, they are broken down by the play of human forces.

There are courses in high school and college whose purpose it is to equip students with desirable attitudes toward certain objects in their environment. Many such courses are to be found in departments of sociology, and the arguments in their favor are at least partly sound. Rigorous academicians object to them because, as they say, it is the business of education to inform; education should be concerned with the intellectual content of the mind and not with the dynamics of its emotional organization. This seems a hasty and ill-considered objection, and one that betokens a narrow view of education, for it is not possible to transmit attitudes without also passing on objects, and "attitude courses" must contribute as much as any others to enabling students to live in a wider and more complexly structured universe.

A more serious criticism of attitude courses is that they do not really affect attitudes. This is as it may be, but academic standards doubtless interfere with the transmission of attitudes. The rigmarole of examinations, grades, and credits prevents the teacher from exerting a personal influence upon his students. Academic standards are preposterous in attitude courses, and either attitude courses must be abandoned or our conception of academic standards revised. For how is it possible to give a grade upon freedom from race prejudice? Or to secure, in a class in which a grade must finally be given, that free expression of one's whole opinion, so different from a servile and tongue-in-cheek repetition of what the teacher and the textbook have said, from which alone can start the sort of social interaction which might result in changed attitudes and opinions?

A like sort of reasoning may be said to hold concerning courses whose aim is to give insight. It is difficult to pass on insight, and its transmission must represent a positive achievement both for student and teacher; this is an important reason for its lack of popularity, but the real reason for the abandonment by teachers of the attempt to pass it on is that it is practically impossible to test it. A teacher who concerned himself mainly with giving insight would not be able to give objective tests, he would not have a proper scatter in his grades, and his marks would not fit the normal curve. He might have a "pipe course" and be outlawed by his colleagues for unfair competition, or he might have an unconscionably hard course, and fail to be elected because of a whispering campaign in the fraternity houses.

Tests and standards are intended to enforce substantial achievement, and to weed out the inept and the lazy. But almost any academic test fails to sort out individuals in the way it is intended to do. Always the mediocre slip through, and always the able and diligent are likely to be penalized with the dull and lazy. In graduate schools there has been of late years a frantic effort to set up requirements which will exclude fools from higher degrees. There has been a multiplication of the hurdles that have to be jumped before one enters into the kingdom. It may be that the ideal of the proper sort of candidate for a Ph.D., as long as it remains an ideal enshrined in the minds of administrators, is not wholly ineffectual. But when that ideal becomes a rule, it is a formal requirement, and dull persons can fulfill it formally without possessing a glimmer of that lively comprehension whose possession it is supposed to insure. It is all very well to have a bridge of asses, but it is well to remember that the trainers of asses are as persistent and ingenious as the builders of bridges.

Although examinations are sometimes pleasant for teachers, they are never pleasant for students, except, perhaps, for those intellectual rarities who, never having experienced a defeat, are anxious to demonstrate their strength again. But it is a matter of common comment among teachers that even the ablest students frequently ask silly questions on examination day. (Some, indeed, have perfected a technique by which, through successive questions as to interpretation of questions, they get their teachers to do the mental work of the examination for them.) Many students are thrown into such a panic that they cannot answer the most elementary questions, and their papers show a marked deterioration from their usual level. (Rule-of-thumb methods allow for a variation of fifteen per cent between daily work and examinations as not abnormal.) Nor should it be thought that the effects of such experiences pass away quickly. There develops a fear of examinations, an examination complex, which remains to bedevil the individual in all the crucial situations of his life. In one case, difficulty with examinations in high school, crystallized by a single experience of failure in college entrance examinations, deterred a young woman from entering college and gave rise to a conflict (expressed in a recurrent dream) which was still fresh eight years later. A proper evaluation of the learning product of the schools would show, however, that one of the chief things which good students have learned is the art of writing examinations.

Some more general questions and problems still await consideration. In the chapter on social mobility we discussed the selective function of the schools. It is obvious that academic requirements are the most important of the selective devices which the schools have at their command. We believe the selective function of the schools to be a legitimate function, and yet we have proposed to relax academic standards in the interest of personality values and a better kind of learning. The relaxation of standards, or the humanization of methods of enforcing them, clearly points toward the development of other testing mechanisms in the school. This need should be filled by the development of the field of vocational guidance, a field which as yet awaits the touch of a master hand.

But it has been with a true intuition that educational theorists have fastened upon this task-performing aspect of education as the most vicious feature of our educational system. We must seek a different kind of education. We must recognize that the education of the understanding, the only kind of education that will ever give us a real mastery of our world, does not proceed so much from acquaintance with a broad range of facts and principles as from the assimilation of a few. The greatest scientific researcher is not always the person who carries the greatest load of concepts in his head. An epigram contrasts two contemporary statesmen as follows: "*A* has read nothing and understands everything; *B* has read everything and understands nothing." It is the undoubted tendency of desiccated and factual instruction to produce the second type of learning. We must aim at a livelier learning. We must aim at assimilation rather than memorization.

All that we have said about academic requirements does not argue against a definite, even a standardized and stereotyped content of education. There are many elements of our culture which it is imperative that any person who is to live in it must assimilate. There is, for instance, arithmetic. Nor can we do away with tasks, for the utility of a definite task roots deep into the construction of the mind. But it is the manner of requiring it that makes the difference. The present mode of enforcing requirements, by recitations and periodic examinations with a system of credits and grades, does not work; at best it enforces a psittaceous repetition of facts committed to memory, and does not assure, perhaps does not even favor, a real assimilation of subject matter. By introducing an element of the artificial and the forced, by placing the emphasis upon the false, objective symbol of the subjective reality of learning, it vitiates the relationship of teacher and taught. A chief merit of some of the recent uses of achievement tests is that they remove this element of artificiality from the school room.

PROJECTS

1. Induce teachers to comment on other teachers who are reputed to be lax in the matter of requirements. Record and analyze.

2. Compare all the courses you have had in college as to exactness, organi-

zation, and susceptibility to being tested. Which courses had the highest standards? Which had the greatest influence upon your attitudes?

3. Make a study of successful examination papers. What were their outstanding characteristics? Compare with badly written examinations. State the technique of writing examinations.

4. Record your introspection while grading a set of examination papers or classroom exercises with a view to ascertaining the factors upon which judgment is actually based. Note especially the chain of reflections involved in the decision as to whether a marginal paper shall be marked pass or fail.

5. Make observations upon persons, their decisions, and incidents of their lives in order to arrive at a statement of the difference between common sense and book knowledge. State the theoretical distinction as clearly as possible.

6. Take notes upon speeches at a convention of specialized teachers. Note shibboleths, collective representations, the buttressing of distorted attitudes by group processes, etc.

7. Make a case study of a specialist whose point of view has apparently suffered no distortion. To what factors in his personality should this freedom from specialism be ascribed?

8. Take careful notes upon an argument between a student and a teacher concerning a grade. Analyze the play of attitudes in the discussion. Compare the techniques of different teachers in meeting or avoiding such arguments.

9. Make observations upon "chiselling" and "handshaking" in your own school. What techniques are employed? Is there a student taboo upon such behavior?

10. Write the history of a teacher who began teaching without any academic standards but was forced to develop them. Analyze group processes at work in the case.

11. Make a case study of a teacher who obtains status in the teacher group by marking students very strictly. Analyze his relation to social groups.

12. Analyze the process of competition for students in a given school. Note the bases, methods, and limitations of competition. Study the personalities of successful and unsuccessful competitors.

13. Record the folk talk of a group of teachers on the topic of academic standards. Get attitudes toward standards, grades, examinations, failures, cribbing, chiselling, etc.

14. Write the history of a projected school reform which foundered as a result of the rebellious attitudes of students and the disciplining attitudes of teachers.

15. Write the history of the honor system in a given school. What makes it work? If it has failed, what was the reason?

16. Make case studies of several students who cheat in examinations. Why do they do it? How do they justify the practice?

17. Compare a teacher in whose classes cheating is rife with a teacher in whose classes students rarely cheat. Analyze and interpret.

18. Describe the social atmosphere of a school or class in which cribbing has become a game. Analyze carefully the involvement of attitudes.

19. Analyze the student relationships of a teacher who attempts to minimize examinations. Compare with the student relationships of a teacher who pays a great deal of attention to examinations. Which is the better course?

20. Make a case study of a student who has a chronic fear of examinations and is always so disorganized by them that he makes a poor showing.

SUGGESTED READINGS

(1) Dawson, C. A., and Gettys, W. E., *An Introduction to Sociology,* pp. 442-447.

(2) Dewey, John, *Democracy and Education.*

(3) Hart, J. K., *A Social Interpretation of Education,* Chapter XVIII.

(4) Kilpatrick, W. H., *Foundations of Method,* Chapter XVII.

(5) Peters, C. C., *Foundations of Educational Sociology,* Chapter VIII.

(6) Rugg, H. O., and Schumaker, Ann, *The Child-Centered School.*

(7) Thayer, V. T., *The Passing of the Recitation.*

PART FIVE

WHAT TEACHING DOES TO TEACHERS

CHAPTER XXII

DETERMINANTS OF THE OCCUPATIONAL TYPE

TEACHING makes the teacher. Teaching is a boomerang that never fails to come back to the hand that threw it. Of teaching, too, it is true, perhaps, that it is more blessed to give than to receive, and it also has more effect. Between good teaching and bad there is a great difference where students are concerned, but none in this, that its most pronounced effect is upon the teacher. Teaching does something to those who teach. Introspective teachers know of changes that have taken place in themselves. Objectively minded persons have observed the relentless march of growing teacherishness in others. This is our problem.

It is necessary to see this inquiry in its true perspective. The question: What does teaching do to teachers? is only a part of the greater problem: What does any occupation do to the human being who follows it? Now that differences of caste and rank have become inconspicuous, and differences that go with the locale are fading, it is the occupation that most marks the man. The understanding of the effects upon the inner man of the impact of the occupation is thus an important task of social science. It is a problem almost untouched. We know that some occupations markedly distort the personalities of those who practice them, that there are occupational patterns to which one conforms his personality as to a Procrustean bed by lopping off superfluous members. Teaching is by no means the only occupation which whittles its followers to convenient size and seasons them to suit its taste. The lawyer and the chorus girl soon come to be recognizable social types. One can tell a politician when one meets him on the street. Henry Adams has expanded upon the unfitness of senators for being anything but senators; occupational molding, then, affects the statesman as much as lesser men. The doctor is always the doctor, and never quite can quit his rôle. The salesman lives in a world of selling configurations. And what preaching most accomplishes is upon the preacher himself. Perhaps no occupation that is followed long fails to leave its stamp upon the person. Certainly teaching leaves no plainer mark than some other vocations, though it is, perhaps, a mark which a larger number of people can recognize. It is our present task to determine, as objectively as may be and as completely as possible, the effect of teaching upon the person.

Before we can understand the occupational type to which the members of any profession belong, we must take account of the operation of four sorts of factors: (1) selective influences affecting the composition of the profession, (2) the set of rôles and attitudes which the member of the profession must play consistently, (3) the effect upon individuals of the opinion which the community has of the profession, and (4) traumatic learning within the occupation.

(1) Following out the operation of the first of these factors, we find that one reason for the similarity of doctors to each other is that there is a type of personality which is especially attracted to medicine. Likewise a certain type is attracted more than others to law, another type to engineering, another to the ministry, etc. There is in no case complete consistency, but there is a sufficiently heavy aggregation of one sort of personality type in a given profession to justify the assumption of a selectivity affecting the composition of the professional population.

(2) Those who follow certain occupations are continually thrown into certain kinds of social situations. These social situations call for, or are best met by, a certain kind of reaction on the part of the professional. The individual thus plays certain rôles and shows certain attitudes habitually, and there is a tendency for him to distort other social situations until they conform to a pattern which can be met by his habitual rôles and attitudes. (This is the transfer joke, the mainstay of overworked humorists.) Training an individual for the practice of such a profession often consists in teaching him what he is expected to do or say upon certain occasions, as when the minister offers the consolations of religion to a bereaved family, a teacher assigns a lesson, a doctor enters a sick room, or a lawyer threatens suit. Long practice in the social techniques enjoined upon one in a profession makes those the deepest grooves, and at length they grow so deep that there is no getting out of them.

(3) From community experience of persons playing certain kinds

of rôles in the practice of certain callings, worked over and somewhat distorted by the conscious and unconscious attitudes of the community toward that profession, arise certain subjective patterns, or stereotypes, which embody the community idea of the individual belonging to a certain occupational group. The stereotype helps to determine the true occupational type, for it affects the selectivity of the occupation, and it limits and canalizes the social experience of the member of the occupation. The attempt of the individual to escape from the stereotype may itself become as in teaching and the ministry one of the important determinants of the occupational type proper.

(4) The social situation surrounding the practice of any occupation is set to inflict upon the individual whose occupational behavior is eccentric certain shocks, or trauma. From the viewpoint of social organization, these shocks or penalties are means of enforcing conformity to social codes. Upon persons they produce special effects due to psychological shock. Though not easily differentiable from situational molding, these effects seem to deserve special discussion.

The selective influences determining the type of person who elects to follow a given occupation are always a little obscure, and to determine them even for a single occupation would require extended research. We must at once confess our inability to map out the set of social influences which lead certain individuals to take up teaching and discourage others from entering the profession. We may attempt an answer in the most general terms by noting briefly some of the conditions which determine the selectivity of any occupation. The economic standing of a vocation is one of the most important factors determining its selective pattern. In this are included the matter of financial return, immediate and future, the opportunity for advancement (more or less graded into steps to constitute a career), and economic security. Economic considerations do not solely determine the power of an occupation to attract desirable individuals, but they are an important part of the general configuration in which the occupation makes its appearance in the minds of individuals, for some callings have a "personality wage," and others have not. The social standing of the occupation is also important. Under this, it needs to be considered what social circles those in the occupation move in, and what stereotyped ideas the community has concerning the profession; for women, the question of marriage opportunities is not a slight one. The nature of the work is another condition of its attractiveness or unattractiveness to particular individuals. Some persons take naturally to routine; others are satisfied only with an occupation which presents a series of crises to be met and conquered. For some, obscurity is no hardship, but for others it is necessary always to be in range of the spotlight. There are yet other persons in whose minds the opportunities which an occupation yields for self-expression outweigh all other factors. The amount and kind of special training required for entry into the ranks of a given occupation are further considerations which select out some few of the many called. This will affect the psychic composition of the profession. It is certain, for instance, that those who come into the medical profession in these days of long and expensive training will always have plenty of patience.

These are the objective considerations which determine the attractiveness or unattractiveness of a given occupation. If choice were rational, these elements would appear in the mind fully, and be weighed the one against the other, and the reliability of every subsidiary inference and of every shred of evidence would be determined logically. But choice is rarely rational. When these considerations appear in the human mind, they are distorted by wishful thinking, altered to conform to the prevalent stereotype, colored by fancy. It is the logic of the impulses that finally determines choice. The choice of a vocation is more likely to be dictated by the family pattern and the supposed conformity of an occupation to class tradition than by a rational consideration of pay, opportunity, and the nature of the work. The social experience of the individual, too, often gives him a preference for a certain occupation on a basis that is scarcely conscious. Not all personal considerations, of course, are irrational in their nature; the possession of special aptitudes or marked disabilities often affects choice. But—so contrary are the workings of our logical machinery—such considerations probably prompt choices that are deliberately wrong as often as choices that are right.

The selective pattern which teaching presents to prospective teachers has never been adequately described, and the present writer does not presume to be able to deal with it any better than have his predecessors. It is a known fact that the financial rewards of teaching are not great; the pay low, the opportunity for advancement, for most teachers, slight; and economic security little. Most writers have concluded that this is in itself an explanation of the known failure of the profession to attract as large a number of capables as it should. Yet one may wonder whether merely raising salaries all around would cause the mediocre to be crowded out by the influx of the talented.

The social standing of the profession is unfortunately low, and this excludes more capable than incapable persons. Particularly damaging, probably, is the belief that is abroad in the community that only persons incapable of success in other lines become teachers, that teaching is a failure belt, the refuge of "unsalable men and unmarriageable women." This belief is the more damaging for the truth that is in it. The nature of the work of teaching, with its overwhelming mass of routine and its few opportunities for free self-expression, may both deter and attract to the ultimate damage of the profession. On the one hand, the drudgery of teaching, combined with the many restrictions which the community places upon the personal conduct of teachers, may eliminate from teaching many of those virile and inspiring persons of whom the profession has such need, for it is a known fact that such pronouncedly individual persons often have little respect for purely negative morality, and react vehemently against living within the community stereotype of the teacher. On the other hand, teaching, along with the ministry, is known as one of the sheltered occupations, as an occupation where those persons who shrink from the daily battle of life, often very estimable persons, by the way, may find refuge. This quality of not wishing to do battle in the front rank, which would perhaps show a high correlation with introversion, by no means detracts from the teaching ability of every person who has it, but on the whole it probably operates to the detriment of the profession.

Perhaps all those who have treated the topic of the selective factors determining the composition of the teaching population have erred by handling the subject too rationalistically. Rarely does an occupational choice result from a process of rigorous reasoning. More often it is the social experience of the individual which gives him a push into teaching that he cannot resist, and the advantages and disadvantages of teaching remain unconsidered. Perhaps it is an inherent need of the personality for being in some sort of managerial position which prompts one to take up teaching as an occupational goal. Perhaps it is a training which has interested one in the things of the mind so that the attractiveness of other occupations has been dulled and that only teaching is left as a compromise (creative art being left out of consideration for lack of talent). Perhaps it is a training which has made one almost able to enter some other profession, such as law or medicine, but has left him at the door. (Students of one midwestern institution refer to the customary fifteen hours of education as an "insurance policy.") Perhaps it is a desire for ready money which prompts the young graduate to take up teaching, where he can command a slightly higher salary as a beginner than he can in business.

Few facts are available as to the composition of the teaching population determined by these selective factors. We know that teachers are predominantly native-born, that the large majority of them come from the rural districts, and that they come from families of the lower middle class. Teachers are fairly young, about two thirds of the women and one half of the men being under thirty. There is little in any of these facts to give occasion for either regret or rejoicing. What we should like to know is the psychic qualities of these something more than eight hundred thousand, native-born, predominantly rural persons who teach. This is precisely what we do not know. The average intelligence quotient of teachers may be high or it may be low. Their will-profile may go this way or again it may go that. Writers on the subject of the teaching population in general seem agreed that there are too many teachers of mediocre personal and mental qualifications, and far too few who would rank in the superior class either as intellectual agents or as persons.[1] Granting that this generalization is as true as such a broad generalization can ever be, we may mention the obviosity that one of the tasks facing the teaching profession is the attraction of superior persons and the gradual displacement of the inferior.

When the mills have ground which supply to each profession its accustomed human material, the teaching profession receives each year a large number of plastic and unformed minds. These new recruits have whatever qualities they may have, and upon the basis of their present personalities their life in the teaching profession will build a different structure. They do not know how to teach, although they may know everything that is in innumerable books telling them how to teach. They will not know how to teach until they have got the knack of certain personal adjustments which adapt them to their profession, and the period of learning may be either long or short. These recruits who face teaching as a life work are ready to learn to teach, and they are ready, though they know it not, to be formed by teaching. When teaching has formed them, what shape will it give them? Their daily work will write upon them; what will it write?

[1] Intelligence tests given in a leading eastern university during the last few years have consistently shown freshman education students to be of lower average intelligence than the freshmen of any other school. Women students seem further below the general average than men students. This is largely remedied by severe elimination in the school of education.

What teaching does to teachers it does partly by furnishing them those rôles which habit ties to the inner frame of personality and use makes one with the self. Our method in this discussion will be to describe those social situations which the teacher most often encounters, and to analyze them to discover how the qualities considered to be characteristic of the teacher are produced in them. We must admit that this is a method of empirical analysis, and that it has its first and most important basis in what the writer has seen and thought and done. The only test of such analysis and of the generalizations which come from it is the judgment of other writers who have had equal opportunity to observe. Although this method is vague and is little subject to control, it is the only method available at the present time for pursuing an inquiry of this sort, and we shall endeavor to apply it in as fair-minded a way as possible. Where there seem to be two sides, we shall state both and leave the reader to choose for himself.

Aside from a scattering company of panegyrists, most of those who have presumed to comment on the teacher as an occupational type have done so in an unfriendly manner. This is perhaps regrettable, but certainly significant, for most of those who have passed unfavorable judgments upon teachers have been teachers themselves; from pondering this, one gets a little insight into the conditions of stress and strain in the teacher mind. Unfriendly commentators upon the manners of teachers are able to compile a long list of unpleasant qualities which, they say, are engendered in the teacher's personality by teaching experience. There is first that certain inflexibility or unbendingness of personality which is thought to mark the person who has taught. That stiff and formal manner into which the young teacher compresses himself every morning when he puts on his collar becomes, they say, a plaster cast which at length he cannot loosen. One has noticed, too, that in his personal relationships the teacher is marked by reserve, an incomplete personal participation in the dynamic social situation and a lack of spontaneity, in psychological terms, by an inhibition of his total responses in favor of a restricted segment of them. As if this reserve were not in itself enough to discourage ill-considered advances, it is supplemented, when one has become very much the teacher, by certain outward barriers which prevent all and sundry from coming into contact with the man behind the mask and discovering those inhibited and hidden possibilities of reaction. Along with this goes dignity, the dignity of the teacher which is not natural dignity like that of the American Indian, but another kind of dignity that consists of an abnormal concern over a restricted rôle and the restricted but well-defined status that goes with it. One who has taught long enough may wax unenthusiastic on any subject under the sun; this, too, is part of the picture painted by unfriendly critics. The didactic manner, the authoritative manner, the flat, assured tones of voice that go with them, are bred in the teacher by his dealings in the school room, where he rules over the petty concerns of children as a Jehovah none too sure of himself, and it is said that these traits are carried over by the teacher into his personal relations. It is said, and it would be difficult to deny it, that the teacher mind is not creative. Even the teacher's dress is affected by his occupational attitudes; the rule is that the teacher must be conservative, if not prim, in manner, speech, and dress. There are other traits which some observers have mentioned: a set of the lips, a look of strain, a certain kind of smile, a studied mediocrity, a glib mastery of platitude. Some observers have remarked that a certain way of standing about, the way of a person who has had to spend much of his time waiting for something to happen and has had to be very dignified about it, is characteristic of the teacher. Sometimes only small and uncertain indications betray the profession. Sometimes, as a cynical novelist has remarked of one of his characters, one cannot see the man for the school master. If these traits, or those essential ones which make up the major outlines of the picture, are found among the generality of teachers, it is because these traits have survival value in the schools of today. If one does not have them when he joins the faculty, he must develop them or die the academic death. Opinions might differ as to how widely these characteristic traits are found among the members of the profession and as to how deeply they are ingrained, as to whether the ordinary man might see them, or only one with the curse of satire. But Henry Adams has said that no man can be a school master for ten years and remain fit for anything else, and his statement has given many a teacher something to worry about.

There is enough plausibility in the above description to make us teachers ponder about the future, if not the present, of ourselves and our friends. But there is another side, and we may well pause to look at it before going on with our analysis. Teaching brings out pleasant qualities in some persons, and for them it is the most gratifying vocation in the world. The teacher enjoys the most pleasant associations in his work; he lives surrounded by the respect of the community and the homage of his students. Teaching affords a splendid opportunity for a self-sacrificing person (how many of these are there?) to realize his destiny vicariously; in any case the teacher is less soiled by life than those who follow more vigorous professions. It may well be questioned, too, whether there is any occupational conscience more strict than that of the teacher. Teaching breeds patience in some teachers, patience and fairness and a reserve that is only gentlemanly and never frosty. There are some persons whom teaching liberates, and these sense during their first few months of teaching a rapid growth and expansion of personality. While we are stating this side of the case, we must record the pointed observation of one person on the constructive side of the argument that those very teachers who are bitterest in the denunciation of teaching would not for a moment consider doing anything else, and that even the most discontented teachers can rarely bring themselves to leave the profession. These considerations should be enough to convince us that there are two sides to everything that can be said about the teacher, perhaps that teaching produces radically different effects upon different types of persons. But whatever the classification of the qualities which are produced in the teacher by teaching, they all mark the occupational type. Our theoretical problem should now be clear; it is to account for the genesis of the character traits belonging to the teacher by showing how they flow out of the action of his life situation upon his personality, if possible, to show how different effects are produced upon different basic personality types.

The weightiest social relationship of the teacher is his relationship to his students; it is this relationship which is teaching. It is around this relationship that the teacher's personality tends to be organized, and it is in adaptation to the needs of this relationship that the qualities of character which mark the teacher are produced. The teacher-pupil relationship is a special form of dominance and subordination, a very unstable relationship and in quivering equilibrium, not much supported by sanction and the strong arm of authority, but depending largely upon purely personal ascendency. Every teacher is a taskmaster and every taskmaster is a hard man; if he is naturally kindly, he is hard from duty, but if he is naturally unkind, he is hard because he loves it. It is an unfortunate rôle, that of Simon Legree, and has corrupted the best of men. Conflict is in the rôle, for the wishes of the teacher and the student are necessarily divergent, and more conflict because the teacher must protect himself from the possible destruction of his authority that might arise from this divergence of motives. Subordination is possible only because the subordinated one is a subordinate with a mere fragment of his personality, while the dominant one participates completely. The subject is a subject only part of the time and with a part of himself, but the king is all king. In schools, too, subordinated ones attempt to protect themselves by withdrawing from the relationship, to suck the juice from the orange of conformity before rendering it to the teacher. But the teacher is doomed to strive against the mechanization of his rule and of obedience to it. It is the part of the teacher to enforce a real obedience. The teacher must be aggressive in his domination, and this is very unfortunate, because domination is tolerable only when it stays within set bounds. From this necessary and indispensable aggressiveness of the teacher arises an answering hostility on the part of the student which imperils the very existence of any intercourse between them. The teacher takes upon himself most of the burden of the far-reaching psychic adjustments which make the continuance of the relationship possible.

That inflexibility or unbendingness of personality which we have mentioned as characterizing the school teacher flows naturally out of his relations with his students. The teacher must maintain a consistent pose in the presence of students. He must not adapt to the demands of the childish group in which he lives, but must force the group to adapt to him, wherefore the teacher often feels that he must take leave of graciousness and charm and the art of being a good fellow at the classroom door. The teacher must not accept the definitions of situations which students work out, but must impose his own definition upon students. His position as an agent of social control, as the paid representative of the adult group among the group of children, requires that when he has found a pose he must hold it; to compromise upon matters where adult morality runs would be thought treason to the group that pays his salary. There is added a necessity of his professional career which, since men and careers are always mingled and never appear separately, is also of the greatest personal importance: he must maintain discipline, and it is easier to maintain discipline by making continual demands of the same sort and by keeping one's social rôle constant in conformity with those constant demands than by changing rôles frequently and making demands consistent with those changing rôles but inconsistent with each other. It is, furthermore, very wearing to change rôles when one is responsible for a group, for one must make the fact of the change and all its implications clear to the entire group; it usually requires a certain effort to constellate all the members of the group in the new set of attitudes which take their key from the teacher's changed rôle; there are laggards who never quite catch the point, and some lacking in social comprehension who cannot know that the teacher is joking or do not observe that he has stopped; there are risks to the teacher-dominated order in the straggling march to a new mental alignment. Therefore the teacher cannot change his rôle as often as the fulfillment of his personal impulses might dictate. When he does change it, he must label the transition in such a manner as to destroy its point, erect sign-posts, take the salt from his humor by broad hints that he is joking now. But the ability of a person to hold our interest as a person depends in large part upon a shifting of social rôles so rapid that the eye must look closely to see it and so subtle that no ready-made labels can fit it.

If there are few rôles which classroom life permits the teacher to play, he must put on each of them many times a day. The teacher must alternate his rôles because he is trying to do inconsistent things with his students, and he can bring them about only by rapid changes from one established pose to another. He is trying to maintain a definite dominance over young persons whose lives he presumes to regulate very completely. This requires of the teacher aggressiveness, unyieldingness, and determination. If persisted in, this attitude would exterminate in students all interest in subject matter and would crush out every faint inclination to participate in the social life of the classroom, which presents no very alluring vistas at the best. And the teacher who went very long upon this tack would be known for a knave and a fool, and justly hated for a martinet. Sometimes an unimaginative teacher runs into just this situation. The solution is found in alternating this authority rôle with some other which is not altogether inconsistent with it but which veils the authority so that hostility is no longer aroused. But the authority impression must be continually renewed, and there ensues a long series of rapid but not subtle changes of rôle. As a result, the limitations and implications of the teacher-pupil relationship are made clear to the pupil group.

A clever friend has perhaps summed up the matter by saying, "The successful teacher is one who knows how to get on and off his high-horse rapidly." (As it happened, the author of this remark did not himself possess this skill, and failed in teaching, as so many other clever men have done, for want of dignity.) Thus one says, "I am your teacher," in a certain unemotional tone of voice. This begets discipline, perhaps some sullenness, certainly emotional and personal frustration on the part of both student and teacher. Before this reaction has been carried through to completion, one says, "But I am a human being and I try to be a good fellow. And you are all fine people and we have some good times together, don't we?" This is rôle number two, and if taken at its face value it begets a desirable cheerfulness and a dangerous friendliness. If he tarries too long upon this grace note, the teacher loses his authority by becoming a member of the group. He must revert to rôle number one, and say, with just a hint of warning and an implication of adult dignity in his voice, "But I am the teacher." All this occurs a hundred times a day in every school room, and it marks the rhythm of the teacher's movements of advancement and retreat with reference to his students, the alternate expansion and contraction of his personality. It does not occur, of course, in so obvious a form as this; it is perhaps only the very unskillful teacher who needs to put such things into words. This pulsation of the teacher's personality, with its answering change of posture on the part of students, is usually reduced to a mere conversation of gestures. This conversation, for all that habit has stripped it so bare of identifying characteristics and drained it so dry of emotion, is the most significant social process of the classroom. It is also a very important determinant of the teacher's personality, and one of the points on which transfer is said to be made most easily. After all, it need cause us no amazement if one who has learned to get his way in the school by alternate applications of hot and cold water should fall into that technique of control in his more intimate relationships. In the life of every teacher there is a significant long-term change in the psychic weight of these rôles, a not unusual result being that rôle number one, the authority rôle, eats up the friendly rôle, or absorbs so much of the personality that nothing is left for friendliness to fatten upon.

The authority rôle becomes very much formalized, both because of the psychological law that performances lose their meaningfulness by frequent repetition and because there is an advantage in having it so. Army men speak of a voice of command, a flat, impersonal, unquestionable, non-controversial tone of voice in which commands are best given. It is a tone of voice without overtones, representing only a segment of the officer's personality and demanding obedience from only a segment of the subordinate. School teachers learn by trial and error, by imitation and practice, to formalize their commands. They develop, too, the voice of exposition, which is a voice perfectly dry and as mechanical as a dictaphone, a voice adapted to the expounding of matter that has long since lost what interest it may have had for the expounder. Lack of enthusiasm has survival value. Hence the paradox that sometimes the best teachers are those least interested in their work, and that others do their best work when least concerned. But all these things contribute to the final flatness and dullness of the teacher who falls a prey to them.

It has often been remarked that a certain kind of dignity is characteristic of teachers. It seems that teachers develop a certain way of carrying themselves which sets them out from the rest of the world. This we may call school-teacher dignity. There seem to be two major roots of school-teacher dignity. One is in the community and in the attitude which the community takes toward the teacher; the other is in the nature of the teacher's work. (These are not unconnected, for the community attitude is determined by the school experience of the adult members of the community.) What happens when a new and unformed teacher first goes about in the community in which he is to teach? Let us say that a person who has never before known deference takes up teaching. Suddenly he finds himself the object of flattering attention from students, catered to by them and addressed respectfully and ceremoniously by fellow teachers. In the community he is called "Professor." Tradesmen approach him obsequiously; plain citizens kow-tow. People profess to show him special consideration on the grounds that he is a teacher. He is supposed to be more trustworthy than other mortals, more moral, more learned. A place of honor is prepared for him. It is a dignity that is unearned, and it is empty because it is unearned. In any other occupation, with the same training and experience, he would still be a menial of low degree, but if he ever fought through the ranks in another profession and attained to his top hat at last, he would merit the distinction, and it would fit him well. Not so teacher dignity, for it is too cheap; only the finest man can give it a high value, and then it is not the profession, but the man, that counts. Some young teachers, knowing that they merit no deference, endeavor to fend it off as gracefully as they can. Others realize vaguely that this external respect of the community is a part of the school-teacher stereotype, that it is the obverse side of a latent hostility and is more than balanced by an inclination to ridicule; sometimes they know that this respect is part of the iron framework that shuts the teacher, as a sacred object,[1] out of society and keeps him from acting as a human being—these rebel against teacher dignity. Perhaps their

[1] Cf. Durkeim, Emile, *Elementary Forms of Religious Life.*

rebellion brings them personal disaster, and they are forced to compromise at last with dignity. Perhaps they merely suffer a myriad of tiny hurts from the satire of the dignity, and that gives them dignity by a process of scar-tissue. But dignity they must get, rebels or no—somehow. Others accept teacher dignity, and make the most of it. It is a flattering rôle. They live it. They live it the more determinedly if they ever become aware of the irony that comes with it to the lips of the average man.

The second root of teacher dignity is in the nature of the teacher's work in the classroom. The teacher lives much by the authority rôle; his livelihood depends upon it. Those who live much by one rôle must learn to defend its ultimate implications. Dignity is a means of defending the authority rôle. The necessity of maintaining dignity is increased by the fact that the rôle which gives rise to it is peculiarly liable to attack. On the objective side this dignity which arises in the classroom is an exaggerated concern over all the ramifications of respect and all the formal amenities due to one who occupies a narrow but well-defined social status. On the subjective side, dignity is first an inhibition of all action tendencies inconsistent with the major rôle of the school teacher. What is inhibited is usually the teacher's responsiveness to the more minute and subtler stimuli; what the teacher must crush out in himself is his alertness for human participation in unimportant by-play. But since it is this little responsiveness that makes us human, or makes us seem to be human, we say that the teacher, when his dignity has become habitual, has lost the human touch. Since, furthermore, the teacher must demand and obtain respect in all the ramifications of his authoritative rôle, he must develop certain mechanisms in himself which will defeat any attacks made by others upon that rôle. Among these mechanisms, perhaps chief among them, is the hair-trigger temper so often observed in the man with the pointer. The person learning to teach must recondition his anger response. The teacher must learn when to get angry and how to get angry quickly. He must learn every by-path of the social interaction of the classroom so that he may know what does and does not constitute an attack upon his dignity. To keep little misdeeds from growing into great ones, he must learn to magnify them to the larger size originally; this is easy because the more his habits are concerned with the established order the more heinous breaches of it will appear. What is even more important, he must learn that breaches of order committed in his presence or when he is responsible constitute direct attacks upon his authority. Teachers are cranky because crankiness helps them to hold their jobs.

If by virtue of unusual personal force or some psychological sleight of hand the teacher is able to dispense with dignity, or if there is in him no need for playing an authoritative rôle, but rather a revulsion against it, so that he pays the price and goes all undignified, he still stands to have dignity forced upon him by others. Though he avoids the open disrespect which most teachers without dignity encounter, or thinks *camaraderie* a compensation for it, he may still be wounded when he learns that his students compare him unfavorably with their other teachers on account of his lack of dignity or his lack of concern for the respect due him. Or he may find that he loses the friendship of the few students who matter to him because of his tolerance for the affronts of those who do not matter. But most of all is dignity enforced by one's fellow teachers. The significant people for a school teacher are other teachers, and by comparison with good standing in that fraternity the good opinion of students is a small thing and of little price. A landmark in one's assimilation to the profession is that moment when he decides that only teachers are important. According to the teacher code there is no worse offence than failure to deport one's self with dignity, and the penalties exacted for the infraction of the code are severe. A more subtle influence of the teacher group arises from the fact that it passes on its tradition to the new member of the profession and furnishes him with his models of imitation.

One has become a school teacher when he has learned to fear the loss of his dignity. Not that a greenhorn can resolve to be very dignified on the morrow, and become a full-fledged teacher by virtue of his resolution. He must learn to be dignified without the slightest effort, and without being conscious of the fact that he is being dignified; it must be so natural for him to ride upon the high horse that he fears alighting as he would fear falling from a balloon. Usually the psychological process by which one comes to fear the loss of dignity and to be bound by iron habit to the dignified pattern is not at all understood by the person who is going through it. He rarely knows that he is acquiring dignity, and when he has acquired it he does not know that he has it. The process by which dignity is built up in the teacher is apparently about as follows. A few unpleasant experiences build up a feeling of insecurity or a fear of what will happen if one lets the situation get out of hand. This fear produces a limitation of intercourse with students to the starkest essentials and an inhibition of other tendencies to respond to the persons about him. One does not love children when they are likely to become dangerous; one does not even trust them. This paralysis of part of the personality and limitation of action is school-teacher poise and school-teacher dignity; it enables one to cut through all extraneous matter to that core of behavior which involves discipline. The teacher who has it is "all business." When it has become habitual and one has built up a new conception of his rôle around his delimited activities, one has acquired dignity and one has become a school teacher. Though confidence returns, as it usually does, and though that confidence grows to great proportions, as it sometimes does, the limitation of behavior remains. It should also be noted that the necessity of treating all students alike contributes to the school teacher's dignity, in so far as that is a matter of the social distance between student and teacher.

This wonted seeking-avoiding balance of the teacher, connected with dignity, is not maintained without some inner conflict. Teachers tend to withdraw from non-institutional contacts the while they yearn for the opportunity and the strength to live a life of dust and danger. Their customary routine of duties, their well-known ceremonial of personal relations, come to be their world, a world which they think of as in some sense a shelter. Thus in one mood the teacher reflects that the school year draws to a close and he shudders slightly at the thought of the new contacts which the summer may bring him. Some budding orators have found their powers deserting them as they developed into school teachers; their growing shell made the self-revelation and expression of emotion which are the soul of successful speech-making increasingly difficult; perhaps they even came to take pride in the fact that "gush" was no longer in their line and to look back with shame to their spectacular behavior in the days when their habits of social expression were less restricted. "Don't be an ass," is a rule of conduct which has a special appeal to teachers and to all others who live much in a dominant rôle. Yet it is a principle that paralyzes, too, and one that cuts the person off from communion with his naïve fellows, and the teacher often feels the isolation which his personality traits impose upon him.

Enthusiasm does not comport well with dignity. Enthusiasm, therefore, is bad form. "I rather resent your inference that anyone who believes in the Dalton plan is a 'progressive' teacher, an enthusiast," said a headmaster at a regional meeting of private-school teachers. Maugham has furnished a classic bit:

It was Winks who summed up the general impression and put it into a form they all felt conclusively damning. Winks was the master of the upper third, a weak-kneed man with drooping eyelids. He was too tall for his strength, and his movements were slow and languid. He gave an impression of lassitude, and his nickname was eminently appropriate.

"He's very enthusiastic," said Winks.

Enthusiasm was ill-bred. Enthusiasm was ungentlemanly. They thought of the Salvation Army with its braying trumpets and its drums. Enthusiasm meant change. They had goose-flesh when they thought of all the pleasant old habits which stood in imminent danger. They hardly dared to look forward to the future.[1]

One is puzzled to explain that peculiar blight which affects the teacher mind, which creeps over it gradually, and, possessing it bit by bit, devours its creative resources. Some there are who escape this disease endemic in the profession, but the wonder is they are so few. That the plague is real, and that it strikes many teachers, the kindest critic cannot deny. Those who have known young teachers well, and have observed the course of their personal development as they became set in the teaching pattern, have often been grieved by the progressive deterioration in their general adaptability. And hardly a college teacher who has taught a class in summer school has failed to lament that lack of supple comprehension and willingness to follow the ball of discussion which characterizes the teacher in class. Teachers make a sad and serious business of learning, and they stand mournfully in contrast with students of the winter session, in whom a reasonable degree of willingness to judge every question on its own merits is much more frequent.[2]

Some of the gradual deadening of the intellect which the observer remarks in the teacher as he grows into his profession may no doubt be explained as an effect of age. Perhaps age does dull some persons, and certainly experience disciplines the creative impulse out of many. But if all the deterioration in the teacher is due to age, there must be a special type of short-blooming mind that is attracted to teaching; if this is so, we are thrown back upon the unanswered question of occupational selection. Another type of explanation could

[1] From *Of Human Bondage* by Somerset Maugham, copyright 1917 by Doubleday, Doran & Company, Inc., pp. 58-59.

[2] The witticism of a clever colleague is perhaps worth recording. It is one of many current in the profession concerning the peculiarities of summer-school students. He said: "The difference between students in the winter term and students in the summer session is this: When I go into my classroom in the winter I look at the class and say, 'Good Morning,' but the students are all making so much noise they don't hear me. When I go into a summer-school class I say, 'Good Morning,' and they all take out their note-books and write it down."

be based upon the tendency inculcated upon one practicing any profession to respond to recurring social situations in stereotyped ways. The deepening of some grooves of social expression is apparently inevitable in any occupation, and this emphasis of the part must involve deterioration of the whole. The mental structure of the unspecialized person is necessarily plastic; by specializing and developing particular proficiency along some one line, one nearly always loses some of his general adaptability. Perhaps that was why the elder James regarded so many of the established pursuits as "narrowing." The extent to which a profession stereotypes and narrows the social expression of the individual depends upon the range of variation in the social situations which the practice of the profession presents. The situations which the teacher faces are somewhat more stereotyped than those which the lawyer and the doctor must confront. Perhaps teaching is only a little more rigid in the social patterning which it imposes upon its devotees, but it is a very important little. The over-attention of teachers to tool subjects must certainly be called in to help explain the smallness and unimportance of the contributions which teachers have made to the arts and sciences. The teacher, from the very nature of his work, must spend most of his time in the classroom in drilling his students upon those subjects which may later open to them the doors that lead to wisdom. Other men, when they have reached maturity, may themselves use those tools to unlock the doors of the palace and enter within. But the teacher, unfortunately, must always sit upon the front steps and talk about the means of opening the door; he must instruct others in the technique of door-opening, and usually he finds when he has finished his task that he has no energy left for explorations of his own. All this is incidental to the fact that the teacher must deal with persons living in a world of childish attitudes and values, and comes himself to live in it part way. This is what one teacher called "the drag of the immature mind."

The routine situations which the teacher confronts give rise to routine habits of social expression adapted to meet them. This we have mentioned. What we have not dealt with is the influence of these routinized reactions upon the selective pattern of experience which the teacher builds up within himself. Actually the teacher faces a narrow but complex and dynamic social situation, one from which he might well receive a liberal education in adaptability, but from this complex network of human attitudes and activities he is forced to select mainly those which affect his discipline. He may peer into the book of human life, a various volume which has many obscure and devious passages, but he is privileged to read in it only the insults to himself. As to subject matter, the teacher's possibilities of reaction are equally limited. Not confutation, nor understanding, nor yet the notation of the heart must be his aim as he reads, but merely the answering of the most obvious questions and the prevention of the most stupid errors. The selectivity which the teacher builds up must be one which will give him a maximum of discipline and a minimum of subject matter. We have noted the partial paralysis of the teacher's personality through a fear of possible consequences if he allows himself freedom in his social life; this is a sort of self-frustration produced by the elaborate system of defence reactions which the teacher builds about himself. We have mentioned, too, a certain tenseness as characterizing the teacher, a tenseness which arises out of the conflict implicit in the inhibition of the major part of his potentialities of response in favor of a few necessary but personally unsatisfactory responses. This tenseness prevents the wholesome fulfillment of creative process. Creation requires motivation with control; the teacher has an excess of motivation with an even greater excess of inhibition.

There is something in the attitude of grading, too, which makes against change, and renders mental growth difficult. One who presumes to rate the performance of another must have a very definite idea of the perfect performance, and he judges other performances, not by their inner, groping onwardness, but simply by their resemblance to the perfect performance. This perfect performance is a thing finished, for nothing can ever be super-perfect except for advertising writers, and so the teacher need not think about it any more. Yet the teacher must have in mind a perfect performance, or he is no very accurate marker. The grading, marking habit assumes increasing importance as one becomes a teacher. The new teacher rarely has definite standards of grading. Often he does not consider that part of his task important. But sceptical though one be concerning the numerical evaluation of so subjective a thing as learning, he must at length conform. From habit, from the importance which others (especially the persons graded) attach to grades, and from the involvement of the teacher's status feelings with the development of rigorous standards, there arises a change in the teacher's attitude. His status feelings become involved when he realizes that students believe that he is "easy," and preen themselves upon their ability to deceive him. (Sometimes there arises a circular interaction as a result of the alternate stiffening and relaxation of academic standards. These changes in the standards produce changes in the attitudes of students, and these in turn work upon the teacher to effect the relaxation or stiffening of standards, according to the place in the cycle where the group happens to be.) The teacher must establish standards of grading; he must identify himself with them and make them a part of himself.

The creative powers of teachers disappear because the teacher tends to lose the learner's attitude. As Burnham has put it, "Again, one's own opinion based upon personal experience and strengthened by daily repetition[1] is apt to develop a didactic attitude that makes learning impossible. With this mental set, teachers cannot learn because so eager to teach; and nothing perhaps wearies them so much as to hear again what they think they already know. This inhibition of learning by the attitude of the teacher as such, combined with the common critical attitude, made it impossible for a large part of the teachers to profit greatly by the teachings of genetic pedagogy and genetic psychology."[2] Now G. Stanley Hall was one of those rare teachers who keep the learner's attitude to the extent of being anxious to learn from their own students, and this was surely not unconnected with the creativeness of his intelligence.

It is likely that the general adaptability of the teacher suffers also from the over-stable adjustment which the teacher makes to a number of simple, changeless rhythms. Teaching, perhaps, exceeds other professions only in the unvarying quality of these rhythms and the tightness with which they are bound together. There is the rhythm of the class period, which becomes so exact and unvarying that the experienced teacher often has a feeling for the end of the hour which no delayed bell can delude. One teacher has reported that when he had taught for some years in a school where the daily regimen was adhered to strictly he developed a time mechanism which always told him when two minutes only were left of the hour; at this time, contrary to the rules of pedagogy, he assigned the lesson for the next day. He said that if he forced himself to assign the lesson at the beginning of the hour, as he occasionally did, he might fail to note the nearness of the end, but if the bell were delayed by so much as two or three minutes, he always noticed it. This is no

[1] Strengthened by repetition, we should say, under circumstances which do not admit of challenge. The preacher and the teacher are infallible because it is not permitted to argue with them.

[2] Burnham, Wm. H., *Great Teachers and Mental Health*, p. 211, New York, 1926. (By permission of D. Appleton & Company.)

doubt rather an unusual case, but similar mechanisms operate in other teachers with less perfection. Then there is the daily rhythm, with its high points and low, its crises relieving monotony, its automatic transition from one class to another, and its alternation of school duties. There is a weekly rhythm, marked by Monday and Friday, and by special days devoted to special tasks. Where the daily routine differs much from one day to the next, the teacher tends to live by the week; this seems to be true of the college teacher. There is a monthly rhythm; payday, quizzes, grades, and the completion of certain tasks mark off the month. In certain communities, the life of the teacher is from one spring to the next, for at that time it is decided what teachers shall be retained and what ones dismissed, and it is never altogether a foregone conclusion in what class one is going to be. In any case, one reckons time from his years of teaching for the first few years. The myriad smaller habits which cluster about teaching (usually interpretable as the manifestations of central, determining rôles) are organized into the pattern of life by being made a part of one of these basic rhythms, and this in part accounts for the meaning which these habits have; a violation of the rhythm in even its smallest detail throws the whole scheme of things out of joint. This extreme routinization amounts almost to stereotypy. Thus a certain man reports that he used to pass a very bad day if he did not have time in the morning to read his paper carefully and smoke his pipe. This external scheme of things, bound together by basic simple rhythms, has a deeper basis in the fundamental motives of the individual, or acquires it by the internal reworking of externals by which time gives values to any life arrangement. Habit, bound together by rhythm, reworked by and in terms of fundamental motives, twisted about until it expresses those motives, accounts for most of the rightness and oughtness of the existent social order. The moss of meaning upon the stone long ago given us for bread can make it bread.

We have touched upon fear in its relation to the non-inventiveness of the teacher mind, and we have elsewhere identified the wish for security with certain mental mechanisms called into action by definite fears. It seems worth while to analyze a little further the results of the dominance of this security motive, based upon fear, in the life of the teacher. That security does receive preferential treatment as contrasted with the other possible values of the teacher's life is obvious enough to one who has known a number of teachers intimately. This preference for security, whether it is a constitutional quality which causes one to choose teaching rather than one of the more risky callings, or whether it is produced by the conditions of teaching, makes for the development of an early and rigid conservatism. When teachers meet and talk freely, one hears talk of positions and the hold that one has upon them; one hears as well of the things that threaten seisin. When it is a group of college teachers, one hears of academic freedom, and though the talk is often bold, one senses the fear it covers up. The established teacher has been playing safe so long that he has lost that necessary minimum of recklessness without which life becomes painful. A realization of the strength of this security motive enables one to understand some of the susipicion with which teachers regard each other; certainly one does not exceed the truth when he asserts that a very large percentage of the numerous quarrels between teachers arise from a belief of one teacher that another is sawing at the strings with which his job is held.

There is basis enough in the conditions of the teacher's life for the existence of many fears and the consequent dominance of security. The teacher's hold upon his students is constantly threatened by the students themselves, and there are many reasons other than inefficiency for a teacher's losing his position. The occupational risks of teaching are high, and there is no Compensation Act which covers them. The insecurity of the teacher's tenure of office profoundly affects the inwardness of the teacher's life. This prevalent insecurity has apparently given rise to a social type which is very common among teachers, that of the "warner." One informant relates his experiences with persons of this species as follows:

One thing I soon noticed about teaching was that wherever I went I had to fight off a whole coterie of "warners." These people, seeing that I was new in the system, would come to me with an offer to set me right about the people there. They would say, "Look out for Smith," "Don't trust Jones," "The less you have to do with Robinson the better," "Johnson's a snake in the grass," "Keep your eye on this chap Brown," "I wouldn't trust Thompson any further than I could throw a bull by the tail," etc. With the utmost show of secrecy, they would announce the generous intention of "giving me a tip." Usually I did not want a tip, but I nearly always got it, and when I did get it it was perfectly meaningless. Sometimes they would hint at dire disclosures they could make about the principal, but when the disclosures were made they were rarely important. Sometimes they would tell one baldly that So-and-So was "making a fight on you," or was "after your job." Details were rarely forthcoming. All this was done in the name of friendliness, but its egotic character was perfectly apparent. These warners got a great deal of ego-gratification from their activities, and demanded a corresponding abasement of self from the warned one. The warners themselves were rarely important in the school system, perhaps because their over-suspicious disposition kept them in trouble; apparently, too, the warning was a compensation for lacks within themselves. Sometimes these warnings covered an opposition of the warner to the administration and at other times they were an attempt to get the newcomer enrolled on the right side in the war of faculty cliques and factions. I found that I did much better to disregard warners altogether. When I did follow their advice it nearly always got me into trouble. (Life history document.)

Undoubtedly these talebearers and self-appointed tipsters contribute much to making the life of the teacher a hard one.

It is odd that this security motive does not usually suffice to make the teacher accumulate extensive savings. For it is generally thought that the savings of teachers do not equal those of business persons in the same income-group. It is quite certain that the savings of teachers are rarely adequate. The high standard of living of the teacher, who has usually travelled a bit further and seen more than the business man of similar income, and the long summer vacation, with its temptation to spend what has been accumulated in the winter, appear to be a basic part of the explanation of the failure of teachers to save. Besides, the check will always be waiting on the first of the month, if only one does not endanger it by unusual doings or unconventional teachings. It is the conduct, then, and not the expenditure, which is controlled. Teachers are crucified between the desire to be safe and the standard of living.

Some observers have spoken of a certain habit of impersonality which grows upon teachers and finally shuts them off from all the subtler kinds of personal interchange with their fellows. In addition to certain things which we have already considered, the fact that the teacher must produce results in human materials conduces strongly to this habit of impersonality. This is an essential of the peculiar distance between teacher and student, that the student is at best material in which the teacher works, at worst, a means for the attainment of the teacher's personal ends. A similar but separate split of the teacher's personality arises because the teacher is forced to say over and over things so elementary that they have no interest for him and so many times repeated that they have lost what meaning they once had. Part of him must serve as an animated phonograph while another part stands aside and jeers. He must inhibit the normal mental processes of the adult in order to think as a child and speak as a child; it follows inevitably that he is shut out from both worlds. If Thornton Wilder had never been a school master he could not have known that it is a luxury to speak out of one's whole mind. Extreme introverts, because of their tendency to speak from the whole mind or not at all, make poor teachers. An additional cause of impersonality, and of unpleasantly toned impersonality, inheres in the fact that the teacher is rarely on good terms with all his students at the same time. As his eye runs over the class he sees two or three particularly interested students and a much larger number of persons who are at best apathetic. Always there are sore spots in the class, and although the teacher averts his gaze from these they still produce an effect upon his attitude. There is Laura Baker; she has always looked a bit disdainfully at him. There is Stanley Brown, who still resents his failing grade in the last examination. There is George Adams, whom only yesterday it was necessary to send from class. Rosie Allen is going to flunk the course; she sits and glares and does not understand. All failing students are potential enemies. And Johnny Jukes, deficient in gray matter and short of food, is a constant worry in the classroom. It will be well to be wary, to watch, watch, watch. One must guard one's behavior in this group.

We have spoken of certain situational necessities which mold the teacher, of the rôles which these situational imperatives impose upon him, and of the enduring effect of these rôles upon personality. It remains to consider in a connected way traumatic learning as a determinant of the occupational type, the effect of shock upon the teacher personality. What we have in mind is that learning which takes place under terrific penalties, and in which the learner is subject to shock if he makes the wrong choices. The pathological effects of shock have been investigated frequently, but these effects have rarely been discussed as learning, nor have they ever been treated in their proper relation to the social organization. Yet, in that learning which involves modification of personality, shock often plays a dominant rôle, and the giving of shocks is one of the principal means by which the social group tailors persons to its specifications. Traumatic learning is therefore important in both sociology and psychology.

This kind of learning is not easily separable from other sorts of learning, and still it has characteristics which seem to justify a distinction. Traumatic learning is continuous with habit formation, being, perhaps, a special instance of the law of effect; the use of slight penalties is also a common incident of laboratory procedure. Traumatic learning is continuous with the normal molding of personality by social conditioning, and we have already discussed minor shocks which mold the teacher's personality. Traumatic learning is continuous with the modification of personality in crisis situations, but represents the reaction of personality to the most sudden and extreme crises. We are justified in regarding traumatic learning as different from ordinary learning because radical differences appear between reactions to slight shocks and reactions to severe shocks. The psychological and psychopathological effects of shock have indeed been investigated, but their meaning in terms of personality and social organization has perhaps not been sufficiently pointed out.

For the teacher, traumatic experiences usually concern the loss of his position, especially the sudden and unforeseen loss of his position. The loss of control over a class may be traumatic in its effect, and so may a quarrel with a colleague. Various minor shocks arise, and we shall need to reconsider all that we have said concerning the molding of personality by the teaching situation in the light of the new insight furnished by the concept of traumatic learning. Individuals, of course, differ greatly in their ability to assimilate shocks without damage to their personalities.

These shocks which teachers experience may induce light dissociation, more pronounced in persons of hysteric constitution, and associated with a tendency to repeat the traumatic experience in a manner akin to that of the war neuroses. The dissociation very likely prolongs and exacerbates the conflict, since it prevents the individual from facing it and reacting to it, but allows the conflict to produce effects indirectly. Whatever the ultimate adjustment, the mind dwells upon such crises a long time, relives them incessantly for months and even years, elaborates reactions to them without end. Usually, a curiously bifurcated adjustment appears. On the one hand, the individual refuses to accept the responsibility for the shocking event and that part of his behavior which led up to it. He multiplies rationalizations to the same end: "It wasn't my fault," "The circumstances were most unusual," "I was the goat," etc. This is often attended by a conscious or unconscious refusal to evaluate the situation correctly, the face-saving rationalizations demanding that the realization of responsibility be shut from consciousness. On the other hand, the individual behaves as if he accepted responsibility completely, something which he does not find at all inconsistent with his conscious insistence that it was not his fault. He multiplies precautions to prevent the recurrence of the unfortunate event, taking an almost obsessive interest in the protection of that which previously was threatened. This, of course, represents the reaction to the other side of the ambivalence. Likewise, an individual may insist that in a certain collapse of his social world he has lost no status, the while he indulges in no end of behavior which can only be interpreted as compensatory for that loss of status. Much of the ruthlessness of teachers toward students is in the nature of compensation for fears traceable to traumatic discipline experiences.

As a result of shocks, too, there appear effects nearly analogous to the specific conditioning of the behaviorists, behavior mechanisms which are very little dependent upon broader associative contexts and which therefore tend to be set off in quite incongruous circumstances if the specific stimulus is presented. Soldiers acquire certain positive behavior patterns which may be set off whenever the stimulus sound is heard. Teachers come likewise to react violently to specific stimuli. A teacher once found on his desk a note from his principal asking him to call at the office the next morning. He called at the office, and was summarily dismissed. Thereafter he experienced acute fear whenever he received a request to call at the office of a school superior, and this reaction did not rapidly suffer attrition in spite of the fact that his behavior did not again expose him to attack.

Conversion, as a sudden change of the working organization of attitudes in personality, may result from a single shocking experience. Traumatic experiences redefine situations. Where this occurs, it is probably correct to speak of it as a change of the dominant attitude; it is likely to take the form of transposition of opposed sides of an ambivalence. Trauma may result in a complete reversal of moral codes or in radical change of policy; such tergiversation is common among teachers who suffer shocks by reason of being kind to students. Conversion usually involves a change of group allegiance.

Most likely to be subject to the cruder types of traumatic learning are ego-centric persons, and other maladjusts of non-conforming type. These persons either fail to observe social necessities, or feel capable of overriding them, and they suffer the consequences. Some persons are completely demoralized by these consequences, and if those consequences are so severe as to entail a collapse of the social world, they usually have most serious results. Undesirable personality traits are in most cases exaggerated rather than remedied by traumatic experiences; these are unusually distressing experiences, and they fall precisely upon the persons least capable of assimilating them. The lunatic fringe of teaching, every year sloughed off and every year renewed, is made up of personalities battered by many trauma.

A minor sort of traumatic learning results from the effect of conflict upon the system of values. Points in one's scheme of life which must be sharply defended come to assume a disproportionate importance. Recurrent crises in the teacher's life, such as inter-departmental squabbles, constellate a temporary organization of personality around the values then to be defended from attack. This temporary organization leaves traces in the nervous system, and as a result of the traces this fighting organization is more easily called into play the next time; the traces may indeed grow so great as to set the tone of the personality. That for which men must often fight is dear to them. This mechanism is very important in the life of the school teacher. The experienced teacher fights harder for discipline than does the novice, and he begins to fight a great deal more readily. The head of the department fights for the privileges of his department much more valiantly than instructors, and has a keener nose for sniffing out conspiracies. In all this the person who has studied the social psychology of conflict groups will find nothing startling or new.

The analysis of dreams is an excellent technique for uncovering the tension points existing within the life-situation of the individual. The dreams of teachers, then, ought to show where the points of stress and strain appear in the school situation as it affects the teacher. Particularly is this true of recurrent dreams, or of similar dreams of different teachers. Any thorough research into this topic would demand that we examine the entire dream life of a number of teachers, but we have chosen to consider here only some highly typical dreams concerning the school situation. Following is the recurrent dream of a male teacher of twenty-six. He has an excellent reputation as a disciplinarian, and has succeeded with some difficult schools.

The record of the dream follows:

Each year as the horrid conflict of the first month was going on and the feeling against me was considerable and bitter, I would have a dream. It ran as follows:

It is morning. The nine o'clock bell calling the school formally to attention has not rung yet. Part of the pupils are in the school building visiting and playing; others are outside doing likewise. All is going nicely. I bend intently over my work at the desk for several minutes.

Finally a noise in the room draws my attention. Annoyed, I look up quickly. To my surprise a big boy is scuffling with a smaller one. I loudly command them to stop. They do, but reluctantly. About that time some girls start running noisily up and down the aisles. This on top of the scuffling is too much. I tell them to take their seats. They do, but I can see by their faces that they have a notion not to. There is rebellion in the air. By this time the boys in the corner are throwing books at each other. I am amazed. Why, what ails them? Throwing things inside is strictly against the rules. And these boys are usually so docile. But there is Alfred Davis among them, and he is a very mischievous boy and antagonistic towards me. And it was Bernice Keller, ever slow to mind, who led the girls in their racing among the seats. I shout at the boys. They do not heed me. I bawl them out and remark that if they can't find anything better to do they had better wash the blackboards for me. They interpret the remark in the imperative mode, which is correct, and scowling and muttering begin the task.

There is a commotion on the playground. From the window I see the boys fighting over a swing. I go out. They do not stop as I approach. I speak to them. I cuff them. They pay no attention. I am aghast. *Neither look, nor speech, nor action, nor presence of the teacher avails.* I note some girls running back and forth across the street in front of the passing automobiles. I call to them, but in vain. Wrathfully I start toward the street. The girls run away down the street. I am no child; I will not run after them. Baffled I ring the school bell. It is past nine o'clock anyhow.

Inside pandemonium reigns. The girls whom I left in their seats are dashing about the room upsetting the loose furniture. The boys at the blackboards are pelting each other with chalk and erasers. They pelt me as I appear. I charge upon them. They elude me. This is terrible, *terrible*!

But where are the boys and girls from outdoors? Why do they not come in? Did they not hear the bell? The boys have stopped fighting and are standing looking sullenly at the building. What shall I do? What can I do? They heed neither teacher nor bell. I attempt to expel them. They will not go home. The girls are standing tantalizingly across the street. I shall take it up with the school board. They laugh at me. They even scorn the board! Then I shall settle this thing by force. I go inside to get a club. They follow me in. The sight of the club quiets them somewhat. They all take their seats.

I preach to them. Smirkingly they listen. We start the lessons, but the conflict reasserts itself everywhere. I leave the desk and the club to help a student whose hand is raised. In the other end of the room a titter arises and increases in volume. Aha! So they're at it again. I seize the club. A few blows restore order. But it is no use. No matter where I turn the club must be used. Nor can I use it fast enough to be effective, to keep order. I shall have to call in the board. I have failed! But no, I will not fail! I redouble my efforts. The students begin breaking up desks and tearing down casements so that they too may have clubs. I seek refuge behind my desk and pound upon it for order. They ignore the act. The whole school gathers itself to rush upon me with clubs. Pale with fear, I square myself for the finish. They start . . . but never reach me because I awake, cold with sweat. Parts of the dream and the faces appear and fade away in the darkness before my eyes. I recall a few pupils—good students, "teacher's pets," friends of mine outside of school, or students with whom my associations in school have been close, who took no part. Vernon Hart, Lucille Ollinger, Harold Childers, and Oscar Olson had nothing to do with it. They stood off in the corners and at the edges staring without expression. They were neutral. They favored neither side. God bless them! I must be better to them in the future. The dream is still real. I begin to plan what I shall do tomorrow to get even with them and to restore order. I excuse myself for letting such a thing get started. I wasn't feeling well, my head ached so, or this would never have happened. Well, if I can't control them, I'll just disappear, I'll skip the country.

Then I become fully conscious. I wonder what I really would do if such a thing should happen. I resolve not to rule with quite such an iron hand. Well, if it ever does happen, they'll never see me again. And thus for an hour or so until I fall asleep again. The dream, however, haunts me for several days.

During my first year of teaching, when this dream came, it frightened me. I thought it must be a bad sign. But nothing of the kind ever happened. Only one little red-haired chap even so much as dared to talk back to me that year. And at the end of the term I was asked to return at an increase in salary; and so in the years of teaching after that I looked upon this dream, when it came, as a good omen, as a portent that the year would be a successful one. (Autobiographical document.)

This dream apparently reveals a fear, grounded in an inferiority complex of long standing, that the situation may get out of control. It is a fear which the teacher refuses to face in his waking hours, so that it is forced to come out in the dream. But it is deeply grounded in his mental life, for the dream, identical in all details, recurs yearly. The energy and activity, as well as the strict discipline of this teacher, may be interpreted as compensation for this underlying fear, and for the inferiority complex which it bespeaks. It is interesting to note that the customary social alignments of the classroom, relations of conflict, alliance, neutrality, etc., had impressed themselves so strongly upon this teacher's mind that the awareness of them was not dimmed in the dream.

The account of this dream was read to a class in Educational Sociology, and the approximate interpretation given above was indicated as accounting for the origin of the dream. On the following day another young man in the class presented the following dream:

'Twas the opening day of the fall term. My good resolutions were to the fore, and I was determined to execute some of the ideas gained during the summer. Chief of them was that I would be masterful as well as understandingly human. The method in which all work was to be done and when had been carefully predetermined.

Of course a good beginning was desirable and an assured means of starting the school in the proper manner. No one should be given permission to speak, nor to leave their seats. The slightest whimper from the newly arrived freshmen would be frowned upon in my most ferocious manner. And as for the new seniors—well, as Juniors they had behaved quite according as their name indicated, but things were going to be different this year.

I had hoped that I would not be troubled with before-school assembly duty as I had been the year before, but evidently the pleasure was still mine. During the period before the nine o'clock bell rang quite a few of the "also-go-to-school" type had entered and seated themselves with evident pleasure at the reopening of school.

Then the bell *rang*.

No delay on the part of the students to respond to the assembly summons. They came pouring in like a herd of excited cattle. As the tardy bell sounded I suggested in a very sarcastic tone, "The summer vacation is a thing of the past. So, if you dear young things will remember that you are again in school and quiet down I shall make a few announcements."

As I had started speaking the magic of my voice had brought about an abrupt silence. But as my tone indicated a period, bedlam broke loose. A general war whoop seemed to come from the throats of every member of the assembly, and seemingly with a fine disregard for my presence each and all began to do as they pleased.

Before I could determine the course to be pursued the infernal disturbance aroused me from slumber.

This dream, less meaningful than the previous one, apparently presents and rejects a solution which this young man has been working out for his teaching problem, that is, his resolution to be masterful. Its occurrence at that particular time was undoubtedly due to the strong suggestion of the day before, but that does not entirely destroy the significance of the dream, for it would be very difficult to get such a dream by such a low degree of suggestion in one who did not already have a predisposition toward it. We are probably justified in saying that the procedure of the day before merely touched off a complex and that the dream is the result. This young man, who characterized himself at another time, rather too unkindly, as "a windy extrovert,'' represents a type, with diffuse and friendly, almost breezy, social expression, which comes very slowly into conformity with the teaching attitude. After a year of none too successful teaching experience, he has reached the point where he resolves to be masterful. How fear-ridden and unstable such a desire is when it first appears seems to come out pretty well from this document. The dream is also very enlightening as an indication of what behavior this young man regarded as ''masterful.''

Subsequent inquiry revealed that the analysis of dreams was potentially of great assistance in interpreting the impact of the teaching situation upon the teacher's personality. Nearly every teacher approached, some in the most casual way, had one or more dreams to contribute, and the list of dreams soon grew to several dozen. Few teachers returned an entirely negative report. There were included in the list, of course, only undisguised teaching dreams, and this means that only the simpler sort of problem was revealed by them. Since thorough analysis of all these dreams was not possible, it seemed best to adopt for all only the simplest and most objective type of interpretation. The underlying assumption was that the dream pointed to something which the teacher did not ordinarily face in his conscious life. Thus these dreams represented repetitions of traumatic experiences, statements of problems, and, perhaps, of solutions, expressions of repressed fears, of worries, wish-fulfillment mechanisms, and the like. We are well aware that more exhaustive analysis by more subjective methods would have revealed a great deal more, but it would so have broadened the scope of the inquiry that it did not seem possible to carry it out. A summary of these materials is presented herewith.

The discipline dream was found to be exceedingly common. It was frequently stereotyped and recurrent. It was protean in its forms. In several cases, it recurred months or even years after the individual quit teaching.

Supervision dreams ranked next in order of frequency. Typical of these was the following:

> I had this dream while I was doing my practice teaching in Richmond the past summer. I might say that I was teaching Ancient History, a subject I had never studied even in high school. Also that I had a particular horror for the supervisor.
>
> The night I had this dream I had gone to bed early without preparing my lessons and had set the alarm in order to get up early the next morning and do it. I dreamed that the alarm had not gone off and that I awoke just

in time to get to school—totally unprepared. I went to my class and decided to give them a study period for fifteen minutes in which I also could prepare the lesson. I had no more than made this decision when in walked the supervisor. I was panic stricken. I opened my book and desperately tried to read a few sentences so that I could ask some questions. I started asking questions that had nothing to do with Ancient History. The supervisor listened for a few minutes and then got up and with a look of scorn started teaching the class herself. I awoke.

Needless to say the affective tone of this dream was most unpleasant.

These supervision dreams were apparently expressions of lightly repressed fears or worries. The situation in which the dreamer was caught in some unethical or tabooed behavior frequently recurred. One man dreamed that his supervisor caught him talking disparagingly about America's entry into the war, and politely reproved him. Another dreamed that two supervisors caught him at a dance with a high-school girl. Others dreamed of detection in lateness to class. These dreams show that supervision can be an important source of strain.

Unpunctuality, interpretable in some cases as wish-fulfillment through the avoidance of teaching, and in others as simple fear, recurred as a feature of quite a number of dreams. In several cases it was complicated by the dreamer's losing his way while going to class; this was always associated with some unusual source of unpleasantness in the teaching situation. The fear dreams also reveal the perfection of the social mechanism by which the threat of classroom disorder enforces punctuality upon the teacher.

Some communication dreams occurred. These revealed the strain upon the teacher of trying to communicate, the nearly impassable barriers set up by the difficulties of language and the breakdown of configurations in communication, a feeling of the uselessness of talk. This is a significant clue to the teacher mind.

Another rather common type of dream represented the teacher as "losing the place" in the text, or unable to "find the place." In one case this was recurrent. It represented, apparently, an unacknowledged fear.

There was one clearly defined executive dream, representing the worry of a school head over the adequacy of supplies and facilities. Interestingly enough, it was still recalled some thirty years after the informant left the profession. There were other dreams which might have been similarly interpreted.

The following dream situations are represented by single examples:

an argument over a grade, going out with a high-school girl, a homosexual dream, a stern attempt to be fair to all students, and deafness (representing a fear of going deaf). Numerous dreams showed rivalry with colleagues, rebellion against executives, or fear of losing one's position.

The author believes that this merely scratches the surface of this subject, and that extended study of teacher dreams involving more subjective techniques, more exhaustive analysis of each dream, and greater penetration into the dreamer's personality, may prove very rewarding in the future. Even the present list of teacher dreams, interpreted most superficially, seems to point to important sources of stress and strain in the teaching situation. An investigator will need to exercise care in evaluating the influence of suggestion, for it has been demonstrated repeatedly that both the form and content of dreams are easily subject to this influence.

The phantasy life of school teachers also gives some interesting clues to the nature of the adjustment they have made to their occupation. These phantasies are sometimes purely compensatory, being unrelated in subject matter to the life of the teacher in the school; the classic example of this is the very common case of the teacher of English mooning about breaking into the *Atlantic* as he corrects examination papers. Those plans which so many teachers have of going into some other occupation which will bring them into the heat and dust of the market place, and into the spotlight of publicity, must be regarded as in this class also, for they are rarely more earnest, and almost never any better adjusted to reality. Many of the phantasies of teachers, however, concern the daily problems of the classroom. There is a troublesome boy whom the teacher daydreams of putting in his place, but whom he never does put in his place. Or there is a fellow teacher who presumes too much upon good nature; the teacher may have long phantasies in which he bests this colleague in a battle of words, but the two may never come to words. Sometimes teachers endowed with less than mediocre literary ability start to write, and when they write their hero so closely resembles themselves that the wish-fulfilling character of the writing is more than obvious. There was the sex-starved teacher who had unrealizable dreams of a lovely young thing who would be exceedingly thrilled by himself; he wrote numerous short stories in which this same theme was repeated: a young man of his age and personal characteristics met a girl in her teens; soon there arose between them a perfect understanding. The episodes and the dialogue, in this case, were often identical from story to story. Another man, a failure in teaching because of his inadequate personality and extreme shortness of stature, made his hero an army officer of very small size, and caused this hero to triumph over all kinds of opposition and persecution. Similar to these self-determined phantasies are the books that the teacher reads, for one obtains phantasy gratification in that way, too. It would be very difficult, however, to trace a pattern in these.

Concerning the sex tensions of teachers, especially women, a great deal has been said and some few things have been written. Amateurs in psychiatry have been free with diagnoses. It is true that the choice of teaching as a career condemns many women to remain unmarried, and that the moral order coils so tightly about the woman teacher that even legitimate courtship is often out of the question. But there is not, apparently, a one to one correspondence between spinsterhood and that nervous, wracked unhappiness which the amateur psychiatrists say attacks the teacher because she is unmarried. The life history of the unmarried teacher seems to follow, a pretty definite pattern. There are a number of years in which the hope of finding a mate is not relinquished. There is a critical period when that hope dies. An informant has suggested that hope has died when a woman buys a diamond for herself. The critical period is an incubation period during which spinsterhood ripens. During this critical period many desperate and pathetic things occur. The woman going through this period falls in love very easily, and may come to make the most open advances upon slight or no provocation. The attentions of a lover being absent, the most perfunctory civility may be magnified to that size, and distorted to fit that configuration. Hence arise deep plots to trick the doctor or the dentist into a declaration. Hence, too, pitiful misinterpretations of the most commonplace remarks. It is a period of the most intense conflicts, and no way of solving the problem is left unthought of; these dignified women sometimes attempt, pathetic to record, to learn the technique of sex lure from the twenty-year-olds of their acquaintance. Perhaps this hope of finding a mate always dies hard and slowly, and requires little stimulant to keep it alive after its time.

The adjustment in which the spinster stabilizes after this critical period tends to be final. Several forms are common. There is the discontented misanthropy of the woman who is bitter because the male sex has passed her by. There is the split-off, phantastic love life of the woman who preserves her susceptibility, perhaps her hope, to an advanced age. There is the sweetly resigned attitude of the woman who accepts celibacy and arranges her life on that basis; this adjustment is easier if the individual is able to live with her own family or with close relatives who have a strong family life which includes her. There is the "bachelor-girl" adjustment, carried off with different degrees of success, and with more or less attendant conflict. There is the adjustment of the teacher who achieves vicarious fulfillment in her students. There is homosexuality, both that which is deeply ingrained and that which is *faute de mieux*, and numerous other adjustments of a pathological nature.

It is true that male values are lacking in the universe in which spinsters live, and that this lack is sometimes sadly obvious. It is a peculiarity of some of these maiden teachers, a peculiarity which has been observed in several widely separated groups, in order to relieve the loneliness of their lives, to give names to inanimate objects. They populate the universe by naming the things about them, especially those articles which are in daily use and may be thought to have something of a character of their own. Thus a car is John, an ashtray Mr. Johnson, a fountain-pen Mr. Wright, and so on. It is significant that most of these names are male. The sex starvation, and its attendant isolation from the procession of the generations, are there, and they materially affect the adjustment of maiden teachers to the teaching profession. Yet it is doubtful whether one can advance his explanation very much by following out this line. Spinster teachers sometimes present a sorry picture and one rightly diagnosed as a picture of frustration. But, then, so do the men who teach; and men teachers are free to marry. It is something in the teaching itself, or something in the life of the teacher, which frustrates. No doubt the sex thwarts of spinsters have some effect upon their personalities, but it is an effect which takes the form of an enhancement of a personality distortion produced otherwise. The woman teacher, furthermore, but for the personal thwarting implicit in the necessity of institutionalized domination, is in a very favorable position, associated, as she is, with many children, to work out a satisfactory sublimation of her sexual life. The major lines of her personality difficulty, therefore, have their causation in the social situations which her profession imposes upon her.

CHAPTER XXIII

TEACHER TYPES; THE TEACHER STEREOTYPE, ETC.

IT WOULD be incorrect to assume that teaching inevitably develops the same character traits in all teachers. The adjustments of personality which different teachers make to the conditions of school life differ as radically as the personalities of those who enter teaching. There are all kinds of teachers. There are "natural born teachers," and made teachers, and different classes of each. "Natural teachers," apparently include both those whose enthusiasm enables them to muddle through in spite of mistakes and those who, by virtue of ballast and inhibitions, make no mistakes. There are problem teachers, persons with definite twists to their personalities, whose adjustment takes them far from contact with reality. There are teachers who come into close but entirely negative contact with reality, and others, just as realistically minded, whose general orientation is positive. And there are both positive and negative orientations in the flight from reality. Especially is it true that there are several kinds of good teachers. Techniques, too, and this is a point of the very first importance, must differ with different personalities.

Two teachers who seem to have been at the opposite poles of teaching technique but were both remarkably successful have been described by Edward Eggleston. We quote his description:

Probably no two teachers of equal ability were ever associated who were more unlike in the constitution of their minds, and who conducted a recitation in modes more dissimilar, than Judge Story and Professor Greenleaf. The latter, the beau ideal of the lawyer in his physique, was severe and searching in the classroom, probing the student to the quick, accepting no half answers or vague general statements for accurate replies, showing no mercy to laziness, and when he commented on the text, it was always in the fewest, pithiest words that would convey the ideas. Language in his mouth seemed to have proclaimed a sumptuary law forbidding that it should in any case overstep the limits of thought. Indolent students who had skimmed over the lesson dreaded his scrutiny, for they knew that an examination by him was a literal weighing of their knowledge—and that they could impose upon him by no shams. Judge Story's forte, on the other hand, was in lecturing, not in questioning, in the communication of information, not in ascertaining the exact sum of the pupil's knowledge. In most cases, his questions were put in such a way as to suggest the answer. For example, having stated two modes of legal procedure under certain circumstances, he would ask the student; "Would you adopt the former course or would you *rather* adopt the latter?" "I would rather adopt the latter," the student would reply, who perhaps had not looked at the lesson. "You are right," would be the comment of the kind-hearted Dane professor; "Lord Mansfield himself could not have answered more correctly." Whether he was too good-natured to put the students on the rack, or thought the time might be more profitably spent, we know not; but no one feared to recite because he was utterly ignorant of the lesson. The manner of the judge, when lecturing, was that of an enthusiast rather than of a professional teacher. . . . He had that rare gift, the faculty of communicating, and loved, above all things, to communicate knowledge."[1]

Judge Story had other qualities which also fitted into this pattern, as Eggleston described him. He suffered fools gladly, and was never out of patience with the slow or the uncomprehending. And the text, for him, was not the sum and substance of knowledge, but something to be used as a point of departure for instructive excursions. He taught unsystematically, one judges, but he put all of himself into his teaching.

One wonders what would happen to a man like Judge Story if he were forced to uphold the academic standards in the conventional way or lose his means of livelihood. One wonders how his type of teaching would stand the goose-step of a large school machine. Unquestionably the best and happiest teachers, and those whose instruction is longest remembered, belong to his type, but it seems certain that such a teacher would lose his effectiveness if he were not free. Such persons need to be judged less harshly by those who conform to the more usual teaching pattern, for it is very difficult for them to canalize their teaching without the loss of all the values inherent in it. There seem to be two opposite techniques of instruction, and it seems that they conform to personality types at opposite poles. There is the technique of formal and carefully delimited drill and recitation; this is the customary pattern of teaching. Then there is the technique of improvisation by teacher and class. The technique of formal drill puts subject matter first, and makes of it the dominant value. It is most effective for the communication of facts. But the technique of improvisation is one which involves both teacher and class in a free and moving interaction, and puts the interchange of per-

[1] Eggleston, Edward, In *Hours With Men and Books*, ed. by Wm. Matthews. (Reprinted by permission of Scott, Foresman and Company.)

sonalities before the values of subject matter. In the formal class the involvement of personalities is a very limited one; there is a tendency for both personalities and interests to shrink. In the informal class, interest in kindled, and whatever is learned is attended to most positively. To be in Judge Story's class must have been a constructive experience, and it may often have been an experience that was very important in the subsequent growth of personality. The technique illustrated by Judge Story is best adapted for the passing on of attitudes and the kindling of interest, perhaps for the awakening of the desire to ponder things and the development of understanding that goes with pondering. It is possible to think of those two contrasting adjustments of personality as characteristic of introversion and extroversion. The introverted teacher reacts in class according to plan and very objectively; he is not at his best in the extemporaneous sort of instruction because it takes him too long to think things through and he must think them through too thoroughly before answering, and therefore he is slow of speech. The extroverted teacher reacts enthusiastically and diffusely; he wears a subject out very quickly and passes easily to another, and therefore the textbook is no anchoring point for him, but the starting point of an excursion.

But there are other points of distinction between these contrasting personalities which the categories of introversion and extroversion do not wholly explain. An introvert who suffers fools as gladly as Judge Story may maintain as favorable a feeling tone with his students. And the immunity which Judge Story had for most of the occupational traits we have discussed depends in part upon group alignments and ego-gratifying devices which enable one to avoid taking hurt when his students do not prepare lessons diligently for him. (Judge Story had gained enviable recognition elsewhere.) The entirely pleasant reaction of such persons to teaching may depend upon a selective pattern in consciousness which enables them to overlook unpleasant things and to forget at once those which impose themselves upon attention. This does not always correspond to the extroverted character. Some extroverts are not wise enough to educate as Judge Story did, and must undergo painful self-discipline to confine their thoughts within reasonable bounds. Some other extroverts are competent but not free, and they are likely if restricted to take a very destructive attitude toward their work. One's willingness to conform is another factor of importance in determining what attitude one will take toward teaching and what configuration of traits teaching will develop in him. The person who accepts the world as it is (usually the extrovert, by the way) develops the more favorable set of qualities; the non-conformist tends to develop a different personality picture. Most teachers represent mixed rather than pure types.

The adjustment of personality to teaching differs according to the grade of teaching and the subject taught. Teachers of home economics, shop-work, and the practical subjects develop the occupational traits little because they are not put into the ordinary classroom situation and do not suffer so much from the strain of giving unwanted instruction. It is said that "the classics make teachers"; if so, it is the necessity of drill and the strain of instructing that bring it about. English teachers have special problems and develop special adjustments to them; it is perhaps more difficult for a teacher of English to take leave of his rôle than for any other teacher. (A realization of the pressure constantly upon them was probably what prompted a group of English teachers at a conference in Missouri to sing a song asserting "We ain't prissy, we ain't prim.") Intellectual racketeers, persons who teach non-existent subjects, subjects which cannot be taught, or subjects which they themselves do not understand, must develop special techniques and special adjustments of personality. (They frequently take refuge in pomposity, verbosity, temperament, etc.) The personality adjustments of teachers and administrators differ somewhat. Administrative posts, with their long hours and their immense amount of detail, appear to make for a falling off in mental content and a deterioration in its quality, but this is probably more than compensated for by a broader range of human contacts. The small-town superintendent of schools is forced to conform to a more rigid pattern than are other teachers, and he is correspondingly biased. Teachers are supposed to develop the teaching personality more rapidly in private schools than in public, especially if the private schools are of the boarding variety; this is because they have fewer opportunities to take leave of their rôle. There are vast differences between the personalities of teachers regarded as successful and those of teachers who are not successful.

The minds of those in different occupations work upon different materials, and the content of thought differs much from one profession to another. Yet mental processes are transposable, and tend to reproduce themselves in every walk of life. There are careers everywhere, rewards, rivals, "politics," right and wrong ways of doing things. One "makes good" even in prison. The product of the working of the mind upon the conditions of life has been called the life organization.[1] The occupational life-organization is an important determiner of the occupational type. The life organization of the rural school teacher is well brought out in the following document:

Mr. Wise was attending the summer session of a midwestern university. He must have a few more hours of college credit in methods of teaching so that he could qualify for a better teaching position. Yes, Mr. Wise was a school teacher. Oh, not so much the school teacher as some school teachers were, but nevertheless a school teacher. He had already had three years of successful experience and was a junior in college and he was, therefore, not only a practical school man but also a professional school man—acquainted not only with the actual but also with the theoretical phases of education.

And this summer-school attendance was quite an important part of the school-teaching game. You got a teacher's certificate as soon as you could after graduation from high school. Then you got a teaching position. It might not be much of a position—out in a one-teacher rural grade school near Podunk—but you got a position, and then you had experience. *Experience*—that was the main thing, that was the magic word, that was the key which unlocked the door to a hundred good jobs. So the teachers' agencies and the normal-school professors told you, anyway.

Well, you got the job and you taught through the year. You went to summer school in the summer. Eventually you got a better certificate. Then you secured a position in a small town. Ah, teaching in town! How you had waited for that moment! You went to summer school some more. You became a principal—perhaps a high-school principal! You took in a few more summer sessions. You got a degree! Then you went out in the field as a small-town superintendent. But you mustn't be satisfied with this. You *must* have a master's degree. So you took a year off or attended a few more summer sessions and you received a *master's*. As a reward for your labors, you were taken into a large school system. Thus you went through college easily—without learning much perhaps but without much inconvenience to yourself. And you were allowed to place an imposing string of letters after your name to impress people with, especially school boards, high-school students, and other persons just like yourself. And thus you became established—*you were fixed for life!* Oh, you might, if you played your cards right, get into a school where so many years of service netted you a retirement pension. Or you might, if you were politician enough, become an

[1] Park says of life organization: "It is this intellectual element that is represented specifically in the life-organization. One might perhaps express the notion by saying that the individual has a conception of himself, and that this conception of himself and his role in society is an integral part of his personality." (Park, Robert E., "The Sociological Methods of William Graham Sumner and of William I. Thomas and Florian Znaniecki," p. 170, *Methods in Social Science*, edited by Stuart A. Rice, University of Chicago Press, Chicago, 1931.)

instructor in a teachers college. But anyway you were "pretty much on top of the world" when you got your master's degree.

Thus ran what Mr. Wise called his vision. (Unpublished manuscript, *The School Teacher in a Restaurant,* Kenneth McGill.)

Summer school, hours of education, qualifications, recommendations, successful experience, professional training, "politics," certificates, advancement to a larger town, teachers' agencies—how familiar all these to every experienced teacher! How thoroughly does the teacher's mind become habituated to the universe in which these are the values! This document calls up also numerous questions concerning the larger organization of the profession.

Those who follow certain occupations play out the rôles which go with it rather consistently. Other persons come to think of these rôles as characterizing the occupation, and when they think of the one they think of the other. Experience of persons playing those rôles leaves residua in the form of imagined constructs relating to the appearance or behavior of persons falling within certain occupational categories. These imagined constructs are stereotypes. When a stereotype has been organized out of the community experience of persons belonging to certain occupational groups and consistently playing out certain rôles that go with it, the members of the community tend to organize all experience of the persons in such an occupation in terms of the existent stereotype; they have a low perceptual threshold for behavior conforming to the stereotype, and a high threshold for facts which argue against the correctness of the stereotype. A stereotype, once established, reenforces itself; it proves its own correctness by arguing in a perfect circle. When a stereotype has once become current, it may be passed from one individual to another by social contagion, and it tends to distort the first naïve experience of new members with persons belonging to the group included in the stereotype. Stereotypes are predominantly visual. Lippmann has aptly called them "pictures in our heads." Some stereotypes have the form of very definite visual images; others merely represent types which we can recognize but not reproduce.

Much of social interaction rests upon stereotypes. The interaction of intimates largely escapes the influence of the stereotype, and so does naïve experience for which no model exists in one's social world. But a very wide range of social interchange is affected by the presence of more or less definite stereotypes, sometimes stereotypes which have currency in an entire group (this is the best use of the term) and sometimes constructs of our own relating to particular persons or classes of persons. This is possible because in many kinds of relations we do not respond to another person directly, but always to a more or less veracious construct of him in our own minds. Certain consequences follow; one of the more important is that an individual's behavior in our presence is no criterion of his behavior in the presence of others, no matter how stabilized his behavior in our presence (unless we have experienced him fully and with no intervening stereotype, and he has presented to us an equally unbiased segment of himself). The error of generalizing an individual's behavior toward us, limited by the possibilities of behavior which we, reacting to our own imagined construct of him, have offered to him, accounts for many of the surprises of social life and for some of the unexpectedness of human nature. The young man's fiancée, worshipped and idealized by him, is seduced by another in an evening. A gruff employer is rendered human by an unusual approach. Disraeli won over Queen Victoria by treating her as a human being. It seems that people gain who treat others as human beings, neglecting as far as possible the conventional restrictions or stereotyped ideas as to how they ought to be treated. In inferiority-superiority relationships the influence of the stereotype is particularly vicious, for the parties involved almost invariably conclude that because the relationship is stereotyped the person is but an enlargement of the stereotyped relation.

Stuart Rice has devised a technique by which he has been able to demonstrate the existence of stereotypes statistically and to measure their effect in biassing personal judgments. His work was largely with occupational stereotypes, and as such is in point here. An experiment similar to the one first devised by Stuart Rice was worked out by Kenneth McGill[1] in the attempt to investigate the school-teacher stereotype. Ten photographs, posed photographs approximately equal in size, were mounted together on a large piece of cardboard. Five of the photographs were of men and five of women. Of the five women, three were teachers, two of whom had been selected for this experiment because of their supposed conformity to the school-teacher stereotype. They "looked like teachers" to the persons carrying on the experiment, and the point of the experiment was to see whether they would look like teachers to others. These photographs were then presented to small groups of students at the University of Nebraska, and students were asked to identify them as

[1] Cf. McGill, Kenneth, "The School-Teacher Stereotype," *Journal of Educational Sociology*, Vol. 9, June, 1931, pp. 642-651.

to occupation. Students were asked to state a reason for each identification. Extreme care was exercised to eliminate all suggestion as to actual occupations of these individuals. In order to keep conditions uniform, instructions were read to each group.

The experiment gave very positive results. One of the women teachers, selected, be it understood, not for her supposed conformity to an actual occupational type but for her conformity to the prevalent stereotype, was identified as a teacher 86 times out of 138. The other carefully selected photograph was identified as a teacher 69 times out of 137. A table showing these results is included. The teachers were numbers 3, 5, and 9 on the table. The identifications of men are omitted from the table.

TABLE I

Occupation	Number of Photograph and Times Identified in Particular Occupations				
	1	3	5	7	9
Teacher	14	32	86	23	69
Housewife	15	3	4	36	20
Office worker	11	33	11	16	5
Musician	36	3		13	3
Nurse	1	3	15	7	13
Saleswoman	6	16	2	3	3
Actress	12	1		13	1
Singer	18			2	
Student	7	3	1	6	
Painter	4	7		2	2
Business woman		6	1		7
Domestic	2	10	1		
Social worker		4		2	5
Writer	1	4	2	2	
Missionary			6	1	1
Mother		2	1		4
Society woman	2	1		3	
Country woman		1	2		2
Beauty operator		1		2	
Church worker			2		
Lawyer			2		
Librarian			2		
Delinquent	1				
Telephone operator					1
Waitress					1
	130	130	138	131	137

Although a more refined treatment of this material may be possible, it is thought that merely calling attention to the bunching of identifications under headings 5, 7, and 9 should be enough to convince the reader of the existence of a school-teacher stereotype. This is pretty good evidence, too, that there is considerable consistency in these stereotypes, for the heavy allocation of teacher identifications occurred precisely at the places where the experimenters had decided to put it. Those who "looked like teachers" to the persons devising the experiment looked like teachers to those who made the identifications.

Students were also asked to state their reasons for identifying individuals as belonging to particular occupational groups. The reasons for the teacher identifications have been compiled and are given in the following table.

TABLE II

What Suggested Identification	Picture No. 1	3	5	7	9	Times Mentioned
General Facial Expression						
Stern, dignified, reserved	1	2	10	2	5	20
Determined, firm, set	1	2	4	1	7	15
Intelligent, capable	1	1	3	1	2	8
Serious, patient, hopeless		2	2		3	7
Thoughtful, sympathetic, composed	1	2	2	1		6
Prim, trim, neat		1	3	1		5
Studious, instructive		2	3			5
Tired, bored, disgusted			3	1	1	5
Leader-like, forceful, brooks no interference			1		3	4
Nervous, strained	1	1		1		3
Old-maidish			2		1	3
Impersonal, hard		1	1			2
Refined	1			1		2
Ascetic			1			1
Minister-like					1	1
No-one-is-right-but-me			1			1
Turn-rise-pass			1			1
Vinegar drinker			1			1
Specific Facial Expression						
Mouth						
Determined, firm, set		4	6	2	6	18
Stern, stony		2	2		2	6
Strained		1	2		1	4
Kindly, pleasant, understanding		1			1	2
Straight-lipped					1	1
Eyes						
Determined, firm, set		2	3	1	4	10
Piercing, staring		1	2		3	6
Straight-forward		1	1		2	4
Dreamy, impractical	1	1	1			3
Kindly, understanding		1	1		1	3
Strained			1	1	2	4
Oh-I-know-all-the-tricks-look			1			1
Chin						
Squared					3	3

Materials of this sort need to be interpreted most cautiously. There is a great temptation to draw from them conclusions much too sweeping and general. We may say, however, that this experiment demonstrates that one or more persons may select photographs which will be consistently identified by others as conforming to the school-teacher stereotype. The reasons presented for the identifications may be taken as giving some hints as to the qualities or expressions which are considered characteristic of the school-teacher stereotype. It would be erroneous to conclude, however, that these traits are present in the photograph and lead to the identification as a teacher, for it is just as possible, and on psychological grounds a good deal more likely, that the identification came first, and was made because the picture conformed to a general configuration, and that the qualities were perceived after the identification was made. This interpretation is made to seem more plausible by the fact that Rice's work shows that identification in a certain stereotype biases judgment of personal qualities. It is perhaps an essential part of the stereotype that it loses its characteristics when subjected to analysis; the whole is not the same as the sum of its parts. This conclusion is supported by the fact that there is little more concentration of opinion as to the distinguishing traits of those persons who conform to the teacher stereotype than with regard to others; column 5 is about as scattering as columns 1 or 3. The chief significance of Table II, then, is the light it sheds upon the qualities which are projected into the face of the person thought of as a teacher.

On the basis of the same kind of empirical insight that made this experiment possible, one may conclude that there are two different stereotypes of the teacher. The more common one is the one which we have been discussing. It is, as we elsewhere point out, the result of a hostile reworking of the residua of community experience with teachers; it is a caricature. There is another stereotype of the teacher, that of the self-sacrificing, gentle, kindly, self-effacing creature, overworked, underpaid, but never out of patience and always ready to "give freely of her time and money" for school purposes. This is the resultant of a friendly reworking of experience; it is an idealization of the teacher. We should not overlook, however, the part which has been played by opposite types of teachers in determining the form of these stereotypes. Both these stereotypes may be present in the same mind, and may supplement each other in determining the standing of a particular teacher. We may say that this favorable stereotype represents the community idea of what a teacher ought to be, and that the unfavorable one represents the common opinion as to what an actual teacher is. The second stereotype carries those ideals for which the school serves as a convenient repository.

Teachers are forced to remain more or less within the boundaries of behavior set up by these stereotypes. It is an odd thing that behavior contrary to the stereotyped pattern should so easily arouse the moral indignation of the community, but it does.[1] The teacher is imprisoned within the stereotype. Our concern here is not so much with the stereotype as with its effect upon the teacher. From long imprisonment within the stereotype the teacher grows unused to freedom. A certain man taught for some years in a private school where a rule of the institution, supported by a clause in his contract, prevented him from smoking in the presence of students. For some years he resented the rule, but obeyed it as well as possible. At length the rule ceased to gall him. One day he stood talking in front of the school with a friend of his who was in business. His friend offered him a cigarette. He replied, very matter-of-factly, "Not now. Thanks."

"Why?" asked his friend.

"I can't smoke here. There are students here."

"Well, what difference does that make?"

"I can't smoke in the presence of students," said the teacher.

"Well," said the other man, "I'm sure I couldn't ever be a teacher. I couldn't stand the restrictions." But habit had made the teacher unaware of the fact that the rule constituted a restriction. When the teacher has internalized the rules which bind him, he has become truly a teacher. Other professions have other rules, and place different restrictions upon behavior. It is not ours to decide here which restrictions are most important. The point is that a person is not free in any occupation until he has made conformity a part of himself. When conformity is the most natural thing for him, and he conforms without thought, the teacher is free, for freedom is only an optical illusion that results from our inability to see the restrictions that surround us.

But another determinant of the teacher is his attempt to escape from the occupational rôle, his attempt to step out of the stereotype and to affect others as a human being rather than a teacher. Each teacher tries to save some segment of himself from the demands of his profession. A young teacher of Latin bore with some patience the exacting drill of the classroom, and submitted to questions concerning Latin when he was on duty in study hall. But one day an over-enthusiastic, somewhat dull student approached him on the campus, during his off hours, with a request that he listen to

[1] Scandalous things happen in every school administration. In most cases the scandal does not inhere in the teacher's behavior, but in the discrepancy between his behavior and the prevalent stereotype.

a paradigm. He turned upon the student furiously, "Why don't you recite it in class? What do you think I am?" It is plain enough what the student thought he was; he was someone who listened to paradigms, he was an enlargement of the teaching relation. Incidents of the sort could be multiplied. A more kindly man fulfilled all demands made upon himself, anywhere and everywhere, apparently, but hotly resented demands which the community and the school made upon his wife. A commercial teacher, a woman who had been very conscientious and very kind throughout the year, reacted in the summer with some temper to a request of a winter student for her professional opinion; it was not, she explained, the time that she minded, but the attempt to force her back into the teaching rôle.

Not only does the teacher attempt to protect himself from the encroachment of the teaching rôle upon other segments of his personality, but he sometimes strives desperately to break through the stereotype which shuts him off from others and to impress himself upon his fellows as a human being of note. Here the teacher's situation is almost exactly similar to that of the minister; it is in the attempt to escape the stereotype that some preachers have developed into such breezy, virile "he-men." The teacher is talking to a tradesman. The teacher says "Damn." The tradesman is startled, and remarks jokingly, "Why, I'm surprised. That's no way for a school teacher to talk." The teacher tries to get some young friends past the school age to call him by his first name. He does not succeed. One of the young friends remarks, "Why, I'd no sooner call Mr. White by his first name than walk up to my father and tell him a dirty joke." Yet, in this case, the age difference was slight. "I am a human being," is the constant cry of the person imprisoned within the stereotype and attempting to shake it off. But it is a cry that is rarely heard, or rarely understood, or rarely believed. School teachers, like negroes and women, can never quite enter the white man's world, and they must remain partial men, except in the society of others who, like themselves, are outcast. School-teacher prejudice is as difficult a thing to combat as negro prejudice. Not only the teacher, but education itself, suffers from the exclusion of the teacher. Theorists may continue to lament the lop-sidedness and one-sidedness of education, but how can an optical illusion educate a whole boy?

The attitudes of teachers toward their profession are very important determinants of the effect which their profession has upon them. We have already indicated the place of a willingness to conform and a cheerful acceptance of things as they are in bringing about the more positive adjustment to teaching. The fact is, however, that a very large number of teachers are extremely discontented with their profession; this seems especially true of the younger teachers. One young teacher (aged twenty-six) told of the attitudes of himself and his friends as follows: "Every summer when you come back to summer school after a winter of teaching you see your old friends and go through the same ceremony of explaining why you are still teaching. Each one tells of flattering offers that he has had to go into business but explains that he can't make quite as much at the start in business so he has decided to teach another year and save his money. Each one ends by saying, 'Well, I thought I'd teach another year, but I'm pretty sure that another year will find me doing something else.' Sometimes hints are dropped about splendid opportunities one is hoping to take up—usually based upon circulars from life insurance companies. But every year it's the same old story." But the low starting salaries of business, and the fact that the teacher is beginning to work up in teaching, make it very difficult for these young teachers actually to carry their plans through.

Teachers make a determined fight, sometimes, against becoming teachers. The younger ones are horrified at the thought that if they go on teaching they may become like their elder colleagues. The cynical Van Druten makes one of his younger teachers express himself as follows:

"My God, Terry, are they all like that?"

"Most of them, more or less. Simmons is a bit worse than the average, perhaps."

"Will you be like that one day?"

"I hope not. That's my one fear, that if I remain a school-master I shall go the same way. They nearly all do."

"I know, but you're not going to remain a school-master."

"How do you know?"

"Oh, but you're not. You know you're not. You know it's only a temporary thing with you."

"That's what they all said once."

"Yes, but you'll get to Cambridge. Or write."

"I expect most of them said that too."

"Terry, how ghastly. What is it that makes them like that? What gives them that . . . that domineering, self-conscious attitude of the pedagogue that hangs around them like a halo?"

"I don't know. Just being in authority perhaps. That, and the rut of it. Never talking to anybody but boys and other school-masters. Always having to think of dignity and position. I dare say Simmons wasn't such a bad chap once. He's a crashing bore, of course, and a self-satisfied prig, but . . ."[1]

Teachers' conventions usually help the morale of the teacher, for they give him a sub-group sanction for his teacher morality. At conferences every teacher has an opportunity to meet persons who are facing the same teaching problems, and the usual effect of their interchange is favorable to all concerned. But sometimes there comes out of the experience of the conference a bitter rejection of the identification of one's self with other teachers. One sees the others, and hates to admit that he and they are of the same flesh.

I used to teach French. I imagine that the situation of a man teaching French is particularly bad when he goes to conferences because of the terribly large percentage of perfect wash-outs among the other men teachers of the subject. So I was always horribly shocked when I looked at a roomful of French teachers and realized that I was one of them, that the world classed me with them already, and that if I kept on in my profession I would be just like all the others. I used to be depressed for several days after such an experience.

I delayed as long as I could before going to the meeting. But finally I had to go, because it was necessary to fill out a card in order to be counted among those present. I found the room at last, and went in, and this was the sight that confronted me.

A frowsy little man is reading a paper. He tells enthusiastically how to teach students to pronounce French. He dilates on the natural method of learning French. He speaks of teaching objectives. Where have I heard all this before? And how often, *mutatis mutandis,* will I hear it again? He gets a great thrill from making his speech, more than I get from listening to it. I look around. They are the same people as last year. Here and there a new face; the new ones look a little less hopeless than the older ones. I think how many years I have been attending this section meeting, and I wonder how I look to a newcomer. I take it all in. The pathetic women. The incredibly feminine men. There is the lame fellow who once tried to hold my hand. He is smiling at me hopefully. I pretend not to see him.

I hear their voices as from a great distance. They are still discussing objectives. One woman has a clever device for making students understand the difference between the accent aigu and the accent grave. She smirks as she tells it. She sits down and smirks. So that is what she thinks about, is it? As if I cared about her or the *accent aigu.*

These people are dead, I reflect. I wonder how long the body can live when the mind has died.

[1] Van Druten, Carl, *Young Woodley*, p. 172. (Reprinted by permission of Simon and Schuster.)

I reflect that in another sense, too, this is a charnel house. This, I say, is really the house of the dead. It is the burying place of dead hopes. All these people had once high ambitions and bright prospects. The women to marry, to love and be loved, to create and procreate. The reason for the unsuccess is clear enough, as plain as the noses on their faces. The men, mingling with all these lost souls of women in this petty hell, what did they once hope? To teach French to bored and self-satisfied youngsters? I doubt it, but perhaps that is what men like these would want to do; I don't know what they would want to do, I am sure, and I care less. But that is not fair; there is defeat in the face of every person here.

I make bold to leave the room, hoping that no one will notice that I just came a few moments before. I try to smooth it over by looking at my watch and pretending that I have an engagement. (Autobiographical document of a man teacher.)

The very bitterness of the above narrative is an incident of the writer's violent reaction to being classed as a teacher. His way of rejecting the school-teacher identification is to express his disgust with the whole profession, but his disgust also covers a real fear that he will himself become like the other members of the group. The attitude of teachers toward teaching is conditioned by the fact that many teachers, and much of the community, regard teaching as a failure belt. Even those teachers who proudly reject this notion sometimes betray themselves by their exaggerated respect and admiration for business men and other "men who are doing things."

The attitudes of teachers toward other teachers are striking marks of the occupational character, and they operate as well to influence the personality adjustment of new teachers. Of much interest are the conflicting and antithetical attitudes of teachers toward executive officers whose duty it is to direct and supervise their labors. Attitudes of teachers toward executives are ambivalent. On the surface appears a loyalty that is highly intense and sometimes verges upon sycophancy. Teachers often feel a very real gratitude to administrators who retain them in their positions. (Perhaps the gratitude that is most outspoken is a "lively anticipation of favors to be received.") This attitude is fostered by the executives themselves, who rate the quality of loyalty to themselves very highly. There is some justification for this attitude in executives, for the school head is held responsible for the acts of his subordinates, and he must therefore exact of them some respect for his personal wishes. There are many names for loyalty and its opposite. The non-cooperative teacher is usually the one who is disloyal to the superintendent. One suspects that "professional ethics," a creation of executives for the guidance of subordinates, is really loyalty under another name. So it is that teachers are usually obedient, and in some systems almost slavishly so. But underneath this obedience is a latent rebellion that sometimes comes to the surface. Then are those quite unpredictable "rows" with the superintendent, those fallings out over trifles, which alter the personnel of every school yearly, and then occur, too, those intrigues whose purpose it is to oust the executive from his job. But teachers who are not loyal must be very guarded in their utterances, must approach carefully those whom they suspect of like disaffection, and must close all windows before conspiring. From the guardedness with which dissatisfaction must usually be expressed arises part of that undue caution in speech which is thought one of the marks of the teacher. A bold speaker is much admired but he rarely stays long in the same place.

The mental operations of teachers and of school executives display some striking differences. The intellectual and verbal facility of executives is probably less than that of teachers of equivalent training, but their ideas, though more limited in scope, have a much closer connection with reality. Elements of social selection and of situational molding enter into the explanation of these differences. We may think of the contrast between able classroom teachers and executives partly in terms of the ancient contrast between talkers and doers. If talkers are proverbially no great doers, then doers are not talkers either, and there must be something in the fundamental economy of the situation that makes it so. The great artist does not talk about art but practices it; the great scientist does not prate about concepts but uses them. College professors are the greatest talkers in the world, but they are no kind of doers at all. Perhaps all persons could be ranged in a series according to the complexity of the configurations into which their world is organized; this would probably correspond roughly to the inverse order of the stability of the configurations. Simple and stable configurations would likewise be relatively easy of access. Doers, then, would be those whose world is contained in many simple configurations, all relatively accessible. Doers know how to manipulate their environment, but they do not find in it much that is worth talking about. Talkers, by virtue of the greater complexity and instability of their world, by virtue, as well, of their greater difficulty of inducing their subtle and intricate configurations to materialize, are notoriously slow and ill-organized doers. The needs of executive work select out doers; and, within limits, use develops executives into doers. There are many persons of middle sort whose natural bent may be inclined either way; either the constant strain to verbalize subtle configurations can make them theorists, or the press of a multitude of new situations to be met can make them into executives.

The cleavage between the executive and the theoretical mentality is a very clear one. It is often difficult for the two to establish an understanding. The executive presents a simple task as if its accomplishment would strain the faculties of the other person to the utmost, and the theorist is puzzled and annoyed. (This mechanism is illustrated in the relations of father and son in *Clayhanger*, by Arnold Bennett.) The theorist must engage in an endless discussion, with many and tortuous complexities, before arriving at a decision regarding a policy, and this leaves the executive, accustomed to pragmatism and the main chance, puzzled and a little out of patience.

Let it be perfectly clear that we have no wish to disparage executive mentality. It is an uncommon gift of considerable social utility, and usually it deserves the greater part of the rewards which it gets. This is especially true of executive ability in its higher reaches, of that ability which enables its possessor to manipulate complex persons. The executive can carry a load of responsibility under which a less balanced personality would disintegrate. He can resist the ceaseless hammering of details.

Executives who have been teachers employ, as might be expected, the same sort of techniques in controlling under-teachers that they once found effective in the classroom. Under-teachers, likewise, build up the same sort of control over them that students are able to exert over teachers. A young practice teacher declares that his supervisor never catches him unready because his behavior always betrays an impending visit. On mornings when a visit is to be expected, the supervisor does not exchange greetings with the young novice; on other mornings he speaks formally. In a very teacherly manner, then, the supervisor hardens his heart with social distance before he strikes. That numerous tribe of teachers who strive to ingratiate themselves by finding out what policy the executive head favors and then proposing it has also its analogue in the classroom; among students such behavior is "chiselling." It needs to be said that this magisterial technique falls short of perfection when it is transmuted into executive policy.

Most school executives have learned that groups of teachers are difficult to handle. The reason for this is partly that the teacher grows accustomed to having his own way in the classroom, and partly that his attitude toward the administration is usually ambivalent. The slightest mistake of an incoming executive is often enough to lose him the support of the entire faculty. Particularly difficult is the situation of an executive succeeding a popular man or a man who has allowed the authority of his office to slip through his fingers. The new executive must guard his speech clearly, and make sure that his new policies are not misunderstood. Sweeping changes are probably more difficult than gradual ones, for in the slower process the executive is able to carry his group with him. But any change is likely to leave one or two faculty members in revolt against it; from then on these persons are isolated from the onmoving current, and they stand out like those hard rocks which the sea cuts off from the land. Some executives have learned to use with the greatest dexterity the technique of deference and willingness to discuss. An executive who is ready to receive ideas from subordinates, or to leave questions of policy to be decided by those subordinates in discussion groups, is often able to gather about him a very enthusiastic faculty; the explanation is simple, for each faculty member is enthusiastic because he feels that he is really the mainstay of the administration. This technique, however, may lead to very bitter quarrels when real differences between teacher and executive arise. When there is exceptionally bitter disagreement between the members of the group, adroit executives contrive to get the subject dropped and delay decision until feeling has subsided. But an executive makes a bad blunder when he submits a matter for discussion among his teachers, and then allows it to become apparent, when his decision is rendered, that the wishes and opinions of the teachers have not been considered. Some executives commit the incredible stupidity of holding a discussion after a decision has already been reached. The executive who expects to profit most from discussion of school matters by his teachers must allow those advisers to be perfectly free in their thinking. Most executives are not so much interested in getting wisdom through discussion as in keeping their teachers in a good humor; sometimes this is best done by an adroit manipulation of the discussion which permits clever members of the faculty to seize upon the executive's unspoken views and reflect them back upon him, often a process of which both executive and sycophant teacher are not fully conscious. Some executives, too, manipulate the situation by giving a biased statement of fact; but this is dangerous. It should be added that the best use of discussion allows each faculty member to state his view and to feel that he is participating in a final decision, but permits the executive to preserve the prerogative of a final decision. As between teacher and executive, there appears a considerable amount of manipulation of the executive by the teacher; the technique of this varies from that of the clinging vine who asks for much advice to that of the most subtle and sophisticated sycophant.

An endless subject, but one which cannot here receive endless treatment, is that of the relation of the teacher to his colleagues. Teachers are a closed group, a dominant group, with the morality of the dominant group; yet they are engaged in rivalry, and are cut off from contact with each other by that rivalry; the school-teacher stereotype cuts down yet further their intimacy with each other, the while it throws them back upon each other for company; close association in their work throws them into constant contact, but the restrictions imposed by the situation prevent the completeness of intimacy. These are some of the more important phases of the relations of teachers to each other.

The teaching group demands the exclusive loyalty of all its members. As one executive has phrased it, the faculty is like a ruling cabinet, all of whose members must stand or fall together. If disagreements appear among the members of the faculty, as they must, the group morality demands that outsiders shall not be admitted to those disagreements. There is a code of "institutional behavior," which imposes upon its members the most rigid restrictions; it is a code which has its niceties and its subtle points which we cannot argue out here. But we can consider the main outlines of that code. Teachers must not speak ill of their colleagues in the presence of students, nor must they permit students to criticize their colleagues to them. This is a rule to which administrators make exceptions constantly, and it has its limits outside which it does not apply. The reason for the rule is that one teacher who sympathizes with students in their disagreements with his colleagues can break that circle of reenforcement of each by each upon which teacher domination rests. Not only is it not morality to base one's judgment of a fellow teacher upon the opinions of students, but it is not good policy, for nothing is more unreliable than students' reports concerning teachers; they are not always truthful, they nearly always reflect an incomplete comprehension of the teacher's action, and in any case they are invariably judgments from the point of view of the student, which differs radically from that of the teacher. Executives have been known to use certain students as stool-pigeons for the purpose of spying out the behavior of subordinates; this is open to numerous objections from the point of view of in-group morality, and to this one objection orientated from the point of view of common sense, that one whose status depends upon making and reporting important discoveries may report such discoveries without making them.

But a satisfactory ethical formula for regulating the relations of members of the profession has by no means been evolved. Should the subordination of the teacher to the executive be complete? If it should not be (and the present writer most emphatically does not believe that it should be), how can unanimity of action be secured in the school? What ethics should govern the inevitable disagreements of teacher and executive? If a final break is reached, what is the ethics of recommendation? (This is a point on which a convention is sorely needed.) In the case of the minor executive, which should be dominant, administrative loyalty or teacher-group loyalty? (Do deans, for instance, hang with teachers or with administrators?)

The rivalry of teachers is keen and often bitter. The prizes of competition are positions, increases in salary, and the good opinion of those persons upon whom advancement depends. Where education is thought of as a process of learning specific facts, the rivalry of teachers often culminates in bitter conflicts over the right to impart certain subject matter to students. Rivalry over subject matter and the manner in which it is imparted comes to light also in the insistence of teachers of all levels that their students have not been properly prepared. Interdepartmental morality arises as a corrective to this rivalry inherent in the situation. In the progressive school, rivalry concerns the initiation of new policies and administrative devices. In the highly stabilized school, an intense rivalry springs up in the enforcement of the status quo. A breach of discipline is observed by several persons; each of them moves quickly in order to be the person from whom the correction comes. And when all are on the spot they vie with each other in the attempt to say the most relevant and pointed thing, each striving to distinguish himself by being the one who has really dealt adequately with this particular offender. All members of the faculty of such a stabilized school are on the alert for the detection of new evasions of the rules, and they bring these to the attention of authorities with zest. It is never any distinction to report a large number of cases of discipline in a group for which one is solely responsible (as the class or the study hall), but it is usually true that one's alertness for offences against the general order is something of a measure of his general efficiency. The enforcement of the status quo becomes a way of life, and it is buttressed by a philosophy. "A punch in reserve, that's my motto," said a belligerent enforcer, knowing well it was a pose that would profit him greatly, feeling also that it was a virtuous thought. Rivalry in this rises to a high point in the stabilized school. Sometimes the teachers, informally and with an appearance of jesting, keep score. Different status-getting mechanisms are in vogue in different groups. On college faculties the pose most in favor is one of broad-mindedness. The conversation of a certain group of younger sociologists is composed chiefly of the boasts of the members concerning their utter freedom from race prejudice. On another plane is the glorified ignorance of critical minds.

As a point of pride, and as a means of defending their own positions, teachers in the stabilized school become very jealous of the prerogative which goes with such position as they may have. Disputes over jurisdiction sunder such a faculty frequently, and with each new dispute there occurs a new alignment of faculty friends and enemies. Sometimes serious cases of discipline are not dealt with because of disputes over the right to prosecute. A description of a faculty row occurs in Young Woodley:

> Having dispatched Riley to the sickroom and the housemaid to the matron, Plunkett went straight to the Head. Ratcliffe, summoned to conference, was bitterly indignant. Riley was in his House, a disgrace to it, but none the less a member of it and the fact that the venue of the crime was Plunkett's did not, in his eyes, excuse Plunkett from coming to him first. He resented Plunkett's direct appeal to the Head, not merely as a breach of etiquette, but as a personal affront, a deliberate act of spite. He found himself almost defending Riley. He went to Simmons and Blakeney, and enlisted them on his side in censuring Plunkett's action. Of the penalty for the offence there was no doubt; Riley's expulsion was inevitable. But the technique of the matter caused a decided split in the Common Room. Once again there was a shuffling of cards, a re-grouping of allies; enemies in old feuds found themselves on the same side in this. Simmons and Plunkett, cordially united in the affair of bounds last term, were now frigid adversaries. In a few weeks something else would arise and involve a further readjustment, but, while this lasted, feeling ran high.[1]

Rivalry, which cuts teachers off from each other, and the constant hunger for shop talk, which brings them together, are distinctive features of the society of school teachers. The lack of spontaneous and whole-hearted participation, the formalization of the

[1] Van Druten, Carl, *Young Woodley,* p. 116. (Reprinted by permission of Simon and Schuster.)

ceremonies of respect, the guards which are set upon the lips, the constant concern over dignity and prerogative—all these things operate to make the society of teachers generally rather disappointing. One observer has put it this way: "When a group of professors get together, each one of them listens only to what he says, and then sits still and thinks of what he is going to say next. Nobody listens to what the other fellow has to say. One just looks at the other fellow and nods politely from time to time. But one is really waiting for a chance to get in his own remarks." The scathing Henry Adams has characterized the society of teachers as follows:

> The same failure marked the society of a college. Several score of the best-educated, most agreeable, and personally the most sociable people in America united in Cambridge to make a social desert that would have starved a polar bear. The liveliest and most agreeable of men—James Russell Lowell, Francis J. Child, Louis Agassiz, his son Alexander, Gurney, John Fiske, William James, and a dozen others, who would have made the joy of London or Paris—tried their best to break out and be like other men in Cambridge and Boston, but society called them professors and professors they had to be. While all these brilliant men were greedy for companionship, all were famished for want of it. Society was a faculty-meeting without business.[1]

It is not easy to return a satisfactory answer to the question, "Why do teachers talk shop?" The fact that they do has sometimes been cited as one of the wholesome and hopeful things about the profession. From one point of view this incessant preoccupation of teachers with teaching is hopeful, for it argues that the task of forming the young is one of great intrinsic interest. This it certainly is, and teachers, who hold the fate of the generations in their hands, have a right to talk about their work. But partly also the unwillingness of teachers to talk about anything but teaching betokens an unhealthy narrowing of their mental horizon. The teacher must, if he is to understand children, remain conversant with the values of the mental universe of childhood, but he must also, if he is to retain his own mental health, keep a strong hold upon the adult world as well. Many younger teachers, when they are thrown into a group of teachers who live teaching, breathe teaching, dream teaching, and have teaching as a garnish for every meal, undergo a personal degeneration sometimes called "the reduction of personality." The reduction of personality results from the transition from a wide and stimulating range of contacts to a much narrower attentional field; a loss of faith in

[1] *The Education of Henry Adams*, p. 307. (Reprinted by permission of Houghton Mifflin Company.)

subtler and less easily accessible personal satisfactions, a regression toward the elemental, an inner grief and longing for the things that were, covered by an outward cynicism of the most callous and brutal sort; these are some of the phenomena thought to be associated with the reduction of personality. The reduction of personality occurs among teachers when they leave the brilliant world of college for the more prosaic world in which they are to teach. On another level it occurs when one departs from graduate school; sometimes, when one enters it. This is what sets the ultimate limit to the amount of shop-talk in which teachers can indulge without incurring those vicious tissue-changes that go with overindulgence.

Yet Bagley, and for the most excellent of reasons, advises that teachers cultivate the craft spirit, turning inward upon their own group for support and encouragement.

> On the other hand, sympathetic intercourse with fellow-workers will constantly emphasize the craft spirit—the most priceless possession of the teacher, and the possession that he is most likely to lose in the earlier stages of his career. His effort should be to keep the craft spirit alive at all hazards. He should constantly look upon his work as professional service, and upon himself as an initiate into the privileges of that service. The free association of kindred minds will do more to keep this craft spirit alive than anything else. Any form of social service must be dreary, discouraging work if the tasks that it imposes are not attacked with enthusiasm. In many cities one may find little coteries of teachers that gather together at stated intervals for the purpose (not always avowed) of cultivating the craft spirit, of keeping alive enthusiasm in the work. From these meetings the pessimist, the malcontent, the teacher ashamed of his calling, and the teacher who works with his eyes upon the clock and his mind upon pay day, are all rigidly excluded. No better lot can befall the beginning teacher than to become identified with one of these guilds—for guilds they are, although not always consciously: There he will find the comfort that really cheers, the advice that really helps, the idealism that really inspires. And there, too, he will receive his due share both of the praise that will not puff him up, and of the blame that will not cast him down. But above all, he will learn from this intercourse that the trials and troubles are not his alone, that many of them are intrinsic in the very nature of his calling, and that the safest and sanest policy is to look upon them as problems of the day's work—problems to be studied in sober reflection, and solved with dispassionate judgment.[1]

Bagley has presented the argument for the in-group of teachers

[1] Bagley, W. C., *Classroom Management*, pp. 100 ff. (Reprinted by permission of The Macmillan Company.)

most ably in this eloquent and sympathetic passage. The present writer can agree to all that Bagley says if the shop-talk of the teachers is limited in amount and does not devour the whole social experience of the teacher. The teacher must, indeed, talk with others whose work suspends them between the two worlds of adult and child, and he can find sympathetic comprehension of his efforts only in such a group. But continuous shop-talk becomes sterile, and it does not nourish the mind that feeds upon it. The teacher needs to belong to many other groups where his teaching personality does not enter, and those other groups must contest the possession of his mind by teaching as determinedly as does his wife. These other groups should certainly preponderate over the teaching group in number and in the amount of time given to them. Lodge work, church work, literary work or esthetic achievement, self-cultivation in lines unconnected with teaching, the self-discipline involved in the care and training of progeny, the absorbing interests of courtship, training in the handling of ideas, keeping informed on questions of public interest, active and persistent participation in community affairs and community conflicts—some of these, not all, for a teacher need not be a dilettante, should absorb the teacher's attention after he has put in a full day's work in the classroom. They will be the best possible prophylactics against degeneration into a mere occupational type. The teacher who spends his energies fully in the main stream of the social process need not fear, if he tries to follow a reasonably enlightened mode of classroom procedure, that his classroom work will mark him unfavorably. Perhaps few communities at present will leave their teachers free to indulge in all these activities without criticism and without interference. If this be true, as it certainly is, it looms up as the next task of the teaching profession to hew its way relentlessly through the social inhibitions which surround it. And this is not simply a struggle for personal liberty, but a struggle to be whole men, and that concerns the first and final purpose of all education, for only whole men can educate whole boys.

Observation of personality changes in young persons just beginning to teach will help us to understand the process of occupational molding. Since the adaptation of personality to teaching takes place rapidly, its true nature may elude research that does not concern itself with the first few weeks of teaching experience. The following document, cast in the form of conversations with an older teacher, illustrates some striking but typical changes of attitude:

Before school began:

"I'm going to like teaching. I'm an idealist. I believe that this course I am giving is of considerable importance to these youngsters and I'm going to give them everything I can. Teaching ought to be fun."

"You may not find it enjoyable," said his friend. "Your enthusiasm may not stand up forever under the strain of saying over and over things so elementary that they have lost their significance for you. And your idealism may be rudely jarred when you find yourself in antagonistic relations with your students. That is, if you allow yourself to come into such relationships with them."

After one week of teaching:

"I enjoy teaching. I get a great kick out of standing up in front of these boys and being the oracle. That gratifies the old ego in great shape."

"It's nice that you enjoy it."

After six weeks of teaching:

"I did something this morning and I want you to tell me whether I did right or wrong. I got so tired of talking to that bunch of mine and looking at their stupid faces. Here I am working myself to death to give them a good course, and they hardly bother to listen. I tell you, it gripes me. And I've had a couple of fellows in there who are repeating the course and they are always trying to make trouble. Well, this morning when I turned to write on the board, somebody let out a great big yawn. I don't know who it was, but I think it was one of those fellows.

"Well, that just set me off, and I turned around and I let 'em have it. I asked them what they'd think of a fellow who went down here to Hansen's and bought a five-pound box of candy, paid for it, left it in the store, and then went around bragging to everybody about the five-pound box of candy he had in the store. I told him that was what a fellow did who came to college and paid out his good money and never tried to learn anything.

"Further, about the noise, I told them that the next fellow that did that was going to be dealt with severely. I told them that I would kick him out of class and flunk him in the course. I said, 'God help the fellow if I catch him.' Did I do right?"

"You did not. You antagonized the whole group. You lost your own poise. You made a threat, and a threat is a challenge. Now my idea is that one should never threaten. One should find one guilty person, and if necessary punish him. But one should never antagonize a group. One should rather use strategy to avert antagonism. And one should never threaten a group. That's a sure way to create disorder."

After three months of teaching:

"Well, I believe that from our discussions I've learned a fundamental principle of human management. The way to get cooperation is just to take it.

Now when I came here I believed that a teacher could get the cooperation of his students by asking for it and by being willing to help them all he could. I think I understand better now. You just have to go in and manage things." (Condensed and arranged from a record of conversations with a beginning teacher.)

Observable in this document are:

(1) Early pleasure in the teaching rôle and expansion of the ego in adapting to it, followed by disappointment and ego frustration through hostile attitudes of students and the discovery of the limitations of the rôle.
(2) Enthusiasm fading under the attack of non-cooperation and repetition.
(3) Dissatisfaction with students growing out of the fact that that which has been taught many times tends to be imparted impatiently.
(4) The necessities of discipline disciplining spontaneity out of the teacher.
(5) Growing insight and conformity to the teaching norm influenced by the older colleague.
(6) Falling into the convenient, logically defensible rut of the profession.

Certain marked contrasts between personalities of experienced and inexperienced teachers are the following:

1. The person who has just started teaching experiences a considerable ego expansion in his work, whereas the dominant tone of the experienced teacher is probably opposite.

2. The more experienced teacher is more inclined to resent the intrusion of his institutional upon his private personality than is the beginning teacher.

3. Discipline is more of a problem, though not recognized as such, to the beginning teacher.

4. A new teacher is more likely to have an idealistic conception of the student-teacher relationship than is an older teacher.

5. The new teacher is much less inhibited in his habits of social expression than is the older teacher, i.e., he talks with students oftener, longer, and more intimately, and explains himself more than an older teacher.

6. Students are more significant as persons to the new teacher. The distorting influence of the directing, managing rôle is less apparent.

7. The young teacher is less likely to be involved in rivalries with

colleagues than the older teacher. The fiercely rivalrous attitude toward colleagues is a late adjustment, often requiring ten years or more for its completion.

8. The executive rôle early produces effects upon the teacher, but these effects are at first favorable to general social adjustment, consisting of an elimination of childish mobility of countenance and a growth of decisiveness in meeting situations. This elimination of expression later grows to impassiveness, and the decisiveness, with the increase by experience of pre-judgment of situations, to inflexibility.

9. The initial pleasure of the teacher in the teaching rôle endures throughout the period in which teaching habits are being formed. During this period the work of teaching furnishes nearly the entire content of consciousness, and is attended to almost exclusively. As habits recede from the consciousness with increasing perfection, satisfaction fades, and discontent grows. This genetic analysis of teacher discontent points toward routinization as one of its major sources.

10. The shift of allegiance from the student group to the teacher group takes place gradually over a period of months.

The study of young persons doing their practice teaching will prove particularly rewarding. The crystallization of occupational attitudes may progress far before the completion of this preliminary training. Alert youngsters may acquire penetrating knowledge, though limited by its basic orientation, in a few weeks of such forcible learning. The value of such experiences could be greatly increased by concurrent instruction directed at giving social insight. The conservatism of the profession, further, is in part due to pressure of the attitudes of experienced teachers upon the unformed novice, and yet these experienced persons who consent to talk to neophytes serve an important function. It is suggested, therefore, that practice-teaching institutions appoint enlightened and progressive teachers to serve as cicerones to youngsters; it would be their function to point out to new teachers the principal landmarks of the social world of school, and to assist the new teacher to form forward-looking rather than excessively conservative attitudes.

The involution of the teacher is of equal scientific importance. This is illustrated among teachers who have changed their profession or retired. There is, it seems, a rapid fading of the mental content of teaching subject matter, so that the teacher who has been out of the classroom a few months can no longer recall the things which were once on the end of his tongue. The complex mental adjustments on which teaching is founded fall rapidly into ruin; the unstable equilibrium of the teaching personality topples. A friend of William James asked him, some two years after he had retired, whether he still felt capable of teaching. He replied, "No, and I don't understand now how I ever could have been capable of it."

PROJECTS

1. Rank the members of your high-school class in intelligence, social flexibility, and determination. Indicate their occupational choices. Where do the teachers fit in?

2. Make a case study of a lawyer, a doctor, merchant, or minister from the point of view of occupational selectivity and molding.

3. Compare students of a school of education with students in another school of the same university as to all measurable traits (including physical traits if possible).

4. Make a case history of a "family of teachers." Analyze the social influences at work within the family to direct the occupational choices of its members.

5. Locate ten persons who once thought of teaching but decided not to do so. What were their reasons for changing their minds? Show the relation of this to the selective pattern of the profession.

6. Make an extended study of school teachers in contemporary novels. Interpret carefully.

7. Study a single teacher (whom you consider typical) in the whole range of his social relations. Use as a check upon the text.

8. If you have taught, write the history of your first year of teaching. Determine by introspection and the comments of others what personality changes were produced and show their relationship to your experiences.

9. Write an objective study covering the last year in college and first year of teaching of an intimate friend. Pay particular attention to personality changes as above.

10. Analyze the intimate letters of a young school mistress in her first year of teaching. Show changes of attitude as above.

11. Make a case study of a teacher in whom teaching has induced favorable personality changes. Compare with a teacher upon whom the effect has been destructive. How do you explain the difference?

12. List the ten teachers whom you know best. Make a list of the most outstanding qualities in their social personalities, and check against the analysis in the text.

13. Induce several teachers to discuss their most unpleasant experiences and to indicate as far as they know it the effect of these experiences upon their personalities.

14. Make a complete study of the routine of life of a particular teacher.

15. Contrast the personality of a "born teacher" with that of someone who has with difficulty learned to teach.

16. Compare the classroom behavior of a group of teachers with that of ordinary undergraduates. How do you explain the difference?

17. Contrast an experienced and an inexperienced teacher with regard to their ability to observe classroom incidents which will affect discipline. How is this related to the development of occupational characteristics?

18. Carefully study a beginning teacher giving an examination, writing questions on the board, watching students write, returning papers, explaining grades, etc. What insight does this give as to the impact of the teacher's work upon his personality?

19. Get a number of teachers to discuss their major fears. Relate these to occupational influences of the profession.

20. Make a case study of a "warner."

21. Trace the development of objectivity in handling students in a particular teacher.

22. Collect as many school-teacher dreams as possible and classify and interpret them. Use as a check upon the text.

23. Study intensively the dream life of a single teacher.

24. Study the phantasy life of school teachers.

25. Make a case study of a problem teacher, showing his initial unadjustment and the effect of teaching experience upon him.

26. Can you find teachers in your own circle of experience who conform to the types of Judge Story and Professor Greenleaf? Describe one of each type, relating characteristic incidents.

27. Study from life the interplay of attitudes in the drill type of recitation, and compare with the recitation of the more discursive type. Analyze the effect of each of these upon the teacher's personality. Which is the more effective in communicating information? In awakening thought?

28. Study, comparatively, the personalities of teachers of different subjects, and draw sucn conclusions as the facts seem to warrant.

29. Write out the projected careers—plans, hopes, and ambitions—of several teachers in training. Compare with the actual careers of a similar number of experienced teachers.

30. Describe your own generalized idea of a school teacher.

31. List all the actions which you have heard to be unbecoming in a school teacher. Classify and analyze.

32. Relate the story of your own experiences with the school-teacher stereotype.

33. Find young men and women teachers who have on various occasions refused to admit that they were teachers. Get them to tell their reasons for this behavior.

34. Conduct an experiment similar to that of Mr. McGill and check your results against his.

35. Relate incidents showing the internalization of school rules in the teacher's personality.

36. Relate incidents showing a continued rebellion of a teacher against certain rules of a school.

37. Study the attitudes of a young teacher in rebellion against his profession. Analyze his discontent.

38. Study the personality of a teacher who has made a good adjustment to his profession. Analyze his technique of adjustment.

39. Study intensively a teacher who has avoided the unpleasant features of the occupational type. What prophylactics has he employed against teacher-mindedness? If possible, make a similar study on other teachers and extend your list of prophylactic measures.

40. State clearly the prophylactics against teacher-mindedness which you intend to employ in your teaching career.

41. "A teacher must be absolutely loyal." When, under what circumstances, and how often have you heard the above? State all its implications.

42. Study the technique employed by a successful high-school principal in handling his teachers.

43. Study the use of discussion of school policies as a means of maintaining faculty morale. Give instances of bad and good uses of discussion.

44. Obtain student judgment upon a particular teacher. Compare with faculty appraisals. Show where each appraisal is most trustworthy; contrariwise, where each falls down.

45. Describe the competition of a group of teachers in enforcing the status quo. At what point is competition most keen? What are the personal characteristics of the outstandingly successful competitors?

46. Record the status-getting mechanisms in a group of teachers known to you.

47. Write a complete and detailed history of a school row.

48. Record the shop-talk of teachers. Make your own interpretation of what it means to every teacher.

49. Make a case study of a young teacher who has suffered a "reduction of personality."

50. Describe and analyze a business meeting of a group of teachers. Who controls? What professional attitudes crop out—what rivalries—what posing for approval—what rapprochements and antagonisms are carried out of the meeting?

51. Study Burnham's *Great Teachers and Mental Health.* What personal characteristics and social techniques saved these men from developing into the teacher type? Is the occupation less hurtful in a radically different kind of school?

52. A caste is a marriage group. Trace out marriages of one hundred teachers. How many of the spouses were teachers? Is there a recognizable tendency for teachers to form a separate caste?

SUGGESTED READINGS

(1) BOGARDUS, E. S., "The Occupational Attitude," *Journal of Applied Sociology,* Vol. VIII, pp. 172-176.

(2) BURNHAM, W. H., *Great Teachers and Mental Health.*

(3) HERRICK, ROBERT, *Chimes.*

(4) HUGHES, E. C., "Personality Types and the Division of Labor," *The American Journal of Sociology,* March, 1928, pp. 754-768.

(5) MAUGHAM, SOMERSET, *Of Human Bondage.*

(6) MILLER, G. F., *Letters From a Hard-Boiled Teacher to His Half-Baked Son.*

(7) PATTON, C. H., and FIELD, W. T., *Eight O'Clock Chapel,* Chapters IV and V.

(8) SCOTT, ELEANOR, *War Among Ladies.*

(9) SELVER, PAUL, *Schooling.*

(10) WHITRIDGE, ARNOLD, *Doctor Arnold of Rugby.*

(11) WRIGHT, H. P., *The Young Man and Teaching.*

Part Six

SUMMARY AND RECOMMENDATIONS

Chapter XXIV

A PRINCIPAL REASON WHY INSTITUTIONS DO NOT FUNCTION

A friend who is a minister is fond of the following story:

"I was walking down the street one morning not long ago. A fine-looking man came alongside and kept pace with me.

" 'I am the devil,' he announced.

" 'Well,' I said, 'I have always been very curious about you and I'm glad to see you at last. And what are you doing this morning?'

" 'Oh, my usual business. I am going about corrupting the works of man.'

"We chatted pleasantly, for I have never been a devil-hater, and kept company for some distance. I was surprised to find the devil such a pleasant and well-spoken gentleman. After a time, we noticed a man in front of us who gave all outward indications of having been struck by a good idea. He stopped suddenly still, his face lighted up, he struck his hand to his head in joy, and rapidly walked away to execute his idea. Thinking that this gave me at least a temporary advantage, I said, 'Now there's a man who has an idea, and I venture to say that it is a good idea. That's a point against you. What are you going to do about that?'

" 'Nothing easier,' said the devil, 'I'll organize it.' "

Something happens to ideas when they get themselves organized into social systems. The ethical ideas of Christ, flexible and universal, have nevertheless been smothered by churches. A social principle degenerates into a dogma when an institution is built about it. Yet an idea must be organized before it can be made into fact, and an idea wholly unorganized rarely lives long. Without mechanism it dies, but mechanism perverts it. This is part of the natural flow and recession—the life principle in society.

Institutions have their informal beginnings in the mores; they are "formal trends in the mores." In Sumner's classic words, "An institution consists of a concept and a structure.'' The structure is defined as ''a number of functionaries set to cooperate in prescribed ways at certain conjunctures.'' Where the structure has become too intricate, or too rigid, or the idea of function has faded from the minds of functionaries, we speak of the institution as suffering from formalism. This clinical entity which we have called formalism is variously designated in sociological literature; Cooley mentions six names for it: institutionalism, formalism, traditionalism, conventionalism, ritualism, and bureaucracy. As Cooley has said, it is difficult to tell when mechanism is in excess; the best rule that can be formulated is perhaps that of Cooley, that mechanism is in excess when it interferes with growth and adaptation.

The school must always function as an organization of personalities bound together in a dynamic relation; this is true whether the school be a live organism or dead matter. But in a living bit of social tissue, persons transcend offices; they embody offices but they engulf them; they are persons first and offices afterwards. But in dead tissue offices transcend persons. In live tissue, the man is always too large for the job, and he is forever bursting his uniform at the elbows and shoulders. In dead tissue the man rattles about in the office like a seed in a gourd. When officers are more concerned with the perquisites of their offices than with the human values of their job, that is formalism.

Every social structure and every system of thought must grow old in time, and every one of them must die. And each of these, in its senescence, grows formal. One aspect of age in the social organism is a disorder of communication, an ''excess of the organ of language'' attended by a lack of real communication, a growth of verbiage and a failure of that inner contact upon which communication depends. This may occur, and often does, within the life cycle of individuals, and it then keeps pace with the mental ossification of men. But this breakdown of communication is most clearly visible when one generation is succeeded by another. It is easy to communicate duties, and it is easy to find men to do duties, but it is difficult to communicate a mission. So that it often happens that what is passed on to the newer generation is not a living insight into function, but dead information about duties.

A fading of the distinction between means and ends is one of the things that marks formalism. The general tendency in human process is for ends to turn into means, and this probably favors a healthy growth of personality and of society. Our achievements range themselves on different levels, and we readjust our standards as we pass from one level to another. But there is an opposite tendency which transforms means into ends; means are at first sub-wholes in greater wholes, but the greater whole fades out and leaves nothing but the part. Then the part is the whole. Man is a stupid child that can understand all the parts of his lesson but cannot understand the whole. This happens in teaching whenever a teacher overemphasizes the intrinsic value of his subject. It happens when learning is for school. It happens when learning is dry and dissected into facts. It happens when children are means and knowledge is an end.

Formalism, as Cooley has noted, is psychically cheap, and that is why an overburdened teacher turns to it. The necessities of the teaching situation may compel even the teacher who has a higher conception of education to turn to routine methods of instruction. The teacher must do something in the classroom, and routine teaching is the easiest thing to do. He must, ordinarily, teach something definite, and from this comes the tendency of the teacher to build up courses from definite but probably unimportant facts. And the teacher must have some standards, in any system, and it is therefore not difficult for him to magnify to the size of the whole that part of his job which consists of keeping lazy students from getting credits too easily. When this easiest way has been transmuted into a self-justifying moral order, formalism has taken possession of the school.

A different kind of social degeneration, characterized also by a maladaptation of mechanism and function, arises as a result of primary group attitudes among the functionaries of a social system. The institutional group becomes a more or less self-sufficient in-group, and conducts the institution for its own benefit rather than its social function. It is very difficult to tell when this kind of institutionalism becomes a vice, for in some of its forms it may be very useful in that it furnishes morale for the discharge of social functions. The *esprit de corps* of the Canadian Mounted Police must in part arise from the fact that the members of the force are bound together by ties of personal acquaintance. But a bureaucracy that has no crises to meet does not find the acquaintance of its members with each other an unmixed profit, and there is a point beyond which it is clear loss.

The typical large school is overridden with this sort of institutionalism. The members of the faculty think of themselves as forming a closed group whose interests are sacrosanct; students must take just what the faculty chooses to give them and ask for nothing more; all members of the faculty unite in condemning any attempt to subject the school to control or regulation from the outside. A different institutionalism grows up among the lesser sort of help, who develop in-group attitudes and a group consciousness from which both faculty and students are excluded. An incident illustrating the bureaucratic attitudes that spring up among the hired help of a university was furnished by a professor in a midwestern university.

I was in the periodical room of the university library. A woman approached the attendant with a special request.

"I'd like to take this back number of *Harper's* with me for a while," she stated.

"I am very sorry," said the attendant, "but that is not permitted."

There was some discussion. Finally the attendant asked the woman her official status in the university. It developed that she was a clerk in a nearby administrative office.

"Oh, take the magazine along. We let the people in the administrative offices have whatever they want. But I thought for a while you were some faculty member!"

It is difficult to believe that the purpose of the university was better served by giving the clerical help free access to such material than it would have been by making it easily available to the faculty.

Institutionalism of this sort in the school is analogous to graft in politics. It springs from the same root. The official, whom society and the law supposes to be actuated by considerations of public service and official duty (secondary group norms), is actually governed by considerations arising from his own little group of friends and acquaintances. Friendship flourishes while official duty suffers. That is why the grafting politician is so hard to oust, for he really is a good fellow, as the saying goes, "if you know him." The institutionalized teacher is in exactly the same situation. The morality of his own primary group takes precedence over that of the secondary group which his group is supposed to serve. The difference between the teacher and the politician is in the nature of the public trust which they handle. The politician handles money. The teacher handles children. The politician steals money. The teacher steals personality values.

This kind of institutionalism is also very common in the schools; these cancerous primary groups flourish in dead tissue where an understanding of function no longer exists. The school is especially liable to institutionalism of this sort because of the presence of a large element of dominance and subordination in the relation of teacher and student. The fact of domination shuts both teacher and student off from real communication with each other. Students as well as teachers have put up walls, as many a teacher has learned who has tried to form a real and vital contact with his students. If the teacher cannot establish contact with his students on a common human level, or if he does not dare, because of the enmity between students and teachers in general, then the teacher is thrown back upon formalism in his classroom and upon the primary groups of the teaching profession for friendship and sanction for his own attitudes and behavior. The isolation of teachers in the community also throws teachers upon each other for society, and this also makes for teaching for teachers.

It does not seem unreasonable to conclude, on the basis of the evidence which has been presented throughout this study, that the schools are a barren ground for the cultivation of personality. Some personal interchange there is in the schools, but it is of a limited sort and is largely vitiated by the limitations placed upon it. For the ordinary student in the ordinary school, and for any but the most exceptional teacher in the ordinary school, there is lacking any opportunity for that full, unforced, and unfettered self-expression from which personal development proceeds. It is necessary to consider the personalities of all who are involved in the social situations of the school, for it is not possible to develop the personalities of students favorably without giving like opportunities to teachers, and it is not possible to liberate students from present inhibitions without also liberating teachers.

We have stated in a previous chapter that the school is a social organism, that it is an artificial social order built on the despotic principle and is in a state of perilous equilibrium. In the light of our study of formalism these statements take on a new interrelation. The school is an organism some of whose tissues are dead; it is this dead tissue which we sense as artificial; it is the deadness of the tissue which makes necessary despotic government within the dead parts. It is this deadness of certain relationships, this artificiality of the conventional order and the despotism that goes with it—it is this which constantly creates the rebellion which the teacher must forever put down. The formal, artificial social order of the school does not furnish a proper milieu for the development of normal personality; that is why students are rebellious: they want to live. Cooley has written, "In the same way a school whose discipline is merely formal, not engaging the interest and good-will of the scholar, is pretty certain to turn out unruly boys and girls, because whatever is most personal and vital to them becomes accustomed to assert itself in opposition to the system."

All this is very far from the discipline of personal leadership. Real leadership is unconscious and informal; it is deeply personal in that it flows out of the man rather than the office. It is domination which the dominant one himself cannot prevent, which he quite possibly did not plan, domination that arises from a mind more complex than the minds of the followers and a hand readier and bolder than theirs. This is a kind of disciplined cooperation into which both leader and follower can enter fully; it is that which is lacking in the schools. Formal leadership, the leadership of the person who must be a leader because of the position he holds, and who, because of his position, is forced to be a purely formal leader, takes the place in the schools of natural leadership.

There is need for a natural social order in the schools. That does not mean a chaotic social order, or an uncontrolled social order, but rather a social order which students and teachers work out for themselves in the developing situation, an order which is intrinsic in the personalities of those involved, a social order resulting from the spontaneous, inevitable, and whole-hearted interaction of personalities. It is the function of the schools to help the individual organize his life out of the social materials which are presented to him. This process is now dominated by groups outside the school and is but little influenced by the school. If the school is to become really important in the lives of its students, it must allow them to be as free in school as they are outside it.

PROJECTS

1. Give instances of the failure of social machinery in the school to discharge its proper function by reason of primary group attitudes among functionaries.

2. Trace successive cycles of senescence and rejuvenation in a particular school.

3. Show by discussion of a particular case the relation between formalism in a teacher's methods and his hardening into the occupational type.

4. Record bits of teacher folk talk which reflect a belief that schools are principally for teachers.

SUGGESTED READINGS

(1) Cooley, C. H., *Social Organization.*

(2) Hart, J. K., *A Social Interpretation of Education,* Chapter XI.

(3) Ross, E. A., *Principles of Sociology.*

(4) Thomas, W. I., *Suggestions of Modern Science Concerning Education.* (With Jennings, H. S., Watson, J. B., and Meyer, Adolph.)

Chapter XXV

RECOMMENDATIONS

It is easier to diagnose social ills than it is to cure them. And it is easier far to criticize institutions than to suggest remedies for the evils that are in them. It is also possible to be much more scientific while criticizing, for criticism may rest upon established facts, whereas remedies are largely unknown and untried. Yet our task of social reconstruction in the schools is great and it presses.

It is here proposed that education should be directed at the development of wholesome personality in children by causing them to pass through a series of interlocking social situations each of which elicits certain unforced achievements and constellates certain attitudes corresponding in complexity and range of adaptation to the age and cultural levels of the particular child.

That is only a formula. A formula does not solve a problem, but it indicates the lines along which a solution might be worked out. Let us see what this formula means.

All education comes from the child's experience of social situations. Personality is forged in adaptation to those situations which the child passes through on the way to adulthood. The real influence of the school rests upon the fact that it confronts the child with social situations of a certain sort and compels adaptation to them. That is why the social machinery of the schools so rarely works according to plan; the meaning of the various mechanical devices that are incorporated into the system depends upon the place of those devices in the total situation which confronts the group of children. What is needful is insight into the nature of the total situation of the school; without it the plans of the elders must always go awry. This insight must come in large part from the study of the educative process as a function of the interaction of personalities. The practice has been to select certain ends of education and then to devise systems of education and schooling to attain them. This must always fail, unless it comes out of a study of the social process of education, for not only must means be ill adapted when chosen without knowledge of causal mechanisms, but even ends must be fallacious unless inductively arrived at; it is senseless to speak of the ends of education unless one knows what education is.

Present-day practice in the schools is still largely based upon the notion that education must proceed by the inculcation of specific habits. This is education that works from without, and that is why it does not work. For we do not now believe that habit is the fundamental motor of human life. Rather do we see human behavior as ensuing from an intricate and subtle, self-directed, self-regulated process of dynamic interchange between the individual and the situation with which he is confronted. The tension points which develop in this system of interchange are the springs of action. Thus no habit has meaning or leads to behavior except as it is connected with a general dynamic set of the organism, and this general attitudinal set is a function of the interchange between the individual and the environment.

Behavior is to be thought of as a reaction of the entire organism flowing out of the relation between that organism and the total situation which confronts it. Beginning with the simple situations presented by the perceptual world of childhood, to which adjustment is direct and uncomplicated, there is an interlocking succession of ever more and more complicated situations, and, to these latter, adaptation must be mediated by ever more roundabout and complicated behavior. There is little place for specific habits, in the older sense, in such a system, except as they serve as tools at the service of the other personality trends or represent refinements and adaptations of generalized tendencies to respond.

This is a doctrine that accords well with the findings of common sense, which has often observed with what difficulty habits which do not seem to fit in with the major trends of personal organization are formed, and with what ease they are broken. A habit cannot be imposed from without; it must have a basis in the interlocking system of attitudes already established. The newer doctrine, too, furnishes the basis for a different attitude concerning the transfer of training. Educators have with reluctance given up the idea that the useful elements in one sort of training are carried over into other situations. But tests of the supposed transfer of specific habits have shown that there is in fact no transfer. A strongly developed habit of neatness in English papers does not perceptibly increase the neatness of papers in mathematics. But if we think of the development of personality as a successively more complicated adjustment based upon the attainment of new levels of insight or the emergence of new perceptual configurations or the perfection of new behavior patterns, we see that some transfer is possible. Human beings are not bundles of specific habits, and any attempt to treat them as such is so artificial that it must always fail to give adequate control of their behavior. Naturally there is little or no transfer of specific habits that have been imposed from without, because those habits are easily split off in a new situation, and are in fact cast away at the earliest possible opportunity as so much surplus baggage. But if we think of processes of personal development first and of specific habits only as they arise from these processes, if we think of education as the development of insight and understanding based upon the formation of new configurations, the growth of general ideas and the amassing of facts as part of them, if we think of developing life as attaining successive levels of complication corresponding to ever more complicated insight, then we see that transfer is natural and inevitable. A child can be the same child after you have taught him neatness, diligence, and the habit of shining his shoes, but he can never more be the same when he no longer considers it a moral problem whether he should bite sister or not. Whatever makes a man more complex must make him respond more complexly to any situation.

We must, then, organize education so that the child will work out attitudes adapted to the life situations he is likely to encounter in his culture group. This education of the attitudes can proceed only when the child is brought to face actual situations. The situations which enter into education must be graded and progressive, so that the older the child is and the longer he has been in school the greater will be the correspondence of his social situation with the situations of adult life. Two means suggest themselves for giving this sort of training.

(1) The school may attempt to reproduce the pattern situations of life itself. As far as this is possible, it seems the most satisfactory method, and the method responsible for such successes in the development of personality as present-day systems of schooling have had.[1]

[1] Unplanned, direct training of this sort is also responsible for many of the failures of the present-day school systems. The most significant training which any school gives is training of this kind. Even in the most formalized school the child forms his attitudes in conformity with the actual world about him rather than with the theoretical and formal world. The regrettable thing is that the social world of the ordinary school is of little value, often of negative value, as a preparation for life. It is interesting that a conservative criminologist has remarked that the best we can say for education (schooling) is that there is no certain proof that education increases crime.

This is the method of "activities," and when the ordinary school gets hold of personalities it usually does so through participation in activities. Increasing participation in activities measures, in the case of many individuals, the gradual catching up of the individual in the social process of the school. The boy entering high school or prep school has all his time and all his self at his disposal. He enters a few activities in his first year, takes interest in a few things, signs away the right to some of his time, assumes a few duties; he is enmeshed a little in the social process. By the time he is a senior his leisure time, very likely, has disappeared, and his life is entirely controlled from without, parcelled out to various groups and "activities" which have a claim upon him. The extent to which individuals become involved in them is a measure of the success of activities. There is, as has been pointed out by certain writers, an opposite danger, that of over-organization. Apparently there are considerable differences in persons as to the amount of outside regulation which they can endure without suffering ill effects.

However, the number of social situations which the school and its activities can imitate is limited. Nor is it possible for the school ever to reproduce complicated situations, or those of any great range. Direct education, then, must be subject to some supplementation.

(2) A second method is that of mediating existent or prospective social situations to the child at second hand. If the approach to this sort of exercise is exclusively intellectualistic, it will have little value for the student, although it may prove edifying for the teacher. If, however, the approach is such as to enlist the spontaneous participation of the student, there may be something to be gained through the use of the technique. Apparently this is the only sort of training which the schools can hope to give for the more complicated conditions of life. A difficulty of a practical sort is that teachers in general do not have that whole and unbiased view of life which would make such training worth while. If, after some experimentation with this technique, we find that it is valueless, the schools may have to limit themselves to the imparting of a few basic skills and a limited amount of training in meeting the basic and relatively simple social situations which underlie modern life, leaving the task of adaptation to the more complicated conditions of life to be met in the child's off hours or after he leaves the school. It may be that we shall need two schools, one for learning facts and skills and another for discussion of the adjustment of the individual to the community.[1] Training of the latter sort would very likely follow the former.

[1] Cf. Hart, J. K., *Light from the North.*

Whatever the method that is used, the school must lead the child to work out the solution of each situation for himself in his own way, for education is in any case an internal achievement. This relative freedom for the child should lead ultimately to a new conception of the nature of school discipline. It will do away with much of the present structure of regimen and reglementation. The school must stop trying to become a machine and strive to realize its destiny as a social organism.

It would hardly be correct to say that children would be free under such a system. They would be living in a natural social order, and would be subjected to the painless leadership of such a situation, but they would not be free, for this sort of leadership that we have in mind is the most compelling of all, and partly because it is gladly borne. Children would be relatively free of obvious and external restraint. The pressure which they should feel is the pressure of the social situation. (It is this soft but overwhelming pressure, not habit, that keeps adults moving in their accustomed grooves.) It is the pressure of one's own needs in the social situation in which he lives. This kind of pressure, in the group of children, makes for advancement to the next grade in the series of stair-stepped primary groups. It is a pressure that is very powerful among children, and if it could be canalized in such a way as to make for achievement along accepted lines no school teacher would ever need to worry about discipline. It is a kind of pressure to which the highest type of mind responds as readily as the lowest. But this is not the same thing as the pressure of teacherish domination and subordination.

Education through social situations can produce favorable results only in a natural social order. The attempt to construct such a social system, or to assemble the materials for it and put them into contact with each other so that they might erect themselves into a social order, would require us to abandon the present type of institutionalized dominance and subordination in the schools. Dominance there would be, but of an unforced and informal character, resulting from informal, non-institutionalized, "natural" leadership. It needs to be emphasized that such results cannot be obtained by patching up existing schools with a new piece of mechanism, or by tearing down the old mechanized social order simply in order to erect a new one upon it. Education through graded situations cannot work as a new bit of machinery. It must result from the interaction of personalities according to a different pattern.

The reformation of education becomes a problem of the teaching personnel. Teachers must be obtained who are capable of non-institutional leadership, who have no need of barriers between themselves and their students, and they must be left free to do with the social order of the schools as they will. They will modify it fast enough if we can get the right persons—not that the good teacher necessarily makes the good school, for that he does not, but the good teacher, free, could not possibly make the same sort of bad school. Teachers must be found who are much more strong and independent than teachers are now. If virile teachers are present, they can make any system of education work; no system can succeed that does not bring students into contact with strong and inspiring minds, and any system can succeed that does.[1] This is the crux of the problem of educational reform. We can accomplish little by having teachers do something different, for they cannot do anything different without being something different, and it is the being something different that matters.

All this is very easy to see and very easy to say. It has been said before, and so often that it savors of platitude. The pertinent question is how to get the strong and worth-while personalities to take up teaching; partly, too, it is a question of offering teachers opportunities to develop into strong and worth-while personalities. The answer ordinarily given for this problem is that teachers must be paid better salaries; the better salaries will attract larger numbers of high-grade individuals. No doubt better salaries for teachers are indicated, but it is questionable whether the mere fact of higher salaries would attract a much higher type of personality to the profession.

It seems to the writer that the low state of the profession is partly due to irrelevant competition. It seems that a start should be made by removing from teachers all restrictions not directly pertinent to their teaching function. It is these restrictions upon conduct which frighten away those honest and forthright persons of whom the teaching profession has need. Requirements not relevant to the teacher's function must always be ultimately deleterious, because they lead to irrelevant competition. And from this pointless competition, persons of strong character are very likely to prefer to remain aloof. The strong are not likely to carry it off over the weak in competition

[1] The moral of our previous analysis of the social interaction of the school seems to be similar. Even in the strictest school, the most desirable personal interchange is set up by the most forceful and positive characters. But this interchange would be even more valuable if the social framework in which it takes place were less rigid.

which has as its point the things they do not do; that is why many competent and desirable personalities decide not to take up teaching, and this is why many weaker persons take refuge in teaching as a means of escaping the competition of the strong.

It is submitted that the personnel of the teaching profession will not show a satisfactory improvement unless these restrictions upon the teacher are removed. We shall return to them in a different connection. We must notice briefly certain other devices by which it seems possible to attract a few vigorous and competent persons into the profession, thereby effecting a corresponding improvement in teaching on the personal side. Formerly a large number of able persons passed through teaching on their way to other professions. Latterly these persons have been excluded, largely by reason of the standards of professional training that have been established. One wonders whether the vigor of these stepping-stone teachers did not more than compensate for their faulty knowledge of the technique of teaching. If a way could be found to admit them without letting in a flood of true incompetents, some of these persons would furnish able, if temporary, recruits to the ranks of the teachers. Unquestionably, too, it is a mistake to exclude married women from teaching. It seems certain that married women are on the average more wholesome and normal than their unmarried sisters, and the schools lose by excluding them.

One wonders what could be done in the schools by way of furthering contact between students and stimulating and vigorous persons who are not teachers. The cause of education as personality development would be greatly furthered if students could be brought into intimate contact, if possible daily contact, with the leaders of the outside world, the leaders of business and society, of sport, and of the intellect. One can imagine a great draft system like compulsory military service, but unlike it in that inclusion in the draft is a special honor, that reaches out and drags in the great men and the great women of the community and forces them to do their bit with the young. The army of teachers, under such a system, would be only a skeleton army, and would be filled in by replacements from the community. Nothing would be gained by having these persons from the outside come to the school to make speeches—nothing is more futile than that; they must come into close and repeated contact with the youngsters of the community. Perhaps the easiest beginning for such informal supplementation of the schools would be by having persons particularly interested and specially qualified take charge of special extra-curricular activities of school children. If a certain amount of the work of instructing the young could be taken care of by the community itself, this might afford a way out for the tax-ridden rural sections, enabling them at once to raise salaries and to reduce taxes. This is no plea for dabblers. What we have in mind is that it is necessary to provide a channel for personal interchange between children and the outstanding men and women of the community, and that possibly the school can reorganize its curriculum in such a way as to bring this about.

Perhaps, however, we are finally committed to the policy of having all our teaching done by professionals. Let us suppose that we are able to recruit vigorous persons for service in the schools. The question then arises, "How shall we keep them vigorous?"

It is obvious that the teacher must be free in his teaching, and that some sort of code must govern both his use of that freedom and attempts by members of the community to interfere with it. It is certain that any advanced thinker will get away from the opinion of the generality of men, and some way needs to be found to insure the teacher freedom in his official utterances. Yet it is obviously unethical for the teacher to use his classroom technique as a vehicle for spreading the doctrines of some tangential group to which he belongs (although the teacher has a perfect right to belong to tangential groups). And it would be too much to expect any community to support a school which spread doctrines too far at variance with the opinion of the community. The education that liberates from community opinion must proceed indirectly and imperceptibly or it cannot proceed at all. It would be possible, however, to work out a code of academic freedom which protected the teacher in the discharge of his teaching functions, but likewise prevented abuse of that freedom.

Certainly teachers must be free outside the school. Teachers must be received as normal and in no way exceptional members of the community; they must neither gain nor lose status by being teachers. But one does not know how such an ideal state might be brought about by any means short of such a concerted revolt of all teachers everywhere as is not likely to occur. But if every teacher should for a period of ten years insist upon being treated not as a teacher but as a human being, the iron stereotype might be broken. If teachers began tomorrow to argue it out and fight it out with their communities, if they insisted upon their right to play golf on the Sabbath, to smoke on the streets, to curse the garage man and kick life-insurance salesmen through the front door, if they invariably met the statement "That's no way for a teacher to act" with a cacophonous jeer, then the social position of the profession might be changed in a very few years. But these things are not likely to take place.

Yet there is no sensible reason for asking teachers to furnish the community with examples of the virtues of restraint. The negative virtues cannot be imposed upon the young through the teacher's example. The picture is too unlovely, and the reaction is usually just the opposite to the one desired. Vice, of which many more examples are present, is much more pleasing, and its exemplars have more prestige than have the professional practitioners of virtue. But if teachers had a wholly positive morality, a morality of social idealism and of deeds rather than of inhibitions, that morality would be imitated because that kind of morality is contagious.

Some words might be directed at teachers themselves relative to their relation to the community. Before teachers can come into contact with the community in which they live they must forsake that rather namby-pamby intellectualism so common in the profession, an intellectualism not self-active or creative and based not so much upon wisdom that one does have as upon ignorance that one does not have. They must limit their participation in the shop-talk of teacher cliques, and seek the vital contacts that the larger community offers. In these contacts they must consistently struggle against the effort to treat them as teachers rather than as persons. Teachers need, nevertheless, to cultivate a quiet and unassertive individualism, and to follow their own lights wherever they may lead, paying little attention to the conventional restrictions upon the attitudes of their profession. But as professionals, teachers need to compromise; they need to correct their intellectualistic and departmental bias with the thought that the fate of nations does not depend upon how much arithmetic Johnny Jones learns, with the thought that Johnny Jones can learn only so much arithmetic anyhow and that in a year or so he will probably forget what he does learn.

Some further suggestions of the most practical sort and requiring little change of the social structure of existing schools remain to be made. The first of these pertains to the establishment of personnel work with students. Bureaus of adjustment should be provided and should be presided over by competent psychologists or psychiatrists. This personnel work should follow the model of social work rather than of personnel work in industry, and should look toward the mental and social adjustment of students. It would do well to avoid over-concern about abnormalities of behavior, and to look rather toward the solution of normal problems of development. Personnel work of this sort would thus be a valuable adjunct to character education. The psychoanalytic technique, or other devices for probing into personality, would best be used, until opinion as to the benefits of child analysis becomes more settled, very sparingly, and only by experts, and only upon children definitely maladjusted.[1] The psychoanalytic procedure should, however, find a considerable use as a means of uncovering the basic drives of the personality and of basing further personality development (secured by suggestion or analytic mechanisms) upon these basic drives. The techniques at present advocated by expert character trainers consist mainly of exhortation and autosuggestion. It seems very obvious that an attempt to remodel character through systems of trait-rating and unguided self-cultivation must produce a very brittle sort of organization. Complete case studies of every child in the school system should be made, and this information, summarized and with confidential details omitted, should be made available for all the child's teachers. These case studies should be prepared by specialists, but ideally every teacher in a system where personnel work had any real value would be something of a practicing psychologist. It is possible that a personnel bureau, established as a further bit of social machinery, could, if it did not itself become too formalized, popularize among teachers the technique of control through understanding, and that it could thereby materially affect the entire social organization of the school.

A second suggestion of major importance concerns psychiatric work with teachers. Most of the programs for the rehabilitation of the schools founder upon the rock of teacher resistance. For the most part, we consider this resistance well placed. The common-sense understanding which teachers have of their problems bites deeper into reality than do the maunderings of most theorists. Teachers will do well to insist that any program of educational reform shall start with them, that it shall be based upon, and shall include, their common-sense insight. But there are numerous teachers whose personal problems affect their teaching. This is only natural, for the present order is rooted in the personalities which teachers of the present day have worked out in adaptation to it, and teachers are unwilling and unable to change. And personnel work with teachers, by enabling

[1] For a sound and well-taken criticism of "mass inquisition into psychopathic traits," see Thomas, W. I., *The Child in America*, pp. 163-5.

such teachers to struggle more successfully against their own interior demons, might bring about radical changes in the social world of school. That some sort of psychiatric service might profitably be furnished teachers seems a very obvious point, and one that it should not be necessary to labor long. Only the normal, happy, and well-poised teacher is capable of discipline that is painless and constructive. Perhaps the strongest argument in favor of psychiatric work with teachers is that unadjusted teachers pass on their personality problems to their students. The teacher with a strong inferiority complex spreads inferiority complexes about her in her classroom. The teacher whose attitude toward sex is not wholesome engenders a similar maladjustment in her students. If the psychologist can help the teacher to organize her life in a more satisfactory and stable fashion—and this is just what personnel work with teachers should attempt to do—the beneficial effects upon students will become immediately apparent. The reformation of the schools must begin with teachers, and no program that does not include the personal rehabilitation of teachers can ever overcome the passive resistance of the old order.

A more superficial sort of personnel work, aiming not at the re-adjustment of the teacher's personality but at fitting that personality into its proper place, might also prove of considerable value. There are certain places in the system where certain teachers belong, and the happy conjunction of the man and the job does not always take place without guidance; it would be part of the personnel program of the school to put teachers in the right place.[1] Another task would be to furnish a social program, inside and outside the school, that would give the teachers as a body such wholesome community contacts as would keep them happy and further their personal growth. This kind of personnel work might also contrive to give teachers a sense of security in their positions. It might, further, endeavor to smooth out such differences as arise between teachers and administrative officers, differences which occasion much loss of teaching talent. It would also be a legitimate function of a bureau of personnel to accumulate information concerning personality types most likely to succeed in teaching and those more apt to fail—which would be of immense value for administrators.

[1] This function of a personnel bureau might well be correlated with a larger organization of the teaching profession, one which would take care of rating and placing teachers, thereby eliminating the problems of recommendation and that of placement. (This would replace the troublesome and expensive process of placement through agencies.) This larger organization of teaching, if perfected, might give teachers a much more secure tenure of their offices.

A final suggestion concerns the training of teachers. The teacher's training should be more to the point of the task that faces the teacher when he leaves training school. The teacher's most important task is to deal with the dynamic social situation of the classroom. And it should be his objective to deal with that situation in such a way as to further the development of the personality values of the children who with the teacher make up that situation. A central point of the teacher's training, then, should be the attempt to give him insight into the nature of the social reality which is the school. This is what teachers usually learn in the hard school of experience, and by those rules of thumb which experience gives, and this is another reason for the conservatism of educational practice. Prospective teachers learn all the new educational theories while they are in school, but they must learn how to teach from horny-handed men who have been teaching a long time. But if theory is ever really to be translated into practice, theorists must learn to follow it through the social dynamics of the school room. Only so can experience be fruitful in the understanding that will make possible a change of things that are. It is to this task that we have tried to make a small beginning.

SUGGESTED READINGS

(1) Charters, W. W., and Waples, D., *The Commonwealth Study of Teacher Training.*
(2) Counts, George S., *The American Road to Culture,* Chapter XI.
(3) Porter, M. P., *The Teacher in the New School.*
(4) Ross, E. A., *Principles of Sociology.*
(5) Washburne, C., and Stearns, M. M., *Better Schools.*

INDEX

DATE DUE

JAN 18 '71	JAN 10 '71		
MAY 16 '72	MAY 14 '73		
GAYLORD			PRINTED IN U.S.A.